Why Do You Need This New Edition?

If you're wondering why you should buy this new edition of *Academic Reading* here are seven good reasons!

① The seventh edition focuses on three elements: (1) active reading skills for academic success; (2) reading skills and strategies for specific academic disciplines; and (3) how to adapt your reading skills to specific college majors and career paths to help you be successful in and out of the classroom.

② An Academic Success for College introduction identifies the ten most popular college majors and offers ten strategies to get you off to the right start in college.

③ Sections on learning about specific academic disciplines in Part Four explain what each discipline involves, the courses it encompasses, its focus of study, and a sampling of the careers it prepares you to pursue.

④ A feature in Part Four emphasizes career opportunities within each academic discipline, identifying which characteristics and habits would make you a successful major in the field, as well as providing study tips for nonmajors.

⑤ Marginal Tips for College Majors appear throughout Chapters 1 to 9, providing suggestions for how students taking the ten most popular college majors can apply the skills taught in each chapter to their discipline.

⑥ Key Strategy boxes highlight important techniques and strategies for academic learning in an easy reference format.

⑦ Thinking Visually Chapter Openers introduce chapter content while emphasizing how the skills taught link to general academic coursework and on-the-job demands.

Academic Reading

College Major and Career Applications

Seventh Edition

Kathleen T. McWhorter
Niagara County Community College

Longman

Boston   Columbus   Indianapolis   New York   San Francisco   Upper Saddle River
Amsterdam   Cape Town   Dubai   London   Madrid   Milan   Munich   Paris   Montreal   Toronto
Delhi   Mexico City   São Paulo   Sydney   Hong Kong   Seoul   Singapore   Taipei   Tokyo

Acquisitions Editor: Kate Edwards
Development Editor: Gillian Cook
Senior Supplements Editor: Donna Campion
Senior Media Producer: Stefanie Liebman
Marketing Manager: Thomas DeMarco
Production Manager: Bob Ginsberg
Project Coordination, Text Design, and Electronic Page Makeup: Nesbitt Graphics, Inc.
Cover Design Manager/Cover Designer: John Callahan
Cover Photos: iStock
Photo Researcher: Jody Potter
Senior Manufacturing Buyer: Dennis J. Para
Printer and Binder: RR Donnelley & Sons Company / Crawfordsville
Cover Printer: Lehigh Phoenix

For permission to use copyrighted material, grateful acknowledgment is made to the copyright holders on pp. 435–440, which are hereby made part of this copyright page.

Library of Congress Cataloging-in-Publication Data
McWhorter, Kathleen T.
  Academic reading : college major and career applications / Kathleen T.
McWhorter. -- 7th ed.
     p. cm.
  Includes index.
  ISBN 978-0-205-73658-4
  1. Reading (Higher education) 2. Study skills. 3. Reading comprehension.
I. Title.
  LB2395.3.M37 2010
  428.4071'1--dc22

                                            2009037016

Copyright © 2010, 2007, 2004, 2001 by Pearson Education, Inc.

Longman
is an imprint of

www.pearsonhighered.com

12345678910–DOC–12 11 10 09

ISBN-13: 978-0-205-73658-4
ISBN-10:   0-205-73658-0

Brief Contents

Detailed Contents

*Directions for Accessing Online Chapter
1. Type in URL http://www.pearsonhighered.com/mcwhorter
2. Click on cover of text
3. Click on link to Online Chapter

Preface

■ Approach

Each academic discipline has its own subject matter, approach, and methodology. Consequently, reading assignments in each discipline require a unique set of reading skills and strategies. Many students have not learned to adapt their reading skills to the demands of different academic disciplines. *Academic Reading: College Major and Career Applications, Seventh Edition*, focuses on developing essential reading skills and showing students how to adapt them to specific academic disciplines. It also shows students how to adapt reading skills to specific college majors and specific career paths.

■ Changes in the Seventh Edition

The seventh edition of *Academic Reading* offers three new emphases: (1) a focus on skills for academic success, (2) an enhanced focus on skill application to specific disciplines, and (3) a new focus on application of skills necessary in the workplace. While maintaining a solid instructional base focused on instruction in essential reading, vocabulary, and critical thinking skills, the seventh edition reaches beyond these skills to academic and career applications in ten top college majors. Specific additions and changes to the text include the following:

- **NEW Academic Success in College Introduction.** This section offers ten strategies that will get first-year students off to the right start in college by providing them with essential learning and study skills. Strategies include getting organized, managing time, balancing school and work, taking lecture notes, taking charge of learning, managing stress, using technology, learning from textbooks, adapting your skills to academic disciplines, and how to use this textbook. This introduction also features quotations from students suggesting specific ways these skills can be applied. This section is a four-color insert and resembles many introductory course texts in format, color, and the number of engaging visual features. The remainder of the text contains fewer visual features and more closely resembles, in both format and design, the texts students will use when taking upper-level courses in their major. The success strategy titled "Get the Most Out of Your Textbooks" addresses the differences between introductory and upper-level textbooks and suggests strategies for handling upper-level texts.

- NEW Emphasis on and Tips for College Majors.   The ten most popular college majors are identified in the Academic Success in College introduction. Throughout Chapters 1–9, marginal tips offer suggestions for applying skills taught in the chapter to these college majors. For example, in Chapter 2 math/physical science majors are advised that main ideas are often spelled out in the form of theorems, principles, or laws. In the same chapter, life science/allied health students are urged to pay attention to details, as exact and detailed procedures are important in lab work and clinical experience.

- NEW Thinking Visually Chapter Openers.   These new openers present a visually engaging introduction to chapter content while emphasizing how chapter content links to both academic course work and on-the-job demands. In Chapter 1, for instance, the "Thinking Visually About Active Reading" offers a photo of jubilant college graduates and commentary that discusses how these students achieved this goal through active reading. "Active Reading: The Academic Link" discusses the importance of reading in all academic courses, and "Active Reading: The Career Link" emphasizes the importance of active reading in career situations.

- NEW Emphasis on Learning About Each Academic Discipline (Part Four).   Many students are unfamiliar with what each academic discipline encompasses. A new section at the beginning of Chapters 10–15 explains what each discipline involves and the courses it involves. Each chapter contains a table that lists the disciplines, describes the focus of study within each, and provides a sampling of related careers.

- NEW Emphasis on Career Applications Within Each Academic Discipline (Part Four).   Many students wander aimlessly from course to course, without a considered career focus. Others are pursuing career fields for which they eventually discover they are ill suited. Chapters 10–15 present an overview of career opportunities for each field within the discipline and offers advice for majors and nonmajors. For example, Chapter 11, "Reading in Business," contains the following sections:
  - "Should You Major in Business"—a discussion of what majoring in business involves and a list of characteristics and habits that lead to success as a business major.
  - "Tips for Studying Business—Even if You Are Not a Major"—a description of the benefits nonmajors can derive from taking a business course.

- NEW Key Strategy Boxes.   Throughout the text, essential techniques and strategies are boxed to emphasize their importance and make them easy to find for future reference. Examples of these boxes include "How to Preview Textbook Assignments," "How to Make Inferences," and "How to Read an Argument."

- **NEW Reading Selections.**   Nine new reading selections have been added to the text, each representing one or more of the top ten college majors. Topics include innovative advertising techniques (marketing), stem cell use (biology), alternatives to imprisonment (criminal justice), the development of spectator sports (history), the music industry (business/art), classroom stereotyping (education), verbal messages (communication) and telenursing (nursing/allied health), and a pair of readings on Internet freedom/censorship (business/technology)

- **NEW Labeling of Exercises.**   Each exercise is now labeled to indicate the skill being practiced.

■ A Unique Focus on Academic Disciplines

Many students are unfamiliar with the content and topics addressed in various academic disciplines or the career paths to which they lead. They drift from one academic course to the next without a clear career focus. This text offers a unique, contextualized approach that focuses on academic reading skills, but also motivates students toward a particular area of interest or field of study. Students learn important comprehension, vocabulary, and critical thinking skills, as well as how to adapt these skills to study specific academic disciplines. While doing so, they also learn what each discipline involves and what career opportunities are available. This book, then, teaches essential reading skills while opening up new worlds and new possibilities to students.

Academic Reading, Seventh Edition, uses several current, effective methodologies to develop reading skills:

- **Active Reading.**   For many students, reading is a passive assimilation process: their goal is to acquire as many facts and as much information as possible. The active reading approach used in *Academic Reading* encourages students to interact with the text by predicting, questioning, and evaluating ideas.

- **Levels of Thinking.** Using Bloom's taxonomy of cognitive skills (updated by Anderson) as a framework, this book shows students how to apply higher-order thinking skills to their course work.

- **Metacognition.**   Metacognition is the reader's awareness of his or her own comprehension processes. Mature and proficient readers exert a great deal of cognitive control over their reading: they analyze reading tasks, select appropriate reading strategies, and monitor the effectiveness of those strategies. This text guides students in developing these metacognitive strategies.

- **Academic Thought Patterns.**   The text describes six common academic thought patterns that are used in various disciplines to organize and structure ideas. Four additional patterns are also discussed. These patterns, presented as organizing schemata, are used to establish order, consistency, and predictability within academic disciplines.
- **Writing as Learning.** Although most students regard writing as a means of communication, few are accustomed to using it as a reading aid to help them organize information, focus ideas, recognize relationships, or generate new ideas. This text introduces writing as a vehicle for learning. Techniques such as highlighting, outlining, note taking, and cognitive mapping are approached as learning strategies.
- **Learning Style.**   Not all students learn in the same way. To help students discover their unique learning preferences, the text includes a Learning Style Questionnaire (Chapter 1) and offers students suggestions for adapting their study methods to suit their learning style characteristics.

■ Discipline-Specific Reading Skills

With the fundamental skills in place, college students are able to develop a diverse repertoire of reading strategies and to select and alternate among them. Professors from each of the academic disciplines worked as consultants during the writing of the book. A new set of specialists was used to develop a revision plan for the previous edition. These consultant teams offered suggestions for both skill coverage and methodology. Some of the discipline-specific reading skills included are the following:

In the Social Sciences

- understanding theories in the social sciences
- reading research reports
- making comparisons and applications

In Business

- reading models
- reviewing case studies
- studying organization charts and flowcharts
- approaching supplemental readings

In the Liberal Arts, Humanities, and Education

- understanding figurative language
- reading poetry and short stories

- working with literary criticism
- studying visual elements in art

In Mathematics

- understanding mathematical language
- reading sample problems
- verbalizing processes
- reading graphics
- approaching word problems

In the Life and Physical Sciences

- previewing before reading
- understanding scientific approaches
- studying sample problems
- learning terminology and notation

In Technical and Applied Fields

- reading illustrations and drawings
- using visualization
- reading technical manuals
- employing problem-solving strategies
- benefiting from practicum experiences

■ Special Features

The following features enhance student learning and skill application:

- **Academic Success in College four-color introduction.** This visually engaging introduction to the text focuses on ten strategies for academic success.
- **"Thinking Visually" Chapter Openers.** Each chapter begins with one or more visuals that link the chapter content to students' interests and their world of experience. The openers in Chapters 1–9 also provide an academic link and a career link that demonstrate the utility of the skills taught in the chapter to other college courses and to workplace demands. The openers in Part 4, Chapters 10–15, offer three visuals that illustrate a topic of study, an academic application, and a career application of the academic discipline to be discussed.
- **Learning Objectives.** Each chapter includes a brief list of learning objectives that establishes the chapter's focus and provides students

with purposes for reading. The objectives can be used as a way to review and check retention after reading the chapter.

- **Discipline Overviews (Part Four).**   The text provides an introduction to six major academic disciplines. Each chapter in this section defines the discipline, explains the fields it encompasses, and briefly describes related career opportunities. Each chapter also discusses what majoring in the discipline involves and offers tips to help students determine whether a major in that discipline is right for them. Tips for nonmajors taking a course in the discipline are also provided.
- **Tips for Majors.**   The top ten college majors are featured in the Academic Success in College introduction. Throughout Chapters 1–9, marginal tips are provided that offer advice to students in specific majors. These tips demonstrate the importance of certain skills and show students how to apply them in specific fields of study.
- **Key Strategy Boxes.**   Throughout the text, important reading and learning strategies are presented as boxed features, emphasizing their importance and making them easy to find for future reference.
- **Self-test Chapter Summaries.**   Each chapter includes a question and answer summary intended to help students review and consolidate chapter content through self-testing.
- **Reading Selections.**   Each chapter concludes with one or more reading selections from a college textbook or related academic source to reinforce the skills and strategies presented in the chapter. Each reading is accompanied by a vocabulary review exercise, comprehension questions, critical thinking questions, and an exercise on applying learning/study strategies.
- **Academic Applications.**   Exercises labeled "Academic Application" require students to apply their reading skills to textbook or course materials from their other college courses.
- **Exercises for Collaborative Learning.**   Additional exercises designated "Collaborative Learning" provide structured activities in which students can learn from one another as they analyze and apply skills introduced in the chapter.

■ Book-Specific Ancillary Materials

The Instructor's Manual and Test Bank

The Instructor's Manual provides numerous suggestions for using the text, including how to structure the course and how to approach each section of the book. The Instructor's Manual also contains a complete answer key for the text and a set of overhead projection transparency masters. The Test Bank section includes chapter review quizzes for each chapter. (ISBN 0-205-73744-7).

■ Acknowledgments

I wish to acknowledge the contributions of my colleagues and reviewers who have provided valuable advice and suggestions for this and previous editions of *Academic Reading*.

Academic Discipline Reviewers

Allied Health: Professor Bradley Foley, Nursing Program, Minneapolis Community and Technical College

Biology: Professor Jan Pechenik, Department of Biology, Tufts University; Professor Dave Baker, Delta College

Business: Professor John Ribezzo, Department of Business, Community College of Rhode Island; Professor Andrew Szilagyi, College of Business Administration, University of Houston; Professor Ernest T. Fitzgerald, Department of Business, Delgado Community College

Liberal Arts, Humanities, and Education: Professor Pat Mathias, Department of English, Itasca Community College; Professor Thomas Hayes, Department of English, John Carroll University; Professor Barbara Klemm, Department of Social Sciences, Broward Community College; Professor Richard Marius, Professor Emeritus, Harvard University; Professor Victor Uszerowicz, Department of English and Communication, Miami-Dade Community College; Professor Jannette Morales, Department of Visual Arts and Technology, San Antonio College

Mathematics: Professor Jerry Muir, Department of Mathematics, University of Scranton; Professor Paul Perdew, Department of Mathematics, University of Scranton; Professor Marvin L. Bittinger, Department of Mathematics, Indiana University–Purdue University; Professor Diana Hestwood, Minneapolis Community and Technical College

Life and Physical Sciences: Professor William Straits, Department of Science Education, California State University, Long Beach; Professor Bill Leonard, Department of Physics, University of Massachusetts

Social Sciences: Professor Bob Schwegler, College Writing Program, University of Rhode Island; Professor J. Ross Eshleman, Wayne State University

Technical and Applied Fields: Professor Jim White, Dean of Technical Engineering, Industrial and Engineering Technology Division, Central Carolina Technical College; Professor Thomas Athey, California State Technical College; Professor Josephine Brankey, New York Technical College

Reading Specialist Reviewers

Betty Andrews-Tobias, Suffolk Community College; Lisa Barnes, Delaware County Community College; Pamela Bourgeois, California State University,

Northridge; Greta Buck, Pima Community College; Janice Buchner, Suffolk County Community College; Terry Bullock, University of Cincinnati; Marilyn Burke, Austin Community College; Steve Cohen, Norwalk Community Technical College; Diane Cole, Pensacola Junior College; Janet Curtis, Fullerton College; Pat D'Allessio, Dutchess Community College; Lisa DeDeppo, Pima Community College; Susan Deese, University of New Mexico; Cathlene Denny, St. Johns River Community College; Marty Frailey, Pima Community College; Helen Gilbart, St. Petersburg Junior College; Ed Gill, Indiana Vocational Technical College; Lori Grimm, Pima Community College; Jon Hanson, Sacramento City College; Brian Holmes, San Jose State University; Peter Incarderone, New Jersey City University; Jenny Joczik, College of Charleston; Sandra Jones, Community College of Baltimore County; Denise Josten, St. Louis Community College; Sandra Keith, St. Cloud State University; Kathleen Kiefer, Colorado State University; Terry Kozek, Housatonic Community College; Linda W. Larou, Dutchess Community College; Beverly Lipper, Dutchess Community College; Alice Mackey, Missouri Western State College; Monique Manning, Brookhaven College; Donna Mayes, Blue Ridge Community College; Gail Moore, York Technical College; David Murphy, Waubonsee Community College; Karen Nelson, Craven Community College; Michael Newman, Hunter College; Michelle Peterson, Santa Barbara City College; Karen Samson, Chicago State University; Anna-Marie Schlender, Austin Community College; Nancy E. Smith, Florida Community College at Jacksonville; Betsy Tobias, Suffolk County Community College; Katherine Wellington, Metropolitan State University; Stephanie Whippo, Community College of Baltimore County; Michaeline Wideman, University of Cincinnati; Mary Wolting, Indiana University–Purdue University; Kimberley Zernechel, Minneapolis Community and Technical College; Lawrence Ziewaz, Michigan State University.

Student Contributors

I would also like to thank the students who shared their knowledge and experience in the Academic Success section of this new edition of *Academic Reading*.

Ebtisam Abusamak, Michael Archer, Julia Mix Barrington, Tessa Dowling, Nora Edge, Veronica Evans-Johnson, Ashley Hatzler, Ben Howard, Andrew Wilton.

I am particularly indebted to Gillian Cook, my development editor, for her most valuable advice and guidance. She has contributed knowledge, creativity, and energy, as well as practicality. I also wish to thank Kate Edwards, acquisitions editor, for her support in developing the revision plan and overseeing its implementation.

KATHLEEN T. MCWHORTER

The Top Ten College Majors

Biology

Business

Communication

Computer Science/Technology

Criminal Justice

Education

Humanities/Liberal Arts

Mathematics/Physical Science

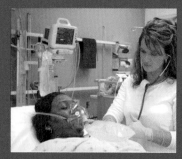

Nursing

Psychology/Social Sciences

Academic Success in College

THIS BOOK WILL HELP YOU SUCCEED IN COLLEGE BY

- Providing you with the skills and strategies that will lead you to success in all of your college courses.

- Showing you how to adapt these essential skills to courses you take as you pursue your college major.

This Academic Success section features general study and learning tips for college. These will jump start your progress as a successful student and help lead you to a successful college career. Then in Chapters 1–9 you will learn the reading skills essential to all college courses. In these chapters you will also find helpful marginal tips for adapting and applying skills to the top 10 college majors. When you reach Part 4 (Chapters 10–15), you will learn specific strategies for adapting those skills to particular fields of study.

STRATEGY #1: Get Organized

Becoming a successful student requires planning and organization. Here are a few suggestions for ensuring your success.

1. **Organize a place to study.** Select a quiet, comfortable location and study in the same place each day. Be sure to have all your materials (paper, pens, etc.) at hand.

2. **Use a pocket or online calendar and a small notebook.** Record exams and due dates for papers on the calendar; record daily assignments in the notebook.

3. **Get to know someone in each class.** You might enjoy having someone to talk to. Also, in case you miss a class, you will have someone from whom you can get the assignment and borrow notes.

4. **Attend all classes, whether or not it is required.** Studies show that successful students attend class regularly, whereas students who do not are unsuccessful.

5. **Get to know your instructors.** Use your instructors' office hours to talk about exams or assignments, ask questions, and discuss ideas for papers.

Michael Archer
Greenfield Community College, Greenfield, MA

Michael has just completed his first year at Greenfield Community College where he is studying fine arts. He plans to transfer to a four-year art college to complete a degree in illustration or sculpture.

"The most important thing is to get an idea of what works for you. Even if you have to take a general class or one you don't think is useful, you can still learn a lot about how your brain works by taking it. It's really important to know how you react to certain assignments, what study techniques work best, and what your strengths and weaknesses are. If you know you're a procrastinator or work slowly, make sure you know the deadline for a project and make time for it. The more you do this the more you can manage your time without thinking about it too much."

STRATEGY #2: Manage Your Study Time

As college students, many of you struggle to divide your time among classes, study, job responsibilities, and friends and family. Here are a few suggestions for managing your study time effectively and avoiding procrastination.

How to Use Your Time Effectively

1. **Develop a weekly study plan.** Allocate time for reading, reviewing, doing homework, and studying for exams. Select several specific times each week for working on each of your courses. As a rule of thumb, reserve two study hours for each hour you spend in class. A sample weekly plan is shown in Figure A-1.

2. **Use peak periods of concentration.** Everyone has high and low periods of concentration and attention. First, determine when these occur for you; then reserve peak times for intensive study and use less efficient times for more routine tasks such as recopying an assignment or collecting information in the library.

3. **Study difficult subjects first.** While it is tempting to get easy tasks and short little assignments out of the way first, do not give in to this approach. When you start studying, your mind is fresh and alert and you are at your peak of concentration. This is the time you are best equipped to handle difficult subjects.

4. **Schedule study for a particular course close to the time when you attend class.** Plan to study the evening before the class meets and soon after the class meeting. For example, if a class meets on Tuesday morning, plan to study Monday evening and Tuesday afternoon or evening. By studying close to class time, you will find it easier to relate class lectures and discussions to what you are reading and studying, to see connections, and to reinforce your learning.

5. **Include short breaks in your study time.** Take a break before you begin studying each new subject. Your mind needs time to refocus so that you can switch from one set of facts, problems, and issues to another. You should also take short breaks when you are working on just one assignment for a long period of time. A 10-minute break after 50 to 60 minutes of study is reasonable.

FIGURE A-1   Sample Weekly Plan

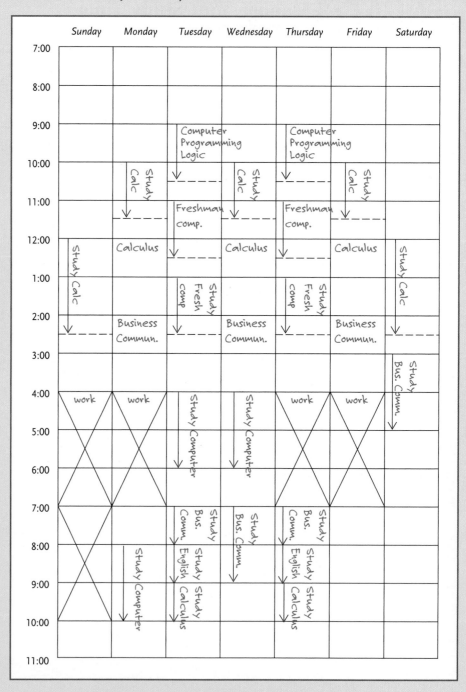

How to Control Procrastination

1. **Clear your desk and give yourself five minutes to start.** Move everything from your desk except materials for the task at hand. Tell yourself that you will work on the task for just five minutes. Often, once you start working, your motivation and interest will build, and you will want to continue working.

2. **Divide the task into manageable parts.** Complicated tasks are often difficult to start because they seem so long and unmanageable. Before beginning such tasks, spend a few minutes organizing and planning. Divide each task into parts, and list what you need to do and in what order. Start somewhere, no matter where or how unimportant it seems.

3. **Recognize when you need more information.** Sometimes, procrastination is a signal that you lack skills or information. You may be avoiding a task because you are not sure how to do it. You may not understand why you use a certain procedure to solve a type of math problem, for example, so you feel reluctant to do math homework. Or selecting a term paper topic may be difficult if you are not certain of the purpose or expected length of the paper. Overcome such stumbling blocks by discussing them with classmates or with your professor.

Nora Edge
St. John's College,
Annapolis, MD

Nora is a junior at St. John's College and is taking a double major in literature and philosophy. She is planning to join the Peace Corps right after graduating; she wants to apply what she has learned, gain work experience, and decide on her future plans.

❝I found writing a schedule was the most useful way to deal with time management. I wrote it out on paper, carried it with me all the time, and checked it constantly. When I had time between classes I knew what I was doing. For example, I would read ahead of time if there was no break between classes, and read for the next class when I did have a break. I found the best way to be successful was give myself time to breathe. I made sure I was exercising three times a week and got 6–8 hours of sleep a night. ❞

STRATEGY #3: Balance School and Work

Many students find they must juggle school responsibilities with their part-time job commitments. Still others must make time for household and/or family responsibilities, as well. Use the following suggestions to help you keep your life running smoothly and efficiently:

1. **Try to choose flexible jobs.** Try to find an employer that is flexible about your work hours. Offer to work unpopular days or times in exchange for fewer hours during busy weeks, such as final exams.

2. **Consider travel time.** Be sure you don't waste too much valuable time traveling from campus to a job.

3. **Build a compact class schedule.** In future semesters, select a class schedule that is compact and convenient, without too many hours between classes. This will free up larger blocks of time for work and study.

4. **Make a schedule to reflect your priorities.** Don't try to fit college into your old weekly schedule before you started college; succeeding in college takes too much time for this to work well. You will need to reserve plenty of time for reading, writing, and studying.

5. **Make a household schedule.** Just as you have planned a weekly study schedule, develop a weekly household schedule. Instead of hoping that all jobs will get done, plan when you or a family member will tackle each. Designate specific times for laundry, shopping, errands, and so forth.

6. **Increase your efficiency by doing things at off-peak times.** Don't go to the grocery store or laundromat on a busy Saturday morning; instead, choose a weekday, early in the morning or later in the evening.

7. **Use weekends for study.** Try to take care of work and household responsibilities during the week by "sandwiching" them between each other. For instance, you could run a load of laundry while washing your car. This will free up larger blocks of time on the weekend for study.

8. **Consider remaining on or returning to campus to study.** If your house or dorm is too distracting a place to concentrate, try studying at the college library or at a local public library. Once you are away from home, you will tend to forget job worries, as well.

Veronica Evans-Johnson

Durham Technical College, Durham, North Carolina

Veronica graduated in May 2007 with an AAS degree in Business Management. She is currently working full-time and taking classes to complete her studies in Clinical Trials Research Level 1. Her goal is to transfer to Strayer University or North Carolina Central University to earn a BA in Business Administration

> 66 You have to prioritize your schedule. I work 8 hours a day. Sometimes I leave my job and go to class, depending on my class schedule, then go back to work and make up the time. Then I go home, take care of my family, cook and clean. Then I go upstairs and work on my school work for 1–3 hours. Last semester I took 8 classes, 5 online. You have to be very disciplined to do online classes, otherwise you'll never make it. You have to set time aside to get work done. It doesn't matter when, but you have to keep up with assignments, because once you fall behind it's very hard to catch up. 99

STRATEGY #4: Take Lecture Notes

In many courses, your instructor will lecture, and you will need to take accurate notes for study and review.

Taking Effective Notes

1. **Read the textbook material on which the lecture will be based before attending the lecture.**
2. **Listen carefully to the lecturer's opening comments;** they often reveal the purpose, focus, or organization of the lecture.
3. **Focus on ideas, not facts.** Do not try to record everything the lecturer says.
4. **Record the main ideas and enough details and examples so that the ideas will make sense later.** Use an abbreviation system for commonly used words (psy = *psychology*, w/ = *with*, etc.) to save time.
5. **Record the organization of the lecture.** Use an indentation system to show the relative importance of ideas. Be sure to leave plenty of space as you take notes so you have room to fill in missed information later.
6. **Review and edit your notes as soon as possible after the lecture.** Fill in missing or additional information. This review will also help you remember the lecture.
7. **Test yourself using the Recall Clue System** (also known as the **Cornell System**). Simply rereading your notes is not an effective study strategy.

Instead, you need to be active and test yourself. Here is how the Recall Clue System works:

- **Leave a 2-inch margin at the left side of each page of notes.** Keep the margin blank while you are taking notes.
- **After you have edited your notes, write words or phrases in the left margin that briefly summarize each section.** You can also write questions that are answered by the information in your notes. These recall clues will help trigger your recall of the details of your lecture notes.
- **To study for tests or exams, cover up your notes, exposing only the left margin.** Read each recall clue and try to remember the information in the corresponding portion of your notes. After you have completed a section, check your notes to see if you were accurate and remembered all of the important points.

Figure A-2 shows an excerpt from a set of notes using the Recall Clue System.

FIGURE A-2   Recall Clue System

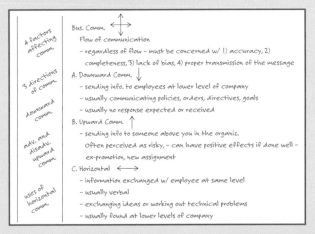

Andrew Wilton
The State University of New York at Buffalo, Buffalo, NY

Andrew is a senior at SUNY, Buffalo. He is pursuing a bachelor's degree in sociology, works part-time in a grocery store, and is interning at a family-counseling center at the Cheektowaga-Sloan intermediate school.

> ❝ I've learned that in a lecture you need to understand the overall patterns and trends and not focus too much on the details used to explain them. I always write down everything that is on the board or an overhead and note anything that's said with emphasis. There are a lot of charts, graphs, and tables in sociology. When they are presented I try to grasp the overall idea the teacher is making, rather than remember every detail. ❞

STRATEGY #5: Take Charge of Your Learning

For each of your courses, you will need to learn many facts, ideas, and concepts. Use the following suggestions to learn most efficiently.

1. **Apply the principle of spaced study.** It is more effective to space, or spread out, study sessions than to study in one or two large blocks of time.

2. **Use immediate review.** As soon as you finish reading or studying, take a few minutes to look back through the material, recalling key points and rereading notes or summaries. If you review immediately after study, you will increase the amount you remember.

3. **Review frequently.** In order to retain information over time, it is necessary to review periodically. Although you are learning new material each week, reserve time to reread notes, material you have highlighted in your textbook, and chapter summaries of previously covered material.

4. **Associate new information with previously learned information.** Call to mind what you already know about a topic before you begin to read or study. Think of it as a process of seeing how new information fits with information already learned.

5. **Use visualization.** Creating a mental picture of what you have read often aids recall. Sometimes you can create mental pictures of people, events, processes, and procedures. Other times, when dealing with more abstract ideas, you may have to visualize the relationships between ideas. When reading arguments about Internet invasion of privacy, for example, you might visualize two lists—pro and con.

6. **Use numerous sensory channels by incorporating writing, speaking, and listening into your study.** For example, consider recording and playing back your history notes or writing a summary sheet of key formulas for a math course.

Tessa Dowling
Bard College, Annandale-on-Hudson, NY

Tessa is a junior at Bard College. She is pursuing a bachelor's degree in liberal arts with a concentration in biology. She plans on interning in her field after she graduates, obtaining a master's degree, and pursuing a career as an environmental conservation biologist.

> ❝I work with my friends to study for tests. In comparative anatomy, we had to learn the names of different types of vertebrae, which are each shaped subtly differently. We made an interpretive dance to help us remember them. For each bone, we would add a movement that helped us to remember a specific shape. For instance, one had a ridge, so we stuck our behinds out for that one. It was really silly, but it worked.❞

STRATEGY #6: Manage Stress

College is a new and challenging experience, and new and challenging experiences tend to produce stress. Consequently, stress is a common problem that many college students face. Complete the Stress Questionnaire shown in Figure A-3 to assess your level of stress.

Figure A-3

STRESS QUESTIONNAIRE

Respond to each of the following statements by checking "Yes," "No," or "Sometimes" in the boxes provided and then adding up the total for each column.

	Yes	No	Sometimes
1. I feel as if I don't have enough time in a week to get everything done.	☐	☐	☐
2. Having at least one healthy meal per day at which I can sit down and relax is unusual.	☐	☐	☐
3. I have more conflicts and disagreements with friends than I used to.	☐	☐	☐
4. I seem to get colds and other minor illnesses (headaches, upset stomachs) more frequently.	☐	☐	☐
5. I find myself confused or listless more than usual.	☐	☐	☐
6. My usual level of physical activity or exercise has decreased.	☐	☐	☐
7. I seldom get six to eight hours of sleep at night.	☐	☐	☐
8. I seldom find time to do some fun things each week.	☐	☐	☐
9. I find myself unable to meet deadlines and am losing track of details (appointments, chores, promises to friends, and so on).	☐	☐	☐
10. I am more short-tempered or more impatient than I used to be.	☐	☐	☐
Total	____	____	____

If you answered "Yes" to more than two or three items or "Sometimes" to more than five or six items, you may be experiencing more stress than you realize. Evaluate the pattern of your responses. Look at the questions to which you answered "Yes" or "Sometimes." Some questions deal with physical habits; others focus on organizational skills. By checking your answers, you will get an idea of your own stress indicators.

How to Reduce Stress

1. **Eliminate stressors.** Identify possible sources of stress, and work toward eliminating them. If a part-time job is stressful, for instance, quit or find another that is less stressful. If a math course is creating stress, take action: go to the learning lab or math lab for assistance, or inquire about tutoring.

2. **Establish a daily routine.** To eliminate daily hassles and make daily tasks as simple as possible, establish a daily routine. A routine eliminates the need to make numerous small decisions, thereby giving you a sense of "smooth sailing."

3. **Accentuate your accomplishments.** When you feel pressured, stop and review what you have already accomplished that day and that week. This review will give you confidence that you can handle the workload. A positive attitude goes a long way in overcoming stress.

4. **Eat nutritious meals and get physical exercise.** Exercise often releases tension, promotes a general feeling of wellness, and improves self-esteem. Many students report that as little as 30 minutes of exercise produces immediate relaxation and helps them to place daily events in perspective. Also be sure to get enough sleep.

5. **Seek knowledgeable advice.** If stress begins to feel overwhelming, seek assistance from the student counseling center. The office may offer workshops in stress-reduction techniques such as relaxation or biofeedback training.

6. **Get involved with campus activities.** Some students become so involved with their course work that they do little else but study or worry about studying. In fact, they feel guilty or stressed when they are not studying. Be sure to allow some time in each day to relax and have fun. Campus activities provide a valuable means of releasing tension and taking your mind off your work.

Ebtisam Abusamak
University of North Carolina at Charlotte, Charlotte, NC

Ebtisam graduated July 1, 2009, with a BSCA in Finance. She is currently working as a waitress and interning at Edward Jones. Her goal is to find a job as financial analyst or asset manager.

"I found the key to managing stress was making sure I had a work/life balance, had enough time to eat healthy, sleep, workout, and being sure I had enough time to see family and friends. It's very hard! My boyfriend was really good for making sure I ate healthy and went to the gym. I would come back from the gym feeling really refreshed and ready to work. I also made sure I stopped every hour when I was studying to have something to eat, go for a walk, or watch TV for 5–10 minutes. If I worked a 2–3 hour stretch, I would take a 20–30 minute break and go for a walk."

STRATEGY #7: Use Technology

A computer's capabilities make it a useful study, learning, and communication tool.

1. **Organize your notes from lectures and textbook assignments.** As you take notes on a lecture or chapter, your notes tend to follow the organization of the lecture or chapter. A computer allows you to reorganize and rearrange your notes and pull together information on the same topic.

2. **Integrate text and lecture notes.** The cut-and-paste function allows you to move sections of your lecture notes to the corresponding sections in your text notes.

3. **Create lists of new terminology for each of your courses.** You can group similar terms, organize them by chapter, or sort them into "know" and "don't know" files.

4. **Choose a study partner or create online study groups.** Instant messaging (IM) allows you to talk back and forth with a classmate, as long as you are both online at the same time. Members can share notes, quiz each other, and discuss course content.

Ben Howard
Brown University,
Providence, RI

Ben is a junior at Brown, where he is majoring in mechanical engineering. He is considering taking a year off after graduation and/or attending graduate school. In his graduate work, he would like to apply his skills in mechanical engineering to video technology.

66 Google Documents is really useful. You go to the site, sign up for your own account, and then either import an existing document or set up a new document, spreadsheet, or slide show for a presentation. It's really cool, because then you can email everyone in the same study project as you, they can sign up as collaborators, and you can all work on the document simultaneously. If you're working in a cell on a spreadsheet you will see it highlighted in one color and as other people work on cells you'll see their work highlighted in a different color. When you're done, you can save the project as a Word file on your computer 99

STRATEGY #8: Get the Most Out of Your Textbooks

There are two types of textbooks: (1) introductory-level texts used by large numbers of beginning college students and (2) advanced, more specialized texts used by students when they pursue their major. These texts differ in appearance, content, and the amount of learning assistance they provide. For example, in an introductory psychology course you would probably use a book with plenty of colorful images, diagrams, charts, boxed inserts, and so on. It would look like this Academic Success introduction. The text would probably also contain plenty of learning aids, such as end-of-chapter study questions and marginal definitions. However, when you start to take courses that are only required of majors, such as Theories of Personality or Child Psychotherapy, the advanced textbooks you will use will look very different. They may be black and white or use only one color; they will have far fewer visual features; they will have far fewer or no learning aids. You will need to learn to work with both types of textbook.

Using Introductory-Level Textbooks

Introductory textbooks help you learn. Be sure to take advantage of all the features offered. On page 14 you will find a list of common features and learning aids along with suggestions about how to use them.

Using Advanced-Level Textbooks

Advanced-level textbooks lack many or most of the features listed in the table on p. 14. The authors assume you are seriously motivated to study the material and do not need photos, boxes, or other features to keep you interested. The authors also assume that you know how to study and do not need help picking out key vocabulary, identifying what is important to learn, and testing your recall of material.

To study advanced-level textbooks, you need to create your own study aids:

- Create your own key vocabulary lists.
- Write questions after each section and practice answering them.
- Write your own chapter summary if none is provided.
- Think of your own applications: What practical situations does the material relate to? What questions does it raise? Why is it important in the field? How can you use this information on the job?
- Working with a classmate, test each other by asking and answering questions.

FEATURE	HOW TO USE IT
Preface or "To the Student"	• Read it to find out how the book is organized, what topics it covers, and what learning features it contains.
Chapter Opener (may include chapter objectives, photographs, and chapter outlines)	• Read it to find out what the chapter is about. • Use it to test yourself later to see if you can recall the main points.
Marginal Vocabulary Definitions	• Learn the definition of each term. • Create a vocabulary log (in a notebook or computer file) and enter words you need to learn.
Photographs and Other Visual Elements	• Determine their purpose: what important information do they illustrate? • For diagrams, charts, and tables, note the process or trend they illustrate. Make marginal notes. • Practice redrawing diagrams without referring to the originals.
Test Yourself Questions (after sections within the chapter)	• Always check to see if you can answer them before going on to the next section. • Use them to check your recall of chapter content when studying for an exam.
Special Interest Inserts (can include profiles of people, coverage of related issues, critical thinking topics, etc.)	• Discover how the inserts are related to the chapter content: what key concepts do they illustrate?
Review Questions/Problems/ Discussion Questions	• Read them once *before* you read the chapter to discover what you are expected to learn. • Use them after you have read the chapter to test your recall.
Chapter Summary	• Test yourself by converting summary statements into questions using the words *Who? Why? When? How?* and *So What?*
Chapter Review Quiz	• Use this to prepare for an exam. Pay extra attention to items you get wrong.

Julia Mix Barrington
Barnard College,
Columbia University,
New York, NY

Julia has just completed her freshman year at Barnard College. She has not declared a major yet, but is very interested in English and is considering a career as a food writer.

66 This year I took earth science and a class on dinosaurs. I realized I didn't have time to read everything. In the earth science text there was this tiny list of 'essential points' at the beginning of each chapter that was absolutely fantastic. I didn't feel I had to read everything about volcanoes, because I knew what I had to focus on. I'm a very visual person so I also go through the text and look at the pictures and read the captions first and that allows me to associate the information with what I read; I still remember this information about how the larger an object that's vibrating the bigger the sound it makes, because of this picture in my freshman physics book of a hillbilly playing a washtub instrument. Reading doesn't take me long, but with the science books I begin to glaze over. If I have a discussion question I can't answer, it sticks in my head, and it helps me latch on better to the information because I'm looking for the answer. 99

STRATEGY #9: Adapt Your Skills to Academic Disciplines

Your tasks as you begin each new college course are:

- to learn how to approach a new field of study.
- to adapt your reading and study strategies to be successful in different disciplines.

Learn How to Approach New Fields of Study

As you pursue your major, you will probably encounter new fields of study, ones you have little background in or experience with. You will have to experiment with how to adapt your reading and study strategies to suit each discipline. Try the following techniques, which can help you adapt:

1. **Spend more time than usual reading and studying.** You are doing more than reading and studying: you are learning how to learn as well.

2. **Since the content is unfamiliar and you don't know the type of exam you will be asked to take, organize the same information in several different ways.** For example, in an anthropology course, you might learn events and discoveries chronologically (according to occurrence in time) as well as comparatively (according to similarities and differences among various discoveries). In an accounting course, you might organize information by procedures as well as by controlling principles.

3. **Use several methods of learning.** Since you are not sure which will be most effective for the types of learning and thinking that are required, try several methods at once. For example, you might highlight textbook information (to promote factual recall) as well as write outlines and summaries (to interpret and consolidate ideas). You might also draw diagrams that map the relations between concepts and ideas. (These learning strategies are discussed in detail in Chapter 9.)

4. **Look for similarities between the new subject matter and other academic fields that are familiar to you.** If similarities exist, you may be able to modify or adapt your existing learning approaches and strategies to fit your new field of study. For example, you may realize that some of the strategies you use for math courses also work for economics or physics.

5. **Get an overview of the course and of the field.** Some college texts delve into a subject immediately, providing only a brief introduction or overview in the first chapter. Spend time studying the table of contents of your textbook; it provides an outline of the course. Look for patterns, progression of ideas, and recurring themes, approaches, or problems. If the field of study is unfamiliar to you, spend an hour or so in the library or online getting a better understanding of what it involves.

Ashley Hartzler
University of Massachusetts,
Amherst, MA

Ashley is a freshman at UMass, Amherst. She is majoring in Japanese, plans to get a master's degree in education and then teach. Eventually, she would like to work as a translator.

66Taking classes that easily integrate helps a lot if you have a very full schedule. It's really helpful if you can to take information you've learned in one class and apply it in another. For example, this semester I took math and economics together and I was able to apply what I learned about a specific equation in math to solve problems in economics. 99

STRATEGY #10: Use This Book

Academic Reading offers a wealth of skills and strategies to guide you through a successful college career. Below are several highlighted features from the text that will be particularly helpful to you.

Tip for Humanities and Social Science Majors

Some students find it useful to use different highlighting colors for different purposes. For example, key vocabulary terms might be highlighted in yellow, while the names of important people might be highlighted in pink. (Be sure to use colors that are easy to read through.) Create a system that works well for you and helps you "chunk" your information into manageable amounts.

Learn to Adapt Specific Skills

In each of Chapters 1–9 and interspersed throughout Chapters 10–15, you will find marginal tips that offer advice on how to adapt the skill being taught to particular college majors. For example, this tip appears next to a discussion of how to highlight textbooks on page 254.

Use the Key Strategy Boxes

Throughout this book you will learn a lot of practical information. Strategies you will want to refer to frequently appear in Key Strategy boxes throughout Chapters 1–9.

KEY STRATEGY: How to Preview Textbook Assignments

Use the following steps to become familiar with a textbook chapter's content and organization:

1. **Read the chapter title.** The title indicates the topic of the article or chapter; the subtitle suggests the specific focus of, or approach to, the topic.

2. **Read the introduction or the first paragraph.** The introduction or first paragraph serves as a lead-in to the chapter by establishing the overall subject and suggesting how it will be developed.

3. **Read each boldfaced (dark print) heading.** Headings label the contents of each section and announce the major topic of the section.

4. **Read the first sentence under each major heading.** The first sentence often states the central thought of the section. If the first sentence seems introductory, read the last sentence; often, this sentence states or restates the central thought.

5. **Note any typographical aids.** Italics are used to emphasize important terminology and definitions by distinguishing them from the rest of the passage. Material that is numbered 1, 2, 3; lettered a, b, c; or presented in list form is also of special importance.

6. **Note any graphic aids.** Graphs, charts, photographs, and tables often suggest what is important in the chapter. Be sure to read the captions of photographs and the legends on graphs, charts, or tables.

In Part 4 (Chapters 10–15), you will also learn more about each discipline and how to be successful in it, including how to adapt and apply your skills to each course you are taking. Here is a sampling of what you will find.

Get an Overview of the Discipline

As you approach new fields of study, it is helpful to know what a specific discipline is about, its subfields, and the job and career opportunities it offers.

TABLE 10–1 The Social Sciences: An Overview		
DISCIPLINE	**SUBFIELDS**	**JOB AND CAREER OPPORTUNITIES**
Anthropology—The study of humanity: Examines concepts, customs, and rules in different societies and cultures.	*Forensic Anthropology*— Seeks to identify human remains through lab techniques	• Forensic scientist • Police lab technician
	Medical and Environmental Anthropology—Studies the factors that influence the health and well being of people	• Environmental worker (local or international) • Public health safety specialist

Learn the Characteristics of Successful Majors

As you select or pursue a major, it is helpful to know what is expected of you. Each chapter in Part 4 offers success strategies for majoring in the discipline.

Should You Major in a Social Science?

Although each social science focuses on a different aspect of human life, they have much in common. Each is interested in general laws, principles, and generalizations that describe how events, facts, trends, and observations are related. Some students believe that the social sciences are somehow less scientific than the physical and life sciences (such as biology, chemistry, engineering, and physics), but social scientists use the same methods that all scientists do: observation, experimentation, testing of scientific theories (called *hypotheses*), and reporting on the results of experiments. So, if you decide to major in a social science, you should expect to conduct and report on a good amount of your own research, as well as read published studies.

What characteristics and habits will make you a successful social science major?

1. **You are expected to understand the roots of the discipline.** This means that you must learn the history of the field and the contributions of the people who are important in that field. In psychology, for example, you must study the work of major figures like Sigmund Freud and Carl Jung; in sociology and anthropology, you will study the work of Margaret Mead.

2. **You must be able to handle a heavy reading load.** In the physical sciences, many complex concepts can be reduced to simple equations. The study of

Use Tips for Studying Disciplines Outside Your Major

Each chapter in Part 4 provides a description of the benefits nonmajors can derive from taking courses in a particular discipline as well as offering valuable study tips for how to get the most out of these classes.

Tips for Studying Social Science—Even if You Are Not a Major

During college you will take at least two or three required social science courses. Here are some tips for making the most of them.

1. **Make time to read**. Although you will devote more time to your major courses, to get the most out of a social science course, read the assignments when you are feeling fresh and not tired. This allows you to better follow the material and appreciate its narrative approach. It can help to think of your textbook as a novel filled with interesting characters, examples, and case studies.

2. **Focus on the big picture**. You may not remember every detail of your textbook after you've taken the final exam, but each time you read a chapter, make a list of the top three things you have learned. Many social science instructors say they feel quite happy if students leave their course with a general level of awareness, so aim for that very achievable goal.

Find Out About Basic Discipline-Specific Strategies

Each chapter in Part 4 offers useful advice specific to the discipline. This advice varies from chapter to chapter and includes topics such as characteristics of textbooks in the discipline, specialized reading techniques, current important topics and issues, and advice to majors.

Social science textbooks tend to share similar characteristics:

1. **The emphasis is on facts**. Especially in introductory courses, an instructor's first task is to acquaint you with known principles, rules, and facts that you can use to approach new problems and situations. Consequently, you must comprehend and retain large amounts of factual information. Refer to "Locating Main Ideas and Supporting Details" in Chapter 2 for specific suggestions, and use a highlighter, take marginal notes, and summarize key information.

2. **Many new terms are introduced.** Each social science has developed an extensive terminology to make its broad topics as objective and quantifiable as possible. To do well on exams, you must understand these terms. Make use of marginal and end-of-text glossaries to test yourself on the meanings of these terms.

3. **Graphics are important.** Social science textbooks include a great deal of information in the form of photographs, diagrams, and other graphics. Be sure to "read" these graphics to learn what they convey about the topic. Refer to Chapter 8, "Reading and Evaluating Graphics and Online Sources," for specific suggestions on how to read and interpret charts, tables, and graphs.

Get Valuable Advice from Professors

Each chapter in Part 4 offers valuable advice from professors teaching in the discipline on how to be successful in the discipline.

Quotes from a Sociology Professor

Advice for Social Science Students

Robert A. Schwegler, Ph.D., Director of Graduate Studies, University of Rhode Island

❝ My students have trouble recognizing the cues that identify a summary of a theoretical approach or research findings. They often read the summaries as statements of fact, not as reports of someone's work, even though they realize that not everything in a textbook or article is fact. I think the problem is that they miss the cues that say, 'This is X's work, etc.' Students need to identify the formal cues, recognize summaries, and deal with the summarized information as the interpretations or conclusions of specific scholars. ❞

1 Strategies for Active Reading

Thinking Visually About Active Reading

The students in this photograph are successful college graduates. They have achieved their goal of earning a degree and are looking forward to successful careers. In the same way that students benefit from planning their college studies, they benefit from setting goals while doing their college reading assignments. The key to effective, goal-oriented reading is *active reading*.

LEARNING OBJECTIVES

- To understand how reading contributes to college success
- To assess your learning style
- To build your concentration skills
- To develop multilevel thinking skills

- To learn to preview and predict before reading
- To develop questions to guide your reading
- To check your comprehension
- To use SQ3R

ACTIVE READING: The Academic Link

When you think of college, you may think of attending classes and labs, completing assignments, studying for and taking exams, and writing papers. A closer look, however, reveals that reading is an important part of all these activities. Reading is at the core of a college education.

ACTIVE READING: The Career Link

Whether in college or in your career, reading is the primary means by which you acquire ideas and gather information. Knowing how to read actively will not only help you earn better grades in college; it will also help you be effective in your chosen profession.

■ Reading and Academic Success

Reading involves much more than moving your eyes across lines of print, more than recognizing words, and more than reading sentences. **Reading is thinking.** It is an active process of identifying important ideas and comparing, evaluating, and applying them.

Have you ever gone to a ballgame and watched the fans? Most do not sit and watch passively. Instead, they direct the plays, criticize the calls, encourage the players, and reprimand the coach. They care enough to get actively engaged with the game. Just like interested fans, active readers get involved. They question, challenge, and criticize, as well as understand. Table 1-1 contrasts the active strategies of successful readers with the passive ones of less successful readers.

Throughout the remainder of this chapter, you will discover specific strategies for becoming a more active learner. Not all strategies will work for everyone. Experiment to discover those that work for you.

| EXERCISE 1-1 | Reading Actively |

Consider each of the following reading assignments. Discuss different ways in which you could get actively involved with them.

1. Reading two poems by e.e. cummings for a literature class
2. Reviewing procedures for your next biology lab
3. Taking notes on an article in *Time* magazine assigned by your political science instructor

Table 1–1   Active Versus Passive Reading

ACTIVE READERS . . .	PASSIVE READERS . . .
Tailor their reading to suit each assignment.	Read all assignments the same way.
Analyze the purpose of an assignment.	Read an assignment *because* it was assigned.
Adjust their speed to suit their purpose.	Read everything at the same speed.
Question ideas in the assignment.	Accept whatever is in print as true.
Compare and connect textbook material with lecture content.	Study lecture notes and textbook separately.
Skim headings to find out what an assignment is about before beginning to read.	Check the length of an assignment and then begin reading.
Make sure they understand what they are reading as they go along.	Read until the assignment is completed.
Read with pencil in hand, highlighting, jotting notes, and marking key vocabulary.	Simply read.
Develop personalized strategies that are particularly effective.	Follow routine, standard methods.

EXERCISE 1-2   **Active Reading Strategies**

Write a list of active reading strategies you already use. Add to your list several new strategies that you intend to begin using. Compare your list with a classmate's.

_____

_____

_____

■ Assessing Your Learning Style

People differ in how they learn and the methods and strategies they use to learn. These differences can be explained by what is known as *learning style*. Your learning style can begin to explain why some courses are easier for you than others and why you learn better from one instructor than another. Learning style also can explain why certain assignments are easy for you and other learning tasks are difficult.

Tip for Education Majors

You have your own distinctive learning style, but the students you'll be teaching will use all of the learning styles listed on the next few pages. To be an effective teacher, you will benefit not only from understanding how different types of students learn, but also from learning to teach the same concept in different ways.

The following brief Learning Style Questionnaire will help you analyze how you learn and show you how to develop an action plan for learning what you read. Complete and score the questionnaire before continuing with this section.

Learning Style Questionnaire

DIRECTIONS: Each item presents two choices. Select the alternative that best describes you. In cases in which neither choice suits you, select the one that is closer to your preference. Write the letter of your choice on the line to the left of each item.

PART ONE

_____ 1. I would prefer to follow a set of
    a. oral directions.
    b. printed directions.

_____ 2. I would prefer to
    a. attend a lecture given by a famous psychologist.
    b. read an online article written by the psychologist.

_____ 3. When I am introduced to someone, it is easier for me to remember the person's
    a. name.
    b. face.

_____ 4. I find it easier to learn new information using

    a. language (words).
    b. images (pictures).

_____ 5. I prefer classes in which the instructor
    a. lectures and answers questions.
    b. uses Powerpoint illustrations and videos.

_____ 6. To follow current events, I would prefer to
    a. listen to the news on the radio.
    b. read the newspaper.

_____ 7. To learn how to operate a machine, I would prefer to
    a. listen to a friend's explanation.
    b. watch a demonstration.

PART TWO

_____ 8. I prefer to
    a. work with facts and details.
    b. construct theories and ideas.

_____ 9. I would prefer a job that involves
    a. following specific instructions.
    b. reading, writing, and analyzing.

_____ 10. I prefer to
    a. solve math problems using a formula.
    b. discover why the formula works.

_____ 11. I would prefer to write a term paper explaining
    a. how a process works.
    b. a theory.

_____ 12. I prefer tasks that require me to
    a. follow careful, detailed instructions.
    b. use reasoning and critical analysis.

_____ 13. For a criminal justice course, I would prefer to
a. discover how and when a law can be used.
b. learn how and why it became law.

_____ 14. To learn more about the operation of a high-speed computer printer, I would prefer to
a. work with several types of printers.
b. understand the principles on which they operate.

PART THREE

_____ 15. To solve a math problem, I would prefer to
a. draw or visualize the problem.
b. study a sample problem and use it as a model.

_____ 16. To best remember something, I
a. create a mental picture.
b. write it down.

_____ 17. Assembling a bicycle from a diagram would be
a. easy.
b. challenging.

_____ 18. I prefer classes in which I
a. handle equipment or work with models.
b. participate in a class discussion.

_____ 19. To understand and remember how a machine works, I would
a. draw a diagram.
b. write notes.

_____ 20. I enjoy
a. drawing or working with my hands.
b. speaking, writing, and listening.

_____ 21. If I were trying to locate an office on an unfamiliar campus, I would prefer
a. a map.
b. printed directions.

PART FOUR

_____ 22. For a grade in biology lab, I would prefer to
a. work with a lab partner.
b. work alone.

_____ 23. When faced with a difficult personal problem, I prefer to
a. discuss it with others.
b. resolve it myself.

_____ 24. Many instructors could improve their classes by
a. including more discussion and group activities.
b. allowing students to work on their own more frequently.

_____ 25. When listening to a lecturer or speaker, I respond more to the
a. person presenting the idea.
b. ideas themselves.

_____ 26. When on a team project, I prefer to
a. work with several team members.
b. divide the tasks and complete those assigned to me.

_____ 27. I prefer to shop and do errands
a. with friends.
b. by myself.

_____ 28. A job in a busy office is
a. more appealing than working alone.
b. less appealing than working alone.

PART FIVE

_____ 29. To make decisions, I rely on
   a. my experiences and gut feelings.
   b. facts and objective data.

_____ 30. To complete a task, I
   a. can use whatever is available to get the job done.
   b. must have everything I need at hand.

_____ 31. I prefer to express my ideas and feelings through
   a. music, song, or poetry.
   b. direct, concise language.

_____ 32. I prefer instructors who
   a. allow students to be guided by their own interests.
   b. make their expectations clear and explicit.

_____ 33. I tend to
   a. challenge and question what I hear and read.
   b. accept what I hear and read.

_____ 34. I prefer
   a. essay exams.
   b. objective exams.

_____ 35. In completing an assignment, I prefer to
   a. figure out my own approach.
   b. be told exactly what to do.

To score your questionnaire, record the total number of a's you selected and the total number of b's for each part of the questionnaire. Record your totals in the scoring grid provided below.

Scoring Grid		
PART	**TOTAL # OF CHOICE "A"**	**TOTAL # OF CHOICE "B"**
One	_____	_____
	Auditory	Visual
Two	_____	_____
	Applied	Conceptual
Three	_____	_____
	Spatial	Verbal
Four	_____	_____
	Social	Independent
Five	_____	_____
	Creative	Pragmatic

Now, circle your higher score for each part of the questionnaire. The word below the score you circled indicates a strength in your learning style. The next section explains how to interpret your scores.

Interpreting Your Scores

Each of the five parts of the questionnaire identifies one aspect of your learning style. These five aspects are explained below.

Part One: Auditory or Visual Learners   This score indicates whether you learn more effectively by listening (auditory) or by seeing (visual). If your auditory score is higher than your visual score, you tend to learn more easily by hearing than by reading. A higher visual score suggests strengths with visual modes of learning such as reading, studying pictures, reading diagrams, and so forth.

Part Two: Applied or Conceptual Learners   This score describes the types of learning tasks and learning situations you instinctively prefer and find easiest to handle. If you are an applied learner, you prefer tasks that involve real objects and situations. Therefore, practical, real-life examples are ideal for you. If you are a conceptual learner, you prefer to work with language and ideas; you tend to rely less on practical applications for understanding than applied learners.

Part Three: Spatial or Verbal Learners   This score reveals your ability to work with spatial relationships. Spatial learners can visualize or mentally "see" how things work or how they are positioned in space. Their strengths may include drawing, assembling, or repairing things. Verbal or nonspatial learners lack skills in positioning things in space. Instead, they rely on verbal or language skills.

Part Four: Social or Independent Learners   This score reveals whether you like to work alone or with others. If you are a social learner, you prefer to work with others—such as classmates and instructors—closely and directly. You tend to be people oriented and enjoy personal interaction. If you are an independent learner, you tend to be self-directed or self-motivated as well as goal oriented.

Part Five: Creative or Pragmatic Learners   This score describes the approach you prefer to take toward learning tasks. Creative learners are imaginative and innovative. They prefer to learn through discovery or experimentation. They are comfortable taking risks and following hunches. Pragmatic learners are practical, logical, and systematic. They seek order and are comfortable following rules.

If you disagree with any part of the Learning Style Questionnaire, go with your own instincts, rather than the questionnaire results. Think of the questionnaire as just a quick assessment, but trust your self-knowledge.

Using Learning Style Effectively

Now that you have completed the Learning Style Questionnaire and know more about *how* you learn, you are ready to develop an action plan for learning what you read. Suppose you are a social learner; you could work with a classmate, the two of you testing each other out loud. Such activities shift the presentation of ideas from visual to auditory form and also give you practice rephrasing ideas.

Table 1-2 (p. 28) lists the different types of learning styles and offers suggestions for how students who exhibit each style might learn most effectively from a reading assignment. You can use this table to build an action plan for more effective learning.

1. Circle the five aspects of learning style in which you received the highest scores on the Learning Style Questionnaire. Disregard the others.

Tip for Nursing and Allied Health Majors

Even if you are not a social learner, many experts note that nursing and allied health students benefit greatly from working in small study groups. Group study helps students with different strengths teach one another. A group member may explain something in a memorable way, catch something you missed, or ask a question you hadn't even considered.

TABLE 1-2   Learning Styles and Reading/Learning Strategies

IF YOUR LEARNING STYLE IS . . .	THEN THE READING/ LEARNING STRATEGIES TO USE ARE . . .	IF YOUR LEARNING STYLE IS . . .	THEN THE READING/ LEARNING STRATEGIES TO USE ARE . . .
Auditory	• Discuss/study with friends. • Talk aloud when studying. • Record self-testing questions and answers.	Verbal	• Translate diagrams and drawings into language. • Record steps, processes, and procedures in words. • Write summaries. • Write your interpretation next to textbook drawings, maps, and graphics.
Visual	• Draw diagrams, charts, and/or tables. • Try to visualize events. • Use DVDs and videos. • Use online tutorials.	Social	• Form study groups. • Find a study partner. • Interact with the instructor. • Work with a tutor.
Applied	• Think of practical situations to which learning applies. • Associate ideas with their application. • Use case studies, examples, and applications to cue your learning.	Independent	• Use online tutorials. • Purchase review workbooks or study guides when available.
Conceptual	• Organize materials. • Use outlining. • Focus on thought patterns (see Chapter 7).	Creative	• Ask and answer questions. • Record your own ideas in the margins of textbooks.
Spatial	• Use mapping. • Use outlining. • Draw diagrams; make charts and sketches. • Use visualization.	Pragmatic	• Study in an organized environment. • Write lists of steps, procedures, and processes. • Paraphrase difficult materials.

2. Read through the suggestions that apply to you.

3. Place a check mark in front of suggestions that you think will work for you. Choose at least one for each of your five learning styles.

4. Experiment with these techniques, one at a time. Use one technique for a while, and then move to the next. Continue using the techniques that seem to work, and work on revising or modifying those that do not. Do not hesitate to experiment with other techniques listed in the table. You may find other techniques that work well for you.

Overcoming Limitations

You should also work on developing learning styles in which you are weak because your learning style is not fixed or unchanging. You can improve areas in which you scored lower. Even though you may be weak in auditory learning, for example, many of your professors will lecture and expect you to take notes. If you work on improving your listening and note-taking skills, you can learn to handle lectures more effectively.

■ Building Your Concentration

Concentration is the ability to focus on the task at hand. Building your concentration can reduce your reading time. It is a two-part process: eliminating distractions, then focusing your attention.

Eliminating Distractions

Activities going on around you can break your concentration. A dog barking, a radio playing, and an overheard conversation are examples of distractions. Use the following suggestions in eliminating distractions:

1. **Choose a place conducive to reading.** The spot you select should be as free of distractions and interruptions as possible. If your home or dorm is too busy or noisy, you will be distracted. Study in a quiet place such as student lounge areas or library study areas. Find a place you can associate with studying so that you are ready to concentrate as soon as you sit down. Although your TV chair or your bed may look like a perfect place to study, you already associate them with relaxation and sleep. If you read and work at the same desk or study carrel regularly, you will find that when you sit down you will feel ready to concentrate, and distractions will be less bothersome.

2. **Notice your physical state.** If you are tired, you will have trouble concentrating. If you are hungry, your thoughts will drift toward food. If you feel sluggish and inactive, you may not be able to focus on your work. Try to schedule reading or studying at times when your physical needs are not likely to interfere. If you are tired, hungry, or sluggish, you may need to take a break or find a better time to complete the assignment.

3. **Have necessary tools and materials available.** Surrounding yourself with any necessary tools creates a psychological readiness for reading and eliminates the distraction created by searching for a book or pen.

4. **Choose your peak periods of attention.** You have a natural time limit for how long you can successfully focus on a task; this is your **attention span.** People experience peaks and valleys in their attention spans. Some people are very alert in the early morning, whereas others find they are most focused at midday. To make concentration easier, try to read during the peaks of your attention span. Choose the times of day when you are most alert and when it is easiest to keep your mind on what you are doing. If you are not aware of your own peaks of attention, keep track of when you read and study for several days and how much you accomplish each time. Then look for a pattern.

Tip for Computer Science/Technical Majors

Working on computers often brings about eyestrain and poor posture. It can be physically draining (and bad for your eyes) to stare at a computer screen for hours at a time. To study and work effectively, take breaks from staring at the computer and allow your eyes to focus farther away. Get up from your chair, stretch, or do a small household chore that doesn't take long.

5. **Keep a list of distractions.** Often, as you are reading or studying, you will be distracted by thoughts of something you must remember to do. If you have a dental appointment scheduled for the next afternoon, you will find that a reminder occasionally flashes through your mind. To help overcome these distractions, keep a list of them. Jot down these mental reminders as they occur. You will find that writing them down temporarily eliminates reminders from your conscious memory.

Focusing Your Attention

Focusing your attention means directing all mental activity to what you are reading. To help focus your attention on the material you are reading, try the following.

1. **Set goals.** Achieving your goals is positive and rewarding; it feels good to accomplish what you set out to do. Before each study or reading session, set specific goals and time limits. Divide large assignments into smaller parts to give yourself the best chance to achieve your goals. One student set the following reading goals for herself for one evening of study.

Reread Psych lecture notes	15 min.
Read first half Chapter 10—Psych	90 min.
Review Chapter 9—Accounting	30 min.
Read short story—English	30 min.

2. **Reward yourself.** Meeting goals within a time limit is a reward in itself. Other rewards could include watching TV, snacking, or checking messages. Schedule rewards to follow periods of reading and studying. You could plan to rewrite your English composition before watching a favorite TV program, for example.

3. **Begin by reviewing previously read material.** Reviewing the preceding assignment will direct your attention to today's work and help you make the "mental switch" from the preceding activity to what you are doing now.

4. **Write and highlight as you read.** Your mind may wander while reading, especially if you find the material dull or boring. To solve this problem, involve yourself in your reading by writing or highlighting the important ideas in each section. Make marginal notes, and jot down questions. These activities force you to think: to identify important ideas, to see how they are related, and to evaluate their worth and importance. Refer to Chapters 2 and 4–6 for specific suggestions on each of these techniques.

5. **Approach assignments critically.** Be an active reader. Instead of simply trying to take in large amounts of information, read critically. Seek ideas you question or disagree with. Look for points of view, opinions, and unsupported statements. Try to predict how the author's train of thought

is developing. Make connections with what you already know about the subject, with what you have read before, and with what the instructor has said in class.

EXERCISE 1-3

LEARNING
COLLABORATIVELY

Listing Distractions

Make a list of common distractions and problems that interfere with your concentration. Next to each item, note how you can overcome it. Discuss with classmates or your instructor any items for which you have no remedy.

_____

_____

_____

_____

EXERCISE 1-4

Improving Your Concentration

Discuss how each student might improve his or her concentration in the following situations.

1. A student cannot concentrate because of frequent interruptions by his two preschool children.
2. A student says she cannot concentrate because she is obsessed with a conflict she is having with her parents.
3. A student says he cannot read sociology for longer than a half-hour because he becomes restless and bored.

■ Developing Levels of Thinking

Tip for
Communication/
Graphic Arts
Majors

The role of communications is often to convey large amounts of complicated information to the general public. Conveying that information effectively requires mastering application, analysis, evaluation, and creation skills.

Throughout your educational career, your primary task is to **remember** and **understand** information. Consequently, you may not be prepared when your instructors ask you to **apply**, **analyze**, **evaluate**, and **create** information.

Table 1-3 (p. 32) describes a hierarchy, or progression, of thinking skills. It was developed by Bloom in 1956 and revised by Anderson (2000) and remains widely used among educators in many academic disciplines. You will notice that the progression moves from basic literal understanding to more complex skills that involve evaluation and creation.

When they write exams, most college instructors assume that you can operate at each of these levels. Table 1-4 (p. 32) shows a few items from an exam for a course in interpersonal communication. Note how the items demand different levels of thinking. You do not need to identify the level of thinking that a particular assignment or test item requires. However, you should be able to think and work at each of these levels.

TABLE 1–3   Levels of Thinking

LEVEL	EXAMPLES
Remembering: recalling information; repeating information with no changes	Recalling dates; memorizing definitions
Understanding: understanding ideas; using rules and following directions	Explaining a law; recognizing what is important
Applying: applying knowledge to a new situation	Using knowledge of formulas to solve a new physics problem
Analyzing: seeing relationships; breaking information into parts; analyzing how things work	Comparing two poems by the same author
Evaluating: making judgments; assessing the worth of information	Evaluating the effectiveness or value of an argument opposing the death penalty
Creating: putting ideas and information together in a unique way; creating something new	Designing a new computer program

---

TABLE 1–4   Level of Thinking Required

TEST ITEM	LEVEL OF THINKING REQUIRED
Define nonverbal communication.	Remembering
Explain how nonverbal communication works.	Understanding
Describe three instances in which you have observed nonverbal communication.	Applying
Study the two pictures projected on the screen at the front of the classroom, and compare the nonverbal messages sent in each.	Analyzing
Evaluate an essay whose major premise is "Nonverbal communication skills should be taught formally as part of the educational process."	Evaluating
Construct, for an international student visiting your hometown, a set of guidelines that will enable him or her to understand local nonverbal communication.	Creating

The following passage is taken from a psychology textbook chapter on memory and learning. Read the passage, and study the list that follows.

Some of the oldest data in psychology tell us that retrieval will be improved if practice (encoding) is spread out over time, with rest intervals spaced in between. . . . In fact, this experiment, first performed in 1946, provides such reliable results that it is commonly used as a student project in psychology classes. The task is to write the letters of the alphabet, upside down and from right to left. (If you think that sounds easy, give it a try.)

Subjects are given the opportunity to practice the task under four conditions. The *massed-practice* group works with no breaks between trials. The three *distributed-practice* groups receive the same amount of practice, but get rest intervals interspersed between each 1-minute trial. One group gets a 3- to 5-second break between trials, a second group receives a 30-second rest, and a third group gets a 45-second break between trials.

Subjects in all four groups begin at about the same (poor) level of performance. After 20 minutes of practice, the performance of all the groups shows improvement, but by far, the massed practice (no rest) group does the poorest, and the 45-second rest group does the best.

The conclusion from years of research is that almost without exception, *distributed practice is superior to massed practice.* There are exceptions, however. Some tasks may suffer from having rest intervals inserted in practice time. In general, whenever you must keep track of many things at the same time, you should mass your practice until you have finished whatever you are working on. If, for example, you are working on a complex math problem, you should work it through until you find a solution, whether it's time for a rest break or not. And of course, you should not break up your practice in such a way as to disrupt the meaningfulness of the material you are studying.

—Gerow, *Psychology: An Introduction,* pp. 217–18

Below you can see how you might use each level of thinking to understand and evaluate this passage on memory and learning.

Remembering	How was the experiment designed?
Understanding	What did the experiment show about learning?
Applying	How can I use distributed practice to plan my study time tonight?
Analyzing	Why is distributed practice more effective?
Evaluating	How effective is distributed practice?
Creating	What kind of experiment could I design to test what types of tasks benefit most (and which least) from distributed practice?

As mentioned earlier, professors use these levels of thinking in writing exams. An effective way to prepare for an exam, then, is to be sure you have thought about the test material at each level. Do this by predicting possible test questions at each level.

EXERCISE 1–5

Applying Levels of Thinking

Read the following excerpt from an interpersonal communications textbook. Demonstrate your ability to think at various levels by answering the questions that follow.

A **friendship relationship** is one marked by very close association, contact, or familiarity. Usually a warm friendship has developed as a result of a long association, but this is not always the case. Sometimes friendship develops suddenly. Friendship relationships are very personal or private, and they are often characterized by different types of communication.

People seek friendship relationships for many reasons. These reasons may operate singly or in conjunction with each other. Many overlap. In some situations, with some people, one of these reasons may sustain a relationship, whereas in others, several are likely to operate. The more needs that are fulfilled in a relationship, the more solid the foundation upon which the relationship rests. You seek friendship relationships to fulfill six basic needs: for enjoyment, security, affection, self-esteem, freedom, and equality. They are not necessarily ranked here in order of importance.

Enjoyment is an important, perhaps the most important, need that friendships fulfill. Simply put, friends enjoy each other's company. The "What do you want to do?" syndrome ("I don't know, what do you want to do?") often occurs because neither friend really cares. Just enjoying being together is enough; *doing* something (anything!) is secondary. . . .

Affection relates to a sense of belonging. This could encompass sexual gratification, but does not need to. Affection suggests a moderate feeling toward or emotional attachment to another person. When you feel tender attachment for others or pleasure in being with them, you are experiencing affection. Abraham Maslow labels this "belonging and love needs," placing this need among the basic or essential needs after "psychological" and "safety" needs.

Self-esteem is felt when you are recognized or appreciated by others. Sometimes being with someone enhances your status. Also, if other people attribute a joint identity to your relationship with another person, this may also increase your self-esteem. Self-esteem is affected because such a high premium is often placed on dating and "going steady." Maslow places self-esteem needs only one step higher than affection—as slightly less essential and more optional.

—Weaver, *Understanding Interpersonal Communication*, pp. 423–26

Remembering and Understanding

1. Define a friendship relationship.
2. List the six basic needs that friendship relationships fulfill.
3. Explain the meaning of the term *self-esteem*.

Applying

4. Name a person with whom you have a friendship that fulfills your need for self-esteem.

Analyzing

5. Think of a long-standing friendship. Analyze that friendship by identifying the needs it fulfills.

Evaluating

6. Do you agree with the author's statement that a high premium often is placed on dating? Why or why not?

Creating

7. The author states that the six basic needs are not necessarily ranked in order of importance. On the basis of your experience with friendships, list these needs in order of importance to you.

EXERCISE 1–6

ACADEMIC
APPLICATION

Creating Questions at Different Levels of Thinking

Select a one- or two-page section from one of your textbooks. Read the section, and then write questions that might be asked to test your thinking at each level.

_____

_____

_____

_____

_____

_____

_____

■ Previewing and Predicting

Previewing and predicting are skills that will help you to think beyond the basic levels of knowledge and comprehension. **Previewing** as described in the Key Strategy box below is a means of familiarizing yourself with the content and organization of an assignment *before* you read it. Think of previewing as getting a "sneak preview" of what a chapter or reading will be about. You can then read the material more easily and more rapidly.

KEY STRATEGY: How to Preview Textbook Assignments

Use the following steps to become familiar with a textbook chapter's content and organization:

1. **Read the chapter title.** The title indicates the topic of the article or chapter; the subtitle suggests the specific focus of, or approach to, the topic.

2. **Read the introduction or the first paragraph.** The introduction or first paragraph serves as a lead-in to the chapter by establishing the overall subject and suggesting how it will be developed.

3. **Read each boldfaced (dark print) heading.** Headings label the contents of each section and announce the major topic of the section.

continued

Key Strategies continued

4. **Read the first sentence under each major heading.**   The first sentence often states the central thought of the section. If the first sentence seems introductory, read the last sentence; often, this sentence states or restates the central thought.

5. **Note any typographical aids.**   Italics are used to emphasize important terminology and definitions by distinguishing them from the rest of the passage. Material that is numbered 1, 2, 3; lettered a, b, c; or presented in list form is also of special importance.

6. **Note any graphic aids.**   Graphs, charts, photographs, and tables often suggest what is important in the chapter. Be sure to read the captions of photographs and the legends on graphs, charts, or tables.

7. **Read the last paragraph or summary.**   This provides a condensed view of the chapter by outlining its key points.

8. **Quickly read any end-of-article or end-of-chapter material.**   This might include references, study questions, discussion questions, chapter outlines, or vocabulary lists. If there are study questions, read them through quickly because they tell you what is important to remember in the chapter. If a vocabulary list is included, skim through it to identify the terms you will be learning as you read.

A section of a speech communication textbook chapter discussing purposes of listening is reprinted here to illustrate how previewing is done. The portions to focus on when previewing are shaded. Read only those portions. After you have finished, test how well your previewing worked by answering the questions in Exercise 1-7 on page 38.

PURPOSES OF LISTENING

Speakers' motivations for speechmaking vary from situation to situation just as listeners' purposes for paying attention vary. Researchers have identified five types of listening (each serving a different purpose): (a) appreciative, (b) discriminative, (c) therapeutic, (d) comprehension, and (e) critical.

Appreciative Listening

Appreciative listening focuses on something other than the primary message. People who are principally concerned with participating in the experience are appreciative listeners. Some listeners enjoy seeing a famous speaker. Other listeners enjoy the art of good public speaking, pleasing vocal modulation, clever uses of language, impressive phraseology, and the skillful use of supporting materials. Still other listeners simply like to attend special occasions such as inaugurations, dedications, and graduations.

Discriminative Listening

Discriminative listening requires listeners to draw conclusions from the way a message is presented rather than from what is said. In discriminative listening, people seek to understand what the speaker really thinks, believes, or feels. You're engaging in discriminative listening when you draw conclusions about how angry your parents are with you, based not on what they say, but on how they say it. Journalists listening to the way that a message is presented often second-guess the attitudes of national leaders on foreign policy. Performers, of course, can convey emotions such as anger or exhilaration to audiences through their delivery alone.

Therapeutic Listening

Therapeutic listening is intended to provide emotional support to the speaker. It is more typical of interpersonal than public communication—the therapeutic listener acts as a sounding board for a speaker attempting to talk through a problem, work out a difficult situation, or express deep emotions. Sometimes, however, therapeutic listening occurs in public speaking situations such as when a sports star apologizes for unprofessional behavior, a religious convert describes a soul-saving experience, or a classmate reviews a personal problem and thanks friends for their help in solving it.

Listening for Comprehension

Listening for comprehension occurs when the listener wants to gain additional information or insights provided by the speaker. This is probably the form of listening with which you are most familiar. When you listen to radio or TV news programs, to classroom lectures on the four principal causes of World War II, or to an orientation official previewing your school's new registration process, you're listening to understand—to comprehend information, ideas, and processes.

Critical Listening

Critical listening requires listeners to both interpret and evaluate the message. The most sophisticated kind of listening is critical listening. It demands that auditors go beyond understanding the message to interpreting it, judging its strengths and weaknesses, and assigning it some value. You'll practice this sort of listening in your class. You may also use critical listening as you evaluate commercials, political campaign speeches, advice from career counselors, or arguments offered by controversial talk show guests. When you listen critically, you decide to accept or reject ideas. You may also resolve to act or delay action on the message. . . .

The variety of listening purposes has serious implications for both listeners and speakers. Appreciative listeners are highly selective, watching for metaphors, responding to speaking tones, and searching out memorable phrasings. At the other extreme, critical listeners work hard to catch relevant details, to judge the soundness of competing arguments and to rationally decide whether to accept ideas. Therapeutic listeners decide when to positively reinforce speakers through applause or other signs of approval, and those listening for comprehension distinguish between important and unimportant information. Finally, discriminative listeners search for clues to unspoken ideas or feelings that are relevant to themselves. As you think about your own listening purposes, you'll find yourself adapting your listening behavior to the speaking situation more carefully.

—Gronbeck et al., *Principles of Speech Communication,* pp. 38–39

EXERCISE 1–7

Evaluating Your Previewing

Without referring to the passage, answer each of the following true/false questions.

_____ 1. Discriminative listening requires listeners to pay attention to how the message is presented rather than to the message itself.

_____ 2. The purpose of therapeutic listening is to provide support for the speaker.

_____ 3. The purpose of listening for comprehension is to acquire information.

_____ 4. In appreciative listening, the listener focuses on the primary message.

_____ 5. Depending on their purpose, listeners pay attention to different parts of a message.

You probably were able to answer all (or most) of the questions correctly. Previewing, then, does provide you with a great deal of information. If you were to return to the passage from the speech communication textbook and read the entire section, you would find it easier to do than if you had not previewed.

Previewing Nontextbook Material

With nontextbook material, you may have to make changes in how you preview. Many articles, essays, and reference books do not have the same features as textbook chapters. They may lack headings or clearly identifiable introductions and summaries. The following hints will help you to preview materials of this sort.

1. **Pay close attention to the title;** it may make a statement about the theme or key focus of the article.
2. **Identify the author and source of the material.** This information may provide clues about the article's content or focus.
3. **Read the first paragraph carefully, searching for a statement of purpose or theme.**
4. **If there are no headings, read the first sentence of each paragraph.** The first sentence of the paragraph is often the topic sentence, which states the main idea of the paragraph. By reading first sentences, you will encounter most of the key ideas in the article.
5. **Pay close attention to the last paragraph.** It probably will not provide a summary, but it usually serves as a conclusion to the article.

Why Previewing Is Effective

Previewing helps you to make decisions about how you will approach the material. On the basis of what you discover about the assignment's organization and content, you can select the reading and study strategies that will be most effective.

Previewing puts your mind in gear and helps you start thinking about the subject.

Also, previewing gives you a mental outline of the chapter's content. It enables you to see how ideas are connected, and, since you know where the author is headed, your reading will be easier than if you had not previewed. Previewing, however, is never a substitute for careful, thorough reading.

EXERCISE 1–8

ACADEMIC
APPLICATION

Practicing Previewing

Select a textbook chapter that you have not read and preview it using the procedure described in this section. When you have finished, answer the following questions.

1. What is its overall subject?
2. What topics (aspects of the subject) does the chapter discuss? List as many as you can recall.
3. How difficult do you expect the chapter to be?
4. How is the subject approached? In other words, is the material practical, theoretical, historical, research oriented, or procedural?
5. How can you apply this material in your class?

Activating Your Background Knowledge

After previewing your assignment, you should take a moment to think about what you already know about the topic. Whatever the topic, you probably know *something* about it: this is your background knowledge. Activating your background knowledge aids your reading in three ways. First, it makes reading easier because you have already thought about the topic. Second, the material is easier to remember because you can connect the new information with what you already know. Third, topics become more interesting if you can link them to your own experiences. The Key Strategy box below offers techniques to help you activate your background knowledge.

KEY STRATEGY: How to Activate Your Background Knowledge

1. **Ask questions, and try to answer them.** If a chapter in your biology textbook titled "Human Diseases" contains headings such as "Infectious Diseases," "Sexually Transmitted Diseases," "Cancer," and "Vascular Diseases," you might ask and try to answer such questions as the following: What kinds of infectious diseases have I seen? What

continued

Key Strategies *continued*

caused them? What do I know about preventing cancer and other diseases?

2. **Draw on your own experience.**   If a chapter in your business textbook is titled "Advertising: Its Purpose and Design," you might think of several ads you have seen and analyze the purpose of each and how it was constructed.

3. **Brainstorm.**   Suppose you're about to read a chapter in your sociology textbook on domestic violence. You might list types of violence (child abuse, rape, and so on), write questions ("What causes child abuse?" "How can it be prevented?"), or list incidents of domestic violence you have heard or read about.

EXERCISE 1-9   ### Activating Your Background Knowledge

Assume you have just previewed a chapter in your psychology text on psychological disorders. Discover what you already know about psychological disorders by using each of the techniques suggested previously. Then answer the questions that follow.

1. Did you discover you knew more about psychological disorders than you initially thought?
2. Which technique worked best? Why?

Making Predictions

We make predictions about many tasks before we undertake them. We predict how long it will take to drive to a shopping mall, how much dinner will cost at a new restaurant, how long a party will last, or how difficult an exam will be. Prediction helps us organize our time and cope with new situations.

Prediction is an important part of active reading as well. It enables you to approach the material systematically. Also, it helps you to read actively because you continually accept or reject your predictions. As you preview, you can predict the development of ideas, the organization of the material, and the author's conclusions. For example, for her philosophy class, a student began to preview an essay titled "Do Computers Have a Right to Life?" From the title, she predicted that the essay would discuss the topic of artificial intelligence: whether computers can "think." Then, as she read the essay, she discovered that this prediction was correct.

In textbook chapters, the boldfaced headings serve as section "titles" and also are helpful in predicting content and organization. Considered together, chapter headings often suggest the development of ideas through the chapter. For instance, the following headings appeared in a sociology text chapter titled "Energy and the Environment":

The Limits of Fossil Fuels

Nuclear Power: High Promises, Serious Risks

Conservation: The Hidden "Energy Source"

Solar Power: An Emerging Role

These headings reveal the author's approach to energy resources. We can predict that the chapter will describe the supply of fossil fuels as finite and nuclear power as risky; conservation and solar energy will be offered as viable alternatives.

| EXERCISE 1-10 | **Making Predictions** |

Predict the subject and/or point of view of each of the following essays or articles.

1. "Reality as Presented by Television News"
2. "TV Violence—The Shocking New Threat to Society"
3. "Professional Sports: Necessary Violence"

| EXERCISE 1-11 | **Making Predictions** |

ACADEMIC
APPLICATION

Turn to the table of contents in one of your textbooks. Study the headings for two or three chapters you have not read. Predict the organization or focus of each chapter. Explain which words in the headings helped you make your prediction.

_____

_____

_____

■ Developing Guide Questions

Have you ever read an entire page or more and forgotten everything you read? Have you found yourself going from paragraph to paragraph without really thinking about what the writer is saying? Because you are not looking for anything in particular as you read, you do not notice or remember anything specific.

Reading should be a purposeful activity. You should have a reason for reading each piece of material that you pick up. Before you begin reading any article, selection, or chapter, you should know what you want to find out.

The easiest way to make certain you are reading purposefully is to use guide questions. These are specific questions that guide or direct your attention to what is important in each chapter section you are reading.

One of the easiest ways to make up guide questions is to turn the chapter title and headings into questions that you will try to answer as you read. Jot them down in the margin of your text, next to each heading, until you get in the habit of forming them. Later, you can form the questions mentally. Here are three examples:

Chapter Title: "Nine Principles of Communication"
Question: What are the nine principles of communication?

Essay Title:	"The Real Way to Prevent Nuclear War"
Questions:	How does the essayist think nuclear war can be prevented?
	Are these preventive measures realistic and practical?
Chapter Heading:	"Theories of Color Vision"
Questions:	What are the theories of color vision?
	How do they differ?

Avoid asking guide questions that have one-word answers or that require recall of details. "How," "what," and "why" questions generally are more useful than those beginning with "who," "when," and "where."

EXERCISE 1-12

Writing Guide Questions

Write at least one guide question for each of the following headings that appear in a criminology textbook.

Headings	Questions
Technology and Criminal Justice	_____
Criminalistics: Past, Present, and Future	_____
The Justice System Today	_____
Cybercrime: The New White-Collar crime	_____
Rules of Terrorism	_____
Controlling Terrorism	_____
Technology and Individual Rights	_____

EXERCISE 1-13

ACADEMIC
APPLICATION

Writing Guide Questions

Select a chapter from one of your textbooks, and write guide questions for each major heading.

■ Checking Your Comprehension

You maintain an awareness or "check" on how well you are performing many of your daily activities. In sports such as racquetball, tennis, and bowling, you know if you are playing a poor game; you actually keep score and deliberately try to correct errors and improve your performance. When preparing a favorite food, you often taste as you cook to be sure the recipe will taste the way you want it. When you wash your car, you check to be sure that you have not missed any spots.

A similar type of checking should occur as you read. You need to "keep score" of how effectively you are comprehending and reacting to content. Because reading is a mental process, it is more difficult to check than is bowling or cooking. You may understand certain ideas you read and be confused by others.

Recognizing Comprehension Signals

What happens when you read material you can understand easily? Does it seem that everything "clicks"? Do ideas seem to fit together and make sense? Is that "click" noticeably absent at other times?

Read each of the following excerpts. As you read, be alert to how well you understand each one.

EXCERPT 1

As you well know, all you have to do to reveal anger is change the way you talk: you may talk louder, faster, and more articulately than usual. You can say exactly the same thing in a fit of anger as in a state of delight and change your meaning by how you say it. You can say "I hate you" to sound angry, teasing, or cruel. Vocal cues are what is lost when your words are written down. The term often used to refer to this quality is paralanguage. As noted before, it includes all the nonlanguage means of vocal expression, such as rate, pitch, and tone. It includes, therefore, what occurs beyond or in addition to the words you speak.

—Weaver, *Understanding Interpersonal Communication,* pp. 226–27

EXCERPT 2

Large-quantity waste generators and SQGs must comply with the RCRA regulations, including obtaining an EPA identification (EPA ID) number, proper handling of the waste transport, manifesting the waste (discussed in the next section), and proper record keeping and reporting. Conditionally exempt SQGs do not require EPA ID numbers. Appropriate transport handling requires suitable packaging to prevent leakage and labeling of the packaged waste to identify its characteristics and dangers.

—Nathanson, *Basic Environmental Technology,* p. 351

Did you feel comfortable and confident as you read Excerpt 1? Did the ideas seem to lead from one to another and make sense? How did you feel while reading Excerpt 2? Probably you found it difficult and felt confused. Unfamiliar terms were used, and you could not follow the flow of ideas, so the whole passage did not make sense.

Table 1-5 (p. 44) lists and compares common signals to assist you in checking your comprehension. Not all the signals appear at the same time, and not all the signals work for everyone. As you study the list, identify those positive signals you sensed as you read the first excerpt about paralanguage. Then identify the negative signals you sensed when reading the excerpt about waste generators.

TABLE 1–5   Comprehension Signals

POSITIVE SIGNALS	NEGATIVE SIGNALS
You feel comfortable and have some knowledge about the topic.	The topic is unfamiliar, yet the author assumes you understand it.
You recognize most words or can figure them out from context.	Many words are unfamiliar.
You can express the main ideas in your own words.	You must reread the main ideas and use the author's language to explain them.
You understand why the material was assigned.	You do not know why the material was assigned and cannot explain why it is important.
You read at a regular, comfortable pace.	You often slow down or reread.
You are able to make connections between ideas.	You are unable to detect relationships; the organization is not apparent.
You are able to see where the author is leading.	You feel as if you are struggling to stay with the author and are unable to predict what will follow.
You understand what is important.	Nothing (or everything) seems important.

EXERCISE 1-14   **Checking Your Comprehension**

ACADEMIC
APPLICATION

Select and read a three- to four-page section of a chapter in one of your textbooks. Be alert for positive and negative comprehension signals as you read. After reading the section, answer the following questions.

1. How would you rate your overall comprehension? What positive signals did you sense? Did you feel any negative signals?
2. Where was your comprehension strongest?
3. Did you feel at any time that you had lost, or were about to lose, comprehension? If so, go back to that part now. What made it difficult to read?

Checking Techniques

At times you may think you have understood a chapter, only to find out later, on a exam, that you did not. To make sure your comprehension is complete and accurate, use the following techniques.

1. **Use your guide questions.** When you finish reading a chapter section, stop and see if you can answer your questions.
2. **Ask application, analysis, evaluation, and creation questions.** When you finish a chapter section, ask questions such as
   - How does this assignment fit with the class lectures?
   - How does this assignment fit with what I know about the topic?
   - How useful is this information in relation to the topic I am studying?
   - How can I use this information in my major or on the job?

3. **Rephrase content in your own words.** If you cannot express an idea in your own words, you probably do not understand it.

| EXERCISE 1-15 | Checking Your Comprehension |

ACADEMIC
APPLICATION

Select another section from one of your textbooks and practice checking your comprehension. On a sheet of paper, describe the technique you used and evaluate its effectiveness.

■ Using the SQ3R Reading/Study System

The SQ3R system has been used successfully for many years and has proved effective in increasing retention of information. It is especially useful for textbooks and other highly factual, well-organized materials. Basically, SQ3R is a way of learning as you read. Its name is taken from the first letter of each step. The box below summarizes the steps, and then you will apply the system to a sample selection.

KEY STRATEGY: Steps in the SQ3R System

Survey Become familiar with the overall content and organization of the material using the steps for previewing in the Key Strategy box on page 35.

Question Ask questions about the material that you expect to be able to answer as you read. As you read each successive heading, turn it into a question.

Read As you read each section, actively search for the answers to your guide questions. When you find the answers, underline or mark the portions of the text that concisely state the information.

Recite Probably the most important part of the system, "recite" means that after each section or after each major heading you should stop, look away from the page, and try to remember the answer to your question. If you are unable to remember, look back at the page and reread the material. Then test yourself again by looking away from the page and "reciting" the answer to your question.

Review Immediately after you have finished reading, go back through the material again, reading headings and summaries. As you read each heading, recall your question and test yourself to see whether you can still remember the answer. If you cannot, reread that section. Once you are satisfied that you have understood and recalled key information, move toward the higher-level thinking skills. Ask application, analysis, evaluation, and creation questions. Some students like to add a fourth "R" step—for "React."

Now, to get a clear picture of how the steps in the SQ3R method work, let's apply them to a textbook reading. Suppose you have been assigned the article on page 46 on nonverbal communication for a communication class. Follow each of the SQ3R steps in reading this section.

Survey Preview the article, noting introductions, headings, first sentences, and typographical clues. From this previewing, you should have a good idea of what information this article will convey and should know the general conclusions the author draws about the subject.

Question Use the headings to ask several questions you expect the article to answer. You might ask such questions as

What are the major types of nonverbal cues?

What are spatial cues?

What messages are communicated at each of the four distances?

Read Now read the selection through. Keep your questions in mind. Stop at the end of each major section and proceed to the next step.

Recite After each section, stop reading and check to see whether you can recall the answer to the corresponding question.

Review When you have finished reading the entire article, take a few minutes to reread the headings, recall your questions, and write answers to your questions to see how well you can remember the answers.

TYPES OF NONVERBAL CUES

You now have a definition of nonverbal communication, you know how much nonverbal communication counts, you understand the characteristics most nonverbal cues share, and you know the functions and forms, so it is time to examine the types of nonverbal cues. In this section, spatial cues, visual cues, vocal cues, touch, time, and silence will be discussed.

Spatial Cues

Spatial cues are the distances we choose to stand or sit from others. Each of us carries with us something called informal space. We might think of this as a bubble; we occupy the center of the bubble. This bubble expands or contracts depending on varying conditions and circumstances such as these:

- Age and sex of those involved.
- Cultural and ethnic background of the participants.
- Topic or subject matter.
- Setting for the interaction.

- Physical characteristics of the participants (size or shape).
- Attitudinal and emotional orientation of partners.
- Characteristics of the interpersonal relationship (like friendship).
- Personality characteristics of those involved.

In his book *The Silent Language,* Edward T. Hall, a cultural anthropologist, identifies the distances that people assume when they talk with others. He calls these distances intimate, personal, social, and public. In many cases, the adjustments that occur in these distances result from some of the factors listed above.

Intimate distance. At an **intimate distance** (0 to 18 inches), you often use a soft or barely audible whisper to share intimate or confidential information. Physical contact becomes easy at this distance. This is the distance we use for physical comforting, lovemaking, and physical fighting, among other things.

Personal distance. Hall identified the range of 18 inches to 4 feet as **personal distance**. When you disclose yourself to someone, you are likely to do it within this distance. The topics you discuss at this range may be somewhat confidential and usually are personal and mutually involving. At personal distance you are still able to touch another if you want to. This is likely to be the distance between people conversing at a party, between classmates in a casual conversation, or within many work relationships. This distance assumes a well-established acquaintanceship. It is probably the most comfortable distance for free exchange of feedback.

Social distance. When you are talking at a normal level with another person, sharing concerns that are not of a personal nature, you usually use the **social distance** (4 to 12 feet). Many of your on-the-job conversations take place at this distance. Seating arrangements in living rooms may be based on "conversation groups" of chairs placed at a distance of 4 to 7 feet from each other. Hall calls 4 to 7 feet the close phase of social distance; from 7 to 12 feet is the far phase of social distance.

The greater the distance, the more formal the business or social discourse conducted is likely to be. Often, the desks of important people are broad enough to hold visitors at a distance of 7 to 12 feet. Eye contact at this distance becomes more important to the flow of communication; without visual contact one party is likely to feel shut out and the conversation may come to a halt.

Public distance. **Public distance** (12 feet and farther) is well outside the range for close involvement with another person. It is impractical for interpersonal communication. You are limited to what you can see and hear at that distance; topics for conversation are relatively impersonal and formal; and most of the communication that occurs is in the public-speaking style, with subjects planned in advance and limited opportunities for feedback.

—Weaver, *Understanding Interpersonal Communications*, pp. 215–18

How SQ3R Improves Your Reading Efficiency

The SQ3R system improves your reading efficiency in three ways. It increases your comprehension, it enhances your recall, and it saves you valuable time by encouraging you to learn as you read.

Because you are learning as you are reading, you will save time later when you are ready to study the material for an exam. Since you already have learned the material through recitation and review, you will find that you need much less time to prepare for an exam. Instead of learning the material for the first time, you can spend the time reviewing. You also will have time to consider applications, to pull the material together, to analyze it, and to evaluate its usefulness.

Adapting SQ3R to Suit Your Learning Style

You have probably found that some learning techniques work better for you than others. Just as everyone's personality is unique, so is everyone's learning style (see p. 23). Use knowledge of your learning style to develop your own reading/study system. Experiment with various study methods and adapt the SQ3R system accordingly. For instance, if writing outlines helps you recall information, then replace the Recite step with an Outline step, and make the Review step a Review of Outline step. Or if you have discovered that you learn well by listening, replace the Recite and Review steps with Record and Listen steps, in which you dictate and record information to be learned and reviewed by listening to the recording.

There are numerous possibilities for developing your own reading/study system. The best approach is to test variations until you find the most effective system.

EXERCISE 1-16	**Adapting the SQ3R System**

Get together with other students taking one of the same courses you are (or courses within the same discipline or department). Discuss and prepare a list of modifications to the SQ3R system that would be appropriate for your course's content and learning requirements.

EXERCISE 1-17	**Using SQ3R**

Apply the SQ3R system to a chapter in one of your other textbooks. List your questions on a separate sheet of paper, and underline the answers in your textbook. Evaluate the effectiveness of your approach and decide on any modifications needed.

Self-Test Summary

1. Why is active reading important for success in college?	Reading is the primary way in which students acquire ideas and gather information.
2. How is active reading different from passive reading?	Active readers analyze an assignment, determine its purpose, and tailor their reading accordingly. Passive readers read only what is assigned. Active readers make notes as they read and make sure they understand what they are reading. Passive readers read everything at the same pace and in the same way, not making the distinction between what is relevant to the information they are getting in class and what is not.
3. People have different learning styles. Why is it important to understand what your learning style is?	A person's learning style can make certain classes or assignments easy and others more difficult. Understanding how you learn can help you form an action plan and develop strategies for tackling the subjects and assignments that are difficult for you.
4. What are some of the things you can do to focus your attention on what you are reading?	Set goals, reward yourself, review previously read material, write notes and underline as you read, and read critically.
5. How can you assess your concentration and what can you do to improve it?	Concentration can be assessed by keeping track of every time your mind wanders and analyzing what happened each of these times to distract you. To improve your concentration, look for patterns and make adjustments to when, where, and how you study.
6. What are the six stages involved in active reading?	The stages of active reading are remembering, understanding, applying, analyzing, evaluating, and creating.
7. Why is previewing important?	Previewing helps you become familiar with the chapter's content and organization and enables you to make predictions.
8. What are guide questions?	Guide questions are specific questions that direct your attention to what is important in each chapter or section you read.
9. How can you check your comprehension?	Use guide questions; ask application, analysis, and synthesis questions; rephrase content.
10. What are the five steps in the SQ3R system?	The steps are survey, question, read, recite, and review.

Factors Affecting Interpersonal Attraction

Josh R. Gerow

Prereading Question

Think of a person to whom you are attracted. Why are you attracted to him or her?

1   Now let's look at some empirical evidence related to attraction. What determines whom you will be attracted to? What factors tend to provide the rewards, or the positive reward/cost ratios, that serve as the basis for strong relationships? Here we'll describe four common principles related to interpersonal attraction.

Reciprocity

2   Our first principle is perhaps the most obvious one. Not surprisingly, we tend to value and like people who like and value us (Backman & Secord; Curtis & Miller). Remember that we've already noted, in our discussion of operant conditioning, that the attention of others often can be a powerful reinforcer. This is particularly true if the attention is positive, supportive, and affectionate. Research indicates that the value of someone

Proximity leads to liking, which is why teenagers who go to the same school are likely to form friendships.

else caring for us is particularly powerful when that someone initially seemed to have neutral or even negative attitudes toward us (Aronson & Linder). That is, we are most attracted to people who like us now, but who didn't originally. The logic here is related to attribution. If someone we meet for the first time expresses nothing but positive feelings and attitudes toward us, we are likely to attribute their reaction internally to the way the person is—rather shallow and the sort who just likes everybody. But if someone at first were to express neutral, or even slightly negative, feelings toward us and then were to become more and more positive, we might have a different, more positive view of their ability to judge others.

Proximity

3   Our second principle suggests that physical closeness, or proximity, tends to produce attraction. Sociologists, as well as your own personal experience, will tell you that people tend to establish friendships (and romances) with others with whom they have grown up, worked, or gone to school. Similarly, social-psychological studies consistently have found that residents of apartments or dormitories tend to become friends with those other res-

idents living closest to them (Festinger et al.). Being around others gives us the opportunity to discover just who can provide those interpersonal rewards we seek in friendship.

4   There may be another social-psychological phenomenon at work here called the **mere exposure phenomenon.** Research, pioneered by Robert Zajonc, has shown with a variety of stimuli that liking tends to increase with repeated exposure to stimuli. Examples of this phenomenon are abundant in everyday life. Have you ever bought a CD that you have not heard previously, assuming that you will like it because you have liked all the other CDs this performer made? The first time you listen to your new CD, however, your reaction may be lukewarm at best, and you may be disappointed in your purchase. Not wanting to feel that you've wasted your money, you play the CD a few more times over the next several days. What often happens is that soon you realize that you like this CD after all. The mere exposure effect has occurred, and this commonly happens in our formation of attitudes about other people as well. Apparently, familiarity is apt to breed attraction, not contempt. I also have to add that although there seems to be ample evidence that the mere exposure phenomenon is real, there remains considerable disagreement about *why* familiarity and repeated interactions breed attraction (e.g., Birnbaum & Mellers; Kunst-Wilson & Zajonc).

mere exposure phenomenon the tendency to increase our liking of people and things the more we see of them

Physical Attractiveness

5   Our physical appearance is one personal characteristic that we cannot easily hide. It is always on display in social situations, and it communicates something about us. People are aware of the role of appearance in nonverbal, interpersonal communication and may spend hours each week doing whatever can be done to improve the way they look.

6   The power of physical attractiveness in the context of dating has been demonstrated experimentally in a classic study directed by Elaine Walster (Walster et al.). University of Minnesota freshmen completed a number of psychological tests as part of an orientation program. The students were then randomly matched for dates to an orientation dance, during which they took a break and evaluated their assigned partners. This study allowed researchers the possibility of uncovering intricate, complex, and subtle facts about interpersonal attraction, such as which personality traits might tend to mesh in such a way as to produce attraction. As it turned out, none of these complex factors, so carefully controlled for, was important. The effect of physical attractiveness was so powerful that it wiped out all other effects. For both men and women, the more physically attractive their date, the more they liked the person and the more they wanted to go out again with that individual.

7   Numerous studies of physical attractiveness followed this one. Some of these studies simply gave subjects a chance to pick a date from a group of several potential partners (usually using descriptions and pictures). Not surprisingly, subjects almost invariably selected the most attractive person available to be their date (Reis et al.).

8   You may have noticed, however, that in real life we seldom have the opportunity to request a date without at least the possibility of being turned down. When experimental studies began to build in the possibility of rejection, an interesting effect emerged: Subjects stopped picking the most attractive candidate and started selecting partners whose level of physical attractiveness was more similar to their own. This behavior has been called the **matching phenomenon,** and it is an effect that has been verified by naturalistic observation studies (Walster & Walster).

matching phenomenon the tendency to select partners whose level of physical attractiveness matches our own

Similarity

9   There is a large body of research on the relationship between similarity and attraction, but the findings are consistent, and we can summarize them briefly. Much of this research has been done by Donn Byrne and his colleagues (e.g., Byrne). It indicates that there is a strong positive relationship between attraction and the proportion of attitudes held in common. Simply put, the more similar another person is to you, the more you will tend to like that person (Buss, Davis, Rubin). Sensibly, we also tend to be repelled, or put off, by persons we believe to be dissimilar to us (Rosenbaum).

10   Perhaps you know a happily married couple for whom this sweeping conclusion does not seem to fit. At least some of their behaviors seem to be quite dissimilar, almost opposite. Perhaps the wife appears to be the one who makes most of the decisions while the husband simply seems to follow orders. It may very well be the case, however, that this apparent lack of similarity in behavior exists only on the surface. There may be an important similarity that makes for a successful marriage here: Both have the same idea of what a marriage should be like—wives decide and husbands obey. In such a case, the observed differences in behavior are reflecting a powerful similarity in the view of the roles of married couples.

—Gerow, *Psychology: An Introduction*, pp. 654–56

Writing About the Reading

CHECKING YOUR VOCABULARY

1. For each of the words listed below, use context; prefixes, roots, and suffixes (see Chapter 3); and/or a dictionary to write a brief definition or synonym of the word as it is used in the reading.

   a. empirical (para. 1) _____

   b. reciprocity (above para. 2) _____

   c. proximity (para. 3) _____

   d. phenomenon (para. 4) _____

   e. invariably (para. 7) _____

   f. dissimilar (para. 9) _____

2. Underline new, specialized terms introduced in the reading.

CHECKING YOUR COMPREHENSION

1. Write a list of guide questions useful in reading and reviewing this reading.
2. Check your level of comprehension. What positive or negative signals did you sense?
3. What are the four principles discussed in this reading?
4. Explain the mere exposure phenomenon.
5. Explain the matching phenomenon.

THINKING CRITICALLY

1. Think of someone to whom you are attracted. Which of the principles of attraction can account for your attraction?
2. Can you think of other factors not discussed in this reading that may account for interpersonal attraction?
3. Describe an instance in which you experienced the mere exposure phenomenon.
4. Have you observed or experienced the matching phenomenon? If so, describe the situation in which it occurred.

LEARNING/STUDY STRATEGY

For each of the four principles of attraction, the author describes one or more experiments that are related to the principle. To review this research, complete the study chart below.

Principle	Author(s)	Summary of Findings
1. Reciprocity		
2. Proximity		
3. Physical attractiveness		
4. Similarity		

MyReadingLab

To practice your active reading skills, go to http://www.myreadinglab.com. Click on "Study Plan," then on "Reading Skills," and then on "Active Reading Strategies."

2 Fundamental Comprehension Skills

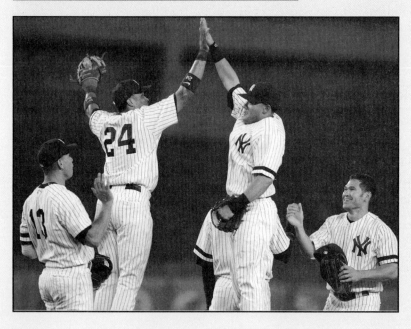

What is happening in this photo? On the face of it, two teammates seem to be celebrating a victory. But there is more to the story. Are they members of an "underdog" team that came from behind to win a championship game? Or did they work together to score the winning point in a particularly tight game with a rival team? Whether you are looking at a photo or reading a college textbook, you are actively seeking to make sense of it, to have a fundamental *comprehension* of the facts.

LEARNING OBJECTIVES

■ To locate main ideas

■ To identify supporting details

■ To learn how to vary your reading rate

READING COMPREHENSION: The Academic Link

This chapter presents techniques that will help you read better and understand more. There are no easy tricks to becoming a faster or better reader; textbook reading must always be relatively slow and deliberate. The key to success when you are faced with large amounts of reading is selectivity: sorting out what is important and focusing your attention on it.

READING COMPREHENSION: The Career Link

The amount of information that will come at you daily—on the TV news, at your desk at work, via the Internet—can sometimes seem overwhelming. To be effective at your job, you must know how to sort out what is more important from what is less important. By understanding how paragraphs are structured, you will find it easier to locate and use key information, which will save you time and make you more effective at your job.

■ Locating Main Ideas and Supporting Details

Not all sentences within a paragraph are equally important. In fact, there are three levels of importance:

> Most important: the main idea
>
> Less important: primary supporting details
>
> Least important: secondary supporting details

Tip for Math/ Physical Science Majors

In mathematics and the physical sciences like chemistry, physics, and engineering, main ideas are often spelled out as *theorems, principles,* or *laws,* which are the principles that guide that discipline. Textbooks in these areas have relatively little text but many problems and examples. Reading the text is important because it is through these brief discussions that important main ideas are conveyed.

As you read a paragraph, you should be sorting ideas according to their relative importance and paying more attention to some than to others. Here, you will learn how to identify these levels of importance as well as how ideas fit and work together in a paragraph.

Finding the Main Idea

A **paragraph** can be defined as a group of related ideas. The sentences are related to one another and all are about the same person, place, thing, or idea. The common subject or idea is called the **topic**—what the focus of the entire paragraph is about. As you read the following paragraph, you will see that its topic is elections.

> Americans elect more people to office than almost any other society. Each even year, when most elections occur, more than 500,000 public officials are elected to school boards, city councils, county offices, state legislatures, state executive positions, the House of Representatives and the Senate, and of

course, every fourth year, the presidency. By contrast with other countries, our elections are drawn-out affairs. Campaigns for even the most local office can be protracted over two or three months and cost a considerable amount of money. Presidential campaigns, including the primary season, last for at least ten months, with some candidates beginning to seek support many months and, as noted earlier, even years before the election.

—Baradat, *Understanding American Democracy*, p. 163

Each sentence of this paragraph discusses or describes elections. To identify the topic of a paragraph, then, ask yourself: *"What or who is the paragraph about?"*

The **main idea** of a paragraph is what the author wants you to know about the topic. It is the broadest, most important idea that the writer develops throughout the paragraph. The entire paragraph explains, develops, and supports this main idea. A question that will guide you in finding the main idea is, *"What key point is the author making about the topic?"* In the paragraph above, the writer's main idea is that elections in America are more numerous and more drawn out than in other countries.

Topic Sentence

Tip for Psychology/Social Science Majors

In general, majors in the social sciences are asked to do a lot of writing of their own because careers in these fields often require detailed reports. Learning how to identify a topic sentence is a valuable skill that you should apply to your own writing. Paragraphs with clear, concise topic sentences make it easy for readers to understand the information that is being conveyed.

Often, but not always, one sentence expresses the main idea. This sentence is called the **topic sentence**.

To find the topic sentence, search for the one general sentence that explains what the writer wants you to know about the topic. A topic sentence is a broad, general statement; the remaining sentences of the paragraph provide details about or explain the topic sentence.

In the following paragraph, the topic is stereotypes. Read the paragraph to find out what the writer wants you to know about this topic. Look for one sentence that states this.

In everyday life, we use a variety of **stereotypes**, which are *static and over-simplified ideas about a group or social category*, that strongly influence our expectations and behaviors. In American society, there are stereotypes of women, men, jocks, the elderly, racial and ethnic minorities, college students, and countless other groups and social categories. When people are identified as belonging to a particular category, we assume they possess particular traits, and we act accordingly. Thus many people believe that redheads should be approached with caution, for they have hot tempers and can "explode at any time." By the same measure, negative stereotypes influence our interactions with racial and ethnic groups. If Scots are believed to be cheap, Italians passionate, and African Americans violent, in the early stages of interaction people will respond to them as if they possess these and other traits associated with their group, whether or not they have them.

—Thompson and Hickey, *Society in Focus*, p. 131

The paragraph opens with a statement and then proceeds to explain it by citing examples. The first sentence of the paragraph functions as a topic sentence, stating the paragraph's main point: Stereotypes exert strong influences on people's expectations and behaviors.

The topic sentence can be located anywhere in the paragraph. However, there are several positions where it is most likely to be found.

Topic Sentence First   Most often, the topic sentence is placed first in the paragraph. In this type of paragraph, the author first states his or her main point and then explains it.

   There is some evidence that colors affect you physiologically. For example, when subjects are exposed to red light, respiratory movements increase; exposure to blue decreases respiratory movements. Similarly, eye blinks increase in frequency when eyes are exposed to red light and decrease when exposed to blue. This seems consistent with intuitive feelings about blue being more soothing and red being more arousing. After changing a school's walls from orange and white to blue, the blood pressure of the students decreased while their academic performance improved.

—DeVito, *Human Communication*, p. 182

Here, the writer first states that there is evidence of the physiological effects of colors. The rest of the paragraph presents that evidence.

Topic Sentence Last   The second most likely place for a topic sentence to appear is last in the paragraph. When using this arrangement, a writer leads up to the main point and then directly states it at the end.

   Is there a relationship between aspects of one's personality and that person's state of physical health? Can psychological evaluations of an individual be used to predict physical as well as psychological disorders? Is there such a thing as a disease-prone personality? Our response is very tentative, and the data are not all supportive, but for the moment we can say yes, there does seem to be a positive correlation between some personality variables and physical health.

—Gerow, *Psychology: An Introduction*, p. 700

In this paragraph, the author ponders the relationship between personality and health and concludes with the paragraph's main point: that they are related.

Topic Sentence in the Middle   If it is placed neither first nor last, then the topic sentence appears somewhere in the middle of the paragraph. In this arrangement, the sentences before the topic sentence lead up to or introduce the main idea. Those that follow the main idea explain or describe it.

   There are 1,500 species of bacteria and approximately 8,500 species of birds. The carrot family alone has about 3,500 species, and there are 15,000 known species of wild orchids. Clearly, the task of separating various living things into their proper groups is not an easy task. Within the insect family, the problem becomes even more complex. For example, there are about 300,000 species of beetles. In fact, certain species are disappearing from the earth before we can even identify and classify them.

—Wallace, *Biology: The World of Life,* p. 283

In this paragraph, the author first gives several examples of living things for which there are numerous species. Then he states his main point: Separating living things into species is not an easy task. The remainder of the paragraph offers an additional example and provides further information.

Topic Sentence First and Last   Occasionally, the main idea is stated at the beginning of a paragraph and again at the end, or elsewhere in the paragraph. Writers may use this organization to emphasize an important idea or to explain an idea that needs clarification. At other times, the first and last sentences together express the paragraph's main idea.

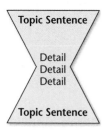

Many elderly people have trouble getting the care and treatment they need for their ailments. Most hospitals, designed to handle injuries and acute illness that are common to the young, do not have the facilities or personnel to treat the chronic degenerative diseases of the elderly. Many doctors are also ill-prepared to deal with such problems. As Fred Cottrell points out, "There is a widespread feeling among the aged that most doctors are not interested in them and are reluctant to treat people who are as little likely to contribute to the future as the aged are reputed to." Even with the help of Medicare, the elderly in the United States often have a difficult time getting the health care that they need.

—Coleman and Cressey, *Social Problems,* p. 277

The first and last sentences together explain that many elderly people in the United States have difficulty obtaining needed health care.

EXERCISE 2-1

Identifying Topic Sentences

Underline the topic sentence(s) of each of the following paragraphs.

1. People of nearly every culture have given names to patterns in the sky. The pattern that the Greeks named Orion, the hunter, was seen as a supreme warrior called *Shen* by the ancient Chinese. Hindus in ancient India also saw a warrior, called *Skanda*, who rode a peacock as the general of a great celestial army. The three stars of Orion's belt were seen as three fisherman in a canoe by Aborigines of northern Australia. As seen from southern California, these three stars climb almost straight up into the sky as they rise in the east, which may explain why the Chemehuevi Indians of the California desert saw them as a line of three sure-footed mountain sheep. These are but a few of the many names, each accompanied by a rich folklore, given to the pattern of stars that we call Orion.

—Bennett et al., *The Cosmic Perspective,* p. 28

2. Language consists of a large number of *symbols.* The symbols that constitute language are commonly referred to as words—labels that we have assigned to

concepts, or our mental representations. When we use the word *chair* as a symbol, we don't use it to label just one specific instance of a chair. We use the word as a symbol to represent our concept of chairs. As symbols, words need not stand for real things in the real world. We have words to describe objects or events that cannot be perceived, such as *ghost* or, for that matter, *mind*. With language we can communicate about owls and pussycats in teacups and a four-dimensional, time-warped hyperspace. Words stand for cognitions, or concepts, and we have a great number of them.

—Gerow, *Psychology: An Introduction*, p. 250

3. Body mass is made up of protoplasm, extracellular fluid, bone, and adipose tissue (body fat). One way to determine the amount of adipose tissue is to measure the whole-body density. After the on-land mass of the body is determined, the under-water body mass is obtained by submerging the person in water. Since water helps support the body by giving it buoyancy, the apparent body mass is less in water. A higher percentage of body fat will make a person more buoyant, causing the under-water mass to be even lower. This occurs because fat has a lower density than the rest of the body.

—Timberlake, *Chemistry: An Introduction to General,*
Organic, and Biological Chemistry, p. 30

4. Early biologists who studied reflexes, kineses, taxes, and fixed action patterns assumed that these responses are inherited, unlearned, and common to all members of a species. They clearly depend on internal and external factors, but until recently, instinct and learning were considered distinct aspects of behavior. However, in some very clever experiments, Jack Hailman of the University of Wisconsin showed that certain stereotyped behavior patterns require subtle forms of experience for their development. In other words, at least some of the behavior normally called instinct is partly learned.

—Mix et al., *Biology, The Network of Life,* p. 532

5. The poorest 20 percent of the elderly, who are primarily unmarried women, minorities, and the physically impaired, possess only 5.5 percent of all of the elderly's resources, whereas the wealthiest 20 percent own 46 percent of the total. Retirement or loss of work due to ill health, decreased physical abilities, or other age-related factors can be economically devastating. While it is a myth that the vast majority of the elderly are poor, those over age 65 have a lower median income than all other adult categories between ages 25 and 64, and elderly members of African American, Hispanic, and other minority groups fare far worse than elderly white Americans. Sixty-two percent of persons over age 65 in this country receive over half their income from Social Security, which is the only source of income for many elderly Americans. In short, the public perception that inequality narrows after age 65 in numbers is inaccurate, and for the aged, even more than for other age cohort, it is true that the rich get richer and the poor get poorer.

—Thompson and Hickey, *Society in Focus,* p. 35

Finding an Implied Main Idea

Detail
Detail
Detail

Although most paragraphs do have a topic sentence, some do not. Such paragraphs contain only details or specifics that, taken together, point to the main idea. The main idea, then, is implied but not directly stated. In such paragraphs, you must infer, or reason out, the main idea. This is a process of adding up the details and deciding what they mean together or what main idea they all support or explain. Use the following steps to grasp implied main ideas:

1. **Identify the topic by asking yourself, "What is the one thing the author is discussing throughout the paragraph?"**
2. **Decide what the writer wants you to know about the topic. Look at each detail and decide what larger idea each explains.**
3. **Express this idea in your own words.**

☑ **Tip for Humanities/ Liberal Arts Majors**

In the humanities and liberal arts, the discussion of various perspectives is often as important as the conclusion that is drawn. When looking for implied main ideas (for example, in history textbooks), be sure that you take into account the differing perspectives and do not overgeneralize.

Here is a sample paragraph; use the preceding steps to identify the main idea.

> As recently as 20 years ago, textbooks on child psychology seldom devoted more than a few paragraphs to the behaviors of the neonate—the newborn through the first 2 weeks of life. It seemed as if the neonate did not do much worth writing about. Today, most child psychology texts devote substantially more space to discussing the abilities of newborns. It is unlikely that over the past 20 years neonates have gotten smarter or more able. Rather, psychologists have. They have devised new and clever ways of measuring the abilities and capacities of neonates.
>
> —Gerow, *Psychology: An Introduction,* p. 319

The topic of this paragraph is the neonate. The author's main point is that coverage of neonates in psychology texts has increased as psychologists have learned more about them.

EXERCISE 2-2

LEARNING
COLLABORATIVELY

Identifying Topic Sentences in a Passage

Read the following section from an ecology textbook and underline the topic sentence in each paragraph. Monitor your comprehension and list positive or negative comprehension signals (see Chapter 1, p. 44) you received while reading. Compare your list with those of other students in the class.

LIVING THINGS ARE BOTH COMPLEX AND ORGANIZED

Life on Earth consists of a hierarchy of structures. Each level is based on the one below it and provides the foundation for the one above it. All of life is built on a chemical foundation of substances called elements, each of which is a unique type of *matter.* An atom is the smallest particle of an element that retains the properties of that element. For example, a diamond is made of the element carbon. The smallest possible unit of the diamond is an individual carbon atom; any further division would produce isolated subatomic particles that would no longer be carbon.

Atoms may combine in specific ways to form assemblies called molecules; for example, one carbon atom can combine with two oxygen atoms to form a molecule of carbon dioxide. Although many simple molecules form spontaneously, only living things manufacture extremely large and complex molecules. The bodies of living things are composed primarily of complex molecules. The molecules of life are called organic molecules, meaning that they contain a framework of carbon, to which at least some hydrogen is bound. Although the chemical arrangement and interaction of atoms and molecules form the building blocks of life, the quality of life itself emerges on the level of the cell. Just as an atom is the smallest unit of an element, so the cell is the smallest unit of life. The differences between a living cell and a conglomeration of chemicals illustrate some of the emergent properties of life.

All cells contain genes, units of heredity that provide the information needed to control the life of the cell: subcellular structures called organelles, miniature chemical factories that use the information in the genes and keep the cell alive; and a plasma membrane, a thin sheet surrounding the cell that both encloses the cytoplasm (the organelles and the watery medium surrounding them) and separates the cell from the outside world. Some life-forms, mostly microscopic, consist of just one cell, but larger life-forms are composed of many cells, each with a specialized function. In multicellular life-forms, related cells combine to form tissues, which perform a particular function. For example, nervous tissue is composed of nerve cells and a variety of supporting cells. Various tissue types combine to form a structural unit called an organ (for example, the brain, which contains nervous tissue, connective tissue, and blood). A group of several organs that collectively perform a single function is called an organ system; for example, the brain, spinal cord, sense organs, and nerves form the nervous system. All the organ systems functioning cooperatively make up an individual living thing, the organism.

Broader levels of organization reach beyond individual organisms. A group of very similar, potentially interbreeding organisms constitutes a species. Members of the same species that live in a given area are considered a population. Populations of several species living and interacting in the same area form a community. A community and its nonliving environment—including land, water, and atmosphere—constitute an ecosystem. Finally, the entire surface region of Earth inhabited by living things (and including its nonliving components) is called the biosphere.

—Audesirk et al., *Biology: Life on Earth,* pp. 2, 4

Positive signals: _____

_____

_____

Negative signals:_____

_____

_____

Identifying Topic Sentences in Textbooks

Select a two- to three-page excerpt from one of your textbooks and underline the topic sentence of each paragraph.

Recognizing Primary and Secondary Details

Supporting details are those facts, reasons, examples, or statistics that prove or explain the main idea of a paragraph. Though all the details in a paragraph support the main idea, not all details are equally important. As you read, try to identify and pay attention to the most important, primary details. These primary details directly explain the main idea. Secondary, less important details may provide additional information, offer an example, or further explain one of the primary details. You might visualize the structure of a paragraph as follows:

```
MAIN IDEA
    Primary detail
        Secondary detail
        Secondary detail
    Primary detail
        Secondary detail
    Primary detail
```

Read the following paragraph. The topic is boxed, the main idea is double-underlined, and primary details are single-underlined.

Our data on the kinds of people who are more likely to read magazines are better than our data on the number who do. Surveys show, not surprisingly, that the amount of magazine reading is highly correlated with education. The more educated people are, the more time they are likely to spend reading magazines. We also know that women tend to read magazines more than men do. This is shown by various kinds of data, including the fact that magazines that appeal primarily to women outsell magazines that appeal primarily to men. There is little evidence that the sexual revolution has erased the clear distinctions between men's and women's tastes in magazines. Men are more likely than women to read magazines that cover news on business and finance, mechanics and science, sports, outdoor life, and those that include photographs of women in various states of undress. Men also have a higher probability of reading the general newsmagazines. Women, on the other hand, are more likely to read magazines with useful household information (recipes, home decor, child care, and gardening) or fashion and beauty information.

—Becker, *Discovering Mass Communication,* p. 159

This paragraph begins with a topic sentence. The primary details present what is known about magazine readership patterns, and the secondary details further explain and offer examples of these patterns.

To determine the importance of a particular detail, decide whether it directly explains the main idea or explains or provides further information about one of the primary details.

EXERCISE 2-4   Identifying Topic Sentences and Supporting Details

Read the following excerpt from a communication textbook. For each paragraph, draw a box around the topic sentence and underline the primary details. What types of details did the authors provide? When you have finished, evaluate your comprehension; summarize the key points of the excerpt in your own words.

COMMUNICATION

YouTube and User-Generated Video

By autumn 2006, users were uploading 65,000 short videos and streaming 100 million a day on the popular website YouTube. Most of these videos were amateur creations, such as altered commercials, music performances, mockumentaries and documentaries, comedy routines, and tapes of cute babies, pet antics, vacations, and local high school bands. Also in the mix were regular television shows, such as *The Daily Show* and *The Colbert Report*. YouTube had become the leader in user-generated content and "clip culture," a convergence of interactive web technologies and television that has transformed the way media producers and many media consumers think about video.

YouTube was founded in early 2005 by Chad Hurley, Jawed Karim, and Steve Chen. Having worked out how to post videos on the web without having to download special software, the team uploaded its first video of Karim standing in front of an elephant at the zoo. Internet users were attracted to other videos of the founders' everyday lives, and word of mouth spread quickly.

As it gained popularity, YouTube received the blessing of mainstream media critics. lonelygirl15's video diary attracted 10,000 subscribers and caught the attention of *New York Magazine* and NPR's *On the Media*, where critics debated issues of art and authenticity in user-generated video. (lonelygirl15 turned out to be a fake, created by a screenwriter and filmmaker.) Discussing lonelygirl15 and other YouTube contributors, former *Spin* editor Michael Hirschorn wrote, "Digital video is doing more than just providing infinite alternatives; it's making network product seem visually slow and outdated." Many media commentators noted the significance of user-generated video as overturning an old broadcast model of delivering content to a relatively passive audience. In the *Los Angeles Times*, media management consultant Randall Rothenberg wrote that YouTube represented "a remarkable, even revolutionary, democratizing of the means of production."

Utopian predictions about the new media were dampened by various issues related to authenticity, proper social conduct, and stealing. Criticisms arose over revelations that advertisers were slipping in fake videos purportedly from YouTube amateurs. During election season, concerns were expressed that negative campaign videos were harming the political process. Always a lurking issue, copyright infringement came to the fore. The Japanese Society for Rights of Authors, Composers and Publishers asked YouTube to remove 30,000 pirated clips, and after

Google purchased the site for $1.65 billion, Comedy Central demanded that all clips of its shows be removed. Only a year before, *The Daily Show's* executive producer had encouraged viewers to share clips online, and in an agreement between Google and Comedy Central's parent, Viacom, the clips were restored.

YouTube had provoked the television networks, including Fox and ABC, into putting their shows online, using their own websites and iTunes. In that way, the networks had a hope of making money through advertising revenues and cross-promotion. However, YouTube had already irrevocably changed the mediascape, technologically economically, aesthetically, and culturally.

Folkerts, et al., *The Media in Your Life,* p. 239

■ Adjusting Your Rate to Meet Comprehension Demands

Do you read the newspaper in the same way and at the same speed at which you read a biology textbook? Surprisingly, many people do.

If you are an efficient reader, however, you read the newspaper more quickly and in a different way than you read a biology textbook. Usually, the newspaper is easier to read, and you have a different purpose for reading it. Efficient readers adapt their speed and comprehension levels to suit the material.

To adapt your rate, you need to decide how you will read a given item. How you will read depends on why you are reading and how much you need to remember. A number of variables work together. To read efficiently, you must create a balance among these factors each time you read.

KEY STRATEGY: Adjusting Rate to Meet Comprehension Demands

The following steps will help you learn to vary your reading rate:

1. **Assess the text's difficulty.**   Factors such as difficulty of the language, length, and organization all affect text difficulty. Usually, longer or poorly organized material is more difficult to read than shorter or well-organized material. Numerous typographical aids (italics, headings, etc.) can make material easier to read. As you preview an assignment, notice these features and estimate how difficult the material will be to read.

2. **Assess your familiarity with and interest in the subject.**   Material you are interested in or that you know something about will be easier for you to read, and you can increase your speed.

3. **Define your purpose.**   Different situations demand different levels of comprehension and recall. For example, you can read an article in *Time* magazine assigned as a supplementary reading in sociology faster than you can read your sociology text because the magazine assignment does not require as high a level of recall and analysis.

4. **Decide what, if any, follow-up activity is required.**   Will you have to pass a multiple-choice exam on the content? Will you be participating in a class discussion? Will you summarize the information in a short paper? The activities that follow your reading determine, in part, the level of comprehension that is required. Passing an exam requires a very high level of reading comprehension, whereas preparing for a class discussion requires a more moderate level of comprehension or retention.

Table 2-1 shows the level of comprehension required for various types of material and gives approximate reading rates appropriate for each level.

TABLE 2-1   Levels of Comprehension

DESIRED LEVEL OF COMPREHENSION	TYPE OF MATERIAL	PURPOSE IN READING	RANGE OF READING RATES
Complete, 100%	Poetry, legal documents, argumentative writing	Analysis, criticism, evaluation	Under 200 wpm (words per minute)
High, 80–100%	Textbooks, manuals, research documents	High comprehension recall for exams, writing research reports, following directions	200–300 wpm
Moderate, 60–80%	Novels, paperbacks, newspapers, magazines	Entertainment enjoyment, general information	300–500 wpm
Selective, below 60%	Reference materials, catalogues, magazines	Overview of material, location of specific facts, review of previously read material	600–800 wpm

EXERCISE 2-5

Identifying Purpose and Level of Comprehension

For each of the following situations, define your purpose and indicate the level of comprehension that seems appropriate.

1. Reading the end-of-chapter discussion questions in a business marketing text as part of your chapter preview.

   Purpose: _____

   Comprehension level: _____

2. Reading a critical essay that analyzes a Shakespearean sonnet you are studying in a literature class.

   Purpose: _____

   Comprehension level: _____

3. Reading an encyclopedia entry on poverty to narrow down a term paper assignment to a manageable topic.

Purpose: _____

Comprehension level: _____

4. Reading a newspaper article on a recent incident in the Middle East for your political science class.

Purpose: _____

Comprehension level: _____

5. Reading an excerpt from a historical novel set in the Civil War period for your American history class.

Purpose: _____

Comprehension level: _____

Reading Selectively to Improve Your Reading Efficiency

Many students falsely believe that anything that appears in print must be true, valuable, and worth reading. Actually, the importance and value of printed information are affected by whether you need to learn it and whether you can use it in a practical way. Depending on the kind of material and your purpose for reading it, many times you may need to read only some parts and may skip over others, as shown in the Key Strategy box below.

KEY STRATEGY: Reading Selectively to Improve Reading Efficiency

Tip for Business Majors

Businesspeople are expected to keep up with what is going on in the world of business. Many make a habit of reading the business press (*The Wall Street Journal*, *The Financial Times*, *BusinessWeek*) on a daily basis. However, nobody has the time to read every page of these periodicals; this is where skimming becomes a very valuable skill. (Note that professionals of all types, not just those in business, are expected to read their industry publications to keep up on current news.)

You might read selectively when:

1. **You are searching for specific information.** If you are looking up the date of a historical event in your history text, you skip over everything in the chapter except the exact passage that contains the information. This technique of skipping everything except the specific information for which you are looking is called *scanning.*

2. **A high level of comprehension is not needed.** If you are not trying to remember a major portion of the facts and details, then you might concentrate on reading only main ideas. This method of reading only main ideas is called *skimming.*

3. **You are familiar with what you are reading.** In a college chemistry course, for example, you might find that the first few chapters of your text are basic if you have already studied high school chemistry. You could afford to skip basic definitions and the explanations and examples of principles that you already know. Do not, however, decide to skip an entire chapter or even large sections within it; there just may be some new information included. You may find that more exact and detailed definitions are given or that a new approach is taken toward a particular topic.

4. **The material does not match your purpose in reading.** Suppose that, in making an assignment in your physics text, your instructor told you to concentrate only on theories, laws, and principles presented in the chapter. As you begin reading the chapter, you find that the first topic discussed is Newton's law of motion, but the chapter also contains a biographical sketch of Newton giving detailed information about his life. Because your purpose in reading the chapter is to focus on theories, laws, and principles, it would be appropriate to skip over much of the biographical information.

5. **The writer's style allows you to skip information (portions).** Some writers include many examples of a particular concept or principle. If, after reading two or three examples, you are sure that you understand the idea being explained, quickly glance at the remaining examples. Unless they present a new aspect or different point of view, skip over them. Other writers provide detailed background information before leading into a discussion of the intended topic. If a chapter starts out by summarizing information that was covered in a chapter you just read last week, it is not necessary to read this information again carefully unless you feel you need to review.

EXERCISE 2-6 ## Practicing Reading Selectively

The following items suggest different reading situations and describe the material to be read. For each item, decide whether you should (a) read the material completely, (b) read parts and skip other parts, or (c) skip most of the material.

1. Your computer science instructor has just returned a test on a chapter of your textbook. She indicates that the class's overall performance on this test was poor and suggests that the chapter be reviewed. You received a grade of 77 on the test. How should you reread this chapter?

2. You have just attended English class, where your instructor discussed Shakespeare's *Richard III*. During his discussion, he made numerous references to Machiavelli's *The Prince*. You have never read this second work but think it's important to know something about it. How would you read it?

3. You are doing research for a sociology term paper on world trends in gender inequality. You are looking for information and statistics on recent income and employment trends. You have located several books from the 1960s on the topic of gender inequality in the United States. How would you read these books?

4. Your American history instructor has assigned each student to read a historical novel for the purpose of getting a realistic picture of what life was like and how people lived during a certain period. As you are reading, you come to a detailed two-page description of decorative glass making in Sandwich, Massachusetts. How should you read these two pages?

5. Your zoology professor has assigned a number of brief outside readings along with the chapters in your regular textbook. He has put them on reserve in the college library for the use of all his classes. This is the only place where they can be used. He did not say whether you would be tested on these readings. How would you read them?

Self–Test Summary

1. What is a paragraph?	A paragraph is a group of related ideas.
2. What is meant by the "main idea"?	The main idea is the most important idea expressed in the paragraph; it is the idea that the remainder of the paragraph explains or supports.
3. What is a primary supporting detail?	A primary supporting detail provides information that backs up the main idea.
4. What is a secondary supporting detail?	A secondary detail provides further explanation of the main idea or of one of the primary details.
5. What is a topic sentence?	A topic sentence is a broad statement that expresses the main idea.
6. What is an implied main idea?	An implied main idea is one that is suggested, but not directly stated.
7. What position can a topic sentence have in a paragraph?	The topic sentence can be the first, last, middle, or first and last sentences in a paragraph.
8. Why should you vary your reading rate?	You should vary your reading rate to suit the material and your purpose for reading it.
9. When is it appropriate to read selectively?	It is appropriate to read selectively when you are reading for only main ideas, a specific fact, or the answer to a question; when you are very familiar with the material; when the material does not match with your purpose; and when the style or type of material is conducive to skipping information.

Diversity in U.S. Families

James M. Henslin

Prereading Questions

1. Is there any such thing as a typical American family?
2. What different types of family structure have you encountered?

1   It is important to note that there is no such thing as *the* American family. Rather, family life varies widely throughout the United States. The significance of social class, noted earlier, will continue to be evident as we examine diversity in U.S. families.

African American Families

2   Note that the heading reads African American *families*, not *the* African American family. There is no such thing as *the* African American family any more than there is *the* white family or *the* Latino family. The primary distinction is not between African Americans and other groups, but between social classes (Willie and Reddick 2003). Because African Americans who are members of the upper class follow the class interests—preservation of privilege and family fortune—they are especially concerned about the family background of those whom their children marry (Gatewood 1990). To them, marriage is viewed as a merger of family lines. Children of this class marry later than children of other classes.

There is no such thing as the *African American family, any more than there is* the *Native American, Asian American, Latino, or Irish American family. Rather, each racial–ethnic group has different types of families, with the primary determinant being social class.*

3   Middle-class African American families focus on achievement and respectability. Both husband and wife are likely to work outside the home. A central concern is that their children go to college, get good jobs, and marry well—that is, marry people like themselves, respectable and hardworking, who want to get ahead in school and pursue a successful career.

4   African American families in poverty face all the problems that cluster around poverty (Wilson 1987, 1996; Anderson 1990/2006; Venkatesh 2006). Because the men are likely to have few skills and to be unemployed, it is difficult for them to fulfill the cultural roles of husband and father. Consequently, these families are likely to be headed by a woman and to have a high rate of births to single women. Divorce and desertion are also more common than among other classes. Sharing scarce resources and "stretching kinship" are primary survival mechanisms. People who have helped out in hard times are considered brothers, sisters, or cousins to whom one owes obligations as though they were blood relatives; and men who are not the biological fathers of their children are given fatherhood status (Stack 1974; Fischer et al. 2005). Sociologists use the term *fictive kin* to refer to this stretching of kinship.

5   From Figure A you can see that, compared with other groups, African American families are the least likely to be headed by married couples and the most likely to be headed by women. Because African American women tend to go farther in school than African American men, they are more likely than women in other racial–ethnic groups to marry men who are less educated than themselves (South 1991; Eshleman 2000).

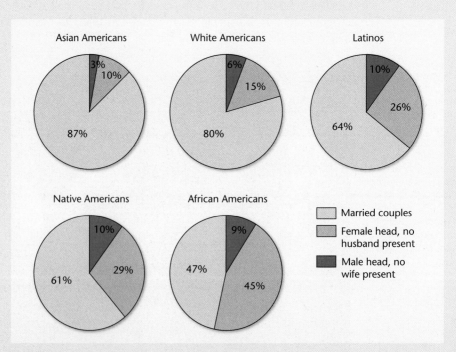

FIGURE A   Family Structure: The Percentage of U.S. Families Headed by Men, Women, and Married Couples

Latino Families

6   As Figure A shows, the proportion of Latino families headed by married couples and women falls in between that of whites and African Americans. The effects of social class on families, which I just sketched, also apply to Latinos. In addition, families differ by country of origin. Families from Mexico, for example, are more likely to be headed by a married couple than are families from Puerto Rico (*Statistical Abstract* 2007:Table 44). The longer that Latinos have lived in the United States, the more their families resemble those of middle-class Americans (Saenz 2004).

7   With such a wide variety, experts disagree on what is distinctive about Latino families. Some point to the Spanish language, the Roman Catholic religion, and a strong family orientation coupled with a disapproval of divorce. Others add that Latinos emphasize loyalty to the extended family, with an obligation to support the extended family in times of need (Cauce and Domenech-Rodriguez 2002). Descriptions of Latino families used to include **machismo**—an emphasis on male strength, sexual vigor, and dominance—but current studies show that *machismo* now characterizes only a small proportion of Latino husband-fathers (Torres et al. 2002). *Machismo* apparently decreases with each generation in the United States (Hurtado et al. 1992; D. B. Wood 2001). Some researchers have found that the husband-father plays a stronger role than in either white or African American families (Vega 1990; Torres et al. 2002). Apparently, the wife-mother is usually more family-centered than her husband, displaying more warmth and affection for her children.

8   It is difficult to draw generalizations because, as with other racial–ethnic groups, individual Latino families vary considerably (Contreras et al. 2002). Some Latino families,

As with other groups, there is no such thing as the Latino family. Some Latino families have assimilated into U.S. culture to such an extent that they no longer speak Spanish. Others maintain Mexican customs, such as this family, which is celebrating quinceañera, the "coming of age" of girls at age 15 (traditionally, an announcement to the community that a girl is eligible for courtship).

for example, have acculturated to such an extent that they are protestants who do not speak Spanish.

Asian American Families

9   As you can see from Figure A on the previous page, Asian American children are more likely than children in any other racial–ethnic group to grow up with both parents. As with the other groups, family life also reflects social class. In addition, because Asian Americans emigrated from many different countries, their family life reflects those many cultures (Xie and Goyette 2004). As with Latino families, the more recent their immigration, the more closely their family life reflects the patterns in their country of origin (Kibria 1993; Glenn 1994).

10   Despite such differences, sociologist Bob Suzuki (1985), who studied Chinese American and Japanese American families, identified several distinctive characteristics of Asian American families. Although Asian Americans have adopted the nuclear family structure, they have retained Confucian values that provide a framework for family life: humanism, collectivity, self-discipline, hierarchy, respect for the elderly, moderation, and obligation. Obligation means that each member of a family owes respect to other family members and has a responsibility never to bring shame on the family. Conversely, a child's success brings honor to the family (Zamiska 2004). To control their children, Asian American parents are more likely to use shame and guilt than physical punishment.

11   The ideal does not always translate into the real, however, and so it is here. The children born to Asian immigrants confront a bewildering world of incompatible expectations—those of the new culture and those of their parents. As a result, they experience more family conflict and mental problems than do children of Asian Americans who are not immigrants (Meyers 2006).

Native American Families

12   Perhaps the single most significant issue that Native American families face is whether to follow traditional values or to assimilate into the dominant culture (Garrett 1999). This primary distinction creates vast differences among families. The traditionals speak native languages and emphasize distinctive Native American values and beliefs. Those who have assimilated into the broader culture do not.

13   Figure A on page 70 depicts the structure of Native American families. You can see how close it is to that of Latinos. In general, Native American parents are permissive with their children and avoid physical punishment. Elders play a much more active role in their children's families than they do in most U.S. families: Elders, especially grandparents, not only provide child care but also teach and discipline children. Like others, Native American families differ by social class.

14   **In Sum:** From this brief review, you can see that race–ethnicity signifies little for understanding family life. Rather, social class and culture hold the keys. The more resources a family has, the more it assumes the characteristics of a middle-class nuclear family. Compared with the poor, middle-class families have fewer children and fewer unmarried mothers. They also place greater emphasis on educational achievement and deferred gratification.

Writing About the Reading

CHECKING YOUR VOCABULARY

1. For each of the words listed below, use context: prefixes, roots, and suffixes (see Chapter 3): and/or a dictionary to write a brief definition or synonym of the word as it is used in the reading.

   a. diversity (para. 1)_____

   b. preservation (para. 2) _____

   c. merger (para. 2) _____

   d. respectability (para. 3) _____

   e. cultural (para. 4) _____

   f. machismo (para. 7)_____

   g. nuclear family (para. 10) _____

   h. assimilate (para. 12) _____

   i. permissive (para. 13)_____

2. Underline new, specialized terms introduced in the reading (see Chapter 3).

CHECKING YOUR COMPREHENSION

1. What is more important than race and ethnicity in understanding family life?
2. What is the primary interest of the upper class?
3. In what ways are Native American and Asian American families similar?
4. Which racial–ethnic group is least likely to be headed by a married couple?
5. Which family structure varies least from racial–ethnic group to racial–ethnic group (refer to Figure A)?
6. Which group has the most similar structure to white (non-Hispanic) American families?

THINKING CRITICALLY

1. Why is there no such thing as *the* African American family?
2. Explain the meaning of *fictive kin*. Give examples of fictive kin in families you know.
3. Discuss possible reasons why machismo decreases with each generation in the United States.
4. Respect for family members is important in Asian American families. Discuss whether respect for elderly family members exists among families you know.
5. Discuss the pros and cons of a racial–ethnic group being assimilated into the dominant culture. What is gained? What is lost?

LEARNING/STUDY STRATEGY

Assume that this reading was assigned as a topic for class discussion by your sociology instructor. Reread and annotate the reading in preparation for the class discussion.

MyReadingLab

To practice identifying the main idea, go to http://www.myreadinglab.com. Click on "Study Plan," then on "Reading Skills," and then on "Main Ideas." To practice identifying details, click on "Supporting Skills." To practice adapting your reading rate, click on "Reading Rate."

3 Essential Vocabulary Skills

Study the photograph. It is interesting and engaging because it reveals a great deal of information about the person shown. Your vocabulary is like a photograph—it can be lively, interesting, and descriptive and convey a great deal of information, or it can be dull and uninteresting and convey minimal information.

LEARNING OBJECTIVES

- To learn techniques for vocabulary development

- To develop skill in using context clues

- To use word parts to expand your vocabulary

- To use word mapping

- To handle technical and specialized vocabulary

VOCABULARY: The Academic Link

Your vocabulary is one of your strongest academic assets or one of your worst liabilities. Language is the primary vehicle of thought, expression, and communication. In addition, each academic discipline has its own vocabulary. In a sense, each course you take in college will be about learning the words used in that discipline.

VOCABULARY: The Career Link

If your vocabulary is limited, your potential for self-expression, effective communication, and adequate comprehension of oral or printed materials is also limited. Conversely, a strong vocabulary makes you a stronger writer and communicator—two skills that are essential for career success.

■ Techniques for Vocabulary Development

Here are some basic techniques for vocabulary development that can produce immediate results.

Use New Words You Have Learned

Make a point of using one new word each day, both in speaking and in writing. Regardless of how much time you spend looking up and recording words, you probably will remember only those that you use fairly soon after you learn them. Forgetting occurs extremely rapidly after learning unless you take action to apply what you have learned.

Acquire the Necessary Tools

To develop a strong vocabulary, you must acquire the necessary tools. These include a dictionary and a thesaurus, as well as access to subject area dictionaries.

Choose the Right Dictionary   There are several different types of dictionaries, each suited to a different purpose, as shown below.

> **☑ Tip for Education Majors**
>
> A dictionary, thesaurus, and encyclopedia are the three reference works most commonly used by elementary school students. As a future teacher, you should be well versed in how to use these reference books. They are invaluable tools for K–12 students. Be sure to know how to use the printed versions of these works as well as the digital or online versions.

TYPE OF DICTIONARY	PURPOSE
Pocket dictionary (small paperback)	Provides a convenient and portable reference for a limited number of words
Desk dictionary (large paperback, hardbound, or online)	Provides a more complete reference source

Tip for Psychology/Social Science Majors

The social sciences rely on the use of specific terminology. Buying a discipline-specific dictionary is always a good idea. Psychology majors might consider purchasing the *Penguin Dictionary of Psychology*; sociology majors might consider the *Penguin Dictionary of Sociology*. Both cost under $15.

Unabridged dictionary (available in the library reference section)	Provides the most complete information on every word in the English language
Online dictionary sites (such as http://m-w.com and http://www.dictionary.com)	Offer audio pronunciation of the word and entries from several different desk dictionaries
Subject area dictionaries (*Taber's Cyclopedic Medical Dictionary* or *Dictionary of Biological Terms*)	Provide listings and definitions of words used in a particular discipline

Figure 3-1 demonstrates the difference between the two most popular types—pocket and desk.

EXERCISE 3-1

Find a Subject Dictionary

For each of the courses you are taking, find out whether there is a subject area dictionary available. If so, make note of its title.

FIGURE 3-1   Comparison of Pocket and Collegiate Dictionaries

Pocket Dictionary Entry	Collegiate Dictionary Entry
di•lem′ma (di-lem′ə) *n.* a choice between alternatives equally undesirable.	di-lem-ma (dĭ-lĕm′ə) *n.* 1. A situation that requires a choice between options that are or seem equally unfavorable or mutually exclusive. 2. *Usage Problem.* A problem that seems to defy a satisfactory solution. 3. *Logic.* An argument that presents an antagonist with a choice of two or more alternatives, each of which contradicts the original contention and is conclusive. [Late Latin, from Greek *dilemma*, ambiguous proposition : *di-*, two; see DI-¹ + *lēmma*, proposition; see LEMMA¹] — dil′em-mat′ic (dĭl′ə-mat′ĭk) *adj.*
	USAGE NOTE: In its primary sense *dilemma* denotes a situation in which a choice must be made between alternative courses of action or argument. Although citational evidence attests to widespread use of the term meaning simply "problem" or "predicament" and involving no issue of choice, 74 percent of the Usage Panel rejected the sentence *Juvenile drug abuse is the great dilemma of the 1980's.* • It is sometimes claimed that because the *di-* in *dilemma* comes from a Greek prefix meaning "two," the word should be used only when exactly two choices are involved. But 64 percent of the Usage Panel accepts its use for choices among three or more options in the example *Ph.D. students who haven't completed their dissertations by the time their fellowships expire face a difficult dilemma; whether to take out loans to support themselves, to try to work part-time at both a job and their research, or to give up on the degree entirely.*

SOURCE: *The New American Webster Handy College Dictionary* (left) and *The American Heritage Dictionary of the English Language* (right)

Use a Thesaurus   A thesaurus is a dictionary of synonyms that groups together words with similar meanings. This type of dictionary is available in print and online (Roget's Thesaurus is at http://www.bartleby.com/62/ and Merriam-Webster Online Thesaurus is at http://www.merriam-webster.com) and is useful for locating a precise descriptive word to fit a particular situation. For example, suppose you are looking for a more precise term for the boldfaced expression in the following sentence in a term paper you are writing:

Whether men and women react differently to similar situations is often **talked about** in popular magazine articles.

Figure 3-2 shows a thesaurus entry for the phrase *talk about.* Right away, you can identify a number of words that are more specific than the phrase *talked about.* The next step is to choose a word from the entry that most closely suggests the meaning you wish to convey. Words such as *debate* and *discuss* would be appropriate. The easiest way to do this is to substitute various choices in your sentence to see which works best; check the dictionary if you are not sure of a word's exact meaning. Many students misuse the thesaurus by choosing words that do not fit the context. Use a word only when you are familiar with all its shades of meaning. Remember, a misused word is often a more serious error than a wordy or an imprecise expression.

FIGURE 3-2   Thesaurus Entry

> 12   discuss, debate, reason, deliberate, deliberate upon, exchange views *or* opinions, talk, talk over, hash over <nonformal>, talk of *or* about, rap <nonformal>, comment upon, reason about, discourse about, consider, treat, dissertate on, handle, deal with, take up, go into, examine, investigate, talk out, analyze, sift, study, canvass, review, pass under review, controvert, ventilate, air, thresh out, reason the point, consider pro and con; kick *or* knock around <nonformal>

SOURCE: *Roget's International Thesaurus*

EXERCISE 3-2   Using a Thesaurus

Use a thesaurus to find a more specific or descriptive word to replace the underlined word in each of the following sentences. Revise the sentence, if necessary.

1. The jury made the <u>right</u> decision in the sexual discrimination case.
2. The DVD on the rights of victims shown in my criminal justice class was <u>dull</u>.
3. After completing three exams in one day, Joe seemed <u>tired</u>.
4. Dr. Rodriguez is a <u>good</u> teacher.
5. My friends thought the biology exam was <u>hard</u>.

■ Use a System for Learning Vocabulary

One of the most practical systems for expanding your vocabulary is the index card system.

KEY STRATEGY: Use the Index Card System

Here is how the system works:

1. **Whenever you hear or read a new word that you want to learn, jot it down in the margin of your notes or mark it in the material you are reading.**

2. **Later, write each word on the front of an index card.**   Then look up the meaning of each word, and write it on the back. You also might record a phonetic key for the word's pronunciation, if it is a difficult one, or a sample sentence in which the word is used. Sample index cards are shown in Figure 3-3 below.

3. **Whenever you have a few spare minutes, go through your pack of index cards.**   For each card, look at the word on the front and try to recall its meaning on the back. Then check the back of the card to see whether you were correct. If you were unable to recall the meaning or if you confused it with another word, retest yourself. Shuffle the cards after each use.

4. **After you have gone through your pack of cards several times, sort the cards into two piles, separating the words you know from those you have not learned.**   Then, putting the known words aside, concentrate on the words still to be learned.

5. **Once you have mastered all the words, periodically review them to refresh your memory and to keep the words current in your mind.**

6. **Once you have learned the words, use them in your speech and/or writing and evaluate how effectively you have used them.**   This step is perhaps the most important of all, because it moves you from the knowledge and comprehension levels of thinking to the applying and evaluating levels (see Chapter 1).

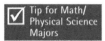
Tip for Math/ Physical Science Majors

The "language" of math and the physical sciences is composed not only of words, but also of numbers and symbols (many of them Greek). The index card system discussed here works not only for vocabulary words, but also for key symbols, formulas, theories, and abbreviations.

FIGURE 3-3   Sample Index Cards

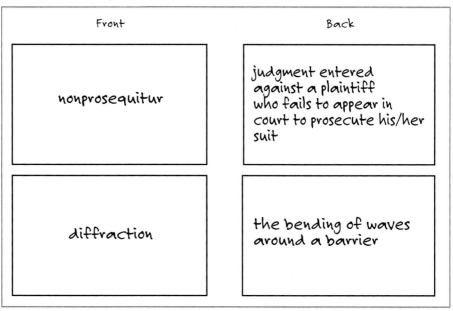

Front

nonprosequitur

diffraction

Back

judgment entered against a plaintiff who fails to appear in court to prosecute his/her suit

the bending of waves around a barrier

The index card system is effective for several reasons.

- You can accomplish it in your spare time; you can even review your cards while you wait for a bus.
- It enables you to spend time learning what you do not know rather than wasting time studying what you have already learned.
- Shuffling the cards enables you to scramble the order of the words and prevents you from learning the material in a fixed order.

EXERCISE 3-3

ACADEMIC
APPLICATION

Creating Index Cards

Over the next week, prepare a set of 15 to 20 index cards for new words used by your professor or introduced in your textbook. Include only words you feel you could use in your own speech or writing.

■ Using Context Clues

Read the following paragraph, from which several words have been deleted. Fill them in after you have read the paragraph through once.

> Karl Marx (1818–1883) was born _____ Germany. _____ father, a lawyer, and his _____ were both descended from long lines of rabbis. Marx _____ college and planned _____ practice law, but after becoming involved with a radical antireligious _____, he decided to devote his _____ to philosophy.
>
> —Eshleman et al., *Sociology, An Introduction*, pp. 34–35

Certainly, you had no trouble filling in the missing words. You were able to do this because the paragraph contained enough information or clues about what was missing. Now imagine that instead of blanks, the paragraph contained several unfamiliar words. Often, you can "fill in" the meaning of the unknown words by using clues contained in the paragraph. Use these clues to determine the meanings of the boldfaced words in the following passage:

> The condition most feared among governments as a cause of war is power **asymmetry**—that is, an unfavorable tilt in the distribution of power. There is widespread conviction that whatever other **impetuses** to war may be present, a careful equilibration of power between **antagonists** will tend to prevent war, while a disequilibrium will invite aggression. . . .
>
> —Jones, *The Logic of International Relations*, p. 379

Although you may not have been able to define exactly words such as *asymmetry, impetuses,* and *antagonists,* you were probably able to make a reasonable guess about their meanings. You used the clues contained in the context (surrounding words and phrases) to arrive at the meaning.

Types of Context Clues

Now, let's look at various types of context clues. Each clue requires analysis of the word's context and the ideas that context contains.

Definition or Synonym   Frequently, a writer gives a brief definition or synonym for a word, usually in the same sentence as the word being defined. The definition may be the key idea of the sentence, as in the following example:

> **Ethology** is the study of the behavior of animals in their natural settings.

At other times, the definition or synonym may be set apart from the key idea of the sentence through the use of commas, dashes, or parentheses.

> Experimental biology includes the study of learning, behavior, memory, perception, and **psychology** (biological bases of behavior).

> Most societies are **patriarchal**—males exert dominant power and authority.

You will find this type of clue used in most introductory college textbooks, especially in the first several chapters in which the "course language" is introduced.

Example Clues   Writers include examples to clarify or illustrate important concepts and ideas. If you are unfamiliar with a word or concept, often you can figure it out by studying the example.

> The use of **nonverbal communication,** such as a smile or gesture, usually reduces the risk of misinterpretation.

From the examples, *smile* and *gesture,* you know that nonverbal communication refers to "body language"—physical movements and facial expressions. Here are two other sentences that contain example clues:

> Collecting **demographic data** on potential consumers, including age, marital status, residency, and income, is an essential part of market research.

> Salary increases, promotions, privileges, and praise are forms of **extrinsic** rewards that motivate behavior.

You may have noticed that the examples in these sentences are signaled by certain words and phrases. *Such as* and *including* are used here. Other common signals are *for instance, to illustrate,* and *for example.*

Contrast Clues   Sometimes, you can determine the meaning of an unknown word from a word or phrase in the context that has an opposite meaning. Note, in the following sentence, how a word opposite in meaning from the boldfaced word provides a clue to its meaning.

> Despite their seemingly **altruistic** actions, large corporations are self-interested institutions that exist to make profits.

Although you may not know the meaning of *altruistic,* you know it means the opposite of *self-interested.* The word *despite* suggests this. *Altruistic,* then, means "interested in the welfare of others." Here are two additional sentences containing contrast clues:

> Studies of crowd behavior suggest that people in a crowd lose their personalities and act **impulsively**, rather than making reasoned decisions.

> Polytheism, the worship of more than one god, is common throughout India; however, **monotheism** is the most familiar religion to Americans.

Each of these examples contains a word or phrase that indicates that an opposite or contrasting situation exists. Two such signals that were used in the examples are *rather than* and *however.* Other signal words that also show a contrasting idea include *but, despite, rather, while, yet,* and *nevertheless.*

Inference Clues   Many times, you can figure out the meaning of a word you do not know by using logical reasoning or by drawing on your own knowledge and experience. From the information given in the context, you can infer the meaning of a word you are not familiar with, as in the following sentence:

> Confucius had a **pervasive** influence on all aspects of Chinese life, so much so that every county in China built a temple to him.

If every county in China built a temple to Confucius, you can imagine that his influence was widespread. You can infer, then, that *pervasive* means "spread throughout."

Similarly, in the following example, the general sense of the context provides clues to the meaning of the word.

> In wind instruments such as the trumpet, sound is **emitted** directly by the vibrations of air columns in the instrument.

In this sentence, *emitted* means "sent out."

Sometimes your knowledge and experience can help you figure out an unknown word. Consider, for instance, the following sentence:

> To **simulate** the weightless environment of outer space, astronauts are placed in a specially designed room.

Here, *simulate* means "to give the appearance of."

Limitations of Context Clues

Although context clues generally are useful, they do not always work. There will be words for which the context provides no clues. Also, you should recognize that context clues give you only a general sense of what the word means— not its exact or complete definition. If you've figured a word out from context clues and you feel it is worth learning, mark it and later check its complete meaning in a dictionary.

A final limitation of context is that it suggests the meaning of the word only as it is used in a particular context. Words have multiple meanings; the meaning you infer from a single context gives you only a limited understanding of the word.

Tip for Life Science/Allied Health Majors

Context clues can help you get a sense of a word you are not familiar with, but in these fields it is essential that you completely understand a word's meaning before you act on instructions or work with a patient or client. Someone's life may depend on it.

EXERCISE 3-4   ## Using Context Clues

Use context clues to determine the meaning of each boldfaced word. Write a brief definition or synonym in the space provided.

1. People who practice **totemism**, the worship of plants, animals, or objects as gods, usually select for worship objects that are important to the community.

   _____

2. The tone of **percussion** instruments, such as drums and cymbals, depends in part on the geometry of the surface area.

   _____

3. A cult may recruit followers through **deception;** potential followers may not be told what the cult involves or what will be expected of them.

   _____

4. **Euthanasia**, sometimes called mercy killing, is a controversial issue among the families of terminally ill patients.

   _____

5. Establishing a buying **motive**, such as hunger, safety, or prestige, is important in developing an advertising plan for a new product.

   _____

6. Our **paleolithic** ancestors relied on their own body power and the controlled use of fire to get things done. In later Stone Age societies, people used animals for muscle power.

   _____

7. Information, as well as rumors and gossip, is quickly spread through the office **grapevine**, although it is not recognized as an official channel of communication.

   _____

8. New hourly employees in the firm are **accountable** to the training director, who, in turn, is accountable to the director of personnel.

   _____

9. In one culture, a man may be **ostracized** for having more than one wife, whereas in other cultures, a man with many wives is an admired and respected part of the group.

   _____

10. **Homogeneous** groups, such as classes made up entirely of teenagers, social organizations of high-IQ people, and country clubs of wealthy families, have particular roles and functions in our society.

    _____

LEARNING
COLLABORATIVELY

Using Context Clues

Working with a classmate, use context clues to determine the meaning of each word in boldfaced print in the following passage. Write a brief definition or synonym for each.

If you have ever tried to perform heavy manual labor on a hot summer day, you may have become weak and dizzy as a result. If your **exertions** were severe, you may have even collapsed and lost **consciousness** momentarily. If this has happened to you, then you have experienced *heat exhaustion*. Heat exhaustion is a **consequence** of the body's effort to regulate its temperature—in particular, its efforts to get rid of **excess** heat. When the body must get rid of a large quantity of heat, **massive** quantities of sweat can be produced, leading to a significant **reduction** in blood volume. In addition, blood flow to the skin increases markedly, which **diverts** blood from other areas of the body. Together, these changes produce a reduction in blood pressure, which reduces blood flow to the brain and **precipitates** the symptoms just described.

A far more serious condition is *heat stroke*, in which the body's temperature rises out of control due to failure of the **thermoregulatory** system. The skin of individuals experiencing heat stroke has a flushed appearance but will also be dry, in contrast to the **profuse** sweating of heat exhaustion. If someone is experiencing heat stroke, immediate medical attention is of the utmost importance.

—adapted from Germann and Stanfield, *Principles of Human Physiology*, p. 9

■ Learning Word Parts: The Multiplier Effect

 **Tip for Criminal Justice Majors**

Criminal justice majors are expected to learn a large amount of legal terminology, much of which is based on Latin words or phrases (for example, *de facto* and *de jure*). Many of the word parts discussed in this section—prefixes, roots, and suffixes—originally come from Latin.

Suppose you want to learn 50 new words. For each word you learn, your vocabulary increases by one word; if you learn all 50, then you've increased your vocabulary by 50 words. The vocabulary of the average young adult is 30,000 words. Adding 50 words is equal to a 0.17 percent increase—negligible at best. You may be thinking, "There must be a better way," and fortunately, there is. If you learn word parts—prefixes, roots, and suffixes (beginnings, middles, and endings of words)—instead of single words, your vocabulary will multiply geometrically rather than increase by one word at a time.

Learning word parts, then, produces a multiplier effect. A single prefix can unlock the meaning of 50 or more words. Think of the prefix *inter-*. Once you learn that it means "between," you can define many new words. Here are a few examples:

intercede	interrupt	interstellar
interconnect	interscholastic	intertribal
interracial	intersperse	intervene
interrelate		

Similarly, knowledge of a single root unlocks numerous word meanings. For instance, knowing that the root *spec* means "to look or see" enables you to understand words such as:

inspect	perspective	spectator
inspector	retrospect	speculate
introspection	retrospection	speculation
introspective		

Learning word parts is a much more efficient means of building vocabulary than learning single words. The following sections list common prefixes, roots, and suffixes and provide practice in learning them. Before you begin to learn specific word parts, study the following guidelines:

1. **In most cases, a word is built on at least one root.**
2. **Words can have more than one prefix, root, or suffix.**
   a. Words can be made up of two or more roots (*geo-logy*).
   b. Some words have two prefixes (*in-sub-ordination*).
   c. Some words have two suffixes (*beauti-ful-ly*).
3. **Words do not always have both a prefix and a suffix.**
   a. Some words have neither a prefix nor a suffix (*read*).
   b. Others have a suffix but no prefix (*read-ing*).
   c. Others have a prefix but no suffix (*pre-read*).
4. **Roots may change in spelling as they are combined with suffixes (arid, arable).**
5. **Sometimes, you may identify a group of letters as a prefix or root but find that it does not carry the meaning of the prefix or root.** For example, in the word *internal,* the letters *i-n-t-e-r* should not be confused with the prefix *inter-,* which means "between." Similarly, the letters *m-i-s* in the word *missile* are part of the root and are not the prefix *mis-,* which means "wrong or bad."

Prefixes

Prefixes appear at the beginning of many English words and alter the meaning of the root to which they are connected. Table 3-1 (p. 86) groups 36 common prefixes according to meaning.

Learning word parts is particularly useful for science courses. Many scientific words are built from a common core of prefixes, roots, and suffixes. Chapter 14 offers several examples on pages 391–392.

EXERCISE 3-6

Using Prefixes

Using the list of common prefixes in Table 3-1 write the meaning of each of the following boldfaced words. If you are unfamiliar with the root, check its meaning in a dictionary.

1. a **multinational** corporation _____

2. **antisocial** behavior _____

3. **inefficient** study habits _____

4. **postglacial** period _____

TABLE 3-1   Common Prefixes

PREFIX	MEANING	EXAMPLE
Amount or Number		
bi-	two	bimonthly
centi-	hundred	centigrade
deci-	ten	decimal
equi-	equal	equidistant
micro-	small	microscope
milli-	thousand	milligram
mono-	one	monocle
multi-	many	multipurpose
poly-	many	polygon
semi-	half	semicircle
tri-	three	triangle
uni-	one	unicycle
Negative		
a-	not	asymmetrical
anti-	against	antiwar
contra-	against, opposite	contradict
dis-	apart, away, not	disagree
in-/il-/ir-/im-	not	illogical
mis-	wrongly	misunderstood
non-	not	nonfiction
pseudo-	false	pseudoscientific
un-	not	unpopular
Direction, Location, or Placement		
circum-	around	circumference
com-/col-/con-	with, together	compile
de-	away, from	depart
ex-/extra-	from, out of, former	ex-wife
hyper-	over, excessive	hyperactive
inter-	between	interpersonal
intro-/intra-	within, into, in	introduction
post-	after	posttest
pre-	before	premarital
re-	back, again	review
retro-	backward	retrospect
sub-	under, below	submarine
super-	above, extra	supercharge
tele-	far	telescope
trans-	across, over	transcontinental

5. **unspecialized** training _____

6. housing **subdivision** _____

7. **redefine** one's goals _____

8. a **semifinalist** _____

9. **retroactive** policies _____

10. a sudden **transformation** _____

EXERCISE 3-7

LEARNING
COLLABORATIVELY

Listing Words with Prefixes

Select two classmates and, working as a team, record as many words as you can that begin with one of the following prefixes. Compare your findings with those of other classroom teams.

1. pre-   2. de-   3. mis-

Roots

Roots carry the basic or core meaning of a word. Hundreds of root words are used to build words in the English language. Table 3-2 lists 30 of the most common and most useful roots.

TABLE 3-2   Common Roots

ROOT	MEANING	EXAMPLE
aster/astro	star	astronaut
aud/audit	hear	audible
bio	life	biology
cap	take, seize	captive
chron(o)	time	chronology
corp	body	corpse
cred	believe	incredible
dict/dic	tell, say	predict
duc/duct	lead	introduce
fact/fac	make, do	factory
geo	earth	geophysics
graph	write	telegraph
log/logo/logy	study, thought	psychology
mit/miss	send	dismiss
mort/mor	die, death	immortal
path	feeling	sympathy
phono	sound, voice	telephone
photo	light	photosensitive
port	carry	transport
sen/sent	feel	insensitive
scop	see	microscope
scrib/script	write	inscription
spec/spic/spect	look, see	retrospect
tend/tent/tens	stretch or strain	tension
terr/terre	land, earth	territory
theo	god	theology
ven/vent	come	convention
vert/vers	turn	invert
vis/vid	see	invisible
voc	call	vocation

Using Roots

Use the list of common roots in Table 3-2 to determine the meanings of the following boldfaced words. Write a brief definition or synonym for each, checking a dictionary if necessary.

1. **bioethical** issues _____

2. **terrestrial** life _____

3. to **desensitize** _____

4. to study **astronomy** _____

5. **synchronize** your watches _____

6. **visualize** the problem _____

7. a religious **missionary** _____

8. **biographical** data _____

9. a **geology** course _____

10. **pathological** behavior _____

Suffixes

Suffixes are word endings that often change the part of speech of a word. For example, adding the suffix *-y* to the noun *cloud* produces the adjective *cloudy*. Accompanying the change in part of speech is a shift in meaning.

Often, several different words can be formed from a single root word with the addition of different suffixes. Some examples follow:

Root: *class*

root + suffix = *class-ify, class-ification, class-ic*

Root: *right*

root + suffix = *right-ly, right-ful, right-ist, right-eous*

If you know the meaning of the root word and the ways in which different suffixes affect the meaning of the root word, you will be able to understand a word's meaning when a suffix is added. A list of common suffixes and their meanings appears in Table 3-3.

TABLE 3-3   Common Suffixes

SUFFIX	EXAMPLE
State, Condition, or Quality	
-able	touchable
-ance	assistance
-ation	confrontation
-ence	reference
-ible	tangible
-ion	discussion
-ity	superiority
-ive	permissive
-ment	amazement
-ness	kindness
-ous	jealous
-ty	loyalty
-y	creamy
"One Who"	
-ee	tutee
-eer	engineer
-er	teacher
-ist	activist
-or	advisor
Pertaining to or Referring to	
-al	autumnal
-hood	brotherhood
-ship	friendship
-ward	homeward

EXERCISE 3-9

Using Suffixes

For each of the words listed, add a suffix so that the word will complete the sentence. Write the new word in the space provided.

1. *behavior*

   _____ therapy attempts to change habits and illnesses by altering people's responses to stimuli.

2. *atom*

   Uranium, when bombarded with neutrons, explodes and produces a heat reaction known as _____ energy.

3. *advertise*

   One important purpose of an _____ is to inform potential customers about the service or product and familiarize the public with the brand name.

4. *uniform*

The _____ of a law requires that it must be applied to all relevant groups without bias.

5. *evolution*

Darwin's theory of natural selection tied the survival of a species to its _____ fitness—its ability to survive and reproduce.

6. *compete*

When food sources are not large enough to support all the organisms in a habitat, environmental _____ occurs.

7. *religion*

During the Age of Reason in American history, _____ revivals swept the nation.

8. *perform*

Perhaps an administrator's most important duty is establishing conditions conducive to high employee motivation, which results in better job

_____.

9. *effective*

A critical factor in evaluating a piece of literature or art is its _____—how strongly and clearly the artist's message has been conveyed to the audience.

10. *theory*

_____ have spent decades studying the theory of relativity.

EXERCISE 3-10   ## Using Context Clues and Word Parts

Use your knowledge of context clues and word parts to determine the meaning of each boldfaced word. On a separate sheet of paper, write a brief definition of each word that fits its use in the sentence.

1. GLOBAL TECHNOLOGY

The advancement of technology is a **global** issue. The United States has been known as a world leader in the advancement of technology. To remain **competitive**, however, global research and development strategies must respond to changes in transportation, communication, information technology, and **merged** national markets. Intellectual capital is the critical resource in the global economy. The ability to **generate**, access, and rapidly use new knowledge and **convert** it (technology transfer) into marketable quality products and processes is the key to competitive advantage.

The **diffusion** of technological capabilities and expansion of the technically trained work force worldwide have strengthened the competitive position of industrialized countries and **enabled** many more to enter the marketplace. As a result, **dominance** by the United States in nearly all high-tech markets is being challenged.

In many countries, government-sponsored programs have reduced the costs and risks associated with technological development by **assuring** long-term financial commitment. Airbus Industries, for example, is a cross-national European consortium that has developed and produced airplanes through support of its partner companies in the form of repayable loans.

—Kinnear et al., *Principles of Marketing*, pp. 57–58

2. LINGUISTIC ANTHROPOLOGY

While all organisms have some way of communicating, and some animals, such as porpoises and chimpanzees, have highly developed means of communicating, humans have evolved a unique and extremely complex system. Without it, human culture as we know it would be impossible. The field of **linguistic anthropology** focuses on this aspect of human life. It is, in turn, divided into a number of **subfields**.

Descriptive linguistics deals with how languages are constructed and how the various parts (sound and grammar) are **interrelated** to form coherent systems of communication. Historical linguistics concerns the **evolution** of language—how languages grow and change. Sociolinguistics studies the relationship between language and social factors, such as class, ethnicity, age, and gender. Finally, a topic of interest to many anthropological linguists is language and culture, which examines the ways that language affects how we think and, **conversely**, how our beliefs and values might influence our linguistic patterns.

—Howard, *Contemporary Cultural Anthropology*, pp. 12–13

■ Using Word Mapping to Expand Your Vocabulary

Word mapping is a visual method of expanding your vocabulary, as described in the Key Strategy box below. It involves examining a word in detail by considering its meanings, synonyms (words similar in meaning), antonyms (words opposite

KEY STRATEGY: Word Mapping

Use the following steps to complete a word map:

1. **Write the sentence containing the word at the top of the map.**

2. **Look the word up in your dictionary.** Figure out which meaning fits the context of the sentence and write it in the box labeled "Meaning (as used in context)."

3. **In the "Part of speech" box, write in the word's part(s) of speech as used in context.**

4. **Study the dictionary entry to discover other meanings of the word.** Write them on the map in the box labeled "Other meanings."

5. **Find or think of two synonyms (words similar in meaning), and write them in the "Synonyms" box.** You might need a thesaurus for this.

continued

Key Strategies *continued*

6. **Analyze the word's parts and identify any prefixes, roots, or suffixes. Write each word part and its meaning in the space provided.**

7. **At the bottom of the map, write two sentences using the word.**

8. **In the box labeled "Other," include any other interesting information about the word.** You might include antonyms, restrictive meanings, or word history.

Word Map

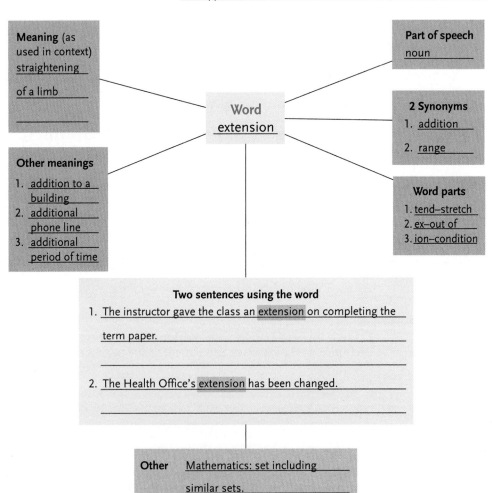

Original sentence using the word Full extension of the leg is necessary in order for the therapy to be effective.

Meaning (as used in context) straightening of a limb

Part of speech noun

Word extension

2 Synonyms
1. addition
2. range

Other meanings
1. addition to a building
2. additional phone line
3. additional period of time

Word parts
1. tend–stretch
2. ex–out of
3. ion–condition

Two sentences using the word
1. The instructor gave the class an extension on completing the term paper.

2. The Health Office's extension has been changed.

Other Mathematics: set including similar sets.

in meaning), part(s) of speech, word parts, and usages. By the time you have completed the map, you will find that you have learned the word and are ready to use it in your speech and writing. On page 92 is a sample map for the word *extension*.

EXERCISE 3-11 | **Creating a Word Map**

Using a dictionary, complete the word map below for a new word you are learning in one of your other courses.

Word Map

Original sentence using the word _____

_____

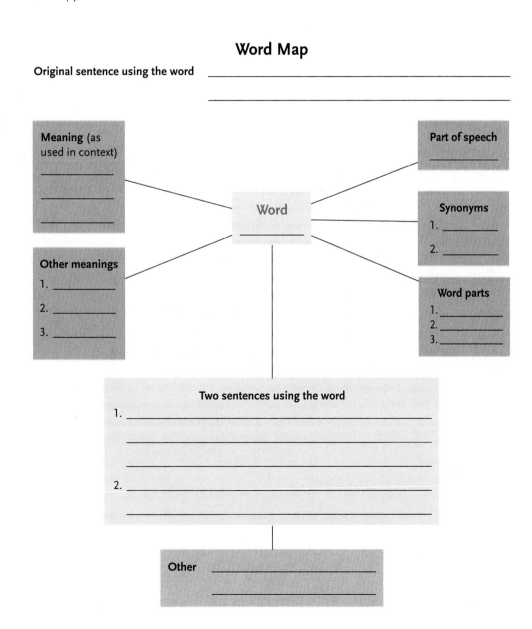

Meaning (as used in context)

_____

_____

_____

Other meanings

1. _____

2. _____

3. _____

Word

_____

Part of speech

_____

Synonyms

1. _____

2. _____

Word parts

1. _____

2. _____

3. _____

Two sentences using the word

1. _____

_____

_____

2. _____

_____

Other _____

_____

■ Learning Specialized and Scientific Vocabulary

You probably have noticed that each sport and hobby has its own language—a specialized set of words with specific meanings. Baseball players and fans talk about *no-hitters, home runs, errors,* and *runs batted in.* Each academic discipline, too, has its own set of specialized words. These terms enable specialists to give accurate and concise descriptions of events, principles, concepts, problems, and occurrences.

One of the first tasks that you face in a new course is to learn its specialized language. In an introductory computer science course, for instance, you often start by learning how a computer functions. From that point, many new terms are introduced: *bit, byte, field, numeric characters, character positions, statements, coding, format,* and so forth. Hundreds of new scientific terms are introduced in each science course. For specific suggestions on learning scientific terminology, refer to Chapter 15, pages 418–420.

> ☑ **Tip for Life Science/Allied Health Majors**
>
> Studying biology, anatomy, physiology, and health-related courses involves learning an entirely new vocabulary. Research suggests students learn more new terms in a year of biology than they do in a year of high school French. Be aware that your major requires you to learn not only many new words, but also new ways of using words you already know.

Specialized Terminology in Class Lectures

Often, the first few class lectures in a course are devoted to acquainting students with the nature and scope of the field and to introducing its specialized language.

- Record each new term accurately for later review and study.
- Look for clues to what terms and definitions are important to record.
- Record words written on the chalkboard.
- Notice repeated words and definitions repeated slowly.
- Develop a consistent way of easily identifying new terms and definitions recorded in your notes. For instance, you might circle or draw a box around each new term or write "def." in the margin.

EXERCISE 3-12

ACADEMIC APPLICATION

Estimating New Terminology

Estimate the number of new terms that each of your instructors introduced during the first several weeks for each of your courses. Now check the accuracy of your estimates by reviewing the first two weeks of your class notes and the first several chapters of the textbook for each course you are taking. How many new terms and definitions were included for each course? Most students underestimate. Did you?

Specialized Terminology in Textbooks

Textbook authors use various means to emphasize new terminology. These include

- New vocabulary printed in italics, boldfaced type, or colored print.
- Marginal definitions.
- "New Terminology" or "Vocabulary" lists that appear at the beginning or end of each chapter.
- A glossary of key terms at the back of the book.

EXERCISE 3-13

ACADEMIC
APPLICATION

Vocabulary in Your Textbooks

Review the first chapter from two of your texts and then answer the following questions.

1. How many new terms are introduced in each?
2. If your texts contain glossaries, are all of these new terms listed?
3. Are most new words technical terms, or are they words in everyday use to which a specialized meaning is attached?
4. How does each textbook author call your attention to these new terms?

Learning Core Prefixes, Roots, and Suffixes

Terminology in a particular academic discipline often uses a core of common prefixes, roots, and suffixes. For example, in the field of human anatomy and physiology, the prefix *endo-* means "inner" and the root *derma* refers to "skin." Thus, the word endoderm refers to the inner layer of cells in the skin. Numerous other words are formed by using the root *derma* in conjunction with a suffix.

As you are learning new terminology for each course, make a point of noticing recurring prefixes, roots, and suffixes. Compile a list of these word parts and their meanings, along with several examples of each one. A partial sample list for anthropology follows.

Key Terminology in Anthropology

	MEANINGS	EXAMPLES
Prefixes		
bi-	two	bipedalism
anti-	against	antibody
poly-	many	polygyny
Roots		
terra	earth, ground	territory
gene	unit of chromosomes	genotype
anthropo	human	anthropoid
Suffixes		
-us	one who	Australopithecus
-cene	era or epoch	Pleistocene
-cide	killing of	infanticide

EXERCISE 3-14

ACADEMIC
APPLICATION

Identifying Commonly Used Word Parts

For one of your courses, identify five commonly used prefixes, roots, and suffixes. If you have difficulty, review the glossary of the text to discover commonly used word parts.

Developing a Course Master File

For each course you are taking, set up a master file that includes new terminology to be learned and a list of essential prefixes, roots, and suffixes. Also include a list of frequently used signs, abbreviations, and symbols and their meanings.

In the sciences, numerous symbols are used in formulas. You'll save time and avoid frequent interruptions if you learn these symbols right away rather than having to refer to the text to translate each sign or symbol. Your course master file can be a big help in this effort.

An abbreviated version of a course master file for a course in American politics is shown in Figure 3-4.

EXERCISE 3-15

ACADEMIC
APPLICATION

Developing a Course Master File

Begin preparing a course master file for one of your courses. Using both your text and your lecture notes, begin with the first chapter and list new terms, prefixes, roots, and suffixes, as well as symbols and abbreviations.

FIGURE 3-4   Excerpt from Course Master File

NEW TERMINOLOGY

Cabinet	Group of presidential advisors made up of the attorney general and the secretaries who head government departments
Deficit	An excess of government expenditures over federal revenues

PREFIXES, ROOTS, SUFFIXES

Prefix	Meaning	Example
anti-	against	antitrust
bi-	two	bicameral

Root	Meaning	Example
pol	political	policy
pluri	many	pluralist

Suffix	Meaning	Example
-ism	a quality, doctrine, theory, or principle	capitalism
-ive	state, condition, or quality	progressive

ABBREVIATIONS

CIA	Central Intelligence Agency
PAC	political action committee
FTC	Federal Trade Commission

Self-Test Summary

1. What are some basic tools for vocabulary development?	Vocabulary development tools are pocket and collegiate dictionaries, thesauruses, subject area dictionaries, and an index card system.
2. What is the difference between a dictionary and a thesaurus?	A dictionary is a nearly complete listing of words and their definitions. A thesaurus is a dictionary of synonyms that groups together words with similar meanings.
3. List the four most common types of context clues.	Types of context clues are definition or synonym, example, contrast, and inference.
4. Name three common word parts and explain where each appears and what it does.	A prefix appears at the beginning of a word and alters the meaning of the root to which it is connected. A root carries the basic or core meaning of a word. A suffix appears at the end of a word and often changes the part of speech of that word.
5. What is a word map?	A word map is a visual method of word study involving examination of meanings, parts of speech, synonyms, and usages.
6. How can you master specialized terminology?	You can master specialized terminology by using subject area dictionaries; learning core prefixes, roots, and suffixes; and keeping a course master file.

Principles of Verbal Messages

Joseph A. DeVito

Prereading Questions

1. What are the five principles of verbal messages?
2. How effective are your verbal messages?

1   Perhaps the best way to study verbal messages is to examine the principles that govern the way verbal messages work. Here we look at five such principles: (1) Message meanings are in *people;* (2) verbal messages are both denotative and connotative and communicate objective meanings as well as attitudes and values; (3) messages vary in directness; (4) messages vary in abstraction; and (5) messages vary in assertiveness.

Message Meanings Are in People

2   If you wanted to know the meaning of the word *love*, you'd probably turn to a dictionary. There you'd find, according to Webster's: "the attraction, desire, or affection felt for a person who arouses delight or admiration or elicits tenderness, sympathetic interest, or benevolence." This is the denotative meaning.

3   But where would you turn if you wanted to know what Pedro means when he says, "I'm in love"? Of course, you'd turn to Pedro to discover his meaning. It's in this sense that meanings are not in words but in people. Consequently, to uncover meaning, you need to look into people and not merely into words.

4   Also, recognize that as you change, you also change the meanings you created out of past messages. Thus, although the message sent may not change, the meanings you created from it yesterday and the meanings you create today may be quite different. Yesterday,

when a special someone said, "I love you," you created certain meanings. But today, when you learn that the same "I love you" was said to three other people, or when you fall in love with someone else, you drastically change the meanings you draw from those three words.

Messages Are Denotative and Connotative

5   Two general types of meaning are essential to identify: denotation and connotation. The term **denotation** refers to the meaning you'd find in a dictionary; it's the meaning that members of the culture assign to a word. **Connotation** is the emotional meaning that specific speakers/listeners give to a word. Take as an example the word *death*. To a doctor this word might mean (denote) the time when the heart stops. This is an objective description of a particular event. On the other hand, to a mother who is informed of her son's death, the word means (connotes) much more. It recalls her son's youth, ambitions, family, illness, and so on. To her *death* is a highly emotional, subjective, and personal word. These emotional, subjective, or personal associations make up the word's connotative meaning. The denotation of a word is its objective definition. The connotation of a word is its subjective or emotional meaning.

6   Semanticist S. I. Hayakawa (Hayakawa & Hayakawa, 1989) coined the terms "snarl words" and "purr words" to further clarify the distinction between denotative and connotative meaning. Snarl words are highly negative ("She's an idiot," "He's a pig," "They're a bunch of losers"). Sexist, racist, heterosexist, and ageist language, and hate speech generally, provide lots of other examples. Purr words are highly positive ("She's a real sweetheart," "He's a dream," "They're the greatest").

7   Snarl and purr words, although they may sometimes seem to have denotative meaning and to refer to the "real world," are actually connotative in meaning. These terms do not describe people or events in the real world but rather reflect the speaker's feelings about these people or events. Compare the term *migrants* (used to designate Mexicans coming into the United States to better their economic condition) with the term *settlers* (used to designate Europeans who came to the United States for the same reason) (Koppelman with Goodhart, 2005). Though both terms describe people engaged in essentially the same activity (and are essentially the same denotatively), one label is often negatively evaluated and the other is more often positively valued (so that the terms differ widely in their connotations).

Messages Vary in Directness

8   Consider your own tendency to be direct or indirect. Imagine you're talking with a friend. Of the four pairs of sentences below, how many would you use from the Indirect column? How many from the Direct column?

Indirect Messages	Direct Messages
Would you like to watch a movie?	I'd like to watch a movie.
Isn't it chilly in here?	Jenny, please close the window.
It must have been expensive.	How much did you pay?
Phone's ringing.	Would you please answer the phone?

9   The messages in the Indirect column, in large part, attempt to get the listener to say or do something without committing the speaker. The messages in Direct column, on the

other hand, express the speaker's preference clearly and/or ask the listener to do or say something. (Note that direct and indirect messages also can be nonverbal. For example, to communicate that it's late, you might use an indirect message such as glancing at your watch; or you might use a more direct message such as getting up and putting on your jacket.)

Messages Vary in Abstraction

10   **Abstract terms** refer to concepts and ideas that have no physical dimensions (freedom, love, happiness, equality, democracy). **Concrete terms,** on the other hand, refer to objects, people, and happenings that you perceive with your senses of sight, smell, touch, hearing, or taste. But between these extremes are degrees of abstraction. Consider the following list of terms:

> entertainment
>
> film
>
> American film
>
> Classic American suspense film
>
> *Psycho*

11   At the top is the general or abstract word *entertainment.* Note that the category "entertainment" includes all the other items on the list plus various other items—television, novels, drama, comics, and so on. The next term, *film*, is more specific and concrete. It includes all of the items below it as well as various other items such as Indian film or Russian film. It excludes, however, all entertainment that is not film. *American film* is again more specific than *film* and excludes all films that are not American. *Classic American suspense film* further limits American film to a genre and time period. *Psycho* specifies concretely the one item to which reference is made.

12   A verbal message that uses the most general term—in this case, *entertainment*—will conjure up many different images in listeners' minds. One person may focus on television, another on music, another on comic books, and still another on radio. To some listeners the word *film* may bring to mind the early silent films; to others it may connote high-tech special effects; to still others it will recall Disney's animated cartoons. *Psycho* guides listeners still further—in this case, to one film. But note that even though *Psycho* identifies a specific film, different listeners are likely to focus on different aspects of the film: perhaps its theme, perhaps the acting, perhaps its financial success. So, as you get more specific—less abstract—you more effectively guide the images that come to your listeners' minds.

13   Effective verbal messages include words that range widely in abstractness. At times a general term may suit your needs best; at other times a more specific term may serve better. The widely accepted recommendation for effective communication is to use abstractions sparingly and to express your meanings explicitly with words that are low in abstraction. However, are there situations in which terms high in abstraction would be more effective than concrete terms? How would you describe advertisements for cosmetics in terms of high and low abstraction? Advertisements for cereals? Advertisements for cat and dog food? How would you describe a political campaign speech in terms of abstraction?

Messages Vary in Assertiveness

14   Assertive messages express your real thoughts—even if they involve disagreeing or arguing with others—but are nevertheless respectful of the other person. Consider your own message behavior. If you disagree with other people in a group, do you speak your mind? Do you allow others to take advantage of you because you're reluctant to say what you want? Do you feel uncomfortable when you have to state your opinion in a group? Questions such as these revolve around your degree of **assertiveness.** Increasing your level of assertiveness will enable you to deal with these experiences positively and productively.

Writing About the Reading

CHECKING YOUR VOCABULARY

1. For each of the words listed below, use context; prefixes, roots, and suffixes; and/or a dictionary to write a brief definition or synonym of the word as it is used in the reading.

    a. denotative (para. 1)_____

    b. connotative (para. 1) _____

    c. benevolence (para. 2) _____

    d. genre (para. 11) _____

    e. conjure (para. 12) _____

    f. sparingly (para. 13) _____

    g. explicitly (para. 13)_____

    h. reluctant (para. 14) _____

2. Underline new, specialized terms introduced in the reading.

3. Draw a word map of one of the words in the reading.

CHECKING YOUR COMPREHENSION

1. List the five principles of verbal messages.
2. Define the terms *denotation* and *connotation.*
3. What are "snarl words" and "purr words"? Are they considered denotative or connotative in meaning?
4. How are indirect messages different from direct messages?
5. Explain the difference between abstract terms and concrete terms.

THINKING CRITICALLY

1. Explain what the author means when he says "message meanings are in people."

2. Choose three words from the essay and give both their denotative and connotative meanings.
3. Write a sentence as an indirect message and as a direct message (see paragraph 8 for examples).
4. Create a list of five words or phrases, beginning with an abstract term such as *entertainment* or *communication*. Make each term more specific, ending your list with a concrete term.
5. How assertive is your message behavior? Describe how you would increase your level of assertiveness, if necessary.
6. Discuss the importance of understanding when to use abstractions in communication. Why do you think abstractions should be used "sparingly" for effective communication? In what situations do you think terms high in abstraction would be more effective?

LEARNING/STUDY STRATEGY

Summarize the most important information in this reading.

MyReadingLab

To practice your vocabulary skills, go to http://www.myreadinglab.com. Click on "Study Plan," then on "Reading Skills," and then on "Vocabulary."

4 Evaluating the Author's Message

Thinking Visually About the Author's Message

Calling **all children**...

help me!

Don't go to the circus.

PeTA People for the Ethical Treatment of Animals
For further information visit our Web site at **www.circuses.com**

Consider the advertisement at left. You certainly see the words and a striking image. How do these two elements work together to create a strong effect or to provoke a strong reaction from you? Because this is an advertisement, it must have a goal—it is designed to make you do something. How does the ad make you want to become involved in this particular cause? How does it use words and images to affect you? Just as advertisements have specific goals to accomplish, so do writers and textbook authors.

LEARNING OBJECTIVES

- To make inferences and understand implied meanings

- To assess the author's credentials

- To distinguish between fact and opinion

- To identify the author's purpose

- To evaluate the data and evidence

- To analyze the author's tone

- To annotate as you read

- To synthesize your ideas

THE AUTHOR'S MESSAGE: The Academic Link

In college you will be reading research articles, essays, critiques, reports, and analyses. Your instructors expect you to be able to do much more than just understand and remember the basic content. They often demand that you read critically—interpreting, evaluating, and reacting to assigned readings. This chapter is all about helping you develop these skills.

THE AUTHOR'S MESSAGE: The Career Link

The analysis of facts and figures is a major part of any career, whether you are a nurse who has to assess a patient's progress or a businessperson trying to find the most profitable investments. Much of the information you come across will be biased in some way. To make informed decisions, you must know how to critically evaluate what you read.

■ Make Inferences as You Read

Reading in college requires you to go beyond what authors *say* and be concerned with what they *mean*. This reasoning process is called "making an inference."

Inferences from the Given Facts

> **Tip for Business Majors**
>
> Learning to make inferences is a valuable skill not only for textbooks but also in the business world. Many of the decisions made by company managers are based on their observations of patterns, on inferences they have made by talking to or studying the behavior of their customers. Good inference skills will not only help you "dig deeper" into buyer behavior, they will also help you in the more quantitative areas of business, such as accounting and finance, where you will have to infer the health of a business from its financial reports.

An **inference** is a reasoned guess about what you don't know made on the basis of what you do know. Inferences are common in our everyday lives. When you enter an expressway and see a long, slow-moving line of traffic, you might predict that there is an accident or roadwork ahead. When you see a puddle of water under the kitchen sink, you can infer that you have a plumbing problem. The inferences you make may not always be correct, even though you base them on the available information. The water under the sink might have been the result of a spill. The traffic you encountered on the expressway might be normal for that time of day, but you didn't know it because you aren't normally on the road then. An inference is only the best guess you can make in a situation, given the information you have.

Inferences from Written Material

When you read the material associated with your college courses, you frequently need to make inferences. Writers do not always present their ideas directly.

There are several reasons why textbook authors and other writers require you to make inferences.

- Information is left out because it would make the message too long or would divert the reader from the central point.

- An author assumes readers know enough to fill in the omitted ideas.
- The writer believes the reader will get more meaning or enjoyment by making an inference.
- Some writers leave out pertinent information in order to make it easier to influence the reader to draw a desired conclusion, especially if he or she might have challenged the details had they been included.

You can see, then, that making inferences is an important first step toward reading critically. Use the steps listed in the Key Strategy box below to make solid and reasonable inferences.

KEY STRATEGY: How to Make Inferences

Each inference you make depends on the situation, the facts provided, and your own knowledge and experience. Here are a few guidelines to help you see beyond the factual level and make solid inferences.

1. **Grasp the literal meaning.**   You should recognize the topic, main idea, key details, and organizational pattern of each paragraph you have read.

2. **Notice details.**   Pay particular attention to details that are unusual or stand out. Ask yourself:

   - What is unusual or striking about this piece of information?
   - Why is it included here?

Read the following excerpt, which is taken from a business marketing text-book, and mark details that are unusual or striking.

MARKETING IN ACTION

Dressing Up the Basics in Idaho

In almost any grocery store across the United States, consumers can purchase ten pounds of Idaho-grown potatoes for less than $5.00. Despite this fact, Rolland Jones Potatoes, Incorporated, has been extremely successful selling a "baker's dozen" of Idaho potatoes for $18.95. The potatoes are wrapped in a decorative box that uses Easter grass.

The Baker's Dozen of Idaho potatoes is only one example of a growing phe-nomenon. Laura Hobbs, marketing specialist for the Idaho Department of Agriculture, reports that more than 200 Idaho farms produce specialty or value-added products. These goods typically consist of basic farm commodities that have been "dressed-up" with packaging. Consumers can choose from these products: microwave popcorn that comes on the cob and pops right off the cob, a bag of complete chili ingredients that makers claim won't cause embarrassing side-effects, and chocolate-covered "Couch Potato Chips."

Idaho farmers are supported by two groups, the Idaho Specialty Foods Association and Buy Idaho, whose goals are to help producers market and

continued

Key Strategies *continued*

promote unique items. With the help of the groups, Idaho farmers are getting quite savvy. The marketers have discovered, for example, that packaging certain items together can increase their attractiveness. Hagerman's Rose Creek Winery found that sales of its wines soared when they were packaged in gift baskets with jars of Sun Valley brand mustard.

According to Hobbs, consumers attracted to the unique packaging provide a market for an endless variety of products, all of which are standard commodities transformed into new products through packaging. The value added through the unique packaging also provides opportunities to charge prices in ranges far above the prices of standard products—like $18.95 for 12 potatoes!

—adapted from Kinnear et al., *Principles of Marketing*, p. 301

Did you mark details such as the price of $18.95 for potatoes, corn that pops right off the cob, and chocolate-covered potato chips?

3. **Add up the facts.** Consider all of the facts taken together. To help you do this, ask yourself such questions as the following:

- What is the writer trying to suggest with this set of facts?
- What do all these facts and ideas seem to point toward or add up to?
- Why did the author include these facts and details?

When you add up the facts in the article "Dressing Up the Basics in Idaho," you realize that the writer is suggesting that people are willing to pay much more than a product is worth if it is specially packaged.

 **Tip for Criminal Justice Majors**

Many criminal justice careers require you to talk with people who have been accused of, convicted of, or implicated in a crime. Talking with these people requires a strong set of inference skills. You must not only listen to what they say, but also listen for what they leave out, or do *not* say. Sometimes very valid inferences can be made based on what is *not* said.

4. **Be alert to clues.** Pay attention to word choice, details included (and omitted), ideas emphasized, and direct commentary to determine an author's attitude toward the topic. In the foregoing excerpt, the authors offer clues that reveal their attitude toward increased prices for special packaging. Terms such as *dressed-up* and the exclamation point at the end of the last sentence suggest that the authors realize that the products mentioned are not worth their price.

5. **Verify your inference.** Once you have made an inference, check that it is accurate. Look back at the stated facts to be sure that you have sufficient evidence to support the inference. Also, be certain that you have not overlooked other equally plausible or more plausible inferences that could be drawn from the same set of facts.

EXERCISE 4-1   **Making Inferences**

Read each of the following statements and the sentences that follow. Place a check mark in front of each sentence that is a reasonable inference that can be made from the statement.

1. Political candidates must now include the Internet in their campaign plans.

_____ a. Political candidates may host online chats to assess voter opinion.

_____ b. Informal debates between candidates may be conducted online.

_____ c. Internet campaigning will drastically increase overall campaign expenditures.

_____ d. Television campaigning is likely to remain the same.

2. Half of the public education classrooms in the United States are now hooked up to the Internet.

_____ a. Children are more computer literate than their parents.

_____ b. Many students now have access to current world news and happenings.

_____ c. Books are no longer considered the sole source of information on a subject.

_____ d. Teachers have become better teachers now that they have Internet access.

3. The Internet can make doctors more efficient through the use of new software and databases that make patient diagnosis more accurate.

_____ a. The cost of in-person medical care is likely to decrease.

_____ b. Doctors may be able to identify patients with serious illness sooner.

_____ c. Doctors are likely to pay less attention to their patients' descriptions of symptoms.

_____ d. Information on the symptoms and treatment of rare illnesses is more readily available.

EXERCISE 4-2   **Making Inferences**

Read the following paragraph. A number of statements follow it; each statement is an inference. Label each inference as either:

PA—Probably accurate—there is substantial evidence in the paragraph to support the statement.

IE—Insufficient evidence—there is little or no evidence in the paragraph to support the statement.

While working for a wholesale firm, traveling to country stores by horse and buggy, Aaron Montgomery Ward conceived the idea of selling directly to country people by mail. He opened his business in 1872 with a one-page list of items that cost one dollar each. People could later order goods through a distributed catalog and the store would ship the merchandise cash on delivery (COD). The idea was slow to catch on because people were suspicious of a strange name. However, in 1875 Ward announced the startling policy of "satisfaction guaranteed or your money back." Contrasting with the former retailing principle of caveat emptor (Latin for "buyer beware"), this policy set off a boom in Ward's business.

—Frings, *Fashion: From Concepts to Consumer*, p. 11

_____ 1. Aaron Ward had experience in sales before he began his own business.

_____ 2. Country people were targeted because they did not have access to stores in cities.

_____ 3. Ward's mistake was to give every item on the list the same price.

_____ 4. Other stores in operation at the time did not offer money back guarantees.

_____ 5. Other mail order business quickly followed Ward's success.

EXERCISE 4–3

Making Inferences

Read the following passages, and then answer the questions. The answers are not directly stated in the passage; you will have to make inferences in order to answer them.

PASSAGE A "IS LAUGHTER THE BEST MEDICINE?"

Lucy went to the hospital to visit Emma, a neighbor who had broken her hip. The first thing Lucy saw when the elevator door opened at the third floor was a clown, with an enormous orange nose, dancing down the hall, pushing a colorfully decorated cart. The clown stopped in front of Lucy, bowed, and then somersaulted to the nurses' station. A cluster of patients cheered. Most of them were in wheelchairs or on crutches. Upon asking for directions, Lucy learned that Emma was in the "humor room," where the film *Blazing Saddles* was about to start.

Since writer Norman Cousins's widely publicized recovery from a debilitating and usually incurable disease of the connective tissue, humor has gained new respectability in hospital wards around the country. Cousins, the long-time editor of the *Saturday Review*, with the cooperation of his physician, supplemented his regular medical therapy with a steady diet of Marx brothers movies and *Candid Camera* film clips. Although he never claimed that laughter alone effected his cure, Cousins is best remembered for his passionate support of the notion that, if negative emotions can cause distress, then humor and positive emotions can enhance the healing process

—Zimbardo and Gerrig, *Psychology and Life*, p. 501

1. What is the purpose of the story about Lucy and Emma?
2. What is a "humor room"?
3. What type of movie is *Blazing Saddles*?
4. Answer the question asked in the title.

PASSAGE B "OPRAH WINFREY—A WOMAN FOR ALL SEASONS"

Oprah Winfrey—actress, talk-show host, and businesswoman—epitomizes the opportunities for America's women entrepreneurs. From welfare child to multimillionaire, Ms. Winfrey—resourceful, assertive, always self-assured, and yet unpretentious—has climbed the socioeconomic ladder by turning apparent failure into opportunities and then capitalizing on them.

With no playmates, Oprah entertained herself by "playacting" with objects such as corncob dolls, chickens, and cows. Her grandmother, a harsh disciplinarian, taught Oprah to read by age 2½, and as a result of speaking at a rural church, her oratory talents began to emerge.

At age 6, Winfrey was sent to live with her mother and two half-brothers in a Milwaukee ghetto. While in Milwaukee, Winfrey, known as "the Little Speaker," was often invited to recite poetry at social gatherings, and her speaking skills continued to develop. At age 12, during a visit to her father in Nashville, she was paid $500 for a speech she gave to a church. It was then that she prophetically announced what she wanted to do for a living: "get paid to talk."

Her mother, working as a maid and drawing available welfare to make ends meet, left Oprah with little or no parental supervision and eventually sent her to live with her father in Nashville. There Oprah found the stability and discipline she so desperately needed. "My father saved my life," Winfrey reminisces. Her father—like her grandmother—a strict disciplinarian, obsessed with properly educating his daughter, forced her to memorize 20 new vocabulary words a week and turn in a weekly book report. His guidance and her hard work soon paid off, as she began to excel in school and other areas.

—Mosley et al., *Management: Leadership in Action*, p. 555

1. What is the author's attitude toward Winfrey?
2. What is the author's attitude toward strict discipline for children?
3. Is the author optimistic about business opportunities for women? How do you know?
4. What factors contributed to Winfrey's success?

■ Assess the Author's Qualifications

Not everything that appears in print is accurate and competently reported. Be sure to assess whether the material you are reading is written by an expert in the field who can knowledgeably and accurately discuss the topic. For example, a sociologist who has studied the criminal justice system is not necessarily an expert on problems of immigrant populations. A scientist who specializes in genetics cannot write authoritatively about the greenhouse effect. In some materials, the author's credentials are footnoted or summarized at the end of the work. In journal articles, the author's college or university affiliation is often included. Authors also may establish their expertise or experience in the field within the material itself.

| EXERCISE 4–4 | **Assessing the Author's Qualifications** |

Read each statement and place a check mark next to the individual who would seem to be the best authority on the subject.

1. One simple way to improve your diet is to put away the salt shaker.
   _____ a. Paula Weigel, registered dietician and nutritionist
   _____ b. John Mishler, life-long dieter
   _____ c. Maria Sanchez, columnist for *Food and Wine* magazine

2. The Dalai Lama is one of the great spiritual leaders of our time.
   _____ a. Richard Gere, film actor and follower of Buddhism
   _____ b. Alice Kohler, college student majoring in religion
   _____ c. Joseph Campbell, author and scholar of religion and mythology

3. Genetic engineering has enhanced both the quality and quantity of many crops, including soybeans, rice, and corn.
   _____ a. Craig Stinson, stockbroker
   _____ b. Andrew Burnette, television news reporter in the Midwest
   _____ c. Charlotte Corbeille, professor of agriculture at Iowa State University

| EXERCISE 4–5 | **Identifying Qualified Experts** |

LEARNING
COLLABORATIVELY

Working together with a classmate, discuss and identify who (title or job description) would be considered a qualified expert on each of the following topics.

1. the side effects of a prescription drug
2. building code laws for an apartment building
3. controlling test anxiety
4. immigration laws
5. influence of video game violence on children

■ Distinguish Between Fact and Opinion

Facts are statements that are verifiably true. **Opinions** are statements that express feelings, attitudes, or beliefs that are neither true nor false. Here are a few examples of each.

Facts

Birthrates declined from 1960 to 1979.

The proportion of married women in the work force has steadily increased in the past 40 years.

Opinions

A drastic change is soon to occur in family structure.

Parenthood is the most rewarding human experience.

There is also what is known as expert opinion or testimony—the opinion of an authority. Ralph Nader represents expert opinion on consumer rights, for example. Here are a few examples of expert opinions.

Bill Gates, former Chairman and Chief Software Architect, Microsoft Corporation	"Right now, we're only scratching the surface of what computing technology can do."
Hubert Williams, President, The Police Foundation	"Unlike the soldier fighting a war on foreign soil, police officers, who provide for our safety at home, have never been given the honor that was their due."

Textbook authors, too, offer expert opinions, especially when they interpret events, summarize research, or evaluate trends. In the following paragraph, the author of a sociology textbook on marriage and the family interprets recent studies on sexuality.

> Recent studies of the history of sexuality in Western society have revealed that dramatic changes have taken place in beliefs and behavior. Among the most striking contrasts with our own times are the acceptance of bisexuality among men in ancient times and the disapproval of sexual pleasure in marriage for many centuries of the Christian era. The new studies also reveal that the sexual culture of any particular place and time is a complex mixture of expressive and repressive codes.
>
> —Skolnick, *The Intimate Environment,* p. 224

Some authors are careful to signal the reader when they are presenting an opinion. Watch for words and phrases such as:

apparently	this suggests	in my view	one explanation is
presumably	possibly	it is likely that	according to
in my opinion	it is believed	seemingly	

Here is an example:

> Among the many moons of Saturn is Titan, Saturn's only large moon and the second-largest in the solar system. Titan's hazy and cloudy atmosphere hides its surface, so we do not know whether Titan is geologically active. However, given its relatively large size and icy composition, it seems likely that Titan has a rich geological history.
>
> —Bennett et al., *The Cosmic Perspective,* pp. 311–12

As you read a work, it is essential to distinguish between fact and opinion. Factual statements from reliable sources can be accepted and used in drawing conclusions, building arguments, and supporting ideas. Opinions, however, are one person's point of view that you are free to accept or reject.

EXERCISE 4-6

Distinguishing Fact and Opinion

Read each of the following statements and identify whether it sounds like fact (F), opinion (O), or expert opinion (EO).

_____ 1. Most Americans feel strongly about the gun control issue.

_____ 2. Mosquitoes can transmit a disease known as encephalitis.

_____ 3. By 2020, the world population is predicted to exceed 8 billion.

_____ 4. Marine biologists use the Internet in researching and identifying plant and animal species.

_____ 5. Computer users often feel guilty and blame themselves when their computer fails or performs an illegal operation.

_____ 6. iTunes is the second biggest United States music retailer.

_____ 7. James Gleick, a well-known author who writes about technology, notes that networked digital devices set the pace of change in the computer field.

_____ 8. An increasing number of private citizens have their own Web sites.

_____ 9. Personal Web sites give people a sense of power and importance.

_____ 10. Capron, an author of a textbook on computers, says Internet traffic jams can be expected, creating slow response times in sending and receiving messages.

EXERCISE 4-7

Identifying Informed Opinion

Read each of the following statements. In each, underline the word or phrase that suggests that the author is offering an informed opinion.

1. According to recent studies, infants who use pacifiers may experience delays in their speech development.
2. The candidate lost the election apparently because voters disapproved of her negative campaigning tactics.
3. In my opinion, the Tour de France is the most demanding athletic event in the world.
4. One explanation for the elementary school's declining enrollment is an aging population in the area.
5. It is likely that the drought will continue through the summer.

EXERCISE 4-8

Distinguishing Fact and Opinion

Each of the following paragraphs contains both fact and opinion. Read each paragraph and label each sentence as fact or opinion.

1.   1 Harriet Tubman was born a slave in Maryland in 1820 and escaped to Philadelphia in 1849. 2 Her own escape presumably required tremendous courage,

but that was just the beginning. 3 Through her work on the Underground Railroad, Harriet Tubman led more than 300 slaves to freedom. 4 During the Civil War, Tubman continued her efforts toward the abolition of slavery by working as a nurse and a spy for the Union forces. 5 Today, Americans of all races consider Harriet Tubman one of the most heroic figures in our country's history.

Sentences: 1. _____ 2. _____ 3. _____ 4. _____ 5. _____

2.   1 Smokeless tobacco is used by approximately 5 million U.S. adults, most of whom are young males. 2 One explanation for the popularity of smokeless tobacco among young men is that they are emulating professional athletes who chew tobacco or use snuff. 3 In any major league baseball game, more than a few players with chewing tobacco bulging in their cheeks apparently believe the myth that smokeless tobacco is less harmful than cigarettes. 4 In reality, smokeless tobacco contains 10 times the amount of cancer-producing substances found in cigarettes and 100 times more than the Food and Drug Administration allows in foods and other substances used by the public. 5 Smokeless tobacco has been banned from minor-league baseball, a move that should be extended to all professional sports to help discourage the use of smokeless tobacco products.

Sentences: 1. _____ 2. _____ 3. _____ 4. _____ 5. _____

3.   1 Managed care plans have agreements with certain physicians, hospitals, and health care providers to give a range of services to plan members at a reduced cost. 2 There are three basic types of managed care plans: health maintenance organizations (HMOs), point-of-service plans (POS), and preferred provider organizations (PPO). 3 The PPO, in my opinion, is the best type of managed care plan because it merges the best features of traditional health insurance and HMOs. 4 As in traditional plans, participants in a PPO pay premiums, deductibles, and co-payments, but the co-pay under a PPO is lower (10 percent or less compared to the 20 percent co-pay under a traditional plan). 5 The best part of a PPO, though, is its flexibility: participants may choose their physicians and services from a list of preferred providers, or they may go outside the plan for care if they wish.

Sentences: 1. _____ 2. _____ 3. _____ 4. _____ 5. _____

■ Identify the Author's Purpose

Writers have many different reasons or purposes for writing. Read the following statements and try to decide why each was written:

1. Acute coronary syndromes are caused by a decrease or interruption of blood flow to the muscular tissue of the heart.

2. The new Slumber-Rest adjustable bed features a patented coil system and a triple-thick mattress for night after night of deep, refreshing sleep. And

Tip for Education Majors

The children you teach often believe that anything in print must be true. One of the most important things you can do as a teacher is to arm your students with the critical thinking skills they need to evaluate a writer's purpose and credentials. For example, if you ask children, "What is the purpose of advertising?" almost none of them will give the correct answer, which is "to sell something."

with any Slumber-Rest bed purchased before January 1, you'll receive two luxurious down pillows.

3. A bad workman quarrels with his tools.

4. If your car engine is overheating, turn on the heater immediately. Pull over to the side of the road and open the hood as soon as possible.

5. Never open an e-mail attachment from an address you do not recognize. It could contain a virus.

Statement 1 was written to give information, 2 to persuade you to buy a bed, 3 to stimulate thought, 4 to explain how to handle an overheated car engine, and 5 to give advice.

In each of the examples, the writer's purpose was fairly clear, as it will be in most textbooks (to present information), newspaper articles (to communicate daily events), and reference books (to compile facts). However, in many other types of writing, authors have varied, sometimes less obvious, purposes. In these cases, an author's purpose must be inferred.

Often a writer's purpose is to express an opinion indirectly. Or the writer may want to encourage the reader to think about a particular issue or problem. Writers achieve their purposes by manipulating and controlling what they say and how they say it. The author's style and intended audience often reveal his or her purpose.

Writers vary their writing styles to suit their intended audience. Their audience may be one of the following:

- **A general interest audience**—people interested in the subject, but not experts
  Examples: newspaper and popular press magazine writers

- **A particular interest group audience**—people with specialized knowledge or interest
  Examples: writers for *Golf Digest* or *World of Antiques*

- **An audience with particular political, moral, or religious attitudes**
  Examples: writers for *Catholic Digest* or *World of Attitudes*

To identify an author's purpose, ask yourself the questions, "Who is the intended audience?" and "Why did the author write this?" In academic reading, you will most often find that the author's purpose is either to inform (present information) or to persuade.

EXERCISE 4-9

Identifying the Author's Purpose

Based on the title of each of the following essays, predict whether the author's purpose is to inform or persuade.

1. Changing Habits: How Shopping Online Is Different
2. I Got Straight A's, but I Wasn't Happy
3. Animals Can't Speak: We Must Speak for Them!
4. Guns Don't Kill People; People Kill People
5. What the Bible Says About the End of the World

EXERCISE 4-10   **Identifying the Intended Audience**

Read each of the following statements and decide for whom each was written. Write a sentence that describes the intended audience.

1. Autumn is the best time of year to plant most trees, shrubs, and perennials. The warm days and cool nights of fall are ideal for root systems to develop, resulting in healthy, hardy plants.

   _____

2. Learning to play a musical instrument can have many rewards for your children. They will develop confidence as a result of successful individual study, and if they choose to play in a band or orchestra, their interpersonal skills and social awareness will be enhanced through their participation in a group. Most important, they will develop a satisfying, lifelong leisure activity.

   _____

3. In the second season of the Women's United Soccer Association, the Carolina Courage defeated Mia Hamm and the Washington Freedom for the WUSA championship. Hamm continues to reign as the leading international scorer in women's soccer history.

   _____

4. For a refreshingly healthy way to quench your thirst, try Pauley's Parrot Juice. Pauley has cleverly combined the juice of pears and carrots to create natural, nutritious, and uniquely delicious Parrot Juice. And while you're quenching your thirst, remember that one-third of all proceeds from Pauley's Parrot Juice goes to conservation efforts in the Amazon rainforest.

   _____

5. When you are choosing a dog, it is important to identify a breed that matches your lifestyle. An apartment with a balcony may lend itself well to smaller breeds that do not require a great deal of outdoor exercise, whereas a house on acreage will provide a larger and more physically demanding dog with the space it needs.

   _____

■ Evaluate the Data and Evidence

Many writers who express their opinions, state viewpoints, or make generalizations provide data or evidence to support their ideas. Your task as a critical reader is to weigh and evaluate the quality of this evidence. You must examine the evidence and assess its adequacy. You should be concerned with two

factors: the type of evidence being presented and the relevance of that evidence. Various types of evidence include

- personal experience or observation.
- statistical data.
- examples, descriptions of particular events, or illustrative situations.
- analogies (comparisons with similar situations).
- historical documentation.
- experimental evidence.

Each type of evidence must be weighed in relation to the statement it supports. Acceptable evidence should directly, clearly, and indisputably support the case or issue in question.

EXERCISE 4-11   Making Inferences

Study the photograph shown above. Place a check mark in front of those statements that seem reasonable based on the evidence shown in the photograph.

_____ 1. The soldier is an American.

_____ 2. The soldier is greeting a close friend or relative.

_____ 3. The soldier has been deployed in Iraq.

_____ 4. The soldier is happy.

_____ 5. The photo was taken in a public place, like an airport.

_____ 6. The soldier will probably be redeployed.

| EXERCISE 4-12 | **Identifying Evidence** |

For each of the following statements, discuss the type or types of evidence that you would need in order to support and evaluate the statement.

1. Individuals must accept primary responsibility for the health and safety of their babies.
2. Apologizing is often seen as a sign of weakness, especially among men.
3. There has been a steady increase in illegal immigration over the past 50 years.
4. More college women than college men agree that abortions should be legal.
5. Car advertisements sell fantasy experiences, not means of transportation.

■ Analyze the Writer's Tone

Tip for Humanities/ Liberal Arts Majors

One of the joys of being a liberal arts major is the many types of reading you are exposed to. Reading in the sciences is usually very fact- and research-based, but in literature, art, and history classes you read a wider range of materials with all very different tones. Many of those who study and love literature and art are drawn to these disciplines precisely because they allow for this wide range of emotions.

Suppose you are a customer service manager and a customer has complained about the assembly instructions for a computer workstation your company sells. You need to write a letter responding to the customer's complaints. You also need to send an e-mail message to the customer support department describing the problem. Would the two messages sound the same? Probably not. The letter to the customer would be friendly, polite, and accommodating, attempting to build goodwill and restore confidence in the company. The message to the customer support would be straightforward, direct, and factual. It would describe the problem and emphasize its seriousness. Each message, then, would have a different tone.

Tone refers to how a writer sounds to readers and how the writer feels about his or her topic. Tone helps to suggest the author's purpose. Tone is revealed primarily through word choice and stylistic features such as sentence patterns and length. Tone, then, can reveal feelings. A writer can communicate surprise, disapproval, hate, disgust, admiration, gratitude, or amusement, for example.

Read the following statement, paying attention to the author's tone:

"Although hazing is considered a time-honored tradition at many fraternities, any activity centered around the senseless humiliation of individuals and the reckless consumption of alcohol has no place on a college campus."

Here the author's disapproval is apparent. Through choice of words such as *humiliation* and *reckless*, as well as choice of detail, she makes the tone obvious. Here are a few examples of different tones. How does each make you feel?

- **Instructive**—"Before you begin any knitting project, always check your gauge. Using the yarn and needles called for in the instructions, knit a 2-inch swatch and then compare it with the scale given in the pattern. By making adjustments before beginning the project, you can avoid problems later on."
- **Sympathetic**—"After the whales had beached themselves for a third time, the exhausted volunteers abandoned their rescue efforts and looked on grimly while the dying whales were euthanized."
- **Persuasive**—"Many frequent flyer programs allow you to donate points to charity. Your frequent flyer points may be used to help people with life-threatening medical conditions travel by plane to obtain the treatment they need, or to transport emergency relief personnel to the site of natural disasters, or simply to enable seriously ill children and their families to enjoy a trip to Disney World."
- **Humorous**—"A boy can run like a deer, swim like a fish, climb like a squirrel, balk like a mule, bellow like a bull, eat like a pig, or act like a jackass, according to climate conditions. A boy is a piece of skin stretched over an appetite. However, he eats only when he is awake. Boys imitate their Dads in spite of all efforts to teach them good manners." (former President Herbert Hoover; source: http://www.hooverassoc.org)
- **Nostalgic**—"The handwritten letter is a vanishing art. Although the convenience of e-mail can't be beat, when someone sits down with pen and paper to write a good, old-fashioned letter, it reminds us of a simpler, more thoughtful time."

Tone can also be used to help establish a relationship between writer and reader. Through tone a writer can establish a sense of a shared communication with the reader, drawing them together. Or a writer may establish a distance from the reader, keeping them apart. In the excerpts that follow, notice how in the first passage a formality, or distance, is evident, and in the second, how a familiarity and friendliness are created.

PASSAGE 1

Meditation, which focuses awareness on a single stimulus, generally brings a subjective sense of well-being and relaxation, along with such physiological changes as decreased heart and respiratory rates and shifting EEG patterns of brain activity. There are three main types of meditation: concentrative, in which the meditator focuses on one chosen image or word; opening-up, in which the meditator's surroundings become part of the meditation; and mindfulness, in which the meditator focuses on whatever is most prominent at the moment.

—Kosslyn and Rosenberg, *Psychology: The Brain, the Person, the World,* p. 162

PASSAGE 2

To begin evaluating a poem, first try to understand your own subjective response—don't pretend it doesn't exist. Admit, at least to yourself, whether the poem delights, moves, bores, or annoys you. Then try to determine what the poem seems designed to make you think and feel. Does it belong to some identifiable form or genre? (Is it, for instance, a love sonnet, narrative ballad, satire, or elegy?)

—Kennedy and Gioia, *Literature,* 2d edition, p. 789

To identify a writer's tone, pay particular attention to the words he or she uses, particularly their connotative meanings. Ask yourself: "How does the author feel about his or her subject and how is that revealed?" It is sometimes difficult to find the right word to describe a writer's tone. Table 4-1 list words that are often used to describe the tone of a piece of writing.

TABLE 4-1   Words Frequently Used to Describe Tone

abstract	condemning	formal	joyful	reverent
absurd	condescending	frustrated	loving	righteous
amused	cynical	gentle	malicious	sarcastic
angry	depressing	grim	melancholic	satiric
apathetic	detached	hateful	mocking	sensational
arrogant	disapproving	humorous	nostalgic	serious
assertive	distressed	impassioned	objective	solemn
awestruck	docile	incredulous	obsequious	sympathetic
bitter	earnest	indignant	optimistic	tragic
caustic	excited	indirect	outraged	uncomfortable
celebratory	fanciful	informative	pathetic	vindictive
cheerful	farcical	intimate	persuasive	worried
comic	flippant	ironic	pessimistic	
compassionate	forgiving	irreverent	playful	

EXERCISE 4-13   **Analyzing Tone**

Read each of the following statements, paying particular attention to the tone. Then write a sentence that describes the tone. Prove your point by listing some of the words that reveal the author's feelings.

1. I could not believe my ears when the boy who bagged my groceries demanded a tip!
2. The spectacular house known as "Falling Waters" illustrates Frank Lloyd Wright's unparalleled genius as an architect.
3. It rained steadily all day, ruining our plans to go out on the boat.
4. The penalty for creating and launching a computer virus should include a personal apology to every single person whose computer was affected by the virus, and each apology should be typed—without errors!—on a manual typewriter.
5. When you are backpacking, you can reduce the risk of back injury by adjusting your pack so that most of its weight is on your hip belt rather than your shoulder straps.

| EXERCISE 4-14 | Thinking Critically |

The following brief excerpt is taken from an American history textbook chapter opening essay. The chapter is titled "American Society in the Industrial Age." Using the guidelines you have learned in this chapter for evaluating the writer's message, answer the questions that follow.

MALLS AS PUBLIC PLACES

The Mall of America outside Minneapolis, Minnesota, is the largest enclosed mall in the United States. It is also the nation's most popular tourist destination, visited by 100,000 people every day. This mall, like many others, was also once a popular hangout for young people. On Friday and Saturday nights, as many as 10,000 teenagers would gather there. But this practice ended in 1996, when the Mall of America instituted a 6:00 P.M. weekend curfew on teenagers under 16 unless accompanied by an adult. Since then, hundreds of malls have adopted similar curfews.

Teenagers, who on the average spend 3.5 hours a week in malls, howled in protest. "We just want to be able to hang out at the mall," complained Kimberly Flanagan, 16, of Charlotte, North Carolina. Kary Ross, an attorney for the American Civil Liberties Union, sided with the teenagers: "We're opposed to curfews that treat all minors as if they're criminals."

Malls insist that as privately owned enterprises, they are exempt from First Amendment protections, such as freedom of speech and the right to assemble. Malls are not public property. Yet recent malls have been designed to evoke the public spaces of the nineteenth-century city. The Mall of America includes an exhibition gallery, amusement park, wedding chapel, assembly hall, school, medical clinic, and a central "Rotunda" for staging "public events" ranging from gardening shows to Hulk Hogan wrestling matches.

In the late nineteenth century, city life was played out in spaces that really were public. Factory hands walked to work along crowded streets or jammed into streetcars or subways. Courting couples strolled through shopping districts or public parks. Children played in streets. "Little Italy" or "Chinatown" provided exotic attractions for all. Amusement parks and sporting events drew huge throngs. In New York City, a journalist explained in 1883, a "huge conglomerate mass" came together in public spaces to form a "vague and vast harmony."

Nineteenth-century cities, though noisy, chaotic, and often ill-governed, exerted a peculiar fascination. There workers, even immigrants and young women, could more easily find jobs. Housing, for all its limitations, was cheap. Urban problems were daunting, but the immense aggregation of peoples constituted a limitless potential for uplift and reform. City life was a great spectacle, played out mostly in public spaces.

—Carnes and Garraty, "Malls as Public Places," *American Destiny*, 3rd edition, pp. 510–511

1. The authors of the history textbook also wrote this opening essay. Evaluate their authority to discuss this topic.
2. Is the article primarily fact, opinion, or expert opinion? Support your answer with examples.
3. What is the authors' purpose?

4. Evaluate the types and adequacy of the evidence the authors provide.

5. Describe the authors' tone.

EXERCISE 4-15

Think Critically

Working with another classmate, review the reading "Factors Affecting Interpersonal Attraction," which appears on page 50 in Chapter 1, and answer questions 2 through 5 from Exercise 4-14.

■ Annotate as You Read

Tip for Computer Science/Technical Majors

Those who work in the technical fields are used to spending their lives on a computer or with a pencil in their hands. In your annotating, do not limit yourself to simply underlining or highlighting key words or passages. Due to the technical nature of your major, it may be more helpful to draw diagrams, flowcharts, and processes. Drawing visuals helps you better learn the processes and procedures.

If you were reading the classified ads in a newspaper in search of an apartment to rent, you probably would mark certain ads. Then, when you phoned for more information, you might make notes about each apartment. These notes would be useful in deciding which apartments were worth visiting.

Similarly, in other types of reading, making notes—*annotating*—is a useful strategy. Annotating is a means of keeping track of your impressions, ideas, reactions, and questions as you read. Reviewing your annotations will help you form a final impression of the work. If a writing assignment accompanies the reading, your annotations will serve as an excellent source of ideas for a paper. This reading strategy is discussed in more detail in Chapter 9.

There are no fixed rules about how or what to annotate. In general, try to mark or note any ideas about the work that come to mind as you read or reread. Underline or highlight within the work and use the margins to write your notes. Use the suggestions in the Key Strategy box below to decide what to annotate.

KEY STRATEGY: What to Annotate

Your annotations might include

- **questions.**
- **opinions.**
- **strong pieces of evidence.**
- **key points.**
- **ideas with which you disagree.**
- **good or poor supporting data or examples.**
- **inconsistencies.**
- **key terms or definitions.**
- **contrasting points of view.**
- **key arguments.**
- **words with strong connotations.**
- **figures of speech (images that reveal the writer's feelings).**

A sample annotation is shown in the following passage on the meaning of color. Read it carefully, noticing the types of markings and annotations that were made.

COLOR AND EMOTIONS

the issue or question

would like reference to these studies

The research in color preference led to a spin-off area of research, that of color and emotional response or moods. Researchers asked whether a reliable mood-color association exists and whether color could influence one's emotional state. Well-controlled research studies have shown that a definite color-mood tone association exists, although the color-mood association differed widely among people participating in the study. In fact, the studies showed all colors to be associated with all moods in varying degrees of strength. Although certain colors are more strongly

does not state nature and strength of evidence
What evidence? describe?

associated with a given mood or emotion, there was evidence to suggest a one-to-one relationship between a given color and a given emotion. What seemed to make the difference was how strongly a person associated a particular color with a particular mood or emotion.

Colors have been stereotyped by the public when it comes to emotions. In spite of physical evidence to the contrary, most people continue to equate red tones with excitement and activity and blue tones with passivity and tranquility in color-mood association research. This is a learned behavior. From the time we are very young we learn to associate red with fire engines, stop lights, and danger signals that cause us to form an alert or danger association with red. Further, the red, orange, and yellow tones in fire further cause association between those colors and heat and kinetic energy. We have seen how cultural biases that are a part of our language further support the red equals excitement myth. These subconscious messages clearly affect the response to red. Blue tones, being associated with cool streams, the sky, and the ocean, continue to be equated with calm and tranquility. This, too, is a learned response with which we are subtly surrounded from early childhood. In understanding color, it is important to

What are the biological ones?

differentiate between these culturally learned color associations and true biological responses.

How?

Clothing design? interior design? building design? —which one?

Research on the emotional aspects of color has for the most part resulted in a gross oversimplification of a very involved process. Unfortunately, this oversimplification has been promoted heavily in the popular press. The design community too has jumped on the bandwagon, often making sweeping statements about color that are totally unsupported by anything but myth or personal belief. For example, one book refers to blue as "communicating cool, comfort, protective,

Could be expert opinion, depending on qualifications of author

calming, although may be slightly depressing if other colors are dark; associated with bad taste." There is of course no basis for these statements except as the personal opinion of the author, but too often these personal opinions become accepted as fact.

Summary

Colors do not contain any inherent emotional triggers. Rather, it is more likely that our changing moods and emotions caused by our own physiological and psychological makeup at the moment interact with color to create preferences and associations that we then link to the color-emotion response itself.

—Fehrman and Fehrman, *Color: The Secret Influence,* pp. 82–83

| EXERCISE 4-16 | **Annotating** |

Review and write annotations for "Malls as Public Places," which appears on page 120.

■ Synthesize Your Ideas

After you have read (and perhaps reread) a piece of writing and made annotations, the final step is to analyze it, pull all your ideas together, and arrive at some conclusions and final impressions of the work. You might think of it as a process similar to evaluating a film after you have seen it or discussing a controversial television documentary.

When analyzing a work, it may be helpful to write lists of words, issues, problems, and questions to discover patterns and evaluate the author's bias. Use the following questions in the Key Strategy box to guide your analysis.

KEY STRATEGY: Analysis Questions

- What did the author intend to accomplish?
- How effectively did he or she accomplish this?
- What questions does the work raise and answer?
- What questions are ignored or left unanswered?
- What contributions to your course content and objectives does this work make?
- How does this work fit with your course textbook?
- How worthwhile is the material? What are its strengths and weaknesses?

| EXERCISE 4-17 | **Analyzing and Evaluating** |

Preview, read, and annotate the following essay titled "The Barbarity of Meat." Assume it is one of several articles your health and nutrition instructor assigned for a class discussion on vegetarianism. Pose several guide questions to focus your reading. Annotate as you read. Then analyze and evaluate the reading using the questions listed on page 124.

THE BARBARITY OF MEAT

The food industry downplays the connection between steak and cows.

If, as some authors suggest, eating meat is indeed an important statement of human power, it might seem strange that we are apparently becoming progressively more uncomfortable with reminders of its animal origins. Consumer attitudes today are in a state of flux, not least for this reason. Whereas once it was sufficient simply to display whole animals and pieces of meat, the packing of the product is now a more delicate task. Most of us prefer not to think too directly about where our meat has come from, and unwelcome reminders can be distinctly off-putting.

As one consumer put it, "I don't like it when you see . . . veins and things coming out of the meat . . . because it always reminds me of my own insides in a funny sort of a way. I suppose it's the idea of, like, blood flowing [that] makes you realize that this slab of meat was once a bit of functioning body, a bit like your own."

Meat marketing has responded accordingly, to assuage customers' sensitivity to the nature of the product. Nowadays, the consumer need never encounter animal flesh in its vulgar, undressed state. Instead it will come cooked and reshaped, in a sesame bun or an exotically flavored sauce, as a turkey roll or as chicken nuggets, in a crumb coating or a vacuum package, with not a hint of blood in sight. More and more butchers' windows sport fresh green vegetables, fragrant herbs, and perhaps a stir-fry mixture. Said one butcher, "I deplore deliveries being carried into the front of my shop on the neck of a van driver—especially if they are not wrapped. . . . I can think of little more guaranteed to turn pedestrians off buying meat than the sight of pigs' heads flopping about as he struggles past them with the carcass."

The number of independent butchers' shops has declined considerably in recent years. Supermarkets have clearly derived particular competitive advantage from presenting meat in conspicuously hygienic conditions with all preparation completed out of sight. Often only the best cuts are displayed; bones, guts, and skin are nowhere to be seen. The hermetically sealed package is effectively dissociated from the animal to which its contents once belonged, a service that is clearly winning customers.

The names we give to the flesh of the main meat animals are another device whereby we reduce the unpleasant impact of having to acknowledge their identity. We do not eat cow, we eat beef; we do not eat pig, we eat pork; we do not eat deer, we eat venison. It is as if we cannot bear to utter the name of the beast whose death we have ordained.

Many first-generation vegetarians and semivegetarians directly trace their abstinence to occasions when, for one reason or another, they were brought face to face with the connection between the meat on their plate and once-living animals. The particular incident related by any individual—be it the sight of carcasses being carried into a butcher's shop, or an encounter with vegetarian polemicism, or a visit to a slaughterhouse on daily business, or merely an unusually vivid flight of imagination—is of minor importance. What matters is that many people, when confronted with this ethical perplexity, seemingly prefer to forgo meat altogether rather than to condone the treatment of animals on their path from birth to plate. And equally important, perhaps, is how new this rebellion is, or rather how rapid its development has been in recent history.

—Fiddes, *Meat: A Natural Symbol*, pp. 100–101

1. Does the author establish his authority on the subject of vegetarianism?
2. Is the article primarily fact or opinion? Justify your answer.
3. What is the author's purpose? How effectively does he accomplish it?
4. Summarize the evidence the author offers in support of his main points.
5. Does the author anticipate and address objections to his argument? If so, what are the objections and how does he refute them?
6. What questions might be raised during a class discussion of this essay?

Self-Test Summary

1. What does critical reading involve?	It involves interpreting, evaluating, and reacting to ideas.
2. What is an inference?	An inference is a reasoned guess about what you do not know based on what you do know.
3. What are the things you must do while you read in order to make inferences?	Know the literal meaning of the stated ideas and facts; notice details; add up the facts; be alert for clues; verify your inference.
4. What are the questions you should ask in order to assess an author's ideas?	• Is the author a qualified expert? • Which are the facts and which are the opinions? • What is the author's purpose? • Is the author biased? • How strong are the data and evidence?
5. What is meant by *tone*?	Tone refers to how writers sound to their readers and how writers feel about their topics.
6. What are two techniques an author uses to convey tone?	An author conveys tone primarily through choice of words and use of stylistic features.
7. Explain what annotating involves.	Annotating involves writing down your reactions during and after reading, and when you have finished, reviewing your notes and evaluating the writer's ideas.
8. What does is mean to synthesize?	Synthesizing involves analyzing a work, pulling your ideas together, and arriving at some conclusions and final impressions.
9. What are the questions you should ask during and after a reading in order to annotate, synthesize, and react to an author's ideas?	• What did the author intend to accomplish? • How effectively did he or she accomplish this? • What questions does the work ask and answer? • What questions are ignored or left unanswered? • What contributions to your course content and objectives does the work make? • How does the work fit with your course textbook? • How worthwhile is the material? What are its weaknesses and strengths?

His Name Is Michael

Donna M. Marriott

Prereading Questions

1. Who is the person described in this essay?
2. Why did the author want to write about her experience?

1   This is a true story—one that both haunts and inspires me. I wish I could say that the names have been changed to protect the innocent. The names were changed, but, sadly, no one was protected.

2   I was teaching that year in a full-inclusion, multiage class. My teaching partner and I had 43 children ranging in age from 5 to 9, ranging in ability from average to labeled, ranging in experience from indulged to adequate. I boasted about being a progressive teacher—a teacher bent on changing the system. As I looked around my classroom, I could see evidence of all the latest and greatest in education: child-directed learning, meaning-driven curriculum, responsive teaching, authentic assessment. It took a little boy to show me what I couldn't see: Beneath this veneer of "best practice," there was a layer of fundamental ignorance.

3   He appeared at my classroom door in the middle of a busy morning gripping the hand of a harried school secretary. He was a tiny child with carefully combed hair, wearing a crisply pressed shirt, tightly clutching his lunch money. The secretary handed this child to me and rattled off the institutional essentials: "His name is Michael. He is a bus rider. He doesn't speak English." Not much of an introduction, but that's how it happens in schools. New students appear in the office at times that make sense in their lives—not in our lives. These children are unceremoniously placed in whatever classroom has an extra chair. It's not very welcoming—but that's the drill. We did all the usual new-kid things that day. We played the name game. The kid of the day gave him the grand tour of our room. He got to sit on the couch even though it wasn't really his turn. The children insisted that Michael have a buddy for absolutely everything—learning buddy, recess buddy, bathroom buddy, lunch buddy, cubby buddy, line buddy, water buddy, rug buddy, bus buddy. They thought it would be great if he had a sleepover buddy, too, but I was able to convince them otherwise. We were genuinely glad to have this youngster in our learning family. But Michael didn't become part of our family.

4   Michael existed marginally on the outside of the group. Sometimes he was on the outside looking in; sometimes he was on the outside looking out. I often saw him with his eyes closed, looking somewhere hidden. He was well-mannered, punctual, respectful, cute-as-a-button—but completely detached from me, from the children, and from the learning.

5   I met with the bilingual resource teacher to chat about concerns and possibilities. She told me she could come do an informal observation "a week from tomorrow." It was a long wait, but that's how it is in schools. She came. She watched. She listened. On her way out she said, "You might have better results, dear, if you call him Miguel."

6   I could not have been more embarrassed or confused. How could I have been calling this child the wrong name? I was a progressive teacher: How could I have made such a mistake? How could the school secretary have made such a mistake? Why hadn't the parents corrected her? Why hadn't the child corrected me?

7   Miguel didn't stay with us for long. His family moved on to follow their own calendar of opportunities. We didn't get to say goodbye, but that's how it happens in schools.

8   Miguel's paperwork arrived about three weeks after he had moved away. I was going through the folder, updating it for his next teacher, when I noticed something that made me catch my breath. His name wasn't Michael. It wasn't Miguel. His name was David.

9   I wondered how it was that this child could have been part of my classroom for more than a month, and in that entire time he never had enough personal power to tell me that his name was David. What was it about me, about the other children, about the school that made David feel he had to give up his name? No child should have to forfeit his identity to walk through our classroom doors. No child. Ever. It is much too high a price to pay.

10   I have to do a bit of guessing about what was going on in David's head. I am guessing that he was told to respect la maestra—to "be good" in school. I am guessing that he thought if the teacher decided to change his name, well then . . . that was that. I am guessing that he didn't connect school to any known reality. He could be David at home, but at school he was expected to become someone else.

11   I don't have to do much guessing at my own complicity. It never occurred to me that his name would be anything other than Michael. In the entire breadth of my experience, people had called me by my given name. In those few instances when someone mispronounced my name, I would offer a polite but prompt correction. I was taught to speak up for myself. I was given the power to be me—in my school, in my neighborhood, in my life. I never considered checking in with David about his name. It was beyond the scope of my experience. It was beyond the lens of my culture.

12   Our power distance was huge. I had all the power. I was white; I was the teacher; I spoke English. David had no power. He was brown; he was a child; he spoke Spanish. Our sense of individualism clashed. I expected him to have a sense of himself—to stand up for himself, to speak up. He denied himself. David expected and accepted that he was "less than" in the culture of school. Our perception of reality was polarized. I trusted in the precision of the system. The name on the registration card just had to be correct. That's how it works in schools. David accepted the imprecision of the system. Having his name changed was just part of the whole befuddling experience.

13   I have learned many difficult lessons in the years since David sat submissively on the edge of my classroom. I have learned lessons about passive racism—the kind that we cannot see in ourselves, don't want to see in ourselves, and vehemently deny. I have learned lessons about implicit power and explicit powerlessness—about those voices we choose to hear and those voices we unknowingly silence. I have learned that being a good teacher is as much about rapport and relationships as it is about progressive curriculum, pedagogy, and assessment.

14   If I could go back to that day when the secretary brought in a little boy with carefully combed hair wearing a crisply pressed shirt, I would shake his hand and say, "Hello. My name is Mrs. Marriott. What's your name?" I believe that if I had simply asked him, he would have told me.

Writing About the Reading

CHECKING YOUR VOCABULARY

1. For each of the words listed below, use context; prefixes, roots, and suffixes (see Chapter 3); and/or a dictionary to write a brief definition or synonym of the word as it is used in the reading.

   a. veneer (para. 2) _____

   b. harried (para. 3) _____

   c. marginally (para. 4) _____

   d. forfeit (para. 9) _____

   e. breadth (para. 11) _____

   f. precision (para. 12) _____

   g. befuddling (para. 12) _____

   h. submissively (para. 13)_____

   i. vehemently (para. 13) _____

   j. rapport (para. 13) _____

2. Underline new, specialized terms introduced in the reading (see Chapter 3).

3. Draw a word map of one of the words in the reading.

CHECKING YOUR COMPREHENSION

1. Who was Michael?
2. What kind of teacher did the author believe herself to be?
3. How did the class treat Michael and how did he fit in?
4. What did the bilingual resource teacher recommend?
5. What did the author discover after Michael had left the school?
6. Why did the boy let people call him by the wrong name?
7. Describe the "difficult lessons" the author learned from this experience.
8. How would the author do things differently if she could?

THINKING CRITICALLY

1. What is the purpose of this essay?
2. Describe the author's tone.
3. What inferences does the author make about her student?
4. Explain what the author means by "power distance."
5. What problems or issues that educators face are addressed in this essay?

LEARNING/STUDY STRATEGY

Assume you are an education major. Use annotations to note the problems and issues that this reading raises that would be important to you as a future teacher.

MyReadingLab

To practice your critical reading skills, go to http://www.myreadinglab
.com. Click on "Study Plan," then on "Reading Skills," and then on
"Critical Reading." To practice identifying purpose and tone, click on
"Purpose and Tone."

5 Evaluating the Author's Techniques

How would you describe the person in the photo at left? Words like *modern*, *individualistic*, and *unique* may come to mind. However, no matter how you would describe her, one thing is clear: she expresses herself very clearly through her sense of style. The same way that people express individual style through hair, clothing, and jewelry choices, authors express themselves with a variety of techniques that move beyond simple words on a page. This chapter discusses various components of an author's "style."

LEARNING OBJECTIVES

- To identify connotative language
- To understand figurative language
- To recognize bias
- To discover missing information

- To evaluate generalizations
- To identify assumptions
- To recognize manipulative language

THE AUTHOR'S TECHNIQUES: The Academic Link

In this chapter you will see how writers can persuade using colorful language, mislead through omissions, make generalizations that may or may not be based on facts, and reveal their biases. You will also examine how writers use language to manipulate readers using clichés, jargon, allusions, euphemisms, double-speak, and hyperbole. Understanding these techniques will greatly improve your critical reading skills and help you master the language arts required for effective academic communication.

THE AUTHOR'S TECHNIQUES: The Career Link

In our lives and careers, we often need to "read between the lines" to have a fuller understanding of what exactly is going on. You can be deceived or taken advantage of if you do not fully understand the ways writers can use language to manipulate the reader.

■ Does the Writer Use Connotative Language?

Tip for Allied Health and Social Science Majors

An understanding of the differences between connotative and denotative language is essential to health workers, who must use great sensitivity in talking with patients and clients. In addition, health workers must be careful about using terminology that their patients may not understand. For example, would you worry if a nurse told you that you had several *benign melanocytic naevi*? If you did not know that this term means "harmless moles," you might very well panic!

If you were wearing a jacket that looked like leather but was made out of man-made fibers, would you prefer it be called *fake* or *synthetic*? Would you rather be part of a *crowd* or a *mob*?

Each of the pairs of words above has basically the same meaning. A *crowd* and a *mob* are both groups of people. Both *fake* and *synthetic* refer to something man-made. If the words have similar meanings, why did you choose *crowd* rather than *mob* and *synthetic* rather than *fake*? While the pairs of words have similar primary meanings, they carry different shades of meaning called connotative meanings.

All words have one or more standard meanings. These meanings are called **denotative meanings.** Think of them as dictionary meanings. They tell us what the words name. Many words also have connotative meanings. **Connotative meanings** include the feelings and associations that may accompany a word. For example, the denotative meaning of *sister* is a female sibling. However, the word carries many connotations. For some, *sister* suggests a playmate with whom they shared their childhood. For others the term may suggest an older sibling who watched over them.

Connotations can vary from individual to individual. The denotative meaning for the word *flag* is a piece of cloth used as a national emblem. To many, the American flag is a symbol of patriotism and love of one's country. To some people, though, it may mean an interesting decoration to place on their clothing.

Writers and speakers use connotative meanings to stir your emotions or to bring to mind positive or negative associations. Suppose a writer is describing how someone drinks. The writer could choose words such as *gulp, sip, slurp,* or *guzzle.* Each creates a different image of the person. Connotative meanings, then, are powerful tools of language. When you read, be alert for meanings suggested by the author's word choice. When writing or speaking, be sure to choose words with appropriate connotations.

EXERCISE 5-1

Recognizing Connotative Meanings

For each of the following pairs of words, underline the word with the more positive connotation.

1. dimple   dent
2. bold   sassy
3. cheap   frugal
4. displease   repel
5. tipsy   drunk
6. ache   agony
7. untidy   grubby
8. haughty   proud
9. deckhand   sailor
10. job   chore

EXERCISE 5-2

Using Connotative Meanings

For each word listed, write a word that has a similar denotative meaning but a negative connotation. Then write a word that has a positive or neutral connotation.

WORD	NEGATIVE CONNOTATION	POSITIVE or NEUTRAL CONNOTATION
Example: costly	extravagant	expensive
1. leisurely	_____	_____
2. small	_____	_____
3. take	_____	_____
4. talk	_____	_____
5. satirize	_____	_____
6. farmer	_____	_____
7. choosy	_____	_____
8. delay	_____	_____
9. desire	_____	_____
10. famous	_____	_____

EXERCISE 5-3

Analyzing Connotative Meanings

Discuss the differences in connotative meaning of each of the following sets of words. Consult a dictionary, if necessary.

1. **painful:** hurtful—sore—excruciating
2. **aware:** familiar—alert—privy
3. **room:** chamber—study—cubicle
4. **someone who travels:** globe-trotter—tourist—pilgrim
5. **understanding:** mastery—insight—comprehension
6. **harmony:** agreement—conformity—order
7. **education:** literacy—schooling—learning
8. **proper:** correct—appropriate—demure
9. **seclusion:** isolation—privacy—withdrawal
10. **lovable:** adorable—attractive—winning

■ Does the Writer Use Figurative Language?

Tip for Math/Physical Science Majors

You might think that figurative language is limited to humanities or liberal arts courses, but the truth is that similes and metaphors are used a great deal in the sciences to help explain concepts. For example, you can probably think of at least a few colorful ways to describe the heat of the sun, the circumference of the Earth, or the distance between Earth and Mars.

Figurative language makes a comparison between two unlike things that share one common characteristic. If you say that your apartment looked as if it had been struck by a tornado, you are comparing two unlike things—your apartment and the effects of a tornado. Figurative language makes sense creatively or imaginatively, but not literally. You mean that the apartment is messy and disheveled. Figurative language is a powerful tool that allows writers to create images or paint pictures in the reader's mind. Figurative language also allows writers to suggest an idea without directly stating it. If you say the councilman bellowed like a bear, you are suggesting that the councilman was animal-like, loud, and forceful, but you have not said so directly. By planting the image of bear-like behavior, you have communicated your message to your reader.

There are three primary types of figurative language—similes, metaphors, and personification. A **simile** uses the words *like* or *as* to make the comparison:

The computer hums like a beehive.

After 5:00 P.M. our downtown is as quiet as a ghost town.

A **metaphor** states or implies the relationship between the two unlike items. Metaphors often use the word *is*.

The computer lab is a beehive.

After 5:00 P.M. our downtown is a ghost town.

Personification compares humans and nonhumans according to one characteristic, attributing human characteristics to ideas or objects. If you say "the wind screamed its angry message," you are giving the wind the humanlike characteristics of screaming, being angry, and communicating a message. Here are two more examples:

The sun mocked us with its relentless stare.

After two days of writer's block, her pen started dancing across the page.

Be sure to analyze the author's motive for using figurative language. Often, a writer uses it as a way of describing rather than telling. A writer could say "The woman blushed" (telling) or "The woman's cheeks filled with the glow of a fire" (describing).

KEY STRATEGY: Evaluating Figurative Language

When evaluating figurative language, ask the following questions:

1. Why did the writer make the comparison?

2. What is the basis of the comparison, that is, the shared characteristic?

3. Is the comparison accurate?

4. What images do you have in your mind? How do these images make you feel?

5. Is the comparison positive or negative?

6. Are several different interpretations possible?

EXERCISE 5-4   **Understanding Figurative Language**

Explain the comparison in each of the following examples of figurative language.

1. The view from the summit was like a painting.
2. Her memory was a blank tablet.
3. The library renovation project was an uncontrollable beast.
4. During the morning commute, the lanes of cars were snarled like a nest of snakes.
5. As the tide rolled in, the waves roared at her to escape quickly.

EXERCISE 5-5   **Analyzing Figurative Language**

Discuss how the writer of each of the following passages uses figurative language to create a specific impression.

1.   As a vacation port of call, Southern California has got it all. It's like a giant geographic theme park. Want to lap up glistening waves and bury your feet in the sand? The beach beckons. How about thick forests with fir- and pine-covered mountains? The majestic Angeles National Forest is a quick drive from Los Angeles. I prefer to use Dante's "Inferno" as my Baedeker [a guidebook for travelers]. Every

summer, whenever I get the itch for a little rest and relaxation, I venture deep into the inner circle of hell—otherwise known as Palm Springs.

—Mark Weingarten, from "Palm Springs in August: The Ducks Use Sunblock,"
The New York Times, August 9, 2002.

2.   Thick as a truck at its base, the Brazil-nut tree rises 10 stories to an opulent crown, lord of the Amazon jungle. It takes the tree a century to grow to maturity; it takes a man with a chain saw an hour to cut it down. "It's a beautiful thing," nods Acelino Cardoso da Silva, a 57-year-old farmer. "But I have six hungry people at home. If the lumberman turns up, I'll sell."

—Margolis, "A Plot of Their Own," *Newsweek*

3.   If parenting is like an endurance race, senior year should be the section where parents triumphantly glide toward the finish line with a smiling graduate-to-be alongside. Instead, it's often more like heartbreak hill at the 20-mile mark of the Boston marathon, the bump that leaves parents exhausted and wondering what they were thinking 17 years ago.

—Dunnewind, "Launching Kids to Independence," *Seattle Times*

EXERCISE 5-6

Writing Figurative Expressions

Convert each of the following statements to an expression of figurative language.

Example: *I am nervous. I feel as if I have a thousand butterflies fluttering in my stomach.*

1. He was hungry. _____
2. The clouds were beautiful. _____
3. Everyone argued. _____
4. The test was hard. _____
5. My friend laughed. _____

■ Is the Author Fair or Biased?

Tip for Business Majors

The written materials produced by companies (for example, on their packages and in their advertising) usually present the product and company in the best possible light. Many business courses now discuss the topic of business ethics, including such topics as how much exaggeration is allowable in an ad.

Think of a television commercial you have seen recently, perhaps for a particular model of car. The ad tells you the car's advantages—why you want to buy it—but does it tell you its disadvantages? Does it describe ways in which the model compares unfavorably with competitors? Certainly not. Do you feel the ad writer is being unfair? We expect advertisers to present a one-sided view of their products. We expect other forms of writing, however, to be honest and forthright; otherwise they present a biased point of view. You can think of bias as a writer's prejudice. If an author is biased, then, he or she is partial to one point of view or one side of a controversial issue.

In the following excerpt from a biology text, the author's choice of words (see highlighting) and sarcastic comment in parentheses reveal his attitude toward seal hunters.

> Greenpeace is an organization dedicated to the preservation of the sea and its great mammals, notably whales, dolphins, and seals. Its ethic is nonviolent but its aggressiveness in protecting our oceans and the life in them is becoming legendary.
> Greenpeace volunteers routinely place their lives in danger in many ways, such as by riding along the backs of whales in inflatable zodiacs, keeping themselves between the animal and the harpoons of ships giving chase. They have pulled alongside Dutch ships to stop the dumping of dangerous toxins into the sea. They have confronted hostile sealers on northern ice floes to try to stop them from bludgeoning the baby seals in the birthing grounds, skinning them on the spot, and leaving the mother sniffing at the glistening red corpse of her baby as its skin is stacked aboard the ship on the way to warm the backs of very fashionable people who gather where the bartender knows their favorite drink. (The mother seal would be proud to know that her dead baby had nearly impressed some bartender.) They have petitioned the International Whaling Commission to establish rules and enact bans.
>
> —Wallace, *Biology: The World of Life*, p. 754

KEY STRATEGY: Detecting Bias

To detect bias, ask the following questions:

1. Is the author acting as a reporter—presenting facts—or as salesperson—providing only favorable information?

2. Does the author feel strongly about or favor one side of the issue?

3. Does the author use connotative or figurative language to create a positive or negative image?

4. Does the author seem emotional about the issue?

5. Are there other views toward the subject that the writer does not recognize or discuss?

EXERCISE 5-7

Detecting Bias

Read each of the following statements, and place a check mark in front of the ones that reveals bias.

_____ 1. Cities should be designed for the pedestrian, not the automobile.

_____ 2. There are more channels than ever before on cable television.

_____ 3. The current system of voter registration is a sham.

_____   4. Professional sports have become elitist.

_____   5. Space exploration costs millions of dollars each year.

EXERCISE 5-8   **Analyzing Bias**

Describe the author's bias in each of the following statements.

1.   Now that Americans are vulnerable to attack in the United States by terrorists, gun control should no longer be an issue for our politicians to waste time debating. Law-abiding, innocent citizens need the means to protect themselves from foreign enemies right here in their homeland. We must reduce the risk of losing more lives to extremists by allowing our people to carry weapons for defense.

2.   I have expressed in the past that police officers should refrain from enforcing immigration laws so that police departments can maintain good relations with Hispanics. If Latinos fear that police will report them or their family members to the immigration service, they might fear coming forward to help solve crimes.
    —Salinas, "Will All Hispanic Men Be Suspect?" *Seattle Post-Intelligencer*

3.   Parents trust their children less and less these days. Convinced beyond a doubt that violent video games will turn their sons and daughters into criminals, parents go to the extreme by banning all forms of electronic entertainment from their homes. Instead of seizing the opportunity to teach a child about limits, self-regulation, and good taste, moms and dads all over America are unwittingly increasing the desire for taboo entertainment. Today's kids are not being allowed to experiment and test themselves while under their parents' supervision. This parental disservice can only lead to a backlash in the future when young men and women experiment with risky behaviors as soon as they leave their parents' tight hold.

4.   Those clamoring to shut down the farmers, however, should look hard at the prospect of a prairie full of subdivisions and suburban pollution: car exhaust, lawn and garden fertilizers, wood stoves, sewage. Certainly, the smoke from field burning is an annoyance, particularly to the hard-hit Sandpoint area, and to some it's a health hazard. But the benefits the sturdy farmers produce 50 weeks of the year shouldn't be dismissed casually.
    —Oliveria, "Burning Will Go; That's Not All Good," *Spokesman Review*

5.   Money doesn't grow on trees, but some trees might as well be pure gold. The world's voracious (and growing) appetite for wood, paper, and other forest products is driving a stampede to mow down forests. Much of this logging is illegal.
    —Haugen, "Logging Illogic," *World Watch*

■ What Isn't the Author Telling Me?

Writers mislead by omission. Here are six common ways writers may mislead their readers:

1. **Omitting essential details.** Suppose, in describing homeschooling, an author states "Many children find homeschooling rewarding." But what is the

author not telling us? If the author does not tell us that some children find homeschooling lonely and feel isolated from their peers, the author is not presenting a fair description of homeschooling. The writer has deliberately omitted essential details that a reader needs to understand homeschooling.

2. **Ignoring contradictory evidence.** Suppose the same writer describes a research study that concludes that homeschooled children excel academically. The writer, to be fair, should also report that other studies have demonstrated that homeschooled children do not differ in academic achievement from traditionally educated students. In this case the writer has ignored contradictory evidence, reporting only evidence that he or she wants the reader to know.

3. **Selectively reporting details.** In describing a homeschool environment, suppose the writer reports that "the home environment is ideal" and goes on to describe features such as comfortable home surroundings, flexible scheduling, and supportive parental mentoring. To be fair, the writer should also point out what the home environment lacks. A home environment may lack a library of instructional software, collaborative learning activities with classmates, or the services of learning support specialists. The writer, then, selectively reported details, telling us what was positive and omitting negative details.

4. **Making an incomplete comparison.** Suppose the writer concludes his or her article on homeschooling by saying, "Homeschooling is the better route to follow to produce a well-educated child." What the writer has not told us is what route homeschooling is better than. Is it better than a private school? Is it better than a public school? Is it better than hiring a private tutor? The writer has made an incomplete comparison.

5. **Using passive voice.** One way writers avoid revealing information is to use a particular sentence structure that does not identify who performed a specified action. In the sentence *The cup broke* you do not know who broke the cup. In the sentence *The bill was paid* you do not know who paid the bill. This sentence pattern is called the passive voice.

6. **Using unspecified nouns and pronouns.** Another way writers avoid revealing information is to use nouns and pronouns that do not refer to a specific person or thing. The sentence *They said it would rain by noon* does not reveal who predicted rain. The sentence *It always happens to me* does not indicate what always happens to the writer.

EXERCISE 5-9   **Analyzing Omissions**

For each of the following statements, indicate what information is missing.

1. Our neighborhood was ruined by the water treatment plant.
2. They raised test scores in that state.
3. People were hurt by welfare reform.
4. Some animal testing has been banned in other countries.
5. Athletes are overpaid.

6. They say the Columbia River has too many dams.
7. Anyone can get on the Internet.
8. They filed charges.
9. Orchestras in many cities have gone out of business.
10. The check was probably forged.

■ Does the Author Make and Support Generalizations?

Tip for Science Majors

Science is all about making generalizations (called *hypotheses*, singular: *hypothesis*) and then using nonbiased research techniques to determine whether those generalizations are valid. As a science major, you will be asked to formulate hypotheses and then test them in a scientifically sound manner and read research reports of others following the same procedure.

Suppose you are reading an article that states, "Musicians are temperamental people." Do you think that every musician who ever wrote or performed a song or played a musical instrument is temperamental? Can you think of exceptions? This statement is an example of a generalization. A **generalization** is a reasoned statement about an entire group (musicians) based on known information about part of the group (musicians the writer has met or observed). A generalization requires a leap from what is known to a conclusion about what is unknown. Generalizations may be expressed using words such as *all, always, none,* or *never.* Some statements may imply but not directly state that the writer is referring to the entire group or class. The statement "Musicians are temperamental people" suggests but does not directly state that all musicians are temperamental. Here are a few more generalizations:

Rich people are snobs.

Chinese food is never filling.

Pets are always troublesome.

The key to evaluating generalizations is to evaluate the type, quality, and amount of evidence given to support them. A critical reader should do the following:

1. **Evaluate types of evidence.** Here are a few more generalizations. What type of evidence would you need to convince you that each is or is not true?

   College students are undecided about future career goals.

   Fast food lacks nutritional value.

   Foreign cars outperform similar American models.

2. **Evaluate the quality of evidence.** For the generalization about college students, you might need to see research studies about college students' career goals, for example. And, then, even if the studies did conclude that many college students are undecided, it would not be fair to conclude that every single student is undecided. If no evidence is given, then the generalization is not trustworthy and should be questioned.

3. **Evaluate the specifics.** For the statement "Pets are always troublesome," ask what kind of pets the author is referring to—a pet potbellied pig, an iguana, or a cat? Then ask what is meant by troublesome—does it mean the animal is time-consuming, requires special care, or behaves poorly?

4. **Think of exceptions.** For the generalization *Medical doctors are aloof and inaccessible*, can you think of a doctor you have met or heard about who was caring and available to his or her patients? If so, the generalization is not accurate in all cases.

EXERCISE 5-10 **Identifying Generalizations**

Read each of the following statements and place a check mark before each generalization.

_____ 1. The Internet is changing America.

_____ 2. Influenza causes severe epidemics every two years.

_____ 3. Most drug cases start with busts of small, local dealers and move to a search of their suppliers.

_____ 4. Attending college is essential for economic success and advancement.

_____ 5. Colds are caused by viruses, not bacteria, not cold weather, and not improper diet.

EXERCISE 5-11 **Identifying Generalizations**

Read each of the following items and underline each generalization.

1. Child care workers are undereducated in relation to the importance of their jobs. A whole generation of children is being left day after day in the hands of women with little more than high-school-level education. These children will suffer in the future for our inattention to the child care employment pool.
2. Americans have had enough of libraries providing Internet pornography to children. They want filtering on all computers or computers out of libraries. When will librarians listen to their customers (who also pay their salaries)?
3. For the past few years, drivers have been getting worse. Especially guilty of poor driving are the oldest and youngest drivers. There should be stricter tests and more classes for new drivers and yearly eye exams and road tests for drivers once they hit age 60. This is the only way to ensure the safety of our roads.

EXERCISE 5-12 **Evaluating Generalizations**

For each of the following generalizations, indicate what questions you would ask and what types of information you would need to evaluate the generalization.

1. Vegetarians are pacifists and they do not own guns.
2. Most crimes are committed by high school dropouts.
3. It always rains in Seattle.
4. Private school students get a better education than public school students.
5. Scientists don't believe in any kind of higher power.

■ What Assumptions Is the Author Making?

Tip for Social Science Majors

Introductory textbooks are often based on a set of assumptions that help the student better understand the discipline. For example, economics textbooks often start with the assumption that "people behave in rational ways," because that assumption is important to the analyses that follow. However, as economics majors learn in upper-level courses, people do not always behave in rational ways, which makes economics considerably more complicated than it at first appears.

Suppose a friend asked you, "Have you stopped cheating on your girlfriend?" This person, perhaps not a friend after all, is making an assumption. He or she is assuming that you already have been cheating. An **assumption** is an idea or principle the writer accepts as true and makes no effort to prove or substantiate. Assumptions often use words such as *since, if,* or *when.* Here are a few more examples:

- You're going to make that mistake again, are you? (The assumption is that you have already made the mistake at least once.)
- When you're mature, you'll realize you made a mistake. (The assumption is that you are not mature now.)
- You are as arrogant as your sister. (The assumption is that your sister is arrogant.)
- My dog is angry. (The assumption is that dogs have and can express emotions.)

Each of the statements above makes no attempt to prove or support the hidden assumption; it is assumed to be true.

Writers often make assumptions and make no effort to prove or support them. For example, an author may assume that television encourages violent behavior in children and proceed to argue for restrictions on TV viewing. If a writer's assumption is wrong or unsubstantiated, then the statements that follow from the assumption should be questioned. If television does not encourage violent behavior, for example, then the suggestion to restrict viewing should not be accepted unless other reasons are offered.

EXERCISE 5–13

Identifying Assumptions

Read each of the following statements and then place a check mark before those choices that are assumptions made by the writer of the statement.

1. Cosmetics should not be tested on animals, since they may cause pain, injury, or even death.

    _____ a. Animals have the right to avoid pain and suffering.

    _____ b. Cosmetics should be tested on people.

    _____ c. Animals should be anesthetized before research is conducted.

2. Teacher's aides lack advanced college degrees: therefore, they are unable to teach children effectively.

    _____ a. Teacher's aides should obtain advanced degrees.

    _____ b. Advanced college degrees are needed in order to teach effectively.

    _____ c. Teachers who hold advanced degrees are not necessarily effective teachers.

3. Border states in the United States must take action to curb illegal immigration; otherwise, state funds will be quickly exhausted.

_____ a. The writer opposes using state funds to help illegal immigrants.

_____ b. Illegal immigrants must enter the United States legally to receive state aid.

_____ c. State funding guidelines should be revised.

EXERCISE 5-14   ## Identifying Assumptions

For each statement listed below, identify at least one assumption.

1. Grocery stores should reduce the number of weekly sale items and lower overall prices.
2. Eliminating essay exams from psychology courses would diminish students' writing abilities.
3. More public transit should be added to our cities to reduce traffic and pollution.
4. Endangered species should be bred in captivity to ensure their survival.
5. Artists do not need grants from the government because they sell their works for such high prices.
6. Hunters serve their communities by keeping down the deer population.
7. Lobbyists hinder the work of our elected officials; these groups should be banned from Washington, DC.
8. Doing away with unions would increase productivity in our country.
9. Learning a foreign language is a waste of time; Americans can get by anywhere.
10. Violence in sports affects everyone. Such brutality corrupts play, a form of free expression.

EXERCISE 5-15   ## Identifying Assumptions

Identify the assumption(s) in each of the following passages.

1.   Most kids, of course, listen barely if at all to what adults say. Instead they watch what adults do. And, for better or worse, there may be no lesson we impart to them so efficiently as how we adults react to events that upset us, from a fender-bender to a threatening new era of conflict.

—Editorial, "Raising the Sept. 11 Generation," *Chicago Tribune*

2.   Speaking from developments in my own family, there are way too many young students out there whose focus centers on partying, dress competition, music, souped-up cars and sex. Goal-setting and accomplishment in their studies as they prepare themselves for what is a highly competitive world do not figure too prominently in their day-to-day lives.

—Editorial, "School's First Week Provides a Few Bright Exceptions," *Toronto Star*

3.   Most products—from cigarette lighters to medicine bottles—have to be designed to protect against foreseeable misuse. But there is no regulator to help the plaintiffs: guns and tobacco are the only products that the Consumer Product Safety Commission does not oversee. And even though lawsuits have often helped push up safety standards elsewhere, there are plenty of conservative judges who do not think it is the courts' job to create gun laws.

—Editorial, "From the hip; Gun control," *The Economist* (U.S.)

4.   In the meantime, a disturbing message is being sent to the guys and girls in the little leagues. Practice hard, work out, eat nutritiously—and sneak illegal steroids because, after all, winning and setting records are everything. And besides, if you make it big, you'll have enough money to care for your broken body.

—Editorial, "Steroids Should Be Tagged Out," *San Jose Mercury News*

5.   Britain on Wednesday marked the 150th anniversary of its public toilets. This reminds us of the barbaric lack of such facilities in the United States. Along with an increasingly chaotic and unfair health system, sparse public transportation and a paucity of neighborhood parks, the absence of public loos here evokes America's depressing distance from the perfect place that pathological patriots assert that it is.

—Editorial, "Sign of Civilization," *Providence Journal*

■ Does the Author Use Manipulative Language?

Writers can shape their readers' thinking and response to their message by the language they choose to express it. Writers use a variety of language manipulation techniques to achieve a particular effect, to communicate their message in a particular way, and to appeal to specific groups of people. These techniques include clichés, jargon, allusions, euphemisms, and doublespeak.

Clichés

A **cliché** is a tired, overused expression. Here are a few examples:

Curiosity killed the cat.

Bigger is better.

He is as blind as a bat.

These everyday expressions have been overused; they are so commonly used that they no longer carry a specific meaning.

Numerous clichés used throughout a piece of writing may suggest that the writer has not thought in depth about the topic or has not made the effort to express his or her ideas in an interesting and unique way.

Because clichés are so common, many readers tend to accept them at face value rather than to evaluate their meaning and appropriateness.

KEY STRATEGY: How to Evaluate Clichés

To evaluate clichés, ask the following questions:

1. **Is the writer trying to gloss over or skip over details by using a cliché?** Clichés often oversimplify a situation that is complex. In trying to decide which courses to register for, a student may say, "Don't put off till tomorrow what you can do today." Actually the student *could* register today, but it may be better to wait until he or she has had time to think, do research, and talk to others about course selection.

2. **Is the writer trying to avoid directly stating an unpopular or unpleasant idea?** Suppose you are reading an article on controlling world terrorism. After describing recent acts of terrorism, the writer concludes the article with the cliché, "What will be, will be." What does this cliché really say? In this context, the cliché suggests (but does not directly state) that nothing can be done about terrorism, an unpopular viewpoint that would receive criticism if directly expressed.

3. **Is the cliché fitting and appropriate?** Suppose in writing an article on college financial aid, the writer admonishes students not to spend their financial aid loan before they receive it, by saying, "Don't count your chickens before they are hatched." Explaining that loan checks are often delayed, and that spending money before it is received may cause serious financial problems would be more meaningful.

4. **What does the use of clichés reveal about the author?** Use of clichés may signal that a writer is not fully aware of his or her audience or interested in accommodating them. A writer who packs an article full of clichés is not aware that his or her readers prefer fresh, descriptive information, rather than standard clichés.

EXERCISE 5-16   ## Understanding Clichés

For each of the following clichés, explain its meaning and then think of a situation in which it would be untrue or inappropriate.

Example:

Cliché: Don't change horses in midstream.

Meaning: You should not try to change course once you have begun.

Situation: If you realize you have made a poor decision and there is a way to correct it, you should correct it. For example, if you realize you are registered for the wrong level math course, try to drop the course or change to the appropriate level course.

1. Better late than never.
2. Opportunity doesn't knock twice.

3. Good fences make good neighbors.
4. Money makes the world go round.
5. If you don't have anything nice to say, don't say anything at all.

EXERCISE 5-17

Rewriting Clichés

Replace each of the following clichés with more specific information that fits the context.

> Example: The university president did not want to "toot his own horn," but he enumerated all his accomplishments of the past year.
>
> Replacement: The university president didn't want to brag . . .

1. My older sister turned 40 this year. She is over-the-hill.
2. The mayor and the governor are like two peas in a pod.
3. Not sure of his itinerary, the salesman decided to play it by ear.
4. The students made sure to read the fine print on their new lease.
5. Our new senator rubs me the wrong way.

Jargon

Jargon refers to words, phrases, and specialized terms used by a particular academic field or special interest group that are not readily understood by the general public. Librarians speak jargon when communicating with each other, for example:

> We are considering several different solutions for the aggregation question that will allow our patrons more targeted periodical database searching.

Doctors use specialized language when communicating treatments to other medical professionals, for example:

> During the technique for nursemaid's elbow reduction, put your thumb in the antecubital fossa, then apply longitudinal traction.

☑ **Tip for Computer Science/Technical Majors**

Avoid the tendency to lapse into "computerese," computer-based jargon that the average person does not understand. Speaking in "plain English" is particularly important when working in a technical support capacity. Employers report that their most valuable technical employees are the ones who are able to communicate effectively with nontechnical workers about computer problems and solutions.

Jargon tends to confuse, isolate, or exclude those readers who are not a member of the group that uses it. A writer may use jargon to appear more knowledgeable or even superior to his or her readers. Unknowing, noncritical readers may accept ideas simply because they are defended by jargon, assuming that the writer must be knowledgeable in order to use complex, unfamiliar terminology.

If a writer uses jargon you do not understand, you may not be the writer's intended audience. If you are the intended audience, the writer may be purposely trying to manipulate you. Writers may intentionally use jargon to assume a position of authority. As another example, a writer of a general interest article on organ transplants may use obtuse medical terminology to present facts that, if presented in layman's terms, may be unpleasant or objectionable.

EXERCISE 5-18

Analyzing Jargon

Underline the jargon in each of the following statements. Can you use context to figure out new terms? Is the jargon confusing or manipulative? Would you continue reading the rest of the article from which each statement is taken?

1.   Place-based education, which draws from local culture, history, and geography to create a meaningful curriculum, can occur in any type of setting, but it holds particular promise for rural homeschooling. Place-based educators use local particulars to teach universal concepts, engage students in community life, and involve people and resources unique to the home community.

    —Jaycox, "Rural Homeschooling and Place-Based *Education,*" *ERIC Digest*

2.   Extinction is actually a normal process in the course of evolution. Throughout geological time, many more species have become extinct than exist today. These species slowly disappeared because of climatic changes and the inability to adapt to such conditions as competition and predation.

    —"Endangered Species," *Funk & Wagnalls New World Encyclopedia*

3.   Dietetic practitioners in need of evidence-based medicine reports should try a new feature available in the periodical literature database CINAHL, which is available through the database vendor EBSCOHost. When conducting a search in this database, the clinician can limit the results to EBM reports. These reports provide data collected through a systematic meta-analysis of randomized controlled trials. The practitioner can then use these recommendations to inform his or her own practice.

Allusions

Allusions are references to well-known religious, literary, artistic, or historical works or sources. A writer may refer to a biblical verse, a character in a famous poem or novel, a line in a well-known song, or a historical figure such as Napoleon or George Washington. Writers usually assume that educated readers will recognize and understand their allusions. Here are a few examples of allusions:

Tip for Humanities/ Liberal Arts Majors

Use of allusions is common in humanities and liberal arts courses, because they often refer to historical and social movements. Religion inspires art and architecture; historical events inspire poetry and literature; philosophers develop theories based on history and personal observation. You may feel overwhelmed by allusions you do not "get." Use footnotes to get more information, and do not worry: as you read more, you'll understand more allusions.

- A writer describes a person as having the patience of Job. In the Bible, Job is a righteous man whose faith was tested by God.
- An article on parental relationships with children refers to the Oedipus complex. Oedipus was a figure in Greek mythology who unknowingly killed his father and married his mother. He blinded himself when he discovered what he had done. The Oedipus complex is controversial but refers to a child's tendency to be attracted to a parent of the opposite sex.

If you encounter an allusion you do not understand, check it on the Internet using a search engine such as Google (http://www.google.com) by typing in the key words of the allusion.

Writers may include numerous literary or scholarly allusions to give their writing the appearance of scholarship. Do not be overly impressed by a writer's use of allusions, particularly obscure ones. A writer may use allusions to divert readers' attention from a lack of substantive detail or support. When evaluating a writer's use of allusions, ask the following questions:

- **What does the allusion mean?**
- **Why did the writer include the allusion?**
- **What does the allusion contribute to the overall meaning of the work?**

| EXERCISE 5-19 | Analyzing Allusions |

For each of the following statements, explain the meaning of the allusion.

1. The mayor looked around the hurricane-ravaged city and pondered the Herculean task that lay ahead in rebuilding the lives and homes destroyed.
2. Emily's mother hoped her new regimen of yoga and raw foods would be her fountain of youth.
3. "Whoa, Twilight Zone," the two new friends said to each other when they realized how many coincidences linked them.
4. Her grandparents finally came out of the Dark Ages and bought a cordless phone.
5. The campaign manager sought to discover and exploit the opponent's Achilles' heel.
6. Many small business people find themselves in a catch-22 when they realize they must compete in a world of e-commerce but cannot afford to create an e-commerce Web site.
7. When she realized her best friend had joined in with others to betray her, she muttered, "Et tu, Brute?"
8. With a grin like the Cheshire Cat, the defendant sat waiting for the jury's verdict.
9. He awoke from a Kafkaesque dream feeling anxious and lonely, frightened of what his day would bring.
10. The little boy likened himself to George Washington as he confessed to breaking the neighbor's window with his baseball.

Euphemisms

What do these sentences have in common?

He suffered combat fatigue.

The company is downsizing.

Capital punishment is controversial.

Each uses an expression called a euphemism. A **euphemism** is a word or phrase that is used in place of a word that is unpleasant, embarrassing, or otherwise objectionable. The expression *combat fatigue* is a less unpleasant way to refer to the psychological problems of veterans caused by their experiences in war, *downsizing* replaces the word *firing*, and *capital punishment* is a substitute for *death penalty*.

Here are a few more examples:

The foreign spy was put out of circulation. (the spy was killed)

He was hit by friendly fire. (accidentally shot by a member of the same army)

My brother works as a sanitation engineer. (janitor or garbage collector)

Euphemisms tend to minimize or downplay something's importance or seriousness. They are often used in politics and advertising. They can be used to camouflage actions or events that may be unacceptable to readers or listeners if bluntly explained. For example, the term *casualties of war* may be used instead of the phrase *dead soldiers* to lessen the impact of the attack. To say that a politician's statement was *at variance with the truth* has less impact and is less forceful than to say that the politician lied.

A writer may use a euphemism to alter your perception of a situation by lessening its harshness, ugliness, severity, or seriousness. When a writer uses a euphemism, substitute the everyday meaning of the euphemism and notice whether the writer's message changes.

EXERCISE 5-20

Rewriting Euphemisms

For each of the underlined euphemisms, write a substitution that does not minimize or avoid the basic meaning of the term.

Example: The theater had only one ladies' room.

The theater had only one women's toilet.

1. The councilman has entered a substance abuse program.
2. Body counts started out high but then were revised to lower numbers.
3. Reporters are not required to reveal their confidential sources.
4. The high school teacher found her senior English students to be unmotivated.
5. A new correctional facility will be built near Deer Run housing development.
6. You may experience precipitation over the holiday weekend.
7. My midwife says I might feel under the weather during the first trimester of my pregnancy.
8. Richard's parents were surprised to see just how cozy his apartment was.
9. Several countries considered a preemptive strike against the uncooperative nation.
10. Everyone wondered how Aurora would make ends meet now that she was between jobs.

Doublespeak

Doublespeak is deliberately unclear or evasive language. Often, it exaggerates or overstates information that could be expressed simply. William Lutz, an expert on doublespeak, defines it as "language that pretends to communicate but does not" in his book *Beyond Nineteen Eighty-Four*. Here is an example: "the letter from the air force colonel in charge of safety said that rocket boosters weighing more than 300,000 pounds 'have an explosive force upon surface impact that is sufficient to exceed the accepted overpressure threshold of physiological damage for the exposed personnel.'" What does the colonel's statement mean in simple words? If a 300,000-pound rocket falls on a person, it will kill that person.

Here is a humorous example of the use of doublespeak, attributed to Everett Dirksen, former U.S. senator:

I am reminded of the man who filled in an application for an insurance policy. One of the questions he had to answer was, "How old was your father when he died and of what did he die?" Well, his father had been hanged, but he did not want to put that on his application. He puzzled it out for a while. He finally wrote, "my father was 65 when he died. He came to his end while participating in a public function when the platform gave way."

—Grazian, "How Much Do Words Really Matter?" *Public Relations* Quarterly

Here are a few more examples, along with their everyday meanings:

detainees—prisoners

downsizing the company—firing employees

vertically deployed antipersonnel devices—bombs

Doublespeak uses euphemisms, but it tangles language in other ways as well that are intended to confuse or overwhelm the listener or reader. Doublespeak often uses technical language (jargon) that is likely to be unfamiliar to the audience. Doublespeak also uses inflated language—words that tend to make something seem more important or complex than it really is. Doublespeak may contain long, polysyllabic words. It may scramble the order of words in a sentence to create confusion or avoid giving complete information. When reading doublespeak, be suspicious of the writer's motives. Ask yourself:

- Why is the writer being purposefully evasive or unclear?
- What is he or she trying to hide?

EXERCISE 5-21

Rewriting Doublespeak

Untangle each of the following examples of doublespeak and write a translation in simple English.

Example: Most hospitals are reluctant to publicize negative patient care outcomes.

Hospitals are reluctant to publicize patient deaths.

1. Jessamyn's advisor suggested she try a course in human kinetics, figuring that the outcomes from this class would cause an upward development in the calculation of her GPA.
2. The positive economic adjustments at our most-liked eating establishment were meant to counter the recent negative contributions to profit.
3. My female sibling went on a caloric reduction program two seasons prior to her nuptials.
4. More than several students have forgone cowhide back-mounted equipment for those of the vegetarian variety.
5. The drug enterprise leader was apprehended following his activation of an intrusion detection device.
6. Large amounts of previously owned parts were strewn about the public waste reception center.
7. How much time do our education users spend on task or attending to their learning facilitators?

8. My personal manual database indicates I must procure a social expression product for my chronologically gifted neighbor.

9. In the event of a nonroutine operation, follow the relocation drill.

10. Preliminary reports show a negative gain in test scores in the state's public schools.

Self-Test Summary

1. What is the connotative meaning of a word?	The connotative meaning of a word includes the feelings and associations that may accompany it, not just its literal meaning (or denotation).
2. What is figurative language?	Writers use figurative language to create vivid images in a reader's mind by comparing two dissimilar things that share a common characteristic.
3. Define three types of figurative language.	• A simile makes a comparison between two unlike things using the words *as* or *like.* • A metaphor states or implies the relationship between two unlike items, usually using the word *is.* • Personification compares ideas or objects to humans by attributing human characteristics to them.
4. What is bias?	Bias is a writer's prejudice, a one-sided viewpoint on a topic or issue.
5. How do writers mislead by omission?	Writers mislead by omission by leaving out, ignoring, or selectively choosing details; by making incomplete comparisons; by using the passive voice; or by using unspecified nouns and pronouns.
6. What is a generalization?	A generalization is a statement about an entire group, based on information known about only part of that group. It is a leap from what is known to a conclusion about what is not known.
7. What is an assumption?	An assumption is an idea or principle a writer accepts as true but makes no effort to prove or substantiate.
8. Why do authors use manipulative language?	Authors use manipulative language to achieve a particular effect, to communicate their message in a particular way, or to appeal to specific groups.
9. Define five commonly used kinds of manipulative language.	• Clichés are tired, overused expressions. • Jargon is the specialized or technical language of a particular field, profession, or group. • Allusions are indirect references to well-known religious, literary, artistic, or historical works or sources. • Euphemisms are words or phrases used in place of ones that are considered unpleasant or objectionable. • Doublespeak is the deliberate use of unclear or evasive language.

Business/Arts

Information Age: How the Music Industry Can Get Digital Satisfaction

L. Gordon Crovitz

Prereading Questions

1. How has digital technology affected the music industry?
2. How have other industries coped with technology?

1   The music industry played one sour note after another as digital technology undermined its traditional business models. But after suing some 35,000 music fans for illegally downloading songs, music honchos decided not to sue the more than seven million others. Instead, the industry has concluded that if it can't beat them, it might as well join them in enjoying the benefits of technology. This marks a milestone in what might be called the Great Unbundling.

2   Digital technology is a powerful disaggregator, giving consumers the power to pick and choose what we want, how we want it, and when and where we want it. Instead of buying a 14-song CD, people can download one favorite. Instead of owning physical CDs, we own access to digital copies. Instead of having to use a stationary stereo, we can play songs on our iPods, phones or laptops.

3   Other industries are still coming to terms with the unbundling power of digital technology—think of video, books and news—which makes the music industry's story timely. Recorded music for decades was sold as physical products, albums via phonographs, cassettes, then CDs. For young programmers, finding ways to download and share songs digitally (and usually illegally) became an early application of the Web. Napster and similar file-sharing services were shut down in the early 2000s as the music industry fought illegal downloads.

4   But shifts in how people access music can mean rethinking the entire value proposition. As music-industry critics David Kusek and Gerd Leonhard predicted several years ago, "Access to music will replace ownership of it. We have passed through the Industrial Age to the Information Age, and music will never be the same again." There are now about half as many CD sales in the U.S. as in 2000. A few years ago, record executives in London were shocked when young people refused even free CDs.

5   The industry should by now understand that the way to get "Back in Black" is not in album CDs, which remain the biggest source of revenue. Instead, the future is sales of digital songs and ring tones, licensing to video games, and trying to get rights to concerts and other revenues associated with the musicians.

6   Just in the past month, the Recording Industry Association of America abandoned its previous theme song of "Bring Lawyers, Guns and Money" by announcing it would no

longer sue downloaders, except in exceptional circumstances. This means kids will no longer be sued for downloading songs for personal use.

7   Instead, the trade group will work with Internet service providers to identify the worst offenders. The association will track people who grossly infringe copyright and alert the ISPs, which will remind users that downloading music illegally is a violation of service agreements that could lead to the service being cut off. A study found that 70% of people in Britain would stop illegally sharing files if their ISP told them it had detected the violation. ISPs would benefit because a limited number of music downloaders hog bandwidth, and they may also hope this approach could work to limit abuse of online video.

8   The music industry also reversed its longtime strategy of limiting digital rights. The recording companies recently agreed that Apple's iTunes Store can sell songs without copy protection, which means that buyers can listen to them on devices other than their iPod or iPhone. They also agreed to price points above and below the flat 99 cents that Apple had used. The iTunes Store has redefined convenience for consumers, last year becoming the world's leading music retailer, dislodging Wal-Mart.

9   Unbundling has made singles—disaggregated from albums—the big winner. Last year was the biggest ever in Britain for the sale of singles, combining downloads and CDs. There can even be new bundles: Buyers of Nokia's "Comes with Music" mobile phone will get the right to download unlimited songs to the owner's phone and computers, with the participating music publisher paid a share of the price of the phone.

10   The music industry is the first disrupted industry to understand that people are willing to pay for what's otherwise free (albeit illegal) if it's convenient, well-packaged and reasonably priced. This is a lesson other parts of the media and entertainment business still fight by making their content available for free in the digital medium while charging for it in other channels.

11   The embrace of technology didn't happen until the traditional music companies had no option. Other industries should stop wailing that they "Can't Get No Satisfaction" and instead work on their own versions of "The Times, They Are A-Changin.'" Consumers will always want choice. When technology provides it, the best response is to find ways to give customers what they want.

Writing About the Reading

CHECKING YOUR VOCABULARY

1. For each of the words listed below, use context; prefixes, roots, and suffixes (see Chapter 3); and/or a dictionary to write a brief definition or synonym of the word as it is used in the reading.

   a. undermined (para. 1) _____

   b. disaggregator (para. 2) _____

   c. stationary (para. 2) _____

   d. timely (para. 3) _____

   e. abandoned (para. 6) _____

   f. infringe (para. 7) _____

g. dislodging (para. 8) _____

h. disrupted (para. 10) _____

2. Highlight new, specialized terms introduced in the reading (see Chapter 3).

3. Draw a word map of one of the words in the reading.

CHECKING YOUR COMPREHENSION

1. Explain what is meant by the "Great Unbundling."
2. According to the author, album CDs are *not* the way for the music industry to make money in the future. What three things does the author say the music industry should focus on instead?
3. How has the Recording Industry Association of America changed its approach to illegal downloaders?
4. Describe how the music industry recently reversed its strategy of limiting digital rights. How is this beneficial to consumers of music?
5. What does the author give as an example of a "new bundle"?

THINKING CRITICALLY

1. What is the author's purpose in writing this article?
2. Why did the author use song titles throughout the article? Evaluate the effectiveness of these references to popular culture.
3. Identify an example of figurative language in the article.
4. What assumptions does the author make? Try to identify at least two in the article.
5. Do you think the music industry's efforts to stop illegal downloading will work? Why or why not?
6. Can you think of any ways that other industries (video, books, news) are coming to terms with digital technology? What opportunities might there be for businesses that recognize the benefits of embracing technology?

LEARNING/STUDY STRATEGY

Assume you are a business major. Highlight and annotate the reading, noting trends and issues that are important in business.

MyReadingLab

To practice your critical thinking skills, go to http://www.myreadinglab .com. Click on "Study Plan," then on "Reading Skills, and then on "Critical Thinking."

6 Reading and Evaluating Arguments

Thinking Visually About Arguments

Study the photo at left that shows a group of students participating in a demonstration. The signs the demonstrators hold take a position on an issue: Rescue Our National Forests. All that is lacking is evidence or reasons to convince us that our national forests should be saved. The photograph, then, presents the beginnings of an *argument*.

LEARNING OBJECTIVES

- To recognize the structure of an argument

- To identify the parts of an argument

- To recognize types of arguments

- To read arguments effectively

- To evaluate evidence used to support an argument

- To recognize opposing viewpoints

- To recognize errors in logical reasoning

ARGUMENTS: The Academic Link

Much of academic thought is based on arguments, which are actually civilized conversations arguing for or against something. For example, in a government course you might read arguments for or against free speech; in a criminal justice course you might read arguments for or against parole for convicted criminals. To understand a situation fully, you need to see it from multiple viewpoints, to consider various perspectives in order to form your own conclusions. College instructors don't want to hear uninformed opinions; they want you to argue your case based on data, research, and a full understanding of the matter at hand.

ARGUMENTS: The Career Link

Most careers will require you to argue your case and to present valid reasons for your recommendations. Learning the elements of argument will make you a more persuasive employee, which will certainly help you the next time you are negotiating for a raise!

■ What Is an Argument?

Here is a brief argument. As you read, notice that the argument offers reasons to support the viewpoint that schools should be allowed to regulate off-campus cyberbullying.

CYBERBULLYING: OFF-CAMPUS REGULATION: PRO

Two high-school students have created a racist profile on a social-networking site, including racist language and cartoons about lynching. Other students are linking to the site and have posted ugly comments. Teachers report that many of the school's minority students are frightened.

At another high school, students created a "We Hate Ashley" profile that includes crude sexual innuendos and cracks about their classmate's weight. Ashley is no longer willing to come to school, and her grades have plummeted. Her parents report she is under psychological care and on suicide watch.

Do school officials have the authority to impose discipline in response to harmful off-campus online speech? Should they? This is a major challenge facing school administrators today.

The problem is grounded in the fact that the most harmful incidents of cyberbullying occur when students post or send material while they are off-campus, because they have more unsupervised time. But the harmful impact is at school, because this is where students are physically together. Cyberbullying incidents lead to school avoidance and failure, youth suicide and school violence.

Studies on cyberbullying reported in the December 2007 *Journal of Adolescent Health* reveal that both perpetrators and targets of cyberbullying report significant psychosocial concerns and increased rates of involvement in off-line physical and relational aggression. Targets of cyberbullying were eight times more likely than other students to report bringing a weapon to school. The concerns for student safety are very real. Students who do not believe school officials can help them may seek their own revenge—or refuse to come to school.

Courts have consistently ruled that school officials can respond to off-campus student speech if that speech has caused—or a reasonable person would anticipate it could cause—a substantial disruption at school or interference with the rights of students to be secure. Situations that have met this standard include violent physical or verbal altercations, a hostile environment interfering with the ability of students to participate in school activities and significant interference with school operations and delivery of instruction.

School officials do not have the authority to respond to off-campus speech simply because they find the speech objectionable or repugnant. Response to such speech is a parent's responsibility. But when off-campus speech raises legitimate concerns about student safety and well-being, school officials must have the authority to respond—because every student faces the potential of harm.

—Nancy Willard, Executive Director, Center for Safe and Responsible Internet Use.
Written for *CQ Researcher*, April 2008.

■ Parts of an Argument

Tip for Allied Health, Science, Business, and Criminal Justice Majors

Almost all colleges offer a course in argument (usually through the English department). Taking this course is excellent preparation for your career, as you will be making arguments in favor of or against ideas or proposals as part of your job. For example, health professionals might have to argue for a specific type of therapy for a patient. A parole officer might have to argue for an opportunity for a rehabilitated criminal.

An argument has four parts:

- **An argument must address an *issue*—a problem or controversy about which people disagree.** Abortion, gun control, animal rights, and drug legalization are all examples of issues.
- **An argument must take a position on an issue.** This position is called a **claim.** An argument may claim that handguns should be outlawed or that medical use of marijuana should be legalized.
- **An argument offers *support* for the claim.** Support consists of reasons and evidence that the claim is reasonable and should be accepted. Emotional appeals (see p. 166) may also be used.
- **A *refutation* considers opposing viewpoints and may attempt to disprove or discredit them.** Not all arguments include refutations.

See Figure 6-1 for an illustration of the structure of an argument.

In the argument above, the issue is regulation of cyberbullying, as announced in the title. The author's claim is that schools should regulate off-campus cyberbullying. The author builds the argument by offering reasons why cyberbullying should be regulated: first, the harmful impact of cyberbullying occurs in school, and second, schools are already allowed to respond to off-campus speech. The author provides evidence that includes examples and citation of research.

FIGURE 6-1   The Structure of an Argument

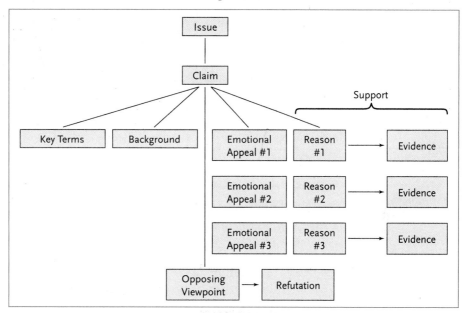

The author does not refute the opposing viewpoint that regulation should not be allowed. An opposing viewpoint may state that regulation of off-campus behavior is the responsibility of parents. To refute this opposing viewpoint, the author may say that parents are reluctant, or do not know how, to provide appropriate supervision and regulation.

Types of Claims

The claim is the position or stand the writer takes on the issue. You might think of it as his or her viewpoint. Here are a few sample claims on the issue of animal rights:

> Animals should have none of the rights that humans do.
>
> Animals have limited rights: freedom from pain and suffering.
>
> Animals should be afforded the same rights as humans.

There are three common types of claims. A **claim of fact** is a statement that can be proven or verified by observation or research, as in the following example:

> Within ten years, destruction of rain forests will cause hundreds of plant and animal species to become extinct.

A **claim of value** states that one thing or idea is better or more desirable than another. Issues of right versus wrong or acceptable versus unacceptable lead to claims of value. An argument about baseball players' use of steroids is a claim of value. Its author argues that steroid use is not acceptable because it is harmful to both the players and the game of baseball.

Here is another example. The following claim of value asserts that mandatory community service is appropriate.

> Requiring community service in high school will produce more community-aware graduates.

A **claim of policy** suggests what should or ought to be done to solve a problem. The following claim of policy states Willard's position on cyberbullying.

> To control harmful cyberbullying, schools should regulate it.

EXERCISE 6-1 | **Identifying Claims**

Identify whether each of the following is a claim of fact (F), a claim of value (V), or claim of policy (P), and label each.

_____ 1. Mandatory jail sentences should be imposed for drivers convicted of more than one drunk driving violation.

_____ 2. Student government elections were largely ignored by the student body due to student satisfaction with current policies and leadership.

_____ 3. Marijuana use and abuse continue to escalate in American society.

_____ 4. A mandatory dress code should be implemented in public schools.

_____ 5. Killing deer and other large animals for sport is wrong.

EXERCISE 6-2 | **Writing Claims**

For two of the following issues, write two claims about the issue. For each issue, try to write two different types of claims.

1. same-sex marriages
2. violence in schools
3. privacy on the Internet
4. drug testing in the workplace

Types of Support

There are three common types of support:

- A **reason** is a general statement that supports a claim. It explains why the writer's viewpoint is reasonable and should be accepted. In "Cyberbullying" on page 155 the author offers two reasons why cyberbullying should be regulated: it is harmful and schools already regulate off-campus speech.
- **Evidence** consists of facts, statistics, experiences, comparisons, and examples that demonstrate why the claim is valid. The author of "Cyberbullying"

on page 155 offers examples of cyberbullying, cites research on the issue, and refers to court rulings.

- **Emotional appeals** are ideas that are targeted toward needs or values that readers are likely to care about. Needs include physiological needs (food, drink, shelter) and psychological needs (sense of belonging, sense of accomplishment, sense of self-worth, sense of competency). In "Cyberbullying" on page 155 the author appeals to the reader's sense of fairness and sympathy for victims of cyberbullying.

EXERCISE 6-3

Identifying Evidence

Identify the type(s) of evidence used to support each of the following brief arguments.

1. Many students have part-time jobs that require them to work late afternoons and evenings during the week. These students are unable to use the library during the week. Therefore, library hours should be extended to weekends.
2. Because parents have the right to determine their children's sexual attitudes, sex education should take place in the home, not at school.
3. No one should be forced to inhale unpleasant or harmful substances. That's why the ban on cigarette smoking in public places was put into effect in our state. Why shouldn't there be a law to prevent people from wearing strong colognes or perfumes, especially in restaurants, since the sense of smell is important to taste?

■ Inductive and Deductive Arguments

Tip for Business Majors

Many decisions made by companies are based on inductive reasoning. For example, the manager of a clothing store might notice that bright colors are selling better than dark; more expensive items are not selling well; that wool shirts are not moving at all. At a buyers' convention, based on inductive reasoning, the manager is likely to decide to purchase light-colored, lower-priced garments made of cotton.

Two types of arguments—inductive and deductive—are common. An **inductive argument** reaches a general conclusion from observed specifics. For example, by observing the performance of a large number of athletes, you could conclude that athletes possess physical stamina. A **deductive argument**, on the other hand, begins with a general statement, known as a major premise, and moves toward a more specific statement, known as the minor premise. For example, from the major premise that "Athletes possess physical stamina," you can reason that because Anthony is an athlete (the minor premise), he must possess physical stamina.

Both types of arguments begin with statements that are assumed to be correct. Basically, both follow a general pattern of "If that is so, then this is so . . ." At times, an argument may be more complex, involving several steps—"If that is so, and this happens, then this should be done." You can visualize each type of argument as shown in Figure 6-2 on page 160.

FIGURE 6-2   Inductive and Deductive Arguments

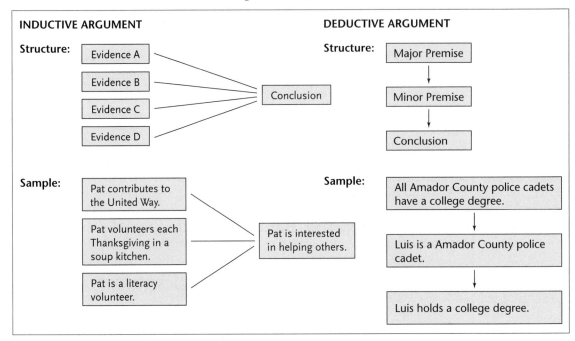

EXERCISE 6-4   **Supplying Evidence**

For each of the following inductive arguments, supply the missing pieces.

1. Evidence: Prof. Hong wears jeans and flannel shirts to class.

   Evidence: Prof. Hutchinson wears khaki pants and running shoes when he lectures.

   Evidence: _____

   Conclusion: Professors on this campus dress casually for class.

2. Evidence: Many people walk down the street talking on their cell phones.

   Evidence: Most families own at least two cell phones.

   Evidence: In restaurants and in shopping malls people can be observed using their cell phones.

   Conclusion: _____

EXERCISE 6-5   **Supplying Conclusions**

For each of the following deductive arguments, supply the conclusion.

1. Major Premise: All students with yearly averages above 3.5 are offered a summer internship.

Minor Premise: Jacqueline has a yearly average of 3.7.

Conclusion: _____

2. Major Premise: Elementary school children's absences from school are due to illness.

Minor Premise: Quinne, a fifth grade student, was absent yesterday.

Conclusion:_____

■ Strategies for Reading an Argument

Arguments need to be read slowly and carefully. Count on reading an argument more than once. The first time you read it, try to get an overview of its three essential elements: issue, claim, and support. Then reread it more carefully to closely follow the author's line of reasoning and to identify and evaluate the evidence provided.

Think Before You Read

1. **What does the title suggest?** Before you read, preview the reading and ask yourself what the title suggests about the issue and claim or support.

2. **Who is the author, and what are his or her qualifications?** Check to see if you recognize the author, and if so, evaluate whether he or she is qualified to write about the issue. For example, an article written by professional golfer Tiger Woods would be an authoritative source on the issue of ethics in professional golf. If the same argument were written by a state senator or a medical doctor, it would have less credibility. The specific qualifications of the author have a bearing on the worth of the evidence provided.

3. **What is the date of publication?** Checking the date will prompt you to consider whether new, even possibly contradictory, evidence has recently developed.

4. **What do I already know about the issue?** Try brainstorming using a two-column list. Label one column "pro" and the other "con," and list as many ideas as you can in each. By thinking about the issue on your own, you are less likely to be swayed by the writer's appeals and more likely to think and evaluate the reasons and evidence objectively.

EXERCISE 6-6   Analyzing an Argument

*Preview but do **not** read the following argument. (For previewing guidelines, see the Strategy box on page 35.) Complete the activities that follow. Read the argument after you have read the Key Strategy box on page 163.*

CYBERBULLYING: OFF-CAMPUS REGULATION: CON

If a school principal observed two students bullying another student at the local park or mall, she might speak to the children, alert the parents or, if really serious, call the police. Most likely she would not, however, contemplate using her principal's authority to suspend or otherwise discipline the bullies. Like most people, she would think that's outside of school and beyond her authority. The same standard should apply to cyberbullying.

School officials act *in loco parentis* (in place of a parent) when children are in school or in school-sponsored activities. Teachers are given leeway to instruct, direct and discipline to ensure a safe environment conducive to learning. And while students don't shed all their constitutional rights at the schoolhouse gate, courts have given administrators some leeway to restrict students' free speech, privacy and other rights while in school custody.

Once students leave the school's custody, they not only reacquire their full constitutional rights, but their parents or guardians regain theirs too, including their right to direct and control their children's upbringing. Parents' values and families' dynamics differ. Some parents prefer to turn the other cheek while others promote an eye for an eye. School officials have their own values and ways of addressing problems, and those may differ from the parents'. When it comes to their children's out-of-school behavior, parents have the right to decide if and how to discipline.

Limiting schools' disciplinary authority for out-of-school speech does not preclude school officials from taking steps, short of discipline, to address problems. Parents typically don't know everything their children do, and that's particularly true for Internet activity. Most parents would probably want school officials to alert them to bullying activity but leave disciplinary decisions to them. And for bullying that may cross the line into criminal behavior, contacting the police might be appropriate.

Finally, while school officials need to recognize that legally they have no authority over students' out-of-school speech, students should understand that Internet speech often carries real-world consequences. Unlike intemperate and stupid things uttered at the mall, speech posted on the Internet endures and is more widely accessible. Colleges, universities and prospective employers increasingly tend to uncover those mean and stupid Internet postings.

In sum, school officials have latitude to discipline students for bullying, cyber or otherwise, that occurs in school, but only parents (or police if necessary) have the authority to handle such matters off campus.

—Witold J. Walczak, Legal Director, American Civil Liberties Union of Pennsylvania.
Written for *CQ Researcher*, April 2008

1. What does the title suggest about the issue, claim, or evidence?
2. What do you already know about the issue? Brainstorm a two-column "Pro–Con" list.

Read Actively

When reading arguments, it is especially important to read actively.

KEY STRATEGY: How to Read an Argument

Use the following specific strategies for reading arguments:

1. **Read once for an initial impression.**   Do not focus on specifics; instead, try to get a general feel for the argument.

2. **Read the argument several more times.**   First identify the specific claim the writer is making and start to identify the reasons and evidence that support it. Read the argument again to examine whether the writer acknowledges or refutes opposing viewpoints.

☑ **Tip for Education Majors**

Helping your students to understand how to read and respond to an argumentative piece of writing will give them an advantage in all areas of their lives by making them better critical readers and thinkers. Emphasize that an effective argument usually acknowledges many sides of an issue, but eventually argues for one specific conclusion or outcome.

3. **Annotate as you read.**   Record your thoughts; note ideas you agree with, those you disagree with, questions that come to mind, additional reasons or evidence overlooked by the author, and the counterarguments not addressed by the author.

4. **Highlight key terms.**   Often, an argument depends on how certain terms are defined. In an argument on the destruction of forests, for example, what does "destruction" mean? Does it mean building homes within a forest, or does it refer to clearing the land for timber or to create a housing subdivision? Highlight both the key terms and the definitions the author provides.

5. **Diagram or map to analyze structure.**   Because many arguments are complex, you may find it helpful to diagram or map them. By mapping the argument, you may discover unsubstantiated ideas, reasons for which evidence is not provided, or an imbalance between reasons and emotional appeals. You can use the format shown in Figure 6-1 (p. 157) to help you analyze an argument's structure.

■ Strategies for Evaluating Arguments

Once you have understood the article by identifying what is asserted and how it is asserted, you are ready to evaluate its soundness, correctness, and worth.

Types of Evidence

The validity of an inductive argument rests, in part, on the soundness and correctness of the evidence provided to draw the conclusion. The validity of a deductive argument, on the other hand, rests on the accuracy and correctness of the premises on which the argument is based. Evaluating each type of argument involves assessing the accuracy and correctness of statements on which the argument is based. Often, writers provide evidence to substantiate their observations or premises. As a critical reader, your task is to assess whether the evidence is sufficient to support the claim.

KEY STRATEGY: How to Evaluate Evidence

☑ Tip for Psychology/ Social Science Majors

In your clinical work and internships, you will probably use all types of evidence—personal experience, examples, statistics, comparisons, and analogies—when reporting on patients' or clients' progress and treatments. Such evidence, when presented alongside accurate data and research, is usually considered acceptable in the social sciences.

Here are some questions to use when evaluating evidence.

1. **Is the observer biased or did he or she exaggerate or incorrectly perceive a situation?**

2. **Are the examples typical and representative?**

3. **Are statistics used fairly and clearly?** Many people are impressed by statistics—the reporting of figures, percentages, averages, and so forth—and assume they are irrefutable proof. Actually, statistics can be misused, misinterpreted, or used selectively to give other than the most objective, accurate picture of a situation. Approach statistical evidence with a critical, questioning attitude.

4. **Are comparisons realistic and true?** The reliability of comparisons depends on how closely the comparison corresponds or how similar it is to the situation to which it is being compared. For example, Martin Luther King, Jr., in his famous letter from the Birmingham jail, compared nonviolent protesters to a robbed man. To evaluate this comparison, you would need to consider how the two are similar and how they are different.

Relevancy and Sufficiency of Evidence

Once you have identified the evidence used to support an argument, the next step is to decide whether there is enough of the right kind of evidence to lead you to accept the writer's claim. This is always a matter of judgment; there are no easy rules to follow. You must determine whether the evidence provided directly supports the claim and whether sufficient evidence has been provided.

Suppose you are reading an article in your campus newspaper that states Freshman Composition should not be required of all students at your college. As evidence, the writer includes the following:

> Composition does not prepare us for the job market. Besides, the reading assignments have no relevancy to modern times.

This reason provides neither adequate nor sufficient evidence. The writer does nothing to substantiate his statements about the irrelevancy of the course to the job market or modern times. For the argument to be regarded seriously, the writer would need to provide facts, statistics, expert opinion, or other forms of documentation.

EXERCISE 6-7   **Analyzing Evidence**

Reread the argument "Cyberbullying: Off-Campus Regulation: Con," on page 162, paying particular attention to the type(s) of evidence used. Then answer the questions that follow.

1. What type(s) of evidence is/are used?
2. Is the evidence convincing?
3. Is there sufficient evidence?
4. What other types of evidence could have been used to strengthen the argument?

Definition of Terms

A clear and effective argument carefully defines key terms and uses them consistently. For example, an essay arguing for or against animal rights should state what is meant by the term, describe or define those rights, and use that definition through the entire argument.

The following two paragraphs are taken from two different argumentative essays on pornography. Notice how in the first paragraph the author carefully defines what he means by pornography before proceeding with his argument, whereas in the second the term is not clearly defined.

PARAGRAPH 1—CAREFUL DEFINITION

There is unquestionably more pornography available today than 15 years ago. However, is it legitimate to assume that more is worse? Pornography is speech, words, and pictures about sexuality. No one would consider an increase in the level of speech about religion or politics to be a completely negative development. What makes speech about sexuality different?

—Lynn, "Pornography's Many Forms: Not All Bad," *Los Angeles Times*

PARAGRAPH 2—VAGUE DEFINITION

If we are not talking about writing laws, defining pornography doesn't pose as serious a problem. We do have different tastes. Maybe some of mine come from my middle-class background (my mother wouldn't think so!). I don't like bodies presented without heads, particularly female bodies. The motive may sometimes be the protection of the individual, but the impression is decapitation, and I also happen to be someone who is attracted to people's faces. This is a matter of taste.

—Rule, "Pornography Is a Social Disease," *The Body Politic*

Cause and Effect Relationships

Arguments are often built around the assumption of a cause and effect relationship. For example, an argument supporting gun control legislation may claim that ready availability of guns contributes to an increased number of shootings. This argument implies that availability of guns causes increased use. If the writer provides no evidence that this cause and effect relationship exists, you should question the accuracy of the statement.

Implied or Stated Value System

An argument often implies or rests on a value system (a structure of what the writer feels is right, wrong, worthwhile, and important). However, everyone possesses a personal value system, and although our culture promotes many major points of agreement (murder is wrong, human life is worthwhile, and so forth), it also allows for disagreement. One person may think telling lies is always wrong; another person may say it depends on the circumstances. Some people have a value system based on religious beliefs; others may not share those beliefs.

In evaluating an argument, look for value judgments and then decide whether the judgments are consistent with and acceptable to your personal value system. Here are a few examples of value-judgment statements:

Financial aid for college should be available to everyone regardless of income.

Capital punishment violates human rights.

Recognizing and Refuting Opposing Viewpoints

Many arguments recognize opposing viewpoints. For example, a writer may argue against gun control, but he or she may recognize the opposing viewpoint that availability of guns allows shootings to occur.

Many arguments also attempt to refute opposing viewpoints (explain why they are wrong, flawed, or unacceptable). Basically, the author finds weaknesses in the opponent's argument. One way to do this is to question the accuracy, relevancy, or sufficiency of the opponent's evidence. Another way is to disagree with the opponent's reasons. The writer against gun control may disagree with the viewpoint that availability of guns causes shootings by stating "Guns don't kill people; people kill people."

When reading arguments that address opposing viewpoints, ask yourself the following questions:

- Does the author address opposing viewpoints clearly and fairly?
- Does the author refute the opposing viewpoint with logic and relevant evidence?

Unfair Emotional Appeals

Emotional appeals attempt to involve or excite readers by appealing to their emotions, thereby shaping the reader's attitude toward the subject. Several types of emotional appeals are described below.

1. **Emotionally charged or biased language.** By using words that create an emotional response, writers establish positive or negative feelings. For example, an advertisement for a new line of fragrances promises to "indulge," "refresh," "nourish," and "pamper" the user. An ad for an automobile uses phrases such as "limousine comfort," "European styling," and "animal sleekness" to interest and excite readers.

2. **False authority.** False authority involves using the opinion or action of a well-known or famous person. We have all seen athletes endorsing underwear or movie stars selling shampoo. This type of appeal works on the

notion that people admire celebrities and strive to be like them, respect their opinions, and are willing to accept their viewpoints.

3. **Association.** An emotional appeal also is made by associating a product, idea, or position with others that are already accepted or highly regarded. Patriotism is valued, so to call a product All-American in an advertisement is an appeal to the emotions. A car named a Cougar reminds you of a fast, sleek animal. A cigarette ad picturing a scenic waterfall or a speaker standing in front of an American flag are other examples.

4. **Appeal to "common folk."** Some people distrust those who are well educated, wealthy, highly artistic, or in other ways distinctly different from the average person. An emotional appeal to this group is made by selling a product or idea by indicating that it is originated from, held by, or bought by ordinary citizens. A commercial may advertise a product by showing its use in an average household. A politician may describe her background and education to suggest that she is like everyone else; a salesperson may dress in styles similar to his clients'.

5. *Ad hominem.* An argument that attacks the holder of an opposing viewpoint, rather than the viewpoint itself, is known as *ad hominem*, or an attack on the man. For example, the statement, "How could a woman who does not even hold a college degree criticize a judicial decision?" attacks the woman's level of education, not her viewpoint.

6. **"Join the crowd" appeal.** The appeal to do, believe, or buy what everyone else is doing, believing, or buying is known as crowd appeal or the bandwagon effect. Commercials that proclaim their product as the "#1 bestselling car in America" are appealing to this motive. Essays that cite opinion polls on a controversial issue in support of a position—"68 percent of Americans favor capital punishment"—are also using this appeal.

■ Errors in Logical Reasoning

Errors in reasoning, often called logical fallacies, are common in arguments. These errors invalidate the argument or render it flawed. Several common errors in logic are described next.

Circular Reasoning

Also known as begging the question, this error involves using part of the conclusion as evidence to support it. Here are two examples.

> Cruel medical experimentation on defenseless animals is inhumane.

> Female police officers should not be sent to crime scenes because apprehending criminals is a man's job.

In circular reasoning, because no evidence is given to support the claim, there is no reason to accept the conclusion.

Hasty Generalization

This fallacy means that the conclusion has been derived from insufficient evidence. Here is one example: you taste three tangerines and each is sour, so you conclude that all tangerines are sour. Here is another: by observing one performance of a musical group, you conclude the group is unfit to perform.

Non Sequitur ("It Does Not Follow")

The false establishment of cause and effect is known as a non sequitur. To say, for example, that "Because my doctor is young, I'm sure she'll be a good doctor" is a non sequitur because youth does not ensure good medical practices. Here is another example: "Arturio Alvarez is the best choice for state senator because he is an ordinary citizen." Being an ordinary citizen will not necessarily make someone an effective state senator.

False Cause

The false cause fallacy is the incorrect assumption that two events that follow each other in time are causally related. Suppose you opened an umbrella and then tripped on an uneven sidewalk. If you said you tripped because you opened the umbrella, you would be assuming false cause.

Either–Or Fallacy

This fallacy assumes that an issue is only two sided, or that there are only two choices or alternatives for a particular situation. In other words, there is no middle ground. Consider the issue of censorship of violence on television. An either–or fallacy is to assume that violence on TV must be either allowed or banned. This fallacy does not recognize other alternatives such as limiting access through viewing hours, restricting certain types of violence, and so forth.

EXERCISE 6-8   **Identifying Logical Fallacies**

Identify the logical fallacy in each of the following statements.

1. All African-American students in my biology class earned A grades, so African-Americans must excel in life sciences.
2. If you are not for nuclear arms control, then you're against protecting our future.
3. My sister cannot do mathematical computations or balance her checkbook because she has math anxiety.
4. A well-known mayor, noting a decline in the crime rate in the four largest cities in his state, quickly announced that his new "get-tough on criminals" publicity campaign was successful and took credit for the decline.
5. I always order a fruit pastry for dessert because I am allergic to chocolate.

EXERCISE 6-9   Analyzing a Pair of Arguments

Read the following pair of arguments that appeared in USA Today, *and complete the items that follow.*

ARGUMENT 1

Misstep on Video Violence

In the booming world of video games, there are more than a few dark corners: Murder and mayhem. Blood and gore. Explicit sex and abuse of women. In one of the best-selling series, Grand Theft Auto, car stealing is accompanied by drug use, shootouts that kill police and bystanders, and simulated sex with comely prostitutes who are beaten with baseball bats afterward.

Small wonder some parents are concerned over what game-crazed teens may be up to. And small wonder, too, that legislators in several states are playing to these concerns by trying to outlaw the sale of violent and sexually explicit games to minors. A bill banning the sale of such games to anyone younger than 18 is awaiting the governor's signature in Illinois. A similar proposal is moving in the Michigan Legislature. The issue has been raised this year in at least nine other states and the District of Columbia. But to what useful end?

This is the latest chapter in a very old story. When teenage entertainment offends adult sensibilities—think Elvis Presley's pulsating hips or the arrival on newsstands of Hugh Hefner's *Playboy*—the first response is to see the new phenomenon as a threat to social order. The second is to attempt to ban it. Parents—former teenagers all—seem to forget history's lesson: The bans never work. And they're probably not constitutional, anyway. Courts have ruled that today's sophisticated video games are protected as creative expression. If communities want to limit access, they must show overriding evidence that the games pose a public threat. That evidence does not exist.

Lawmakers and activist groups assert that the thrill of engaging in virtual criminal activity will spur teens to try the real thing. But the violent crime rate has gone down nearly 30% since the first bloody shoot-'em-up games debuted in the early 1990s. Youth crime rates have dropped even more. And a Federal Trade Commission survey found parents already involved in 83% of video-game purchases and rentals for minors.

Judges have repeatedly rejected as flawed the studies that advocates say show a link between fantasy violence and anti-social behavior. To the extent there is a threat, it is mainly to the individual, vulnerable teenager, and it can be addressed only by parents.

Unknown to many parents, they're getting some help. The game industry's rating system classifies games in six categories from "early childhood" to "adults only" and requires detailed content descriptions. Also, newer models of popular games include parental controls that can block their use for age-inappropriate games. Manufacturers have announced an expanded ratings-education program, and major retailers are tightening their restrictions on sales to minors.

There will always be a market for the dark, tasteless, even the outrageous, and parents ought to keep kids away from it. But even with the best intentions of legislators, the problem is beyond their reach. New laws are likely to give parents only the false impression that someone else is solving that problem for them.

—*USA Today,* June 6, 2005

ARGUMENT 2

Parents Need Our Help

When I was growing up, my parents used to worry if I was hanging out with the wrong kids in the neighborhood. Today, parents have even more to worry about: instead of playing basketball at the schoolyard, our children are spending their afternoons at the controls of a Sony PlayStation simulating acts of murder, dismemberment, decapitation and sexual seduction.

Games such as Grand Theft Auto and Halo 2 use the same techniques the U.S. military uses to train our soldiers to kill the enemy. Another game, JFK Reloaded, re-enacts the assassination of the late president. As a parent, this is the last thing I want my 8-year-old exposed to.

But the truth is that 92% of children between the ages of 2 and 17 are playing video games—and it's taking a toll on them.

A recent study at Iowa State University tied playing video games with an area of the brain directly linked to extreme behavioral disorders. Another study found that kids who play violent games have lower test scores. As one parent told me, we're "competing with video games for the minds and souls of our children." From what I can tell, the video games are winning.

That's why—as both a parent and a governor—I was delighted we passed legislation last week making Illinois the first state in the nation to prohibit the sale or rental of excessively violent or sexually explicit video games to children under 18.

We don't let our kids buy cigarettes. We don't let them buy alcohol. We don't let children purchase pornography. So why should we let them purchase video games that we know can cause them long-term harm?

Many retailers will argue that they don't sell these kinds of games to kids. But a study by the Federal Trade Commission found that 69% of teenage boys were able to purchase violent and sexually explicit games without permission from their parents. I don't believe we should ever put profits ahead of what's best for our children.

I know that some interest groups don't like the idea of limiting anything. But when it comes to our children and their well-being, how about a little common sense? Telling kids they can purchase violent and sexually explicit video games sends the wrong message and reinforces the wrong values.

Parents deserve a fighting chance. It's our responsibility to give it to them.

—*USA Today,* June 6, 2005

For each argument:

1. Identify the claim.
2. Outline the primary reasons used to support the claim.
3. What types of evidence are used?
4. Evaluate the adequacy and sufficiency of the evidence.
5. What emotional appeals are used?
6. Does the author recognize or refute counterarguments?

Compare the arguments:

1. Compare the types of evidence used.
2. Which argument did you find more convincing? Why?
3. What further information would be useful in assessing the issue?

Self-Test Summary

1. What are the three essential parts of an argument?	The three essential parts of an argument are • the issue—a problem or controversy about which people disagree. • the claim—the position the writer takes on the issue. • the support—the reasons and evidence that suggest the claim is reasonable and should be accepted.
2. What is a refutation?	A refutation is the part of an argument that considers opposing viewpoints and attempts to disprove or discredit them.
3. What is a claim of fact?	A claim of fact is one that can be verified through observation or research.
4. What is a claim of value?	A claim of value states that one thing or idea is better or more desirable than another.
5. What is a claim of policy?	A claim of policy suggests what should or ought to be done to solve a problem.
6. What are the three common types of support?	Three common types of support are reasons, evidence, and emotional appeals.
7. What is an inductive argument?	An inductive argument reaches a general conclusion from observed specifics.
8. What is a deductive argument?	A deductive argument begins with a general statement (major premise), moves toward a more specific statement (minor premise), then reaches a conclusion.
9. What are six types of emotional appeals writers use?	Types of emotional appeals include emotionally charged language, false authority, association, appeal to "common folk," *ad hominem*, and "join the crowd."
10. What are five common errors in logical reasoning?	Common errors in logical reasoning include circular reasoning, hasty generalization, non sequitur, false cause, and either–or fallacy.

Should Online Sites Ban Postings by Groups the Government Identifies as Terrorists?

Sen. Joseph I. Lieberman PRO

Leslie Harris and John Morris CON

Prereading Questions

1. Do you think online sites should ban postings by groups identified as terrorists?
2. Should the Internet be subject to more or less censorship?

Reading 1: Pro

Sen. Joseph I. Lieberman, I-Conn.

Chairman, Senate Committee on Homeland Security and Governmental Affairs. From the Committee Web site, May 19 and May 20, 2008, http://hsgac.senate.gov.

1   Islamist terrorist organizations rely extensively on the Internet to attract supporters and advance their cause. This Internet campaign is described in a bipartisan staff report by the Senate Committee on Homeland Security and Governmental Affairs. . . . The report explains how al-Qaeda manages an online media operation intended to enlist followers. Central to it is the branding of content with an icon to guarantee that the content was produced by al-Qaeda or allied organizations like al-Qaeda in Iraq. All of these groups have been designated Foreign Terrorist Organizations by the Department of State.

2   Searches on YouTube return dozens of videos branded with an icon or logo identifying the videos as the work of one of these Islamist terrorist organizations. A great majority document horrific attacks on American soldiers in Iraq and Afghanistan. Others provide weapons training, speeches by al-Qaeda leadership and general material intended to radicalize potential recruits.

3   In other words, Islamist terrorist organizations use YouTube to disseminate propaganda, enlist followers and provide weapons training—activities that are all essential to terrorist activity. The online content produced by al-Qaeda and other Islamist terrorist organizations can play a significant role in the process of radicalization, the end point of which is the planning and execution of a terrorist attack. YouTube also, unwittingly, permits Islamist

terrorist groups to maintain an active, pervasive and amplified voice, despite military set-backs or successful operations by the law-enforcement and intelligence communities.

4   Protecting our citizens from terrorist attacks is a top priority for our government. The private sector can help us do that. By taking action to curtail the use of YouTube to disseminate the goals and methods of those who wish to kill innocent civilians, Google will make a singularly important contribution to this effort.

5   Google apparently has taken 80 videos off YouTube that violated the company's own guidelines against gratuitous violence. That is a start, but it is not enough. Videos produced by al-Qaeda and al-Qaeda affiliates showing attacks on American troops remain on YouTube's Web site and violate YouTube's own community guidelines. Those should be taken down immediately. Furthermore, Google continues to allow the posting of videos by organizations the State Department has designated as foreign terrorist organizations. No matter what their content, videos produced by terrorist organizations like al-Qaeda, that are committed to attacking America and killing Americans, should not be tolerated. Google must reconsider its policy.

Reading 2: Con

Leslie Harris, John Morris

President and CEO, Center for Democracy & Technology. General Counsel, Center for Democracy & Technology. From *The Huffington Post*, May 28, 2008, http://www.huffingtonpost.com

1   Sen. Joe Lieberman took a step backward in America's "war on terrorism," by demanding that YouTube censor hundreds of videos allegedly posted by Islamic terrorist groups. And when the Google-owned site responded by promptly removing a large number of videos, which violated its guidelines against hate speech and violence, he insisted that action was "not enough."

2   What would be "enough" in the senator's estimation? The removal of all tainted videos, even those that were plainly constitutionally protected advocacy, albeit abhorrent, and a plan "to prevent the content from reappearing"?

3   Civil liberties continue to be a casualty in our efforts against terrorism. So far, broad Internet censorship has not taken root, but censorship is the path we would take if Google acceded to Lieberman's demand.

4   The system we have devised, in which online services establish rigorous terms of service and enforce them, is a wise one. Users help police the system, and sites that are notified of potentially offensive content generally take down content that violates their rules. In the spirit of self-policing, Lieberman's request to review specific videos is fair, but demanding ongoing review of all videos, and removal of those that don't meet with self-selected criteria, crosses the line. . . .

5   For the last year, Congress has made the Internet a focus of anti-terrorism activities. The Violent Radicalization and Homegrown Terrorism Prevention Act, which has already passed the House, specifically finds that the Internet "aided in facilitating violent radicalization, ideologically based violence and the homegrown terrorism process in the United States by providing access to broad and constant streams of terrorist-related propaganda."

6   Congress can take away two diametrically opposed lessons from this finding. The first is that the Internet is an essential communications tool that America should learn to better use to counter terrorism and tout our values. The other is to fight terrorism by censoring the Internet and destroying our first freedom.

7   Ironically, while Lieberman's letter was being delivered to Google a Senate panel on human rights was hearing testimony on threats to Internet freedom from repressive regimes. Some, like China, have built a network of gatekeepers to block content that challenges the government's official messages. Congress cannot [advocate] Internet freedom with one voice and [call] for censorship with another.

Writing About the Reading

CHECKING YOUR VOCABULARY

1. For each of the words listed below, use context; prefixes, roots, and suffixes (see Chapter 3); and/or a dictionary to write a brief definition or synonym of the word as it is used in the reading.

Reading 1

a. bipartisan (para. 1) _____

b. radicalize (para. 2) _____

c. disseminate (para. 3) _____

d. unwittingly (para. 3) _____

e. pervasive (para. 3) _____

f. curtail (para. 4) _____

g. gratuitous (para. 5) _____

Reading 2

h. allegedly (para. 1) _____

i. abhorrent (para. 2) _____

j. acceded (para. 3) _____

k. rigorous (para. 4) _____

l. facilitating (para. 5) _____

m. tout (para. 6) _____

n. repressive (para. 7) _____

2. Highlight new, specialized terms introduced in the reading (see Chapter 3).

3. Draw a word map of one of the words in the reading.

CHECKING YOUR COMPREHENSION

Reading 1

1. According to the reading, for what two purposes do Islamist terrorist organizations rely on the Internet?
2. Describe the content of the YouTube videos identified as the work of Islamist terrorist organizations.
3. What activities are described as essential to terrorist activity?
4. According to Sen. Lieberman, what is the "end point" of the process of radicalization?
5. What does Sen. Lieberman want Google to do?

Reading 2

1. Why did YouTube remove videos allegedly posted by Islamist terrorist groups?
2. What do the authors refer to as a "casualty" of antiterrorism efforts?
3. How does the current system work to control online content?
4. According to the authors, what two possible lessons can Congress take away from the findings of the Violent Radicalization and Homegrown Terrorism Prevention Act?

THINKING CRITICALLY ABOUT READINGS 1 AND 2

1. Compare the authors' credentials. How qualified are they to write about the issue?
2. Highlight words in each reading that have strong positive or negative connotations.
3. Compare the tones of the two readings.
4. Which argument attempts to refute the other? How successful is it?
5. Which reading is more persuasive? Explain your answer.
6. In what ways do the authors support their arguments? Evaluate the types of evidence used in each reading.

LEARNING/STUDY STRATEGY

Assume you will be participating in a debate on the topic of censoring Internet content the government considers to be the work of terrorist groups. Create a "pro/con" study sheet that summarizes each side of the argument.

MyReadingLab

To practice your critical reading skills, go to http://www.myreadinglab .com. Click on "Study Plan," then on "Reading Skills," and then on "Critical Reading."

7 Patterns of Academic Thought

Thinking Visually About Thought Patterns

What do all the snowflakes shown here have in common? Each has a unique and intricate pattern. Upon closer inspection, many common objects, other than snowflakes, that we take for granted have underlying patterns that help us better understand and classify them. Think of a leaf, or the wings of a butterfly, for example. The same way we can look closely and see patterns in nature, in people's behavior, and in weather, we can see specific patterns in the way writers choose to organize information.

LEARNING OBJECTIVES

- To use thought patterns to focus your reading

- To understand the definition pattern

- To use classification to break a topic into categories

- To understand chronology, process, order of importance, and spatial arrangement

- To use cause and effect to understand relationships

- To recognize how comparison and contrast emphasize similarities and differences

- To understand the listing pattern

- To recognize the statement and clarification, summary, generalization and example, and addition patterns

ACTIVE READING: The Academic Link

You are probably taking courses in several different disciplines. In one day, you may read a poem, solve math problems, and study early developments in psychology. These tasks may seem widely different, but they have more in common than you may think. Few students realize that a biologist and a psychologist, for example, approach their subject matter in similar ways. Both carefully define terms, examine causes and effects, study similarities and differences, describe sequences of events, classify information, solve problems, and enumerate characteristics. All of these are patterns of thought used in all disciplines, and the more familiar you become with these patterns, the easier your reading assignments will be.

ACTIVE READING: The Career Link

Many people think of their jobs as a place where are paid to *do* something. But the truth is that most careers require you to *think*, not just do. Training yourself to see thought patterns in information will help you better memorize the information you need to do your job well, and it is good practice for management, where you will have to train others how to do the job.

■ Patterns: A Focus for Reading

Let's begin by trying a few learning experiments.

Experiment 1. Supply the missing numbers in the following numeric sequence:

1, 5, 7, 8, 12, 14, 15, _____, _____, _____

Experiment 2. Study each of the following drawings briefly, and then continue reading.

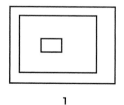

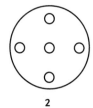

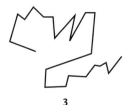

1   2   3   4   5

Next, close the book and quickly sketch each of the drawings you studied.

Now let's analyze your performance. In the first experiment, the last three numbers are 19, 21, and 22. If you were correct, you realized the numbers increased successively by 4, by 2, and by 1, and then the pattern repeated. Now supply the next three numbers. Did you get 26, 28, and 29? It is an easy task now that you know the pattern. Reconstructing the entire sequence from memory also is a simple task now that you know the pattern.

For the second experiment, you probably sketched some or all of drawings 1, 2, 4, and 5 correctly. But did you get drawing 3 correct? Probably not. Why? Drawing 3 is irregular and has no pattern.

From these experiments, you can see that patterns make certain tasks easier to complete and that they facilitate your memory and recall. Patterns exist for ideas as well; we will refer to them as **thought patterns.**

You will find textbook chapters easier to read if you can identify the thought pattern(s) by which they are organized. The same patterns also are used by your professors as they lecture. Lectures will be easier to follow and your notes will be better organized if you can identify these patterns.

Commonly used academic thought patterns include:

- **definition**
- **classification**
- **order or sequence**
- **cause and effect**
- **comparison and contrast**
- **listing/enumeration**

These patterns can work for you in several ways.

1. **Patterns provide a focus for reading by enabling you to anticipate the author's thought development.** For example, from a heading or topic sentence alone, you often can predict the thought pattern that the section or paragraph will follow. When you encounter "Types of Government Spending," you might expect to read about how government spending is divided or classified.

2. **Patterns help you remember and recall what you read.** Information that is grouped, chunked, or organized is easier to store than single, unrelated bits of information. Also, the manner in which information is stored in memory influences the ease with which it is retrieved. Thought patterns help you organize information, and they function as retrieval clues for subsequent recall.

3. **Patterns are useful in your own writing;** they help you organize and express your ideas in a more coherent, comprehensible form. As you write essay exam answers, class assignments, or term papers, thought patterns will provide a base or structure around which you can effectively develop ideas.

■ The Definition Pattern

Each academic discipline has its own specialized vocabulary (see Chapter 3). One of the primary purposes of introductory textbooks is to introduce students to this new language. Consequently, definition is a commonly used pattern throughout most introductory-level texts.

Suppose you were asked to define the word *comedian* for someone unfamiliar with the term. First, you would probably say that a comedian is a person who entertains. Then you might distinguish a comedian from other types of entertainers by saying that a comedian is an entertainer who tells jokes and makes others laugh. Finally, you might mention, by way of example, the names of several well-known comedians who have appeared on television. Although you may have presented it informally, your definition would have followed the standard, classic pattern. The first part of your definition tells what general class or group the term belongs to (entertainers). The second part tells what distinguishes the term from other items in the same class or category. The third part includes further explanation, characteristics, examples, or applications.

Here are two additional examples:

TERM	GENERAL CLASS	DISTINGUISHING CHARACTERISTICS
Stress	Physiological reaction	A response to a perceived threat
Mutant	Organism	Carries a gene that has undergone a change

See how the term *genetics* is defined in the following paragraph.

Term ——————— ⎯ **Genetics is the scientific study of heredity,** the transmission of characteristics
General Class ⎯⎯⎯ from parents to offspring. Genetics explains why offspring resemble their parents
and also why they are not identical to them. Genetics is a subject that has considerable economic, medical, and social significance and is partly the basis for the
Distinguishing modern theory of evolution. Because of its importance, genetics has been a topic of
Characteristics central interest in the study of life for centuries. Modern concepts in genetics are
fundamentally different, however, from earlier ones.

—Mix et al., *Biology: The Network of Life,* p. 262

Writers often provide clues that signal the thought pattern being used. These signals may occur within single sentences or as transitions or connections between sentences. Examples of transitional words or phrases used for the definition pattern are shown below. (Transitional words that occur in phrases are italicized here to help you spot them.)

TRANSITIONS FOR DEFINITION

genetics *is* . . .   aggression *can be defined as* . . .

bureaucracy *means* . . .   deficit is *another term* that . . .

patronage *refers to* . . .   balance of power *also means* . . .

EXERCISE 7–1   ## Analyzing Definition: Paragraphs

Read the following paragraphs and answer the questions that follow.

A.   The French satirist and social reformer Voltaire (1694–1778) once defined the family as a "group of people who cannot stand the sight of each other but are forced to live under the same roof." The American poet Robert Frost (1875–1963) in his narrative poem *Death of the Hired Man* has one character observe, "Home is the place where, when you have to go there, They have to take you in." Whether home and family prove burdensome depends upon one's maturity level, emotional stability, and willingness to work on the difficulties which arise from close relationships. Most would agree, however, that there are few households which glide serenely along on a perpetually even keel.

—Janaro and Altshuler, The Art of Being Human, pp. 334–35

1. What is the definition of family as used in this paragraph?
2. How is home defined?
3. What transitional word(s) is/are used with family?
4. What transitional word(s) is/are used with home?
5. What general class do both home and family belong to according to this paragraph?

B.   The integumentary system is the external covering of the body, or the skin. It waterproofs the body and cushions and protects the deeper tissues from injury. It also excretes salts and urea in perspiration and helps regulate body temperature. Temperature, pressure, and pain receptors located in the skin alert us to what is happening at the body surface.

—Mareib, Essentials of Human Anatomy and Physiology, p. 3

1. What is the definition of the integumentary system?
2. What transitional word is used in this paragraph?
3. List three things the integumentary system does.
4. How does the skin alert us to what is happening at the body surface?
5. What does the integumentary system excrete?

C.   One of the emerging specialties in psychology is concerned with brain functioning. Neuropsychologists are trained to diagnose disorders of the brain. Using various tests, they try to identify specific brain areas that may be malfunctioning. They often conduct research to identify early symptoms that predict the development of disorders such as Huntington's disease. They also devise rehabilitation programs to help patients regain as much of their abilities as possible after suffering brain damage, strokes, or traumatic brain injury.

—Davis and Palladino, Psychology, p. 40

1. What general class do neuropsychologists belong to?
2. What is a distinguishing characteristic of neuropsychologists?
3. How do neuropsychologists identify specific brain areas that may be malfunctioning?
4. What kind of research do neuropsychologists often perform?
5. Why do neuropsychologists devise rehabilitation programs?

EXERCISE 7-2   **Analyzing Definition: Textbook Excerpt**

Read the following passage about polarization and answer the questions that follow.

Another way in which language can obscure differences is in its preponderance of extreme terms and its relative lack of middle terms, a system that often leads to polarization. **Polarization** is the tendency to look at the world in terms of opposites and to describe it in extremes—good or bad, positive or negative, healthy or sick, intelligent or stupid. It's often referred to as the fallacy of "either-or" or "black or white." Most people exist somewhere between the extremes. Yet there's a strong tendency to view only the extremes and to categorize people, objects, and events in terms of these polar opposites.

Problems are created when opposites are used in inappropriate situations. For example, "The politician is either for us or against us." The politician may be for us in some things and against us in other things, or may be neutral.

In correcting this tendency to polarize, be aware of implying (and believing) that two extreme classes include all possible classes—that an individual must be one or the other, with no alternatives ("Are you pro-choice or pro-life?"). Most people, most events, most qualities exist between polar extremes. When others imply that there are only two sides or alternatives, look for the middle ground.

—DeVito, *Human Communication*, p. 124

1. What is the purpose of the passage?
2. Highlight the topic sentence of each paragraph. If there is no stated main idea, write a sentence expressing the main idea.
3. Highlight all transitional words.
4. What is the definition of polarization?
5. Why is polarization often a problem?
6. What are some examples of polarized opposites?
7. What do polarized opposites exclude?
8. What is the solution to the problem of polarization?

EXERCISE 7–3

LEARNING
COLLABORATIVELY

Writing a Definition

Using the definition pattern described above, work with a classmate to write a two-part definition for each of the following terms.

1. robot
2. age discrimination
3. fiction
4. adolescence
5. social network

■ The Classification Pattern

If you were asked to describe types of computers, you might mention desktop, laptop, and Netbook computers. By dividing a broad topic into its major categories, you are using a pattern known as **classification**.

This pattern is widely used in many academic subjects. For example, a psychology text might explain human needs by classifying them into two categories: primary and secondary. In a chemistry textbook, various compounds may be grouped and discussed according to common characteristics, such as the presence of hydrogen or oxygen. The classification pattern divides a topic into parts on the basis of common or shared characteristics.

Here are a few examples of topics and the classifications or categories into which each might be divided:

movies: comedy, horror, mystery

motives: achievement, power, affiliation, competency

plant: leaves, stem, roots

Note how the following paragraph classifies the various types of cancers:

Term

Types

The name of the cancer is derived from the type of tissue in which it develops. Carcinoma (carc = cancer; omo = tumor) refers to a malignant tumor consisting of epithelial cells. A tumor that develops from a gland is called an adenosarcoma (adeno = gland). Sarcoma is a general term for any cancer arising from connective tissue. Osteogenic sarcomas (osteo = bone; genic = origin), the most frequent type of childhood cancer, destroy normal bone tissue and eventually spread to other areas of the body. Myelomas (myelos = marrow) are malignant tumors, occurring in middle-aged and older people, that interfere with the blood-cell-producing function of bone marrow and cause anemia. Chondrosarcomas (chondro = cartilage) are cancerous growths of cartilage.

—Tortora, *Introduction to the Human Body*, p. 56

Tip for Psychology and Science Majors

Many of the social and physical sciences are concerned with classification and categorization. For example, clinical psychologists need to be very familiar with the entire classification of mental disorders, while introductory biology students are required to learn the different types of life, sometimes known as the "march through the phyla."

Examples of transitional words and phrases that indicate the classification pattern follow.

TRANSITIONS FOR CLASSIFICATION

there are *several kinds of* chemical bonding . . .

there are *numerous types of* . . .

reproduction can be *classified as* . . .

the human skeleton is *composed of* . . .

muscles *comprise* . . .

one type of communication . . .

another type of communication . . .

finally, there is . . .

EXERCISE 7–4   Analyzing Classification: Paragraphs

Read the following paragraphs and answer the questions that follow.

A.   The reptiles made one of the most spectacular adaptive radiations in all of Earth history. One group, the pterosaurs, took to the air. These "dragons of the sky" possessed huge membranous wings that allowed them rudimentary flight. Another group of reptiles, exemplified by the fossil *Archaeopteryx,* led to more successful flyers: the birds. Whereas some reptiles took to the skies, others returned to the sea, including fish-eating plesiosaurs and ichthyosaurs. These reptiles became proficient swimmers, but retained their reptilian teeth and breathed by means of lungs.

—Tarbuck and Lutgens, *Earth Science*, p. 309

1. List the classifications of reptiles included in this paragraph.
2. Highlight the transitional words in this paragraph that signal the classification pattern.
3. Which classification does *Archaeopteryx* belong to?
4. Which classification of reptiles could swim proficiently?
5. What is another name for pterosaurs?

B.   From the hundreds of billions of galaxies, several basic types have been identified: spiral, elliptical, and irregular. The Milky Way and the Great Galaxy in Andromeda are examples of fairly large spiral galaxies. Typically, spiral galaxies are disk-shaped with a somewhat greater concentration of stars near their centers, but there are numerous variations. Viewed broadside, arms are often seen extending from the central nucleus and sweeping gracefully away. One type of spiral galaxy, however, has the stars arranged in the shape of a bar, which rotates as a rigid system. This requires that the outer stars move faster than the inner ones, a fact not easy for astronomers to reconcile with the laws of motion. Attached to each end of these bars are curved spiral arms. These have become known as barred spiral galaxies. The most abundant group, making up 60 percent of the total is the elliptical galaxies. These are generally smaller than spiral galaxies. Some are so much smaller, in fact, that the term dwarf has been applied. Because these dwarf galaxies are not visible at great distances, a survey of the sky reveals more of the conspicuous large spiral galaxies. As their name implies, elliptical galaxies have an ellipsoidal shape that ranges to nearly spherical, and they lack spiral arms. Only 10 percent of the known galaxies lack symmetry and are classified as irregular galaxies. The best-known irregular galaxies, the Large and Small Magellanic Clouds in the Southern Hemisphere, are easily visible with the unaided eye.

—Tarbuck and Lutgens, *Earth Science*, pp. 620–21

1. What are the three primary classifications of galaxies?
2. What determines how a galaxy is classified?
3. Highlight the transitional words that signal the classification pattern.
4. How can the types of spiral galaxies be classified?
5. What is another name for elliptical galaxies?

EXERCISE 7–5   Analyzing Classification: Textbook Excerpts

Read the following passages and answer the questions that follow.

PASSAGE A
Types of Bones

The bones of the body may be classified into four principal types on the basis of shape: long, short, flat, and irregular. **Long bones** have greater length than width and consist of a shaft and extremities (ends). They are slightly curved for strength.

Long bones consist mostly of compact bone (dense bone with few spaces) but also contain considerable amounts of spongy bone (bone with large spaces). The details of compact and spongy bone are discussed shortly. Long bones include bones of the thighs, legs, toes, arms, forearms, and fingers.

Short bones are somewhat cube-shaped and nearly equal in length and width. They are spongy except at the surface where there is a thin layer of compact bone. Short bones include the wrist and ankle bones.

Flat bones are generally thin and composed of two more or less parallel plates of compact bone enclosing a layer of spongy bone. Flat bones afford considerable protection and provide extensive areas for muscle attachment. Flat bones include the cranial bones, the sternum (breastbone), ribs, and the scapulas (shoulder blades).

Irregular bones have complex shapes and cannot be grouped into any of the three categories just described. They also vary in the amount of spongy and compact bone present. Such bones include the vertebrae (backbones) and certain facial bones.

—Tortora, *Introduction to the Human Body*, p. 100

1. What is the purpose of this passage?
2. Highlight the topic sentence of each paragraph. If there is no stated main idea, write a sentence expressing the main idea.
3. Highlight transitional words that signal the classification pattern.
4. What are the four principal types of bones?
5. What is the basis of classification (how are they divided)?
6. How can long bones be classified?
7. Why are irregular bones a separate classification?

PASSAGE B
Types of Fossils

Fossils are of many types. The remains of relatively recent organisms may not have been altered at all. Such objects as teeth, bones, and shells are common examples. Far less common are entire animals, flesh included, that have been preserved because of rather unusual circumstances. Remains of prehistoric elephants called mammoths that were frozen in the Arctic tundra of Siberia and Alaska are examples, as are the mummified remains of sloths preserved in a dry cave in Nevada.

Given enough time, the remains of an organism are likely to be modified. Often fossils become *petrified* (literally, "turned into stone"), meaning that the small internal cavities and pores of the original structure are filled with precipitated mineral matter. In other instances *replacement* may occur. Here the cell walls and other solid material are removed and replaced with mineral matter. Sometimes the microscopic details of the replaced structure are faithfully retained.

Molds and casts constitute another common class of fossils. When a shell or other structure is buried in sediment and then dissolved by underground water, a *mold* is created. The mold faithfully reflects only the shape and surface marking of the organism; it does not reveal any information concerning its internal structure. If these hollow spaces are subsequently filled with mineral matter, *casts* are created.

A type of fossilization called *carbonization* is particularly effective in preserving leaves and delicate animal forms. It occurs when fine sediment encases the remains of an organism. As time passes, pressure squeezes out the liquid and gaseous components and leaves behind a thin residue of carbon. Black shales deposited as organic-rich mud in oxygen-poor environments often contain abundant carbonized remains. If the film of carbon is lost from a fossil preserved in fine-grained sediment, a replica of the surface, called an *impression,* may still show considerable detail.

—Tarbuck and Lutgens, *Earth Science,* pp. 278–79

1. What is the purpose of the passage?
2. Highlight the topic sentence of each paragraph. If there is no stated main idea, write a sentence expressing the main idea.
3. Highlight all transitional words.
4. What are the three main classifications of fossils?
5. What are the two types of modified fossils?
6. How are molds and casts distinguished?
7. Which type of fossilization is most effective for leaves?

EXERCISE 7-6   **Writing Using Classification**

Divide each of the topics listed below into several groups or categories.

1. foods _____

2. cars _____

3. arts _____

4. laws _____

5. pollutants _____

■ The Order or Sequence Pattern

If you were asked to summarize what you did today, you probably would mention key events in the order in which they occurred. In describing how to write a particular computer program, you would detail the process step by step. If asked to list what you feel are your accomplishments so far this week, you might present them in order of importance, listing your most important accomplishment first. In each case, you are presenting information in a particular sequence or order. Each of these examples illustrates a form of the thought pattern known as **order,** or **sequence.** Let us look at several types of order.

Chronology

Chronological order refers to the sequence in which events occur in time. This pattern is essential in the academic disciplines concerned with the interpretation of events in the past. History, government, and anthropology are prime examples. In various forms of literature, chronological order is evident; novels, short stories, and narrative essays rely on chronological order.

The following paragraph uses chronology to describe how full-scale intervention in Vietnam began.

topic sentence —————— The pretext for full-scale intervention in Vietnam came in late July 1964. On July 30,

event 1 —————— South Vietnamese PT (patrol torpedo) boats attacked bases in the Gulf of Tonkin

event 2 — inside North Vietnamese waters. Simultaneously, the *Maddox, an American destroyer, steamed into the area* to disrupt North Vietnamese communication facilities. On August 2, possibly seeing the two separate missions as a combined

event 3 — maneuver against them, the North Vietnamese sent out several PT boats to attack the destroyer. The *Maddox* fired, sinking one of the attackers, then radioed the

event 4 —————— news to Washington. Johnson ordered another ship into the bay. On August 3 both destroyers reported another attack, although somewhat later, the commander of

event 5 — the *Maddox* radioed that he was not sure. Nonetheless, the president ordered American planes to retaliate by bombing inside North Vietnam.

—Wilson et al., *The Pursuit of Liberty: A History of the American People,* pp. 492–93

Tip for Humanities/ Liberal Arts Majors

Many humanities courses, such as world history and art history, take a chronological approach, separating history into periods such as "ancient," "medieval," "Renaissance," "modern," and so on. While newer textbooks in these fields have made an effort to become more story oriented, with less of an emphasis on memorizing dates, keeping track of chronology is still a key component to success in these majors.

Examples of transitional words and phrases that indicate chronological order and process include the following.

TRANSITIONS FOR CHRONOLOGICAL ORDER AND PROCESS

in ancient times . . .   the *first* primate species . . .

at the start of the battle . . .   *later* efforts . . .

on September 12 . . .

Other transitional words are:

then, before, during, by the time, while, afterward, as, after, thereafter, meanwhile, at that point

---

Process

In disciplines that focus on steps or stages by which actions are accomplished, writers often employ the **process** pattern. These subjects include mathematics, natural and life sciences, computer science, and engineering.

Note how this pattern is used in a paragraph explaining what occurs in the brain during sleep.

topic sentence — Let us track your brain waves through the night. As you prepare to go to bed, an

background information — EEG records that your brain waves are moving along at a rate of about 14 cycles per second (cps). Once you are comfortably in bed, you begin to relax and your brain waves slow down to a rate of about 8 to 12 cps. When you fall asleep, you enter

stage 1 — your *sleep cycle,* each of whose stages shows a distinct EEG pattern. In Stage 1 sleep, the EEG shows brain waves of about 3 to 7 cps. During Stage 2, the EEG is charac-

stage 2 — terized by *sleep spindles,* minute bursts of electrical activity of 12 to 16 cps. In the

stages 3 & 4 — next two stages (3 and 4) of sleep, you enter into a very deep state of relaxed sleep. Your brain waves slow to about 1 to 2 cps, and your breathing and heart rate

stage 5 ⎡ decrease. In a <u>final stage</u>, the electrical activity of your brain increases; your EEG looks very similar to those recorded during stages 1 and 2. It is during this stage that you will experience REM sleep, and you will begin to dream.

—Zimbardo and Gerrig, *Psychology and Life*, p. 115

Order of Importance

This pattern of ideas sometimes expresses order of priority or preference. Ideas are arranged in one of two ways: from most to least important, or from least to most important. In the following paragraph, the causes of the downward trend in the standard of living are arranged in order of importance.

topic sentence⎯⎯⎯ The United States' downward trend in standard of living has many different causes, of which only a few major ones can be identified here. Most important is

most important⎯⎯ probably deindustrialization, the massive loss of manufacturing jobs as many U.S. Corporations move their production to poor, labor-cheap countries. But deindustrialization hurts mostly low-skilled manufacturing workers. Most of the well-educated, high-skilled employees in service industries are left unscathed. Deindustrialization alone is therefore not enough to explain the economic decline. Another major factor

less important⎯⎯ is the great increase in consumption and decrease in savings. Like their government, people spend more than they earn and become deeply in debt. Those who do practice thrift still have an average rate of savings significantly lower than in countries with fast-growing economies. The habits of high consumption and low saving may have resulted from the great affluence after the Second World War up until the early 1970s (Harrison, 1992).

—Thio, *Sociology*, p. 255

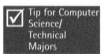

Tip for Computer Science/ Technical Majors

Writing computer programs, or assembling or fixing machinery, requires doing things in the right order. (This is true for many other professions as well, including the medical field.) Many textbooks in the technical fields use the process pattern to provide step-by-step directions for doing something correctly. It is wise to read directions from start to finish *before* beginning a job and follow these directions in the sequence provided.

Order of importance is used in almost every field of study.

> **TRANSITIONS FOR ORDER OF IMPORTANCE**
>
> is *less* essential than . . .
>
> *more* revealing is . . .
>
> of *primary* interest is . . .
>
> Other transitional words are:
>
> *first, next, last, most important, primarily, secondarily*

Spatial Order

Information organized according to its physical location, or position or order in space, exhibits a pattern known as **spatial order.** Spatial order is used in academic disciplines in which physical descriptions are important. These include numerous technical fields, engineering, and the biological sciences.

You can see how the following description of a particular type of blood circulation relies on spatial relationships.

topic sentence⎯⎯⎯ Pulmonary circulation conducts blood between the heart and the lungs. Oxygen-poor, CO_2-laden blood returns through two large veins (venae cavae) from tissues within the body, enters the right atrium, and is then moved into the right ventricle of the heart. From there, it is pumped into the pulmonary artery, which divides into two branches, each leading to one of the lungs. In the lung, the arteries undergo extensive branching, giving rise to vast networks of capillaries where gas exchange takes place, with blood becoming oxygenated while CO_2 is discharged. Oxygen-rich blood then returns to the heart via the pulmonary veins.

—Mix et al., *Biology: The Network of Life*, pp. 663–64

Diagramming is of the utmost importance in working with this pattern; often, a diagram accompanies text material. For example, a diagram makes the functions of the various parts of the human brain easier to understand. Lecturers often refer to a visual aid or chalkboard drawing when providing spatial descriptions.

TRANSITIONS FOR SPATIAL ORDER

the *left side* of the brain . . .   the *outer* covering . . .

the *lower* portion . . .   *beneath* the surface . . .

Other transitional words are:

next to, beside, to the left, in the center, externally

EXERCISE 7-7

Analyzing Order and Sequence: Paragraphs

Read the following paragraphs and answer the questions that follow.

A. *The following paragraph uses the spatial pattern.*

Skeletal muscle tissue is named for its location—attached to bones. Skeletal muscle tissue is also *voluntary* because it can be made to contract by conscious control. A single skeletal muscle fiber (cell) is cylindrical and appears *striated* (striped) under a microscope; when organized in a tissue, the fibers are parallel to each other. Each muscle fiber has a plasma membrane, the **sarcolemma**, surrounding the cytoplasm, or **sarcoplasm**. Skeletal muscle fibers are multinucleate (more than one nucleus), and the nuclei are near the sarcolemma.

—Tortora, *Introduction to the Human Body*, p. 77

1. Briefly describe skeletal muscle tissue.
2. Highlight the transitional words used to indicate the spatial pattern.
3. How are skeletal muscle fibers or cells arranged in a tissue?
4. Where can the sarcolemma (or plasma membrane) be found in muscle fibers?
5. Where are the nuclei in skeletal muscle fibers located?

B. *The following paragraph uses the chronology pattern.*

Only two presidents have been impeached. The House impeached Andrew Johnson, Lincoln's successor, in 1868 on charges stemming from his disagreement with radical Republicans. He narrowly escaped conviction. Richard Nixon came as close to impeachment as anyone since. On July 31, 1974, the house Judiciary

Committee voted to recommend his impeachment to the full House as a result of the **Watergate** scandal. Nixon escaped a certain vote for impeachment by resigning. In 1998, the House voted two articles of impeachment against President Clinton on party-line votes. The public clearly opposed the idea, however, and the Senate voted to acquit the president on both counts in 1999.

—Edwards, *Government in America*, p. 416

1. How many events are described in this paragraph?
2. Highlight the transitional words that are used to indicate the chronology pattern.
3. Which event occurred most recently?
4. When was Andrew Johnson impeached?
5. Whose impeachment episode occurred in 1974?

C. *The following paragraph uses the process pattern.*

BMI [body mass index] is an index of the relationship of height and weight. It is one of the most accurate indicators of a person's health risk due to excessive weight, rather than "fatness" per se. Although many people recoil in fright when they see they have to convert pounds to kilograms and inches to meters to calculate BMI, it really is not as difficult as it may seem. To get your kilogram weight, just divide your weight in pounds (without shoes or clothing) by 2.2. To convert your height to meters squared, divide your height in inches (without shoes) by 39.4, then square this result. Sounds pretty easy and it actually is. Once you have these basic values, calculating your BMI involves dividing your weight in kilograms by your height in meters squared.

$$BMI = \frac{\text{Weight (in lbs)} \div 2.2 \text{ (to determine weight in kg)}}{(\text{Height [in inches]} \div 39.4)^2 \text{ (to determine height in meters squared)}}$$

Healthy weights have been defined as those associated with BMIs of 19 to 25, the range of the lowest statistical health risk. A BMI greater than 25 indicates overweight and potentially significant health risks. The desirable range for females is between 21 and 23; for males, it is between 22 and 24. A body mass index of over 30 is considered obese. Many experts believe this number is too high, particularly for younger adults.

—Donatelle, *Access to Health*, p. 264

1. What process is being described in this paragraph?
2. Highlight the transitional words that are used to signal the process pattern.
3. What is the first step in the process?
4. Is a BMI of 23 considered healthy?
5. How do you convert height to meters squared?

D. *The following paragraph uses the spatial order pattern.*

The nucleus is bound by a double membrane barrier called the **nuclear membrane** or **nuclear envelope**. Between the two membranes is a fluid-filled "moat," or space. At various points, the two layers of the nuclear membrane approach each other and fuse, and nuclear pores penetrate through the fused regions. Like other cellular membranes, the nuclear membrane is selectively permeable, but passage of substances through it is much freer than elsewhere because of its relatively large pores. The nuclear membrane encloses a jellylike fluid called **nucleoplasm** in which the nucleoli and chromatin are suspended.

—Mareib, *Essentials of Human Anatomy and Physiology*, p. 55

1. What is being described in this paragraph?
2. Highlight the transitional words that are used to signal the spatial order pattern.
3. What is between the two outer membranes of a nucleus?
4. What is inside the nucleoplasm?
5. If you read this description in a textbook, what would you expect to accompany it?

E. *The following paragraph uses the order of importance pattern.*

Media resources are being reassembled in a new pattern, with three main parts. The first is the traditional mass media that will continue to be for a long time the most important element in the pattern in terms of their reach and influence. The second consists of the advanced electronic mass media, operating primarily within the new information utility, and competing increasingly with older media services. Finally, there are newer forms of personal electronic media, formed by clusters of like-minded people to fulfill their own professional or individual information needs. Internet chat rooms and personalized Web pages are fast-expanding examples of this development. Each of these parts of the evolving mass-communications pattern deserves separate scrutiny.

–Dizard , *Old Media, New Media*, p. 179

1. What does this paragraph describe?
2. Highlight the transitional words that are used to signal the pattern.
3. Why is traditional mass media the most important type of resource?
4. Which type of media resource competes the most with the traditional mass media?
5. What are some examples of personal electronic media?

EXERCISE 7-8   Analyzing Order and Sequence: Textbook Excerpts

Read the following passages and answer the questions that follow.

PASSAGE A

The shape of a state may affect its ability to consolidate its territory and control circulation across its borders. A circle would be the most efficient shape on an isotropic plain because a circular state would have the shortest possible border in relation to its territory, and that shape would allow all places to be reached from the center with the least travel. States with shapes closest to this model are sometimes called *compact states*. Bulgaria, Poland, and Zimbabwe are examples. *Prorupted states* are nearly compact, but they have at least one narrow extension of territory. Namibia and Thailand are examples. If these extensions reach out to navigable waterways, the extensions are called *corridors. Elongated states* are long and thin, such as Chile or Norway, and *fragmented states* consist of several isolated bits of territory. *Archipelago states,* made up of several strings of islands, such as Japan or the Philippines, are fragmented states. Still other states, called *perforated states*, are interrupted by the territory of another state enclosed entirely within them. South Africa, for example, is perforated by Lesotho, and Italy is perforated by the Vatican and by San Marino.

The shape of a state's territory may influence the government's ability to organize that territory, but this is not always true. A topographic barrier such as a mountain chain may effectively divide even a compact state. Bolivia and Switzerland, for example, are compact in shape, but mountain chains disrupt their interiors. For some of their regions, trade across international borders is easier than trade with other regions of their own country. The people throughout an archipelago state, by contrast, may be successfully linked by shipping.

Before drawing any conclusions about political control from the shape of a state alone, one must consider the distribution of topographic features, the state's population and resources, and whether any centrifugal forces such as economic or cultural ties straddle the state's borders.

—Bergman and Renwick, *Introduction to Geography*, pp. 442–43

1. What is the purpose of the passage?
2. Highlight the topic sentence of each paragraph. If there is no stated main idea, write a sentence expressing the main idea.
3. Highlight all transitional words.
4. What kind of study aid would help you understand this passage?
5. What is a state that is nearly circular in shape called?
6. What is a corridor?
7. What is a perforated state?

PASSAGE B

The first American daily newspaper was printed in Philadelphia in 1783, but such papers did not proliferate until the technological advances of the mid-nineteenth century. The ratification of the First Amendment in 1791, guaranteeing freedom of speech, gave even the earliest American newspapers freedom to print whatever they saw fit. This has given the media a unique ability to display the government's dirty linen, a propensity that continues to distinguish the American press today.

Rapid printing and cheap paper made possible the "penny press," which could be bought for a penny and read at home. In 1841, Horace Greeley's *New York Tribune* was founded, and in 1851, the *New York Times* started up. By the 1840s, the telegraph permitted a primitive "wire service," which relayed news stories from city to city faster than ever before. The Associated Press, founded in 1849, depended heavily on this new technology.

At the turn of the century, newspaper magnates Joseph Pulitzer and William Randolph Hearst ushered in the era of "yellow journalism." This sensational style of reporting focused on violence, corruption, wars, and gossip, often with a less than scrupulous regard for the truth. On a visit to the United States at that time, young

Winston Churchill said that "the essence of American journalism is vulgarity divested of truth." In the midst of the Spanish-American conflict over Cuba, Hearst once boasted of his power over public opinion by telling a news artist "You furnish the pictures and I'll furnish the war."

Newspapers consolidated into **chains** during the early part of the twentieth century. Today's massive media conglomerates (Gannet, Knight-Ridder, and Newhouse are the largest) control newspapers with 78 percent of the nation's daily circulation. Thus, three of four Americans now read a newspaper owned not by a fearless local editor but by a corporation headquartered elsewhere. Often these chains control television and radio stations as well.

—Edwards, *Government in America*, pp. 223–24

1. What is the purpose of the passage?
2. Highlight the topic sentence of each paragraph. If there is no stated main idea, write a sentence expressing the main idea.
3. Highlight all transitional words.
4. How did the American print media begin?
5. When was the *New York Times* founded?
6. What era began at the turn of the century?
7. How are most newspapers owned today?

PASSAGE C

Even before you take your first bite of pizza, your body has already begun a series of complex digestive responses. Your mouth prepares for the food by increasing production of **saliva**. Saliva contains mostly water, which aids in chewing and swallowing, but it also contains important enzymes that begin the process of food breakdown, including amylase, which begins to break down carbohydrates. Enzymes are protein compounds that facilitate chemical reactions but are not altered in the process. From the mouth, the food passes down the **esophagus**, a 9- to 10-inch tube that connects the mouth and stomach. A series of contractions and relaxations by the muscles lining the esophagus gently move food to the next digestive organ, the **stomach**. Here food mixes with enzymes and stomach acids. Hydrochloric acid begins to work in combination with pepsin, an enzyme, to break down proteins. In most people, the stomach secretes enough mucus to protect the stomach lining from these harsh digestive juices.

Further digestive activity takes place in the **small intestine**, a 20-foot coiled tube containing three sections: the *duodenum,* the *jejunum,* and the *ileum.* Each section secretes digestive enzymes that, when combined with enzymes from the liver and the pancreas, further contribute to the breakdown of proteins, fats and carbohydrates. Once broken down, these nutrients are absorbed in the bloodstream to supply body cells with energy. The liver is the major organ that determines whether nutrients are stored, sent to cells or organs, or excreted. Solid wastes consisting of fiber, water, and salts are dumped into the large intestine, where most of the water and salts are reabsorbed into the system and the fiber is passed out the anus. The entire digestive process takes approximately 24 hours.

—Donatelle, *Access to Health*, pp. 223–24

1. What is the purpose of the passage?
2. Highlight the topic sentence of each paragraph. If there is no stated main idea, write a sentence expressing the main idea.
3. Highlight all transitional words.
4. What pattern is used to describe digestion?
5. How does food travel from the mouth to the stomach?
6. What role does the liver play?
7. What happens in the stomach?

EXERCISE 7-9   ## Anticipating Thought Patterns

Read each of the following opening sentences from a textbook reading assignment, and anticipate whether the material will be developed using chronology, process, order of importance, or spatial order. Then underline the portion(s) of the sentence that suggest(s) the pattern you choose.

1. Several statistical procedures are used to track the changes in the divorce rate.

   _____

2. The immune system's ability to defend against an almost infinite variety of antigens depends on a process called clonal selection.[1]

   _____

3. We have no idea how many individuals comprised the human species in our earliest days, and we don't know much more about our numbers in recent times.[2]

   _____

4. There are sources of information about corporations that might help an investor evaluate them. One of the most useful is the *Value Line Investment Survey.*

   _____

5. Human development begins at conception, when the father's sperm cell unites with the mother's ovum.[3]

   _____

6. In the human digestive system, the breakdown of food particles begins in the mouth, where chewing breaks food apart and increases the surface area on which enzymes can act.[4]

   _____

7. The two atrioventricular (AV) valves, one located at each atrial-ventricular junction, prevent backflow into the atria when the ventricles are contracting.[5]

   _____

8. One of the most significant benefits of family therapy is the strengthening of the family unit.

_____

9. The spinal cord is located within the spinal column; it looks like a section of rope or twine.

_____

10. The transition from medieval to modern societies occurred from approximately 1400 to 1800.

_____

■ The Cause and Effect Pattern

The **cause and effect** pattern expresses a relationship between two or more actions, events, or occurrences that are connected in time. The relationship differs, however, from chronological order in that one event leads to another by *causing* it. Information that is organized in terms of the cause and effect pattern may

- explain causes, sources, reasons, motives, and action
- explain the effect, result, or consequence of a particular action
- explain both causes and effects

Cause and effect is clearly illustrated by the following passage, which gives the sources of fashions or the reasons why fashions occur.

topic ─────────────────────┐

Why do fashions occur in the first place? One reason is that some cultures, like ours, *value change:* what is new is good, what is newer is even better. Thus, in many modern societies clothing styles change yearly, while people in traditional societies may wear the same style for generations. A second reason is that many industries promote quick changes in fashion to increase sales. A third reason is that fashions usually trickle down from the top. A new style may occasionally originate from lower-status groups, as blue jeans did. But most fashions come from upper-class people who like to adopt some style or artifact as a badge of their status. But they cannot monopolize most status symbols for long. Their style is adopted by the middle class, maybe copied or modified for use by lower-status groups, offering many people the prestige of possessing a high-status symbol.

—Thio, *Sociology,* p. 534

(margin labels: 1st reason, 2nd reason, 3rd reason)

All disciplines that ask the question "Why" employ the cause and effect thought pattern. It is widely used in the sciences, technologies, and social sciences.

Many statements expressing cause and effect relationships appear in direct order, with the cause stated first and the effect following: "When demand for a product increases, prices rise." However, reverse order is sometimes used, as in the following statement: "Prices rise when a product's demand increases."

| EXERCISE 7-10 | **Identifying Cause and Effect** |

Identify the cause and the effect in each of the following statements. Circle the cause and underline the effect.

1. Most nutritionists agree that long-term weight loss involves a combination of moderate dieting (say, eating 200 to 500 fewer calories a day than your body requires) and moderate exercise, both of which usually involve some behavior modification.[6]
2. When the body loses fluids, the kidneys stimulate the production of a hormone that activates the thirst drive.
3. Anorexia nervosa—a type of self-starvation—may be caused, in part, by our culture's emphasis on thinness.
4. The decrease in tensions between the former Soviet Union and the Western world has made it possible for the UN to become much more active than in the past.[7]
5. A computer program is easy or difficult to run, depending in part on the data entry system you choose.

☑ **Tip for Physical Science Majors**

The physical sciences (chemistry, physics, engineering) are all about cause and effect. Chemists need to know what happens when elements are mixed; engineers need to know about the effects of various weather conditions on roads and bridges. Often, causes and effects in the physical sciences are expressed by mathematical equations. Equations can always be translated into words, and a complete understanding of the equation requires exactly that.

The cause and effect pattern is not limited to an expression of a simple one-cause, one-effect relationship. There may be multiple causes, or multiple effects, or both multiple causes and multiple effects. For example, both slippery road conditions and your failure to buy snow tires (causes) may contribute to your car's sliding into the ditch (effect).

In other instances, a chain of causes or effects may occur. For instance, failing to set your alarm clock may force you to miss your 8:00 A.M. class, which in turn may cause you not to submit your term paper on time, which may result in a grade penalty. Transitional words or phrases that suggest the cause and effect pattern follow.

TRANSITIONS FOR CAUSE AND EFFECT

For causes	**For effects**
because, due to, one cause is . . . ,	*consequently, as a result, thus,*
another is . . . , since, for, first,	*resulted in, one result is . . . ,*
second	*another is . . . , therefore*

| EXERCISE 7-11 | **Identifying Cause and Effect** |

Determine whether each of the following statements expresses single or multiple causes and single or multiple effects. Circle each cause; underline each effect.

1. Heavy drinking (three drinks or more per day) significantly increases the chance of having smaller babies with retarded physical growth, poor coordination, poor muscle tone, intellectual retardation, and other problems, collectively referred to as fetal alcohol syndrome (FAS).[8]

2. Psychogenic amnesia—a severe and often permanent memory loss—results in disorientation and the inability to draw on past experiences.

_____

3. Social loafing, the tendency to work less when part of larger groups, may account for declining worker productivity and corporate profits in rapidly expanding businesses.

_____

4. The world price of an internationally traded product may be influenced greatly, or only slightly, by the demand and supply coming from any one country.[9]

_____

5. Insulin's main effect is to lower blood sugar levels, but it also influences protein and fat metabolism.[10]

_____

EXERCISE 7-12   Analyzing Cause and Effect: Paragraphs

The following paragraphs are organized using the cause and effect pattern. Read them and answer the questions that follow.

PARAGRAPH A

All objects continually radiate energy. Why, then, doesn't the temperature of all objects continually decrease? The answer is that all objects also continually absorb radiant energy. If an object is radiating more energy than it is absorbing, its temperature does decrease; but if an object is absorbing more energy than it is emitting, its temperature increases. An object that is warmer than its surroundings emits more energy than it receives, and therefore it cools; an object colder than its surroundings is a net gainer of energy, and its temperature therefore increases. An object whose temperature is constant, then, emits as much radiant energy as it receives. If it receives none, it will radiate away all its available energy, and its temperature will approach absolute zero.

—Hewitt, *Conceptual Physics*, p. 272

1. Explain why not all objects that radiate energy drop in temperature.
2. What happens to an object that radiates energy but does not absorb any?
3. Highlight the transitional words that signal the cause and effect pattern.
4. What causes an object's temperature to remain constant?
5. What is the effect of an object radiating away all of its available energy?

PARAGRAPH B

It's the end of the term and you have dutifully typed the last of several papers. After hours of nonstop typing, you find that your hands are numb, and you feel an intense, burning pain that makes the thought of typing one more word almost unbearable. If you are like one of the thousands of students and workers who every year must quit a particular task due to pain, you may be suffering from a **repetitive stress injury (RSI).** These are injuries to nerves, soft tissue or joints that result from the physical stress of repeated motions. One of the most common RSIs is **carpal tunnel syndrome,** a product of both the information age and the age of technology in general. Hours spent typing at the computer, flipping groceries through computerized scanners, or other jobs "made simpler" by technology can result in irritation to the median nerve in the wrist, causing numbness, tingling, and pain in the fingers and hands.

—Donatelle, *Access to Health,* p. 516

1. What is the cause of RSIs?
2. Highlight the transitional words that are used in this paragraph.
3. What kind of damage causes carpal tunnel syndrome?
4. What do students often do that can be a cause of RSIs?
5. What kinds of symptoms can result from RSI?

PARAGRAPH C
Causes of Fitness-Related Injuries

There are two types of injuries stemming from participation in fitness-related activities: overuse and traumatic. **Overuse injuries** occur because of cumulative, day-after-day stresses placed on tendons, bones, and ligaments during exercise. The forces that occur normally during physical activity are not enough to cause a ligament sprain or muscle strain, but when these forces are applied on a daily basis for weeks or months, they can result in an injury. Common sites of overuse injuries are the leg, knee, shoulder, and elbow joints. **Traumatic injuries,** which occur suddenly and violently, typically by accident, are the second major type of fitness-related injuries. Typical traumatic injuries are broken bones, torn ligaments and muscles, contusions, and lacerations. Most traumatic injuries are unavoidable—for example, spraining your ankle by landing on another person's foot after jumping up for a rebound in basketball. If your traumatic injury causes a noticeable loss of function and immediate pain or pain that does not go away after 30 minutes, you should have a physician examine it.

—Donatelle, *Access to Health,* p. 300

1. What is the cause of overuse injuries?
2. Highlight the transitional words that are used in this paragraph to signal the cause and effect pattern.
3. How do traumatic injuries often occur?
4. What kinds of injuries are typical traumatic injuries?
5. When should you have a traumatic injury examined?

EXERCISE 7-13   **Analyzing Cause and Effect: Textbook Excerpt**

Read the following passage about alcohol and answer the questions that follow.

IMMEDIATE EFFECTS OF ALCOHOL

The most dramatic effects produced by ethanol occur within the central nervous system (CNS). The primary action of the drug is to reduce the frequency of nerve transmissions and impulses at synaptic junctions. This reduction of nerve transmissions results in a significant depression of CNS functions, with resulting decreases in respiratory rate, pulse rate, and blood pressure. As CNS depression deepens, vital functions become noticeably depressed. In extreme cases, coma and death can result.

Alcohol is a diuretic, causing increased urinary output. Although this effect might be expected to lead to automatic **dehydration** (loss of water), the body actually retains water, most of it in the muscles or in the cerebral tissues. This is because water is usually pulled out of the **cerebrospinal** fluid (fluid within the brain and spinal cord), leading to what is known as mitochondrial dehydration at the cell level within the nervous system. Mitochondria are miniature organs within the cells that are responsible for specific functions. They rely heavily upon fluid balance. When mitochondrial dehydration occurs from drinking, the mitochondria cannot carry out their normal functions, resulting in symptoms that include the "morning-after" headaches suffered by some drinkers.

Alcohol irritates the gastrointestinal system and may cause indigestion and heartburn if taken on an empty stomach. Long-term use of alcohol causes repeated irritation that has been linked to cancers of the esophagus and stomach. In addition, people who engage in brief drinking sprees during which they consume unusually high amounts of alcohol put themselves at risk for irregular heartbeat or even total loss of heart rhythm, which can cause disruption in blood flow and possible damage to the heart muscle.

—Donatelle, *Access to Health*, pp. 337–38

1. What is the purpose of the passage?
2. Highlight the topic sentence of each paragraph. If there is no stated main idea, write a sentence expressing the main idea.
3. Highlight all transitional words.
4. What does the reduction of nerve transmissions result in?
5. What is the result of the diuretic effect of alcohol?
6. Why does drinking alcohol sometimes result in indigestion and heartburn?
7. If alcohol causes irregular heartbeat or loss of heart rhythm, what can result?

■ The Comparison and Contrast Pattern

The **comparison** thought pattern is used to emphasize or discuss similarities between or among ideas, theories, concepts, or events, whereas the **contrast** pattern emphasizes differences. When a speaker or writer is concerned with both similarities and differences, a combination pattern is used. The comparison and contrast pattern is widely used in the social sciences, where different groups, societies, cultures, or behaviors are studied. Literature courses may require comparisons among poets, among literary works, or among stylistic features. A business course may examine various management styles, compare organizational structures, or contrast retailing plans.

A contrast is shown in the following paragraph, which contrasts small and large businesses.

Difference #1: purchase process

    Small businesses are likely to have less formal purchasing processes. A small retail grocer might, for example, purchase a computer system after visiting a few suppliers to compare prices and features, while a large grocery store chain might collect bids from a specified number of vendors and then evaluate those bids on pre-established criteria. Usually, fewer individuals are involved in the decision-making process for a small business. The owner of the small business, for example, may make all decisions, and a larger business may operate with a buying committee of several people.

Difference #2: decision-making

—Kinnear et al., *Principles of Marketing*, p. 218

Depending on whether a speaker or writer is concerned with similarities, differences, or both similarities and differences, the pattern might be organized in different ways. Suppose a professor of American literature is comparing two American poets, Whitman and Frost. Each of the following organizations is possible:

1. **Compare and then contrast the two.** That is, first discuss how Frost's poetry and Whitman's poetry are similar, and then discuss how they are different.

2. **Discuss by author.** For example, discuss the characteristics of Whitman's poetry; then discuss the characteristics of Frost's poetry; then summarize their similarities and differences.

3. **Discuss by characteristic.** For example, first discuss the two poets' use of metaphor; next discuss their use of rhyme, and then discuss their common themes.

Examples of transitional words and phrases that reflect these patterns follow.

> ☑ **Tip for Education (and All) Majors**
>
> Essay questions on exams in many courses (especially those in education, the liberal arts, the humanities, and the social sciences) often ask students to compare and contrast. By studying this pattern of organization when you find it in textbooks, you will simultaneously develop your test-taking skills.

TRANSITIONS FOR CONTRAST

unlike Whitman, Frost . . .

less wordy than Whitman . . .

contrasted with Whitman, Frost . . .

Frost *differs from* . . .

Other contrast transitional words are:

in contrast, however, on the other hand, as opposed to, whereas

TRANSITIONS FOR COMPARISON

similarities between Frost and Whitman . . .

Frost is *as* powerful *as* . . .

like Frost, Whitman . . .

both Frost and Whitman . . .

Frost *resembles* Whitman in that . . .

Other comparison transitional words are:

in a like manner, similarly, likewise, correspondingly, in the same way

---

EXERCISE 7-14   **Analyzing Comparison and Contrast: Paragraphs**

Read the following paragraphs and answer the questions that follow.

A.   When considering the relationship of Congress and the president, the basic differences of the two branches must be kept in mind. Members of Congress are elected from narrower constituencies than is the president. The people usually expect the president to address general concerns such as foreign policy and economic prosperity, while Congresspersons are asked to solve individual problems. There are structural differences as well. Congress is a body composed of hundreds of independent people, each with a different power base, and it is divided along partisan lines. Thus, it is difficult for Congress to act quickly or to project unity and clear policy statements.

—Baradat, *Understanding American Democracy,* p. 300

1. What two branches of the government are discussed?
2. Explain how these two branches are similar and/or different.
3. Highlight the transitional words that signal the comparison and contrast pattern.
4. Does this paragraph mainly use comparison, contrast, or both?
5. Why is it difficult for Congress to act quickly?

B.   What are the main characteristics of this new postindustrial society? Unlike the industrial society from which we are emerging, its hallmark is not raw materials and manufacturing. Rather, its basic component is *information*. Teachers pass on knowledge to students, while lawyers, physicians, bankers, pilots, and interior decorators sell their specialized knowledge of law, the body, money, aerodynamics, and color schemes to clients. Unlike the factory workers in an industrial society, these workers don't *produce* anything. Rather, they transmit or use information to provide services that others are willing to pay for.

—Henslin, *Social Problems,* p. 154

1. What two things are being compared or contrasted?
2. Highlight the transitional words used to indicate the comparison and contrast pattern.
3. What is the postindustrial society based upon?
4. What did most workers in industrial society do at their jobs?
5. How is information connected to money in a postindustrial society?

C.   You have already seen that homosexuality is more common among males than females, a finding that is supported by all researchers who have reported on this matter. Let's see what other differences they have found. One of the most significant is that lesbians are more likely to seek lasting relationships, place a premium on emotional commitment and mutual fidelity, and shun the bar scene. Consequently, while most male homosexuals have "cruised" (sought impersonal sex with strangers), fewer than 20 percent of lesbians have done so. As a result, lesbians tend to have fewer sexual partners than do male homosexuals. Psychologist Alan Bell and sociologist Martin Weinberg interviewed about 1500 homosexuals. They found that almost half the white and one third the African-American homosexual males had at least

500 different sexual partners. About 28 percent of the white sample had more than 1000 different partners. Although their sample is large, it is not representative of homosexuals, because their research focused heavily on bars and steam baths. Bell's and Weinberg's findings do, however, support other studies indicating promiscuity among male homosexuals.

—Henslin, *Social Problems,* p. 74

1. What are two differences between lesbians and gay males?
2. Highlight the transitional words that are used to indicate the comparison-and-contrast pattern?
3. Why is the research cited in this paragraph not representative of all homosexuals?
4. What does it mean to "cruise"?
5. What percent of white homosexual males had more than 1000 partners?

EXERCISE 7–15   **Analyzing Comparison and Contrast: Textbook Excerpt**

Read the following passage about behavior and answer the questions that follow.

MODELS OF ABNORMAL BEHAVIOR

In their efforts to identify and explain abnormal behaviors, psychologists often adopt models, or general views of what causes those behaviors. Models help by pointing out which symptoms are most important, directing attention to their likely causes and suggesting possible treatments.

The Medical Model

Near the end of the eighteenth century, physicians began to document their patients' symptoms and to note which ones occurred together. The occurrence of groups of symptoms, called *syndromes,* helped physicians identify underlying diseases and develop treatments. Approaching abnormal behaviors just as one would approach medical illnesses is known as the **medical model.**

Psychiatrist Thomas Szasz (1993) argues for limiting the medical model to conditions resulting from actual brain dysfunctions. In his opinion, this model has been expanded to cover behaviors that are perhaps annoying or inappropriate but do not constitute diseases of the brain. For example, the list of proposed or recognized diseases includes shoplifting, pathological gambling, and nicotine dependence. According to Szasz, applying the medical model to such behaviors does not advance our understanding of the causes of the problems and allows people to avoid taking responsibility for their problems by attributing them to a disease process.

Accumulating evidence shows that a number of psychological disorders are related to elevated or reduced levels of certain neurotransmitters or structural abnormalities in the brain. What's more, evidence is increasing that heredity plays a significant role in the development of some psychological disorders.

The Psychological Models

In contrast to the medical model, various *psychological models* emphasize the importance of mental functioning, social experiences and learning histories in trying to explain the causes of abnormal behaviors. Sigmund Freud's **psychodynamic model** focuses on unconscious conflicts involving the id, ego and superego or fixations at an early stage of psychosexual development. For example, anxiety is seen as a warning that the ego is about to be overwhelmed by conflict. The **behavioral model,** by contrast, focuses on environmental factors that mold human and animal behaviors. Behavioral theorists such as John B. Watson and B. F. Skinner propose that we learn both normal and abnormal behaviors through the principles of classical conditioning, operant conditioning, and modeling. In contrast to the behavioral model, the cognitive model focuses on understanding the content and processes of human thought. Cognitive psychologists claim that to understand human behavior, we must look beyond actual events to understand how people interpret those events.

—Davis and Palladino, *Psychology*, pp. 535–36

1. What is the purpose of the passage?
2. Highlight the topic sentence of each paragraph. If there is no stated main idea, write a sentence expressing the main idea.
3. Highlight all transitional words.
4. What is the medical model of approaching abnormal behavior?
5. How do psychological models contrast with the medical model?
6. Which psychological model relies on understanding the content and processes of human thought?
7. Why does Szasz argue for limiting the use of the medical model?

EXERCISE 7-16   ### Anticipating Thought Patterns

Read each of the following opening sentences from a textbook reading assignment and predict whether a comparison, contrast, or combination pattern will be used.

1. In Rembrandt's *Self-Portrait* and Frank Auerbach's *Head of Michael Podro,* the artists' responsiveness to both the reality of their subjects and the physical nature of paint and painting is clearly visible.[11]

_____

2. The Enlightenment celebrated the power of reason; however, an opposite reaction, Romanticism, soon followed.[12]

_____

3. The small group develops in much the same way that a conversation develops.[13]

_____

4. Think of the hardware in a computer system as the kitchen in a short-order restaurant: It's equipped to produce whatever output a customer (user) requests, but it sits idle until an order (command) is placed.[14]

_____

5. One important conceptual issue that arises frequently in economics is the distinction between stock and flow variables.[15]

_____

EXERCISE 7-17   **Writing Using Comparison and Contrast**

LEARNING
COLLABORATIVELY

Write five sentences that express either a comparison or a contrast relationship. Exchange your sentences with a classmate, asking him or her to identify the pattern used.

■ The Listing/Enumeration Pattern

If asked to evaluate a film you saw, you might describe the characters, plot, and technical effects. These details about the film could be arranged in any order; each detail provides further information about the film, but they have no specific relationship to one another. This arrangement of ideas is known as **listing** or **enumeration**—giving bits of information on a topic by stating them one after the other. Often, there is no particular method of arrangement for those details.

The following list of managers' difficulties in problem solving could have been presented in any order without altering the meaning of the paragraph.

topic sentence——— Although accurate identification of a problem is essential before the problem can be solved, this stage of decision making creates many difficulties for managers.
difficulty 1 ——— Sometimes managers' preconceptions of the problem prevent them from seeing the situation as it actually is. They produce an answer before the proper question
difficulty 2 ——— has ever been asked. In other cases, managers overlook truly significant issues by
difficulty 3 ——— focusing on unimportant matters. Also, managers may mistakenly analyze problems in terms of symptoms rather than underlying causes.

—Pride et al., *Business,* p. 189

This pattern is widely used in college textbooks in most academic disciplines. In its loosest form, the pattern may be simply a list of items: factors that influence light emission, characteristics of a particular poet, a description of an atom, a list of characteristics that define poverty.

Somewhat tighter is the use of listing to explain, support, or provide evidence. Support may be in the form of facts, statistics, or examples. For instance, the statement "The incidence of white collar crime has dramatically increased over the past 10 years" would be followed by facts and statistics documenting the increase. The transitional words or phrases used for this pattern include the following.

TRANSITIONS FOR LISTING/ENUMERATION

one aspect of relativity . . .

a second feature of relativity . . .

also, relativity . . .

there are *several* characteristics of . . .

(1) . . . , (2) . . . , and (3) . . .

(a) . . . , (b) . . . , and (c) . . .

Other transitional words are:

in addition, first, second, third, finally, another

EXERCISE 7-18 **Analyzing Listing: Paragraphs**

Read the following paragraphs and answer the questions that follow.

A.   By far the most important committees in Congress are the standing committees. Currently 16 standing committees in the Senate and 22 in the House receive the bills that are introduced in Congress. The standing committees are assigned subject-matter jurisdiction by the rules of their respective house, and their titles reflect their general area of expertise. Hence, we have the Senate Finance Committee, the House Agriculture Committee, the Senate Budget Committee, the House Judiciary Committee, and so on. The authority of the standing committees includes the power to study legislation, to subpoena witnesses or information, to remand bills to subcommittees, to vote bills dead, to table bills (putting them aside, thus allowing them to die quietly at the end of the congressional term), to amend bills, to write bills (amending a bill or writing an entirely new version of a bill is called **marking-up**), or to report the bill to the floor.

—Baradat, *Understanding American Democracy,* p. 202

1. What is the topic of the paragraph?
2. What types of information does this paragraph list?
3. Highlight the transitional words used in this paragraph to indicate the listing pattern.
4. What is the purpose of standing committees in general?
5. List two powers of standing committees.

B.   Minorities come into existence, then, when, due to expanded political boundaries or migration, people with different customs, languages, values or physical characteristics come under control of the same state organization. There, some groups who share physical and cultural traits discriminate against those with different traits.

The losers in this power struggle are forced into minority group status; the winners enjoy the higher status and greater privileges that their dominance brings. Wagley and Harris noted that all minorities share these five characteristics: (1) They are treated unequally by the dominant group. (2) Their physical or cultural traits are held in low esteem by the dominant group. (3) They tend to feel strong group solidarity because of their physical or cultural traits—and the disabilities these traits bring. (4) Their membership in a minority group is not voluntary but comes through birth. (5) They tend to marry within their group. Sharing cultural or physical traits, having similar experiences of discrimination, and marrying within their own group create a shared identity—sometimes even a sense of common destiny. These shared experiences, however, do not mean that all minority groups have the same goals.

—Henslin, *Social Problems*, p. 252

1. How do minorities come into existence?
2. Highlight the transitional words used to indicate the listing pattern.
3. How does minority status impact marriage?
4. At what stage of life does a person enter an already existing minority group?
5. How is a shared identity or destiny created among minorities?

C.   Voters make two basic decisions at election time. The first is whether to vote. Americans' right to vote is well established, but in order to do so citizens must go through the registration process. America's unique registration system is one major reason why turnout in American elections is much lower than in most other democracies. The 1996 election was another in a long string of low-turnout elections. Second, those who choose to vote must decide for whom to cast their ballots. Over a generation of research on voting behavior has helped political scientists understand the dominant role played by three factors in voters' choices: party identification, candidate evaluations, and policy positions.

—Edwards, *Government in America*, p. 330

1. What two categories are listed or enumerated in this paragraph?
2. What transitional words are used to indicate the listing or enumeration pattern?
3. What is a major reason why voter turnout is low in America?
4. List the factors involved in voters' choices.
5. What is the first decision a voter must make in an election?

EXERCISE 7-19   **Analyzing Listing: Textbook Excerpt**

Read the following excerpt from a nursing textbook and answer the questions that follow.

THEORIES OF PAIN

The neurophysiologic basis of pain can be explained by several theories, none of which is mutually exclusive nor totally comprehensive.

Specificity Theory

This theory suggests that certain pain receptors are stimulated by a specific type of sensory stimuli that sends impulses to the brain. This theory deals with the physiologic basis for pain but does not take into account the psychologic components of pain, nor the degree of pain tolerance.

Pattern Theory

This theory attempts to include factors that were not adequately explained by the specificity theory. This theory suggests that pain originates in the dorsal horn of the spinal cord. A certain pattern of nerve impulses is produced and results in intense receptor stimulation that is coded in the central nervous system (CNS) and signifies pain. Like the specificity theory, the pattern theory does not explain the psychologic factors of pain.

Gate Control Theory

One of the most popular and credible concepts is the gate control theory. The first premise of the gate control theory is that the actual existence and intensity of the pain experience depends on the particular transmission of neurologic impulses. Secondly, gate mechanisms along the nervous system control the transmission of pain. Finally, if the gate is open, the impulses that result in the sensation of pain are able to reach the conscious level. If the gate is closed, the impulses do not reach the level of consciousness and the sensation of pain is not experienced.

—Smith, et al., *Clinical Nursing Skills*, p. 510

1. What is the purpose of the excerpt?
2. Highlight the topic sentence of each paragraph. If there is no stated main idea, write a sentence expressing the main idea.
3. Highlight any transitional words.
4. What is the limitation of the specificity theory?
5. Explain the gate control theory.

EXERCISE 7-20 | **Identifying the Listing Pattern**

Identify and circle the topics listed below that might be developed by using the listing pattern.

1. The Impact of Budget on Crime Prevention
2. The Aims of Legal Punishment
3. America: A Drugged Society?
4. Varieties of Theft
5. Homicide and Assault: The Current Picture

■ Mixed Patterns

Thought patterns are often combined. In describing a process, a writer may also give reasons why each step must be followed in the prescribed order. A lecturer may define a concept by comparing it to something similar or familiar. Suppose an essay in your political science textbook opens by stating, "The distinction between 'power' and 'power potential' is an important one in considering the balance of power." You might expect a definition pattern (where the two terms are defined), but you also might anticipate that the essay would discuss the difference between the two terms (contrast pattern).

In the passage below, the author uses both definition and listing to explain child abuse.

CHILD ABUSE

definition

Children raised in families in which domestic violence and/or sexual abuse occur are at great risk for damage to personal health and well-being. The effects of such violent acts are powerful and can be very long-lasting. **Child abuse** refers to the systematic harm of a child by a caregiver, generally a parent. The abuse may be sexual, psychological, physical, or any combination of these. Although exact figures are lacking, many experts believe that over 2 million cases of child abuse occur every year in the United States, involving severe injury, permanent disability, or death. Child abusers exist in all gender, social, ethnic, religious, and racial groups.

listing of characteristics

Certain personal characteristics tend to be common among child abusers: having been abused as a child, having a poor self-image, feelings of isolation, extreme frustration with life, higher stress or anxiety levels than normal, a tendency to abuse drugs and/or alcohol, and unrealistic expectations of the child. It is also estimated that from one half to three quarters of men who batter their female partners also batter children. In fact, spouse abuse is the single most identifiable risk factor for predicting child abuse. Finally, children with handicaps or other "differences" are more likely to be abused.

—Donatelle, *Access to Health,* p. 107

EXERCISE 7-21   **Analyzing Patterns**

The following paragraph describes the beginnings of Earth's atmosphere. Read the paragraph and answer the questions that follow.

Earth's very earliest atmosphere probably was swept into space by the *solar wind,* a vast stream of particles emitted by the sun. As earth slowly cooled, a more enduring atmosphere formed. The molten surface solidified into a crust, and gases that had been dissolved in the molten rock were gradually released, a process called **outgassing**. Outgassing continues today from hundreds of active volcanoes worldwide. Thus, geologists hypothesize that Earth's original atmosphere was made up of gases similar to those released in volcanic emissions today: water vapor, carbon dioxide, nitrogen, and several trace gases.

—Tarbuck and Lutgens, *Earth Science,* p. 298

1. Which patterns are used in this paragraph?
2. Highlight the transitional words used to indicate the patterns.
3. What happened to the first atmosphere the Earth had?
4. How does outgassing occur?
5. What was the original atmosphere probably composed of?

EXERCISE 7-22   **Analyzing Patterns**

The following passage uses mixed patterns. Read the passage and answer the questions that follow.

WEATHERING

All materials are susceptible to weathering. Consider, for example, the synthetic rock we call concrete, which closely resembles the sedimentary rock called conglomerate. A newly poured concrete sidewalk has a smooth, fresh look. However, not many years later, the same sidewalk will appear chipped, cracked, and rough, with pebbles exposed at the surface. If a tree is nearby, its roots may grow under the concrete, heaving and buckling it. The same natural processes that eventually break apart a concrete sidewalk also act to disintegrate natural rocks, regardless of their type or strength.

Why does rock weather? Simply, weathering is the response of Earth materials to a changing environment. For instance, after millions of years of uplift and erosion, the rocks overlying a large body of intrusive igneous rock may be removed. This exposes the rock to a whole new environment at the surface. The mass of crystalline rock, which formed deep below ground where temperatures and pressures are much greater than at the surface, is now subjected to very different and comparatively hostile surface conditions. In response, this rock mass will gradually change until it is once again in equilibrium, or balance, with its new environment. Such transformation of rock is what we call *weathering.*

There are two kinds of weathering—mechanical and chemical. Mechanical weathering is the physical breaking up of rocks into smaller pieces. Chemical weathering actually alters a rock's chemistry, changing it into different substances. Although we will consider these two processes separately, keep in mind that they usually work simultaneously in nature.

—Tarbuck and Lutgens, *Earth Science*, p. 61

1. What is the purpose of the passage?
2. Highlight the topic sentence of each paragraph. If there is no stated main idea, write a sentence expressing the main idea.
3. Highlight all transitional words.
4. Which patterns are utilized in this passage?
5. Why do rocks weather?
6. What is the difference between mechanical and chemical weathering?
7. What kind of rock is concrete similar to?

EXERCISE 7-23   **Anticipating Thought Patterns**

For each of the following topic sentences, anticipate what thought pattern(s) the paragraph is likely to exhibit. Record your prediction in the space provided. Underline the word(s) that suggest the pattern(s) you chose.

1. Another form of learning that does not fit neatly into the mold of classical or operant conditioning is learning through insight.

2. GNP (gross national product) is an economic measure that considers the total value of goods and services that a country produces during a given year.

_____

3. Diseases of the heart and blood vessels—cardiovascular diseases—are the leading cause of death in the United States today.[16]

_____

4. Impulse conduction in neurons has been compared to electrical impulses in, say, a copper wire, but the analogy is not a good one.[17]

_____

5. The body's first line of defense against infection consists of several kinds of nonspecific resistance, so named because they do not distinguish one invader from another.[18]

_____

6. Research suggests that obsessive-compulsive disorder has a biological basis.[19]

_____

7. Nervous systems consist of two major types of cells: neurons (nerve cells), which are specialized for carrying signals from one location in the body to another, and supporting cells, which protect, insulate, and reinforce neurons.[20]

_____

8. Both Neoclassicism and Romanticism had their beginnings in rebellion.[21]

_____

9. Anthropology is the study of human beings from their origins to the present time.

_____

10. Before the twentieth century, most of the population of Latin America resembled the populations of antiquity, with high birthrates offset by high death rates.[22]

_____

EXERCISE 7-24

ACADEMIC
APPLICATION

Identifying Thought Patterns

Choose a one- or two-page section of one of your textbooks and determine the pattern of each major paragraph. Then identify the overall pattern of the section as a whole.

EXERCISE 7-25	**Predicting Thought Patterns**

LEARNING
COLLABORATIVELY

Turn to the table of contents of this text. Predict the thought pattern(s) that any five of the readings will follow. Ask a classmate to confirm or disagree with the patterns you identified.

■ Other Useful Patterns of Organization

The patterns presented in the previous sections are the most common. The Key Strategy box "A Review of Common Patterns and Transitions" presents a brief review of those patterns and their corresponding transitional words. However, writers do not limit themselves to these six patterns. Especially in academic writing, you may find one or more of the patterns listed in the Key Strategy box "A Review of Additional Patterns and Transitions" (p. 212), as well. Here is a brief overview of each of these additional patterns.

Statement and Clarification   Many writers make a statement of fact and then proceed to clarify or explain that statement. For instance, a writer may open a paragraph by stating that "The best education for you may not be the best education for someone else." The remainder of the paragraph would then discuss that statement and make its meaning clear by explaining how educational needs are individual and based on one's talents, skills, and goals. Transitional words associated with this pattern are listed in the Key Strategy box on page 212.

In the following paragraph about sex ratios, the writer uses statement and clarification.

statement

clarification

Sex ratios in the poor countries do not show a consistent pattern. In some poor countries men outnumber women, but in others, in tropical Africa, for example, women outnumber men. In fact, variations in sex ratios can be explained only by a combination of national economic and cultural factors. In the countries of North America and Europe and in Japan, women may suffer many kinds of discrimination, but they are not generally discriminated against when it comes to access to medical care.

—Bergman and Renwick, *Introduction to Geography*, p. 185

Notice that the writer begins with the statement about sex ratios in poor countries and then goes on to clarify this fact. The author uses the transitional words "in fact."

Summary

A summary is a condensed statement that provides the key points of a larger idea or piece of writing. The summaries at the end of each chapter of this text provide a quick review of the chapter's contents. Often writers summarize what they have already said or what someone else has said. For example, in a psychology textbook you will find many summaries of research. Instead of asking you to read an entire research study, the textbook author will summarize the

KEY STRATEGY: A Review of Common Patterns and Transitions

PATTERN	CHARACTERISTICS	TRANSITIONS
Definition	Explains the meaning of a word or phrase	*is, refers to, can be defined as, means, consists of, involves, is a term that, is called, is characterized by, occurs when, are those that, entails, corresponds to, is literally*
Classification	Divides a topic into parts based on shared characteristics	*classified as, comprises, is composed of, several varieties of, different stages of, different groups that, includes, one, first, second, another, finally, last*
Order or Sequence	Describes events, processes, procedures, spatial relationships, and order of importance	*first, second, later, before, next, as soon as, after, then, finally, meanwhile, following, last, during, in, on, when, until*
Cause and Effect	Describes how one or more things cause or are related to another	***Causes:*** *because, because of, for, since, stems from, one cause is, one reason is, leads to, causes, creates, yields, produces, due to, breeds, for this reason* ***Effects:*** *consequently, results in, one result is, thus, therefore, as a result, hence*
Comparison and Contrast	Discusses similarities and/or differences among ideas, theories, concepts, objects, or persons	***Similarities:*** *both, also, similarly, like, likewise, too, as well as, resembles, correspondingly, in the same way, to compare, in comparison, share* ***Differences:*** *unlike, differs from, in contrast, on the other hand, instead, despite, nevertheless, however, in spite of, whereas, as opposed to*
Listing/ Enumeration	Organizes lists of information, characteristics	*the following, several, for example, for instance, one, another, also, too, in other words, first, second*

KEY STRATEGY: A Review of Additional Patterns and Transitions

PATTERN	CHARACTERISTICS	TRANSITIONS
Statement and Clarification	Indicates that information explaining an idea or concept will follow the topic sentence	*in fact, in other words, clearly, evidently, obviously*
Summary	Indicates that a condensed review of an idea or piece of writing will be given	*in summary, in conclusion, in brief, to summarize, to sum up, in short, on the whole*
Generalization and Example	Provides examples that clarify a broad, general statement	*for example, for instance, that is, to illustrate, thus*
Addition	Indicates that additional information will follow the topic sentence	*furthermore, additionally, also, besides, further, in addition, moreover, again*

study's findings. Other times a writer may repeat in condensed form what he or she has already said as a means of emphasis or clarification. Transitional words associated with this pattern are listed in the Key Strategy box on the facing page.

In the following paragraph about the magazine industry, the author uses the summary method of organization.

Indicates summary is to follow

In summary, the magazine industry is adapting to the new world of electronic multimedia information and entertainment, with formats that will be quite different from the familiar ones. Computer-generated publishing has become the norm in the magazine business, expanding beyond its uses in producing newsletters and other specialized publications. Most general circulation magazines already rely heavily on desktop computers, interacting with other electronic equipment to produce high-quality, graphics-filled products.

—Dizard, *Old Media, New Media*, p. 169

Notice that the writer summarizes many facts about how the magazine industry uses electronic multimedia information and that the transitional words "in summary" are used.

> ☑ **Tip for Health and Life Science Majors**
>
> Many allied health and biology textbooks include mini-summaries within each chapter, often at the end of each major heading. These summaries are designed to help students pace their learning and test their understanding before they move on to the next section of a chapter. Section summaries are very useful, so be sure to read them. (They often make excellent review tools for exams.)

Generalization and Example

Examples are one of the best ways to explain something that is unfamiliar or unknown. Examples are specific instances or situations that illustrate a concept or idea. Often writers may present a general statement, or generalization, and then explain it by giving examples to make its meaning clear. In a social problems textbook, you might find the following generalization: Computer theft by employees is on the increase. The section might then go on to offer examples from specific companies in which employees insert fictitious information into the company's computer program and steal company funds. Transitional words associated with this pattern are listed in the Key Strategy box on the facing page.

In the following paragraph about dreams, the writer uses generalization and example.

generalization

example

Different cultures place varying emphases on dreams and support different beliefs concerning dreams. For example, many people in the United States view dreams as irrelevant fantasy with no connection to everyday life. By contrast, people in other cultures view dreams as key sources of information about the future, the spiritual world, and the dreamer. Such cultural views can influence the probability of dream recall. In many modern Western cultures, people rarely remember their dreams upon awakening. The Parintintin Of South America, however, typically remember several dreams every night (Kraeke, 1993) and the Senoi of Malaysia discuss their dreams with family members in the morning (Hennager, 1993).

—Davis and Palladino, *Psychology*, p. 210

Notice that the writer begins with the generalization that different cultures place different emphases on dreams and then goes on to give examples of the way specific cultures treat dreams. Note the use of the transitional words "for example."

Addition

Writers often introduce an idea or make a statement and then supply additional information about that idea or statement. For instance, an education textbook might introduce the concept of homeschooling and then provide in-depth information about its benefits. This pattern is often used to expand, elaborate on, or discuss an idea in greater detail. Transitional words associated with this pattern are listed in the Key Strategy box on page 212.

In the following paragraph about pathogens, the writer uses addition.

statement ——————   Some pathogens [disease-causing organisms] evolve and mutate naturally. Also, patients who fail to complete the full portion of their antibiotic prescriptions allow drug-resistant pathogens to multiply. The use of antibiotics in animal feed and sprayed on fruits and vegetables during food processing increases opportunities for resistant organisms to evolve and thrive. Furthermore, there is evidence that the disruption of earth's natural habitats can trigger the evolution of new pathogens.

additional information

—Bergman and Renwick, *Introduction to Geography*, p. 182

Notice that the writer states that some pathogens mutate naturally and then goes on to add that they also mutate as a result of human activities. Note the use of the transitional words "also" and "furthermore."

| EXERCISE 7-26 | Identifying Thought Patterns |

For each of the following statements, identify the pattern that is evident and write its name in the space provided. Choose from among the following patterns: statement and clarification, summary, generalization and example, *and* addition.

1. _____ In short, physical anthropologists are still waiting to locate the remains that will connect present day humans with early hominids.

2. _____ Humans have been using pictures to communicate and make sense of their environment since they first evolved. Cave paintings and the creation of constellation figures are just a few examples.

3. _____ Anthrax is a strain of bacteria that is spread through inhalation. Anthrax can also be contracted cutaneously, through contact with the skin.

4. _____ Pedophiles (criminals who molest children) generally cannot be rehabilitated. In fact, many types of therapy have been tried without success.

5. _____ Internet bulletin boards and listservs make it possible for people to casually meet other people who they would not otherwise come into contact with. For instance, a popular listserv made up of tea enthusiasts comprises members from all over the globe.

6. _____ Frogs are able to breathe underwater by absorbing oxygen from the water through their skin. Besides breathing underwater,

frogs are also able to breathe while in air, but their skin must be wet in order to absorb oxygen from the air.

7. _____ The Moro reflex in human infants is best summed up as a holdover from life in the trees. When the infant perceives the feeling of falling, it spreads its arms and hands in an attempt to prevent a fall from the branches.

8. _____ What is considered as instinct in animals is often the manifestation of a highly developed sense. As a case in point, salmon are able to return to their spawning stream using a highly developed sense of smell.

9. _____ Crustaceans have exoskeletons instead of internal skeletons. To illustrate this, think of how a lobster has a shell on the outside that can be removed and that once inside the shell, there is only meat.

10. _____ Circulation numbers are crucial in increasing ad revenues for magazines. In fact, many magazines give free or very low cost subscriptions in order to boost their circulation numbers and support increases in ad revenues.

EXERCISE 7-27   ## Identifying Thought Patterns

Read each of the following paragraphs and identify the predominant organizational pattern used. Write the name of the pattern in the space provided. Choose from among the following patterns: statement and clarification, summary, generalization and example, and addition.

1. **Managing Emotional Responses**

   Have you gotten all worked up about something you thought was happening only to find that your perceptions were totally wrong or that a communication problem had caused a misrepresentation of events? If you're like most of us, you probably have. We often get upset not by realities but by our faulty perceptions. For example, suppose you found out that everyone except you is invited to a party. You might easily begin to wonder why you were excluded. Does someone dislike you? Have you offended someone? Such thoughts are typical. However, the reality of the situation may have absolutely nothing to do with your being liked or disliked. Perhaps you were sent an invitation and it didn't get to you.

   —Donatelle, *Access to Health*, p. 81

   Pattern: _____

2.   A serious problem with some drugs is **addiction,** or **drug dependence.** That is, people come to depend on the regular consumption of a drug in order to make it through the day. When people think of **drug addiction,** they are likely to think of addicts huddled in slum doorways, the dregs of society who seldom venture into daylight—unless it is to rob someone. They don't associate addiction with "good," middle-class neighborhoods and "solid citizens." But let's look at drug addiction a

little more closely. Although most people may think of heroin as the prime example of an addictive drug, I suggest that nicotine is the better case to consider. I remember a next-door neighbor who stood in his backyard, a lit cigarette in his hand, and told me about the operation in which one of his lungs was removed. I say "I remember," because soon after our conversation he died from his addiction.

—Henslin, *Social Problems*, p. 93

Pattern: _____

3. **The Challenges of Cable TV**

The more immediate challenge to the Big Three television networks, however, came from cable television. The networks were at a structural disadvantage in their attempts to match cable's appeal. They had only one channel with which to reach the home audiences that advertisers wanted. Moreover, network program costs rose as advertising revenues fell. This was especially true of the more popular programs networks had to offer in order to keep what was left of their competitive prime-time edge.

—Dizard, *Old Media, New Media*, p. 87

Pattern: _____

4.   Like previous major wars, Vietnam profoundly affected the lives of mainly African Americans. For black soldiers who served in Vietnam, the war offered an opportunity to demonstrate once again that they were prepared to fight for freedom on many fronts. However, controversies in the United States over civil rights and black power reverberated in Vietnam, while at the same time disagreements concerning American intervention in Vietnam affected the civil rights and black power movements. On both the home front and the battlefields, the backdrop of violence shaped the way racial issues were viewed and discussed. Daily newscasts brought the war to the television sets of civilians; some called it the "living room war." The brief tours of duty—no more than a year in Vietnam for most soldiers—reduced the isolation of soldiers. Moreover, as King pointed out in his antiwar speech at Riverside Church, the war affected domestic racial policies by diverting federal funds that might otherwise be spent on the war on poverty and other Great Society social programs.

—Carson et al., *African American Lives*, pp. 490–91

Pattern: _____

5.   In summary, the publishing industry is undergoing major changes, brought on by demographic shifts, financial upheavals, and the pressure of new technologies. Instability and reassessment are common to all parts of the industry—newspapers, magazines, and books—but the situation in each sector is distinct enough to warrant examining them separately.

—Dizard, *Old Media, New Media*, p. 157

Pattern: _____

6.   For each American who commits suicide, about ten attempt it. Although many more women than men attempt suicide, more men than women succeed at it. This

is likely because the women's attempts are more a "cry for help," while the men are more serious about accomplishing the act. In addition, men tend to choose methods that allow less intervention, such as guns, while women are more likely to use pills. Also guns provide less time to change one's mind or to allow someone to intervene.

—Henslin, *Social Problems,* p. 336

Pattern: _____

7.   Be careful not to evaluate negatively the cultural differences you perceive. Be careful that you don't fall into the trap of ethnocentric thinking, evaluating your culture positively and other cultures negatively. For example, many Americans of Northern European descent evaluate negatively the tendency of many Hispanics and Southern Europeans to use the street for a gathering place, for playing Dominoes, and for just sitting on a cool evening. Whether you like or dislike using the street in this way, recognize that neither attitude is logically correct or incorrect. This street behavior is simply adequate or inadequate for *members of the culture.*

—DeVito, *Human Communication,* p. 103

Pattern: _____

8.   In short, the view that a drug is good or bad depends not on objective conditions but on subjective concerns. It is a matter of how people define matters. People's definitions, in turn, influence how they use and abuse drugs, whether or not a drug will be legal or illegal, and what social policies they want to adopt. This is the central sociological aspect of drug use and abuse, one that we shall stress over and over in this chapter.

—Henslin, *Social Problems,* p. 91

Pattern: _____

9.   Human migration has by no means come to an end. Large-scale migrations still make daily news. The United Nations' Universal Declaration of Human Rights affirms anyone's right to leave his or her homeland to seek a better life elsewhere, but it cannot guarantee that there will be anyplace willing to take anyone. As in the past, the major push and pull factors behind contemporary migration are economic and political. Also, people are trying to move from the poor countries to the rich countries and from the politically repressed countries to more democratic countries. In addition, millions of people are fleeing civil and international warfare. Pressures for migration are growing, and in coming years they may constitute the world's greatest political and economic problem.

—Bergman and Renwick, *Introduction to Geography,* p. 197

Pattern: _____

10.   "I'll lose my job if they find out what I sent you." Most companies keep copies of all e-mail that is sent and received, and most do spot checks of the contents. When the above statement was discovered among an employee's outgoing messages, a company security officer wondered whether she had uncovered corporate espionage.

Was the message sender giving away—or perhaps selling—company secrets? In this case it was easy to find out: The security officer simply extracted the attachment that had been sent with the message. It turned out to be pornographic material—and the employee did indeed lose his job over this incident.

—Capron and Johnson, *Computers: Tools for an Information Age,* p. 328

Pattern: _____

Self-Test Summary

1. What are six common thought patterns used by authors to aid a reader's comprehension?	The patterns are definition, classification, order or sequence, cause and effect, comparison and contrast, and listing/enumeration.
2. What are the three parts of a definition?	The three parts are the term, the general class, and the distinguishing characteristics.
3. What is classification?	Classification breaks a broad topic into its major categories.
4. What are four ways order and sequence can be arranged?	The four ways are chronology, process, order of importance, and spatial arrangement.
5. Define cause and effect.	Cause and effect examines the relationship between two or more actions, events, or occurrences that are connected in time, with one being the direct result of the other.
6. What is the difference between comparison and contrast?	Comparison is used to emphasize similarities, while contrast emphasizes differences in ideas, theories, concepts, or events.
7. Describe the pattern called "listing/enumeration."	Listing/enumeration is a means of presenting supporting details that have no specific relationship to one another.
8. Besides the six common thought patterns you were asked to identify in the first question, what are some other patterns that are often used?	The patterns are • statement and clarification. • summary. • generalization and example. • addition.

The Development of Spectator Sports

Mark C. Carnes and John A. Garraty

Prereading Questions

1. What thought pattern(s) do you anticipate this reading will use?
2. What do you already know about the development of sports such as basketball, football, and baseball?

The Cincinnati Redstockings

1   The postwar era saw the first important development of spectator sports, because cities provided the concentrations of population necessary to support them. Curious relationships developed between upper- and working-class interests and between competitive sports as pure enjoyment for players and spectators and sports as something to bet on. Horse racing had strictly upper-class origins, but racetracks attracted huge crowds of ordinary people more intent on picking a winner than on improving the breed.

2   Professional boxing offers an even better example. It was in a sense a hobby of the rich, who sponsored favorite gladiators, offered prizes, and often wagered large sums on the matches. But the audiences were made up overwhelmingly of young working-class males, from whose ranks most of the fighters emerged. The gambling and also the brutality of the bloody, bare-knuckle character of the fights caused many communities to outlaw boxing, a fact that added to the appeal of the sport for some.

3   The first widely popular pugilist was the legendary "Boston Strong Boy," John L. Sullivan, who became heavyweight champion in 1882 by disposing of one Paddy Ryan in nine rounds. Sullivan was an immensely powerful man whose idea of fighting, according to his biographer, "was simply to hammer his opponent into unconsciousness," something he did repeatedly during his ten-year reign. Sullivan became an international celebrity and made and lost large

sums during this period. He was also the beneficiary of patronage in such forms as a diamond belt worth $10,000 presented to him by some of his admirers. Yet boxing remained a raffish, clandestine occupation. One of Sullivan's important fights took place in France, on the estate of Baron Rothschild, yet when it ended both he and his opponent were arrested.

4   Three major team games—baseball, football, and basketball—developed in something approaching their modern form during the last quarter of the century. Various forms of what became baseball were played long before that time. Organized teams, in most cases made up of upper-class amateurs, first emerged in the 1840s, but the game only became truly popular during the Civil War, when it was a major form of camp recreation for the troops.

5   After the war professional teams began to appear (the first, the Cincinnati Red Stockings, paid players between $800 and $1,400 for the season), and in 1876 teams in eight cities formed the National League. The American League followed in 1901. After a brief period of rivalry, the two leagues made peace in 1903, the year of the first World Series.

6   Organized play led to codification of the rules and improvements in technique and strategy, for example, the development of "minor" leagues; impartial umpires calling balls and strikes and ruling on close plays; the use of catcher's masks and padded gloves; the invention of various kinds of curves and other erratic pitches (often enhanced by "doctoring" the ball). As early as the 1870s, baseball was being called "the national game" and losing all upper-class connotations. Important games attracted crowds in the tens of thousands; betting became a problem. Despite its urban origins, its broad green fields and dusty base paths gave the game a rural character that only recently has begun to fade away.

7   Nobody "invented" baseball, but both football and basketball owe their present form to individuals. James Naismith's invention of basketball is undisputed. In 1891, while a student at a YMCA school, he attached peach baskets to the edge of an elevated running track in the gymnasium and drew up what are still the basic rules of the game. The first basketball was a soccer ball. The game was popular from the start, but because it was played indoors it was not an important spectator sport until much later.

8   Football was not created by one person in the way that basketball was; it evolved out of English rugby. For many decades it remained almost entirely a college sport (and thus played almost entirely by upper- and middle-class types). Organized collegiate sports dated back to before the Civil War; the first intercollegiate matches were rowing races between Harvard and Yale students. The first intercollege football game occurred when Rutgers defeated Princeton in 1869, and by the 1880s college football had become extremely popular.

9   Spectator sports had little appeal to women at this time and indeed for decades thereafter. And few women participated in organized athletics. Sports were "manly" activities; a woman might ride a bicycle, play croquet and perhaps a little tennis, but to display any concentrated interest in excelling in a sport was considered unfeminine.

Writing About the Reading

CHECKING YOUR VOCABULARY

1. For each of the words listed below, use context; prefixes, roots, and suffixes (see Chapter 3); and/or a dictionary to write a brief definition or synonym of the word as it is used in the reading.

   a. gladiators (para. 2) _____

   b. beneficiary (para. 3) _____

   c. raffish (para. 3) _____

   d. clandestine (para. 3) _____

   e. codification (para. 6) _____

   f. impartial (para. 6) _____

   g. erratic (para. 6) _____

   h. evolved (para. 8) _____

2. Underline new, specialized terms introduced in the reading (see Chapter 3).

3. Draw a word map of one of the words in the reading.

CHECKING YOUR COMPREHENSION

1. What aspect of the postwar era enabled the development of spectator sports?
2. What are the four major sports discussed in this reading?
3. Describe when and why baseball became popular.
4. List four examples of changes in baseball that resulted from organized play.
5. Who invented basketball? Describe how he did it.
6. From what sport did football evolve?
7. Why did few women participate in organized athletics in the postwar era?

THINKING CRITICALLY

1. What thought patterns are used in this reading?
2. Why does the author describe the relationships between upper and working classes as "curious" with regard to spectator sports?
3. What is the author's tone?
4. Describe the evidence provided by the author and evaluate its effectiveness.
5. Are you a sports fan? What did this reading teach you that you did not already know about your favorite sport(s)?

LEARNING/STUDY STRATEGY

Write a summary of this selection.

MyReadingLab

To practice recognizing thought patterns, go to http://www.myreadinglab .com. Click on "Study Plan," then on "Reading Skills," and then on "Patterns of Organization."

Thinking Visually About Graphics

Study the photo at left. Why was it included in a sociology textbook chapter that discusses deviance and conformity? What point does the photograph make? In what ways are the bride and groom conforming to society's norms? In what ways are they deviating from them?

LEARNING OBJECTIVES

- To develop strategies for reading graphics

- To learn to read different types of graphics

- To understand the use of cartoons and photographs

- To read online text

- To develop new reading and thinking strategies for reading electronic sources

- To evaluate Internet sources

- To avoid plagiarism

GRAPHICS: The Academic Link

Introductory textbooks in all the college disciplines, even math, are filled with photos, graphics, and diagrams. In fact, many textbooks have visual elements *on every single page*. Textbook authors have developed these tools to help visual learners understand and master the material. Graphics are more than just illustrations; they are *learning tools* that are intended to help you grasp the concepts and do well on examinations. Learning how to read and interpret these graphics is essential to doing well in your coursework.

GRAPHICS: The Career Link

Graphics are not exclusive to textbooks; you will see them everywhere, from magazines and newspapers to journals and billboards. Graphics have become exceedingly popular everywhere because they can be used to summarize large amounts of information in a visually appealing way. Thus you will encounter them regularly in your job, where you may even be required to *create* your own graphics.

■ How to Read Graphics

Tip for Communication/ Graphic Arts Majors

As you read graphics, you should always be asking yourself, "How can these graphics be made *better*? How could they be easier to read or more informative? How would I have formatted the material to make it accessible to my audience?

Many college textbooks include graphics and visuals such as tables, graphs, diagrams, maps, cartoons, and photographs. Some students find graphics intimidating, mainly because they have not learned how to approach them. All graphic devices serve an important function: they summarize and condense written information and make it easier to comprehend and retain. Graphics actually save you time by eliminating lengthy written explanations. To illustrate, first study the table in Figure 8-1 on page 224. Then read the paragraph in Figure 8-2 on page 224 that begins to present the factual information contained in the table.

Which would you rather read, the table or the paragraph? The table presents the same information concisely and in a more interesting format. The table also makes it easier to understand the relationship between individual bits of information. A glance at the table tells you that 19.1 percent of adolescent boys engaged in three problem behaviors, compared with 2.6 percent of girls. (Locating this information would be much more difficult if it were presented only in paragraph form.) By providing a visual picture of the information, graphics also make relationships, trends, and patterns easier to grasp.

FIGURE 8-1   Sample Table

Co-occurrence of Three Serious Problem Behaviors Among Adolescent Girls and Boys

NUMBER OF SERIOUS PROBLEM BEHAVIORS	FEMALES	MALES
None	57.4%	21.9%
One		
Sex	15.5	26.6
Substance use	7.9	2.8
Total	23.4	29.4
Two		
Sex/substance use	14.0	27.0
Substance use/assault	2.6	2.5
Total	16.6	29.5
Three		
Sex/substance use/assault	2.6	19.1

SOURCE: Conger and Galambos, *Adolescence and Youth,* pp. 296–97

FIGURE 8-2   Table in Paragraph Format

Paragraph:

57.4 percent of females exhibited no serious problem behaviors, 23.4 percent engaged in one (sex or substance use), 16.6 percent reported serious engagement in two problem behaviors, and 2.6 percent had been involved in all three. The males in the sample were more generally involved than females in problem behaviors, but 21.9 percent had not engaged seriously in any of the three problem behaviors. About 29 percent of the males had engaged seriously in one problem behavior (primarily sex), nearly 30 percent had engaged in two (primarily sex combined with substance use), and 19.1 percent had engaged in all three.

KEY STRATEGY: How to Read Graphics

Use the following suggestions to read graphics:

1. **Read the title or caption.**   The title tells you what situation or relationship is being described.

2. **Determine how the graphic is organized.**   If you are working with a table, note the column headings. For a graph, note what is marked on the vertical and horizontal axes.

3. **Note any symbols and abbreviations used.**

Tips for Education Majors

The students you will be teaching are used to and expect visuals. In fact, textbooks used in grades K–12 have more visual information than ever before. The teaching materials you'll be using will contain all the types of graphics shown in this chapter.

4. **Determine the scale or unit of measurement.**   Note how the variables are measured. For example, does a graph show expenditures in dollars, thousands of dollars, or millions of dollars?

5. **Identify the trend(s), pattern(s), or relationship(s) the graphic is intended to show.**   The following sections will discuss this step in greater detail.

6. **Read any footnotes.**   Footnotes, printed at the bottom of a graph or chart, indicate how the data were collected, explain what certain numbers or headings mean, or describe the statistical procedures used.

7. **Check the source.**   The source of data is usually cited at the bottom of the graph or chart. Unless the information was collected by the author, you are likely to find listed a research journal or publication from which the data were taken. Identifying the source is helpful in assessing the reliability of the data.

■ Types of Graphics

All graphics describe some type of relationship. Not coincidentally, these relationships correspond to the thought patterns we examined in Chapter 7.

Tables: Comparison and Classification of Information

Sociologists, psychologists, scientists, economists, and business analysts frequently use tables to organize and present statistical evidence. A table is an organized display of factual information, usually numbers or statistics. Its purpose is to classify information so that comparisons can be made between or among data.

Take a few minutes now to study Figure 8-3 (p. 226), using the suggestions listed on page 224 and above. Then use the following steps to analyze the table.

Tip for Math and Physical Science Majors

Because tables are an effective format for presenting numerical data, they are used frequently in the scientific disciplines. In fact, there are some tables that majors need to learn in detail to be proficient in their discipline. For example, chemistry majors will need to know the *periodic table of the elements* almost by heart.

1. **Determine how the data are classified, or divided.** This table classifies sources of sound according to level of intensity. Note that the relative sound intensity and the effects of prolonged exposure are also included.

2. **Make comparisons and look for trends.** This step involves surveying the rows and columns, noting how each entry compares with the others. Be sure to compare columns and rows, noting both similarities and differences and focusing on trends. In Figure 8-3, you might compare the relative intensities of several common sounds to which you are exposed.

3. **Draw conclusions.** Decide what the data show. You can conclude from Figure 8-3 that prolonged exposure to some sounds is dangerous. Often you will find clues, and sometimes direct statements, in the paragraphs that correspond to the table. The portion of the text that refers you to the table often makes a general statement about what the table is intended to highlight.

FIGURE 8-3 Sample Table

The Intensity of Some Common Sounds

SOUND SOURCE EXPOSURE	DECIBELS (dbA)	RELATIVE SOUND INTENSITY	EFFECT ON HEARING (PROLONGED EXPOSURE)
	0*	1	Audibility threshold
Breathing	10	10	
Whisper, rustling leaves	20	100	Very quiet
Quiet rural nighttime	30	1000	
Library, soft music	40	10,000	
Normal conversation	50	100,000	Quiet
Average office	60	1,000,000	
Vacuum cleaner	70	10,000,000	Annoying
Garbage disposal	80	100,000,000	Possible hearing damage
City traffic, diesel truck	90	1,000,000,000	Hearing damage (8 hours or more exposure)
Garbage truck, chain saw	100	10,000,000,000	Serious hearing damage (8 hours or more exposure)
Live rock band; portable stereo held close to ear	110	100,000,000,000	
Siren (close range); jet takeoff (200 yds)	120	1,000,000,000,000	Hearing pain threshold
Crack of gunfire	130	10,000,000,000,000	
Aircraft carrier deck	140	100,000,000,000,000	Eardrum ruptures
Jet takeoff (close range)	150	1,000,000,000,000,000	

*The threshold of hearing is 0 decibels because the scale is logarithmic, and the logarithm of 1 is 0.

SOURCE: Byer and Shainberg, *Living Well: Health in Your Hands*, p. 788

Once you have drawn your conclusions, stop, think, and react. For example, you might consider what the data in Figure 8-3 suggest about your daily activities.

EXERCISE 8-1

Interpreting a Table

Study the table shown in Figure 8-3 and answer the following questions.

1. What is the decibel level of a normal conversation?
2. At what decibel level does hearing damage become possible?
3. What sound source has the highest relative sound intensity?
4. What sound sources are associated with the hearing pain threshold?

Graphs: Relationships Among Variables

Graphs depict the relationship between two or more variables such as price and demand or expenditures over time. Put simply, they are pictures of relationships

☑ Tip for Business Majors

The data and information collected by businesses—showing important variables like income and profit—are often portrayed in graphs in key business documents (such as annual reports) and presentations. It is important that you understand not only how to read these graphs, but also how to create them using common computer programs such as Microsoft Excel.

between two or more sets of information. As you read and study in various academic disciplines, you will encounter many variations of a few basic types of graphs.

Line Graphs   In line graphs, information is plotted along a vertical and a horizontal axis, with one or more variables plotted on each. The resulting graph makes it easy to see the relationship between the variables. A sample line graph is shown in Figure 8-4. The line graph compares population statistics and change for four racial/ethnic groups in the United States.

In addition to comparison, the graph also allows you to see changes in population within each group throughout the years. The graph enables you to determine the general trend or pattern among the variables. For example, this graph shows a steady decrease in the White, non-Hispanic population.

FIGURE 8-4   A Sample Line Graph

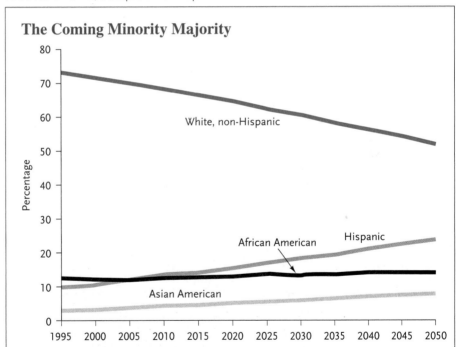

Based on current birthrates and immigration rates, the Census Bureau estimates that the demographics of the country should change as shown in the accompanying graph. Extend the lines a bit beyond the year 2050, and it is clear that the minority groups will soon be in the majority nationwide. Of course, should the rates of birth and immigration change, so will these estimates. But already there are 65 congressional districts with a minority majority, about 85 percent of which are represented in the House by an African American, a Hispanic, or an Asian American.

Source: Edwards et al., *Government in America,* Twelfth Edition

EXERCISE 8-2   **Interpreting a Line Graph**

Study the line graph shown in Figure 8-4 (p. 227) and answer the following questions.

1. What are the four racial/ethnic groups depicted on the graph?
2. Which two groups show a steady increase in population over all the years?
3. In what ten-year period are the African-American and Hispanic populations almost the same?
4. What general trends does this graph reveal?

Circle Graphs   A circle graph, also called a pie chart, is used to show the relationships of parts to the whole or to show how given parts of a unit have been divided or classified. Figure 8-5 is a circle graph that shows the breakdown of a typical person's carbon footprint. (The text originally accompanying this graph explained that a carbon footprint is the impact of human activities on the environment in terms of the percentages of greenhouse gases produced.) In this graph, 12 categories of human activities are presented.

FIGURE 8-5   *Sample Circle Graph*

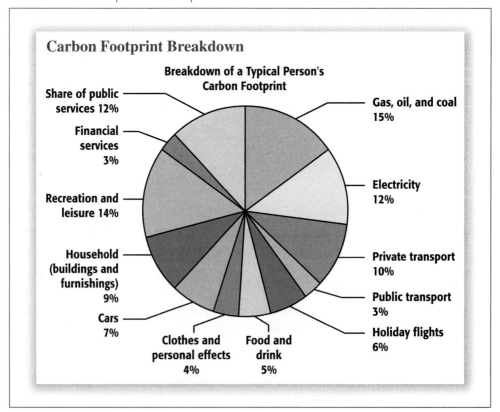

Carbon Footprint Breakdown

Breakdown of a Typical Person's Carbon Footprint

Share of public services 12%
Financial services 3%
Recreation and leisure 14%
Household (buildings and furnishings) 9%
Cars 7%
Clothes and personal effects 4%
Food and drink 5%
Gas, oil, and coal 15%
Electricity 12%
Private transport 10%
Public transport 3%
Holiday flights 6%

SOURCE: Solomon, *Consumer Behavior,* p. 160.

Circle graphs often are used to emphasize proportions or to show the relative size or importance of various parts. You can see from this graph that gas, oil, and coal make up the largest part of a typical person's carbon footprint.

EXERCISE 8-3

Interpreting a Circle Graph

Study the circle graph shown in Figure 8-5 and answer the following questions.

1. What portion of a typical person's carbon footprint is attributed to recreation and leisure activities?
2. What portion is attributed to buildings and furnishings?
3. Which category of human activities has a greater impact: public or private transport? By how much?
4. What are the four categories that make the largest impact? What are the four categories with the smallest impact?

Bar Graphs   A bar graph is often used to make comparisons between quantities or amounts. The horizontal scale often measures time and the vertical scale quantity. A sample bar graph is shown in Figure 8-6. It depicts the number of species known to have become extinct since 1600.

FIGURE 8-6   Sample Bar Graph

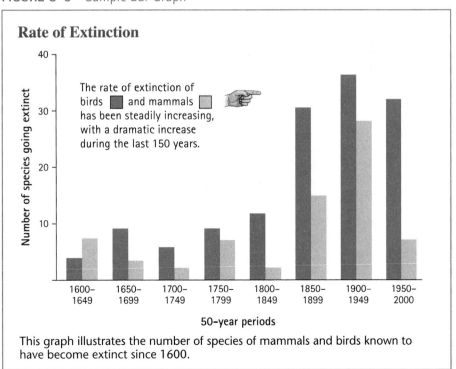

This graph illustrates the number of species of mammals and birds known to have become extinct since 1600.

SOURCE: Belk and Borden, *Biology*, Second Edition, p. 363.

Interpreting a Bar Graph

Study the bar graph in Figure 8-6 (p. 229) and answer the following questions.

1. What two groups are shown on this graph?
2. In which 50-year periods did more than 30 species of birds go extinct?
3. In which 50-year period did the largest number of mammals go extinct?
4. In which 50-year periods did the rate of extinction for birds decrease?
5. What major trend is shown on this graph?

Diagrams: Explanations of Processes

Tip for Nursing, Allied Health, Life Science, and Technical Majors

Diagrams are common in biology, nursing, and health textbooks because they provide a visual summary of processes that cannot be seen directly. For example, biologists need to know what is going on at a cellular level inside the body, and nurses need to know how germs are spread. Diagrams can make complicated concepts easier to understand and provide an excellent review when you are preparing for exams.

Diagrams are often included in technical and scientific as well as business and economics texts to explain processes. Diagrams are intended to help you see relationships between parts and understand sequences. Figure 8-7, which is taken from a geography textbook, shows how the food chain works. It shows how plant-eating animals, called herbivores, begin the food chain by eating plants, how carnivores (meat-eating animals) consume herbivores, and how animal bodily wastes return nutrients to the soil. These nutrients may be used for new plant growth, thus creating a cyclical relationship.

Reading diagrams differs from reading other types of graphics in that diagrams often correspond to fairly large segments of text. This means you have to switch back and forth frequently between the text and the diagram to determine what part of the process each paragraph is discussing.

Because diagrams of processes and the corresponding text are often difficult, complicated, or highly technical, plan to read these sections more than once. Use the first reading to grasp the overall process. In subsequent readings, focus on the details of the process, examining each step and understanding how the process unfolds.

One of the best ways to study a diagram is to redraw it without referring to the original, including as much detail as possible. Redrawing is a true test of whether you understand the process you have diagrammed. Alternatively, you can test your understanding and recall of the process illustrated in a diagram by explaining it step by step in writing, using your own words.

Interpreting a Diagram

Study the diagram in Figure 8-7 and answer the following questions.

1. Cover the diagram and try to redraw it from memory. When you have finished your drawing, compare it with the original and fill in any details you may have left out.
2. Explain the process illustrated in the diagram using your own words to describe each step.

FIGURE 8-7   Sample Diagram

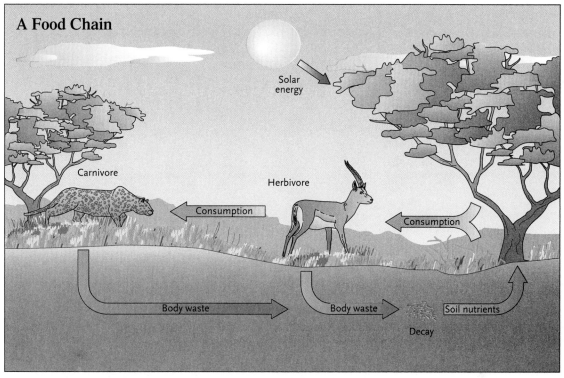

SOURCE: McKnight, *Physical Geography: A Landscape Appreciation,* p. 148

Maps: Physical Relationships

Maps describe relationships and provide information about location and direction. They are commonly found in geography and history texts, and they also appear in ecology, biology, and anthropology texts. Most of us think of maps as describing distances and locations, but maps are also used to describe placement of geographical and ecological features such as areas of pollution, areas of population density, or political data (voting districts).

When reading maps, use the following steps:

1. **Read the caption.** This identifies the subject of the map.
2. **Use the legend or key to identify the symbols or codes used.**
3. **Note distance scales.**
4. **Study the map, looking for trends or key points.** Often, the text that accompanies the map states the key points that the map illustrates.
5. **Try to visualize, or create a mental picture of, the map.**
6. **As a learning and study aid, write, in your own words, a statement of what the map shows.**

FIGURE 8-8 Sample Map

The location of the worst hazardous waste sites.

Source: Henslin, *Essentials of Sociology*, Seventh Edition, p. 431.

Now refer to the map shown in Figure 8-8, which is taken from a sociology textbook.

This map shows the locations of the worst hazardous waste sites in the United States.

EXERCISE 8-6 ### Interpreting a Map

Study the map in Figure 8-8 and answer the following questions.

1. In what area of the country are most of the hazardous waste sites located?
2. Which three states have the highest numbers of hazardous waste sites?
3. Which state has no hazardous waste sites?
4. Is the map more or less effective than a table containing the same data? Why?

EXERCISE 8-7 ### Creating a Graphic

Use the following statistics to construct a graphic that organizes some or all of this information on world population growth. Exchange your graphic with a classmate, and offer each other ideas for improvement.

1. In 1970, the world population was 3,632 million.
2. In 1990, the world population was 5,320 million.
3. In 2000, the world population was 6,080 million.
4. In 1970, the population of Africa was 344 million.

5. In 1990, the population of Africa was 660 million.
6. In 2000, the population of Africa was 805 million.
7. In 1970, the population of Asia was 2,045 million.
8. In 1990, the population of Asia was 3,111 million.
9. In 2000, the population of Asia was 3,688 million.
10. In 1970, the population of Europe was 462 million.
11. In 1990, the population of Europe was 499 million.
12. In 2000, the population of Europe was 729 million.

EXERCISE 8-8

Analyzing Graphics

Select two different graphic devices used in a textbook chapter you have read recently, and answer the following questions about each.

1. What is the subject of the graphic?
2. What is its purpose?
3. If it presents data, how is it organized? If it is a diagram, how does it achieve its purpose?
4. What is its source, and how recent is it?

■ Understanding Visuals

Many textbooks contain numerous cartoons and photographs, always related in some way to chapter content. Be sure to study both cartoons and photographs closely to determine why they were included.

Cartoons

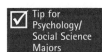

Tip for Psychology/ Social Science Majors

While most college textbooks feature many photographs, they are particularly important in social science textbooks, where they are often used to illustrate concepts taken directly from "real life." Photos used to speak for themselves, but today they are often accompanied by extended captions with critical thinking or other questions to help you connect the image to content: use them to help you learn new concepts.

Cartoons are a visual feature included in textbooks to make a point quickly or simply to lighten the text by adding a touch of humor about the topic at hand. Cartoons usually appear without a title or legend, and there is usually no reference within the text to the cartoon.

Cartoons can make abstract ideas and concepts concrete and real. Pay close attention to cartoons, especially if you are a visually oriented learner. They may help you recall ideas easily by serving as a recall clue that triggers your memory of related material. The cartoon in Figure 8-9 (p. 234) appears in a sociology textbook chapter, Thinking Visually About Graphics. Notice that it humorously illustrates the concept of conformity and deviance.

Photographs: A Visual Impression

Photographs are often considered an art form, but they serve some of the same purposes as other graphics: they are used in textbooks in place of verbal descriptions to present information. Photographs are also used to spark your interest and, often, to draw out an emotional response or impression. Study the photograph shown in Figure 8-10 (p. 235) that follows.

The photograph of Dian Fossey, a scientist who studied gorilla behavior, reveals the trusting relationship she established with gorillas. Use the following steps to understand photographs:

FIGURE 8–9

1. **Read the caption to discover the subject and context of the photograph.**
2. **If the photo is referred to in the text, read the text before studying the photograph.** What details are emphasized? What conclusions are drawn?
3. **Study the photograph.** What is your first overall impression? What details did you notice first? Answering these questions will lead you to discover the purpose of the photograph.

EXERCISE 8-9

Interpreting a Photograph

Study the photograph shown in Figure 8-10 (p. 235) and answer the questions below.

1. What emotional reaction does this photograph elicit?

   _____

   _____

2. What details do you notice in the photograph that would be less effective expressed in words alone?

   _____

   _____

■ Reading Online Text

Reading online text is very different from reading traditional printed text such as textbooks or magazines or newspaper articles. Because Web sites differ from print sources, they require a different mind-set and different reading strategies.

FIGURE 8-10   Sample Photograph

Much of what we know in science is due to simple observation. Dian Fossey told us a great deal about mountain gorillas by being able to move among them. The arrogant, tough, and dedicated Fossey was instrumental in protecting these shy beasts from poachers (who sell gorilla hands to wealthy Europeans to be used for ashtrays) until she was killed by an assailant in her mountain cabin.

Source: Wallace, *Biology*, p. 38 (text); The Gorilla Organization (photo).

■ Developing New Ways of Thinking and Reading

Reading online sources demands a different type of thinking from reading print sources. A print source is linear—it goes in a straight line from idea to idea. Online sources, due to the presence of links, tend to be multidirectional and let you follow numerous paths (see illustration).

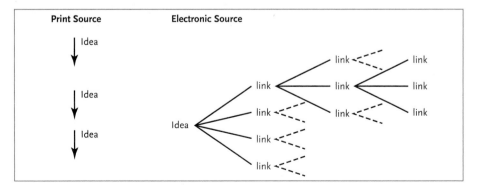

Reading online also requires new strategies. To read online easily and effectively you must adapt how you read.

KEY STRATEGY: How to Read Online

Here are some specific suggestions for reading online.

1. **Focus on your purpose.**   Focus clearly on your purposes for visiting the site. What information do you need?

2. **Spend a few minutes discovering how the site is organized.**   Scroll through it quickly, and use the site map if one is provided, to determine how it is organized and what information is available.

3. **Expect the first screen to grab your attention and make a main point.** Web site authors know that many people who read a Web page do not scroll down to see the next screenful.

4. **Get used to the Web site's design before you attempt to obtain information from the site.**   Your eye may have a tendency to focus on color or movement, rather than on print. Because some Web sites are highly visual, they require visual as well as verbal thinking. The author intends for you to respond to photos, graphics, and animation.

5. **Consider the order in which you want to take in information.**   Choose an order in which to explore links; avoid randomly clicking on them. Doing so is somewhat like randomly choosing pages to read out of a reference book.

6. **Expect shorter, less detailed sentences and paragraphs.**   Much online communication tends to be briefer and more concise than in traditional sources. As a result, you may have to mentally fill in transitions and make inferences about the relationships among ideas. For example, you may have to infer similarities and differences or recognize cause and effect connections.

| EXERCISE 8–10 | **Comparing Print and Online Sources** |

Locate a Web site on a topic related to one of the end-of-chapter readings in this text. Write a list of characteristics that distinguish the site from the print readings.

| EXERCISE 8–11 | **Analyzing Learning Styles** |

LEARNING
COLLABORATIVELY

In groups of two or three students, consider at least two aspects of learning style. For each, discuss the tendencies, limitations, and implications these particular learning styles may have for reading online text. For example, consider how a visual learner would approach a Web site with numerous links and buttons. Then consider how a creative learner's approach might differ.

■ Evaluating Internet Sources

Although the Internet contains a great deal of valuable information and resources, it also contains rumor, gossip, hoaxes, and misinformation. In other words, not all Internet sources are trustworthy. You must evaluate a source

TABLE 8-1   Types of Web Sites

TYPE	PURPOSE AND DESCRIPTION	DOMAIN	SAMPLE SITES
Informational	To present facts, information, and research data. May contain reports, statistical data, results of research studies, and reference materials.	.edu or .gov	http://www.haskins.yale.edu/ http://www.census.gov/
News	To provide current information on local, national, and international news. Often supplements print newspapers, periodicals, and television news programs.	.com or .org	http://news.yahoo.com/ http://www.theheart.org/
Advocacy	To promote a particular cause or point of view. Usually concerned with a controversial issue; often sponsored by nonprofit groups.	.com or .org	http://www.goveg.com/ http://www.bradycampaign.org/
Personal	To provide information about an individual and his/her interests and accomplishments. May list publications or include the individual's résumé.	Varies. May contain .com, .org, .biz, .edu, .info. May contain a tilde (~).	http://www.jessamyn.com/ http://www.mitra.biz/resume.htm http://www.maryrussell.info/ http://www.plu.edu/~chasega/
Commercial	To promote goods or services. May provide news and information related to products.	.com, .biz, .info	http://www.nmgroup.biz/ http://www.alhemer.com/ http://www.vintageradio.info/

before accepting it. Here are some guidelines to follow when evaluating Internet sources.

Discover the Purpose of Web Sites

There are thousands of Web sites, and they vary widely in purpose. Table 8-1 summarizes five primary types of Web sites.

EXERCISE 8-12   **Determining the Purpose of Web Sites**

Determine the purpose of each of the following Web sites using the information in Table 8-1. Some sites may have more than one purpose. Be sure to investigate the whole site carefully and explain your choices.

1. College Finder: http://www.college-finder.info/
2. Israel—A Country Study: http://lcweb2.loc.gov/frd/cs/iltoc.html
3. Senator Chuck Schumer: http://schumer.senate.gov/
4. Center for Science in the Public Interest: http://www.cspinet.org/
5. Meridian: http://www.ncsu.edu/meridian/
6. Professor Hunt's Dog Page: http://www.cs.duke.edu/~rodger/whoami/

Evaluate the Content of a Web Site

It is always important to evaluate the content of a Web site to determine if it is appropriate for your intended use.

KEY STRATEGY: Evaluating a Web Site's Content

Use the following strategies to evaluate content:

1. **Evaluate the site's appropriateness.** To be worthwhile a Web site should contain the information you need. It should answer one or more of your search questions. If the site touches upon answers to your questions but does not address them in detail, check the links on the site to see if they lead you to more detailed information. If they do not, search for another, more useful site.

2. **Evaluate the source.** Another important step in evaluating a Web site is to determine its source. Ask yourself "Who is the sponsor?" and "Why was this site put up on the Web?" The sponsor of a Web site is the person or organization that paid for it to be created and placed on the Web. The sponsor often suggests the purpose of a Web site. For example, a Web site sponsored by Nike is designed to promote its products, whereas a site sponsored by a university library is designed to help students use its resources more effectively.

   If you are uncertain of who sponsors a Web site, check its URL, its copyright, and the links it offers. The ending of the URL often suggests the type of sponsorship, as shown in Table 8-1. The copyright indicates the owner of the site. Links may also reveal the sponsor. Some links may lead to commercial advertising; others may lead to sites sponsored by nonprofit groups, for example.

   Another way to check the ownership of a Web site is to try to locate the site's home page. You can do this by using only the first part of its URL—up to the first slash (/) mark. For example, suppose you found information on animal welfare laws in America on the Internet and you wanted to track its source. Its URL is http://www.defra.gov.uk/animalh/welfare/act/affect.htm#7. This page deals with some sort of animal welfare act, but you are not sure it deals with the United States. If you go back in the URL to http://www.defra.gov.uk/ you will discover that the sponsoring organization is the Department for Environment, Food and Rural Affairs in the United Kingdom.

3. **Evaluate the level of technical detail.** A Web site should contain the level of detail that is suited to your purpose. Some sites may provide information that is too sketchy for your search purposes; others assume a level of background knowledge or technical sophistication that you lack. For example, if you are writing a short, introductory-level paper on global warming, information on the University of New Hampshire's NASA Earth Observing System site (http://www.eos-ids.sr.unh.edu/) may be too technical and contain more information than you need, unless you have some previous knowledge in that field.

4. **Evaluate the presentation.** Information on a Web site should be presented clearly; it should be well written. If you find a site that is not clear and well written, you should be suspicious of it. If the author did not take time to present ideas clearly and correctly, he or she may not have taken time to collect accurate information, either.

5. **Evaluate completeness.** Determine whether the site provides complete information on its topic. Does it address all aspects of the topic that you feel it should? For example, if a Web site on important twentieth-century American poets does not mention Robert Frost, then the site is incomplete. If you discover that a site is incomplete, search for sites that present a more thorough treatment of the topic.

6. **Evaluate the links.** Many reputable sites supply links to related sites. Make sure that the links work and are current. Also check to see if the sites to which you are sent are reliable sources of information. If the links do not work or the sources appear unreliable, you should question the reliability of the site itself. Also determine whether the links provided are comprehensive or present only a representative sample. Either is acceptable, but the site should make clear the nature of the links it is providing.

EXERCISE 8-13

Evaluating the Content of Web Sites

Evaluate the content of two of the following sites. Explain why you would either trust or distrust each site for reliable content.

1. http://www.luminarium.org/
2. http://www.earlham.edu/~peters/knotlink.htm
3. http://www.age-of-the-sage.org/psychology/

Evaluate the Accuracy and Timeliness of a Web Site

When using information on a Web site for an academic paper, it is important to be sure that you have found accurate information. One way to determine the accuracy of a Web site is to compare it with print sources (periodicals and books) on the same topic. If you find a wide discrepancy between the Web site and the printed sources, do not trust the Web site. Another way to determine the accuracy of a site's information is to compare it with other Web sites that address the same topic. If discrepancies exist, further research is needed to determine which site is most accurate.

The site itself will also provide clues about the accuracy of its information.

KEY STRATEGY: Evaluating a Web Site's Accuracy

 Tip for Education Majors

Because school-age children often believe whatever they read, it is important to teach them how to determine the accuracy and validity of Web sites. Younger children need simpler information. For instance, one good guideline is that Web addresses ending in ".edu" (for a college or university) or ".gov" (for a government organization) are usually reliable.

Ask yourself the following questions:

- **Are the author's name and credentials provided?** A well-known writer with established credentials is likely to author only reliable, accurate information. If no author is given, you should question whether the information is accurate.
- **Is contact information for the author included on the site?** Often, sites provide an e-mail address where the author may be contacted.
- **Is the information complete or in summary form?** If it is a summary, use the site to find the original source. Original information has less chance of error and is usually preferred in academic papers.
- **If opinions are offered, are they presented clearly as opinions?** Authors who disguise their opinions as facts are not trustworthy.
- **Does the writer make unsubstantiated assumptions or base his or her ideas on misconceptions?** If so, the information presented may not be accurate.
- **Does the site provide a list of works cited?** As with any form of research, sources used to put information up on a Web site must be documented. If sources are not credited, you should question the accuracy of the Web site.

It may be helpful to determine whether the information is available in print form. If it is, try to obtain the print version. Errors may occur when the article or essay is put up on the Web. Web sites move, change, and delete information, so it may be difficult for a reader of an academic paper to locate the Web site that you used in writing it. Also, page numbers are easier to cite in print sources than in electronic ones.

Although the Web is well known for providing up-to-the-minute information, not all Web sites are current. Evaluate the timeliness by checking

- the date on which the Web site was mounted (put on the Web).
- the date when the document you are using was added.
- the date when the site was last revised.
- the date when the links were last checked.

This information is usually provided at the end of the site's home page or at the end of the document you are using.

EXERCISE 8-14

Evaluating the Accuracy of Web Sites

Evaluate the accuracy of two of the following Web sites.

1. http://www.idausa.org/facts/pg.html
2. http://www.smokingsection.com/issues1.html#smoke
3. http://www.fairus.org/

EXERCISE 8-15

Evaluating the Timeliness of Web Sites

Evaluate the timeliness of two of the following Web sites, using the directions on page 240.

1. http://www.rmc.sierraclub.org/ipg/curriss.htm
2. http://www.mhric.org/mozart/index2.html
3. http://www.genome.gov/10001676

EXERCISE 8-16

Evaluating Web Sites

Evaluate each of the sites you examined for Exercise 8-12. Assign each a rating of 1–5 (1 = low reliability; 5 = high reliability). Be prepared to discuss your ratings.

EXERCISE 8-17

Evaluating a Web Site

Visit a Web site and become familiar with its organization and content. Evaluate it using the suggested criteria. Then write a brief paragraph explaining why the Web site is or is not a reliable source.

■ Avoiding Plagiarism

 Tip for Humanities/ Liberal Arts Majors

Most English courses have heavy writing requirements, including research papers. (In fact, research papers are very common regardless of your major.) Be aware when writing research papers that it is essential you confirm the validity and quality of any Web materials you use.

As you write papers for college classes, you will probably use electronic sources to locate the information you need. As you read and take notes, and later, as you write the paper, you need to know the rules for indicating that you have taken information or ideas from the work of other people. You identify your sources in order to help readers find a source if they want to look further into the ideas of that author, as well as to give credit to the person who originally wrote the material or thought of the idea.

Plagiarism means borrowing someone else's ideas or exact wording without giving that person credit. If you take information on Frank Lloyd Wright's architecture from a reference source, but do not indicate where you found it, you have plagiarized. If you take the six-word phrase "Martinez, the vengeful, despicable drug czar" from an online news article on the war on drugs without putting quotation marks around it and noting the source, you have plagiarized. Plagiarism is intellectually dishonest because you are taking someone else's ideas or wording and passing it off as your own.

The Internet, though a tremendous source of information, makes it easy for a person to copy something from a document and paste it into his or her own paper without giving credit to the source. Numerous Web sites offer student papers for sale on the Internet. Using these papers and submitting them as one's own is also considered plagiarism.

What Constitutes Plagiarism

Plagiarism can be intentional (planned) or unintentional (done by accident or oversight). Either way it carries the same academic penalty. If you buy a paper from an Internet site or deliberately copy and paste a section of an article from a Web site into your paper, your plagiarism is intentional. If you take notes from a source and copy exact wording, forget to enclose the wording in quotation marks, and later use that exact wording in your paper, your plagiarism is unintentional, but it is still dishonest.

KEY STRATEGY: What Is Plagiarism?

Here are some guidelines that will help you understand exactly what is considered plagiarism:

- **Plagiarism** is the use of another person's words without giving credit to that person.
- **Plagiarism** uses another person's theory, opinion, or idea without listing where the information was taken from.
- **Plagiarism** results when another person's exact words are not placed inside quotation marks. Both the quotation marks and a citation (reference) to the original source are required.
- Paraphrasing (rewording) another person's words without giving credit to that person is **plagiarism.**
- Using facts, data, graphs, charts, and so on without stating where they were taken from is **plagiarism.**
- Using commonly known facts or information is not **plagiarism** and you need not give a source for your information. For example, the fact that Neil Armstrong set foot on the moon in 1969 is widely known and so does not require documentation.

There are academic penalties for plagiarism. You may receive a failing grade on your paper or you may fail the entire course. At some institutions you can even be academically dismissed.

KEY STRATEGY: Avoiding Online Plagiarism

Use the following suggestions to avoid unintentional plagiarism:

- **If you copy exact words from any source, put them in quotation marks in your notes, along with the publication information: the author, title, publisher, date of publication, and page number of the source, or, for**

Web sites, the author, the name of the site or page, its date of publication, the date you accessed the Web site, and its URL.** Be sure to consult a style manual for details on how to indicate in your paper which material is borrowed and how to set up a list of the works you used in your paper.

- **List sources for all the information you include in your notes,** regardless of whether the information takes the form of direct quotations, paraphrases, or summaries of someone else's ideas.
- **Never copy and paste directly from a Web site into your paper without enclosing the words in quotation marks and listing their source.**
- **When paraphrasing someone else's words, phrase the information in your own words.** Try not to follow the exact same organization of information. Credit where the information came from.
- **Write paraphrases without looking at the original text** so you will rephrase it in your own words.

EXERCISE 8-18   Identifying Plagiarism

Read the following passage from Sociology for the Twenty-First Century *by Tim Curry, Robert Jiobu, and Kent Schwirian. Place a check mark next to each statement that follows that is an example of plagiarism.*

Mexican Americans. Currently, Mexican Americans are the second-largest racial or ethnic minority in the United States, but by early in the next century they will be the largest group. Their numbers will swell as a result of continual immigration from Mexico and the relatively high Mexican birth rate. Mexican Americans are one of the oldest racial-ethnic groups in the United States. Under the terms of the treaty ending the Mexican-American War in 1848, Mexicans living in territories acquired by the United States could remain there and were to be treated as American citizens. Those that did stay became known as "Californios," "Tejanos," or "Hispanos."

_____ a. Mexican Americans are the second-largest minority in the United States. Their number grows as more people immigrate from Mexico.

_____ b. After the Mexican-American War, those Mexicans living in territories owned by the U.S. became American citizens and were called "Californios," "Tejanos," and "Hispanos" (Curry, Jiobu, and Schwirian, 207).

_____ c. "Mexican Americans are one of the oldest racial-ethnic groups in the United States."

_____ d. The Mexican-American War ended in 1848.

Self-Test Summary

1. What are the functions of graphics?	Graphics summarize and condense information and emphasize or clarify relationships.
2. What is it important to do when reading graphics?	It is important to read the caption; determine the organization of the graphic; note symbols, abbreviations, and/or scales; identify trends or patterns; study footnotes; and check the source of information.
3. Name three different types of graphs and explain how they work.	Line graphs plot information along a vertical and horizontal axis, with one or more variables on each; circle graphs, or pie charts, show the relationships of parts to the whole; and bar graphs make comparisons between quantities or amounts.
4. Describe the following types of graphics in terms of how they supply information: Tables Graphs Diagrams	• Tables are used to compare and classify data or information. • Graphs depict relationships among variables. • Diagrams present visual representations of processes or sequences.
5. Describe the function of each of the following graphics: Maps Cartoons Photographs	• Maps are used to describe physical relationships. • Cartoons make abstract ideas concrete and real, or may be used to add a touch of humor. • Photographs provide visual impressions and often provoke an emotional response.
6. What factors should you take into consideration when evaluating a Web site?	To evaluate a Web site consider content (appropriateness, source or sponsor, level of technical detail, presentation, completeness, links), accuracy, and timeliness.
7. What should you do when you read online text?	• Identify the purpose of the site. • Familiarize yourself with the site's design and layout. • Pay attention to how the information is organized. • Use links to find additional information.
8. What are plagiarism and online plagiarism?	Plagiarism is presenting someone else's work or ideas as your own. Online plagiarism refers to borrowing information, ideas, or papers found on the Internet and presenting them as your own.

Biology

Biodiversity Loss and Species Extinction

Scott Brennan and Jay Withgott

Prereading Questions

1. What is biodiversity?
2. What species are considered endangered or extinct?

1 Biodiversity at all levels is being lost to human impact, most irretrievably in the extinction of species, which, once vanished, can never return. Extinction occurs when the last member of a species dies and the species ceases to exist. In contrast, the extinction of a particular population from a given area, but not the entire species globally, is called **extirpation.** The tiger has been extirpated from most of its historic range, but it is not yet extinct. Although a species that is extirpated from one place may still exist in others, extirpation is an erosive process that can, over time, lead to extinction.

Extinction Is "Natural"

2 Extirpation and extinction are natural processes. If organisms did not naturally go extinct, we would be up to our ears in dinosaurs, trilobites, ammonites, and the millions of other types of organisms that vanished from Earth long before humans appeared. Paleontologists estimate that roughly 99% of all species that have ever lived are already extinct; that is, the wealth of species on our planet today comprises only about 1% of all the species that ever lived. Most extinctions preceding the appearance of humans have occurred one by one, at a rate that paleontologists refer to as the **background rate of extinction.** For example, the fossil record indicates that for both birds and mammals, one species in the world typically became extinct every 500–1,000 years.

The Earth Has Experienced Five Previous Mass Extinction Episodes

3 Extinction rates have risen far above this background rate during several mass extinction events of Earth's history. In the last 440 million years, there have been five major episodes of mass extinction (Figure A, p. 246), each of which has taken more than one-fifth of life's families and at least half its species (Table B, p. 247). The most severe episode occurred at the end of the Permian period, approximately 248 million years ago, when close to 54% of all families, 90% of all species, and 95% of marine species became extinct. The best-known episode occurred at the end of the Cretaceous period, 65 million years ago, when an apparent asteroid impact brought an end to the dinosaurs and many other groups. In addition, there is evidence for further mass extinctions in the Cambrian period and earlier, more than half a billion years ago.

FIGURE A

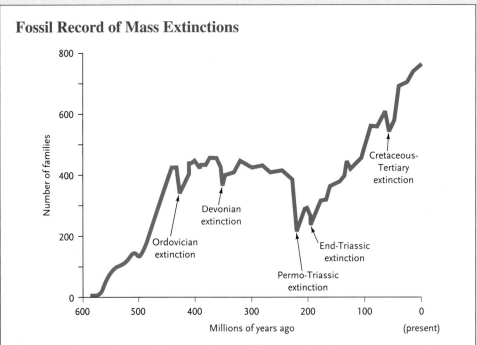

Fossil Record of Mass Extinctions

Figure A   The fossil record shows evidence of five episodes of mass extinction during the past half-billion years of Earth history. At the end of the Ordovician, the end of the Devonian, the end of the Permian, the end of the Triassic, and the end of the Cretaceous, 50%–95% of the world's species appear to have gone extinct. Each time, biodiversity has later rebounded to equal or higher levels, but the rebound has taken millions of years in each case.

4   If current trends continue, the modern era, also known as the Quaternary period, may see the extinction of more than half of all species. Although similar in scale to previous mass extinctions, today's ongoing mass extinction is different in two primary respects. First, humans are causing it. Second, humans will suffer as a result of it.

Humans Set the Sixth Mass Extinction in Motion Years Ago

5   In our written history, we have recorded many instances of human-induced species extinction over the past few hundred years. Sailors documented the extinction of the dodo on the Indian Ocean island of Mauritius in the 17th century, for example, and we still have a few of the dodo's body parts in museums. Among North American birds in the past two centuries, we have lost the passenger pigeon, Carolina parakeet, great auk, Labrador duck, and probably the Bachman's warbler and ivory-billed woodpecker. Several more species, including the whooping crane, California condor, and Kirtland's warbler, teeter on the brink of extinction.

6   However, species extinctions caused by humans likely precede written history; people may have been hunting species to extinction for thousands of years. Scientists have inferred

Table B   Mass Extinctions

EVENT	DATE (MYA: MILLIONS OF YEARS AGO)	CAUSE	TYPES OF LIFE MOST AFFECTED	PERCENT OF LIFE DEPLETED
Ordovician	440 mya	unknown	marine organisms; but terrestial record unknown	>20% of families
Devonian	370 mya	unknown	marine organisms; but terrestial record unknown	>20% of families
Permo-Triassic (P-T)	250 mya	possibly volcanism	marine organisms; but terrestial record less known	>50% of families; 80–95% of species
end-Triassic	202 mya	unknown	marine organisms; but terrestial record less known	20% of families; 50% of genera
Cretaceous-Teritary (K-T)	65 mya	asteroid impact	marine and terrestial organisms, including dinosaurs	15% of families; >50% of species
Current	Beginning 0.01 mya	human impact *via* habitat destruction, land and resource use, hunting, and promoting invasive species	large animals, specialized organisms, island organisms, organisms hunted or harvested by humans	ongoing

this from archaeological evidence in areas of the world that humans have colonized relatively recently. In case after case, a wave of extinctions has seemingly followed close on the heels of human arrival (Figure C, p. 248). After Polynesians reached Hawaii, for instance, many birds went extinct, and evidence of an extinction wave also exists from larger island nations, such as New Zealand and Madagascar. The pattern also holds for at least two continents; large vertebrates died off in Australia after Aborigines arrived roughly 50,000 years ago, and North America lost 35 genera of large mammals after humans arrived in the continent at least 10,000–13,000 years ago. Although some scientists hold that climate variation instead of hunting may be responsible for the North American extinctions, the fact that human arrival co-occurs with extinction waves independently in several regions at different times in history is certainly strongly suggestive.

Current Extinction Rates Are Much Higher than Normal

7   Humans have raised the rate of extinction above the background rate for centuries now. However, today species loss is proceeding at a still more accelerated pace as our population growth and resource consumption put ever-increasing strain on habitats and wildlife.

FIGURE C

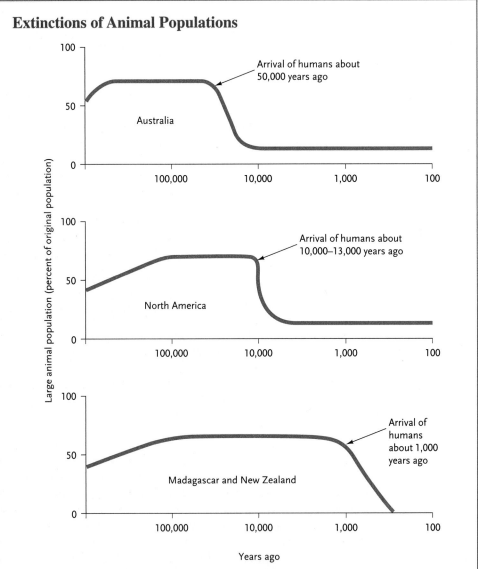

Extinctions of Animal Populations

Figure C Shortly after humans arrived in Australia, North America, Madagascar, and New Zealand a large number of species of large mammals and flightless birds became extinct. It is thought that this did not occur in Africa because humans and other animals evolved together there for many millions of years.

8   In late 1995, 1,500 of the world's leading scientists reported to the United Nations that the current global extinction rate was more than 1,000 times greater than it would have been without human destruction of habitat. The scientists went on to report in their Global Biodiversity Assessment that more than 30,000 plant and animal species face

extinction and that in the preceding 400 years, 484 animals and 654 plant species were known to have become extinct. The scientists also reported that mammals—like the tiger—were becoming extinct 40 times faster than ever before. Independent estimates by UNEP in 2002 reported that extinction is occurring 50–100 times faster than the background rate and that 45% of Earth's forests, 50% of its mangrove ecosystems, and 10% of its coral reefs had been destroyed by recent human activity.

9   To keep track of the current status of endangered species, the World Conservation Union (IUCN, the acronym derived from the name in which the organization was founded—the International Union for Conservation of Nature and Natural Resources (1956)) maintains the Red List, an updated list of species facing unusually high risks of extinction. The 2003 Red List reported that 24% (1,130) of mammal species and 12% (1,194) of bird species are threatened with extinction. Among other major groups (for which assessments are not fully complete), estimates of the percentage of species threatened ranged from 39% to 89%. From 1996 to 2003, the total number of vertebrate animals listed as threatened climbed by 6%, from 3,314 to 3,524. Since 1970, at least 58 fish species, 9 bird species, and 1 mammal species have become extinct, and in the United States alone over the past 500 years, 236 animals and 17 plants are confirmed to have gone extinct. For all of these figures, the *actual* numbers of species extinct and threatened, like the actual number of total species in the world, are doubtless greater than the *known* numbers.

10   Among the 1,130 mammals facing possible extinction on the IUCN's Red List is the tiger, which despite—or perhaps because of—its tremendous size and reputation as a fierce predator, is one of the most endangered large animals on the planet. In 1950 eight tiger subspecies existed. Today three are extinct. The Bali tiger, *Panthera tigris balica*, went extinct in the 1940s; the Caspian tiger, *Panthera tigris virgata*, during the 1970s; and the Javan tiger, *Panthera tigris sondaica*, during the 1980s. In each case, overhunting and habitat alteration were responsible.

The Major Causes of Species Loss Spell "HIPPO"

11   The overharvesting that decimated Siberian tiger populations in the early 20th century is only one form of human activity that has reduced the populations of many species. Overexploitation provides the "O" in **HIPPO,** an acronym scientists have coined to denote the five primary causes of species decline and extinction: Habitat alteration, Invasive species, Pollution, Population growth, and Overexploitation. The most prevalent and powerful of these five causes is habitat alteration.

Writing About the Reading

CHECKING YOUR VOCABULARY

1. For each of the words listed below, use context; prefixes, roots, and suffixes (see Chapter 3); and/or a dictionary to write a brief definition or synonym of the word as it is used in the reading.

   a. irretrievably (para. 1) _____

   b. paleontologists (para. 2) _____

c. episodes (para. 3) _____

d. colonized (para. 6) _____

e. vertebrates (para. 6) _____

f. co-occurs (para. 6) _____

g. consumption (para. 7) _____

h. ecosystems (para. 8) _____

i. overexploitation (para. 11) _____

2. Underline new, specialized terms introduced in the reading (see Chapter 3).

3. Draw a word map of one of the words in the reading.

CHECKING YOUR COMPREHENSION

1. What is *extirpation*?
2. Explain what is meant by the "background rate of extinction."
3. Give two reasons why today's period of mass extinctions differs from previous mass extinctions.
4. What is the Red List?
5. What are the five primary causes of species decline and extinction, as denoted by the acronym HIPPO? Which is the most prevalent and powerful of these causes?

THINKING CRITICALLY

1. Using Figure A, list the five mass extinction episodes that have taken place in the last 500 million years and note the approximate number of families in each episode.
2. According to Table B, which period experienced the most severe episode of mass extinction? What may have caused the episode?
3. According to Figure C, when did humans arrive in Madagascar and New Zealand?
4. What pattern of extinction is depicted in Figure C?
5. What kind of graphic would you use to depict the information about endangered species given in paragraphs 9 and 10? Explain why.
6. According to the reading, some scientists believe that climate variation, not hunting, is responsible for the extinctions in North America. What is your opinion, based on what you have learned from this article and on your previous knowledge?
7. Explain the statement, "For all of these figures, the *actual* numbers of species extinct and threatened, like the actual number of total species in the world, are doubtless greater than the *known* numbers" (para. 9).

LEARNING/STUDY STRATEGY

Assume you are taking a biology course. Predict an essay question that might be based on this reading.

MyReadingLab

To practice reading graphics and visuals, go to http://www.myreadinglab .com. Click on "Study Plan," then on "Reading Skills," and then on "Graphics and Visuals."

9 Using Writing to Learn

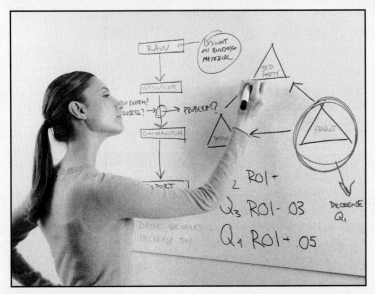

In the photo at left, a student is actively engaging with the information she is learning. Such white board work is common because educators know that writing helps students learn better. Whether taking notes in a notebook, keeping a journal, drawing diagrams, or working equations, many students have an intuitive understanding that taking pen (or chalk) in hand is the best way to learn new material.

LEARNING OBJECTIVES

- To use writing to monitor your comprehension

- To use highlighting to improve textbook reading

- To use note taking to organize, synthesize, and retain ideas

- To use mapping to show relationships

- To use summaries to condense information

- To use writing as a discovery process

WRITING TO LEARN: The Academic Link

Research studies indicate that you learn information more easily if you elaborate upon it. *Elaboration*, which means "building upon," is a process of expanding your thinking. It involves the multilevel skills discussed in Chapter 1: building connections, developing associations, seeing relationships, and considering applications. Elaboration makes information meaningful and, therefore, easier to recall. Writing is one way to help you elaborate, make connections, and memorize. This chapter discusses ways to use writing to help strengthen your comprehension and critical thinking skills. Not all strategies work equally well for everyone. Experiment to discover which work best for you.

WRITING TO LEARN: The Career Link

Business owners and managers consistently indicate that one of the most highly prized skills in an employee is the ability to write. We live in a society in which we are judged on our ability to write. Excellent writing skills are essential to career success.

■ Writing to Assess and Strengthen Comprehension

Writing is an excellent learning and study tool. Use writing to:

- **Test whether you understand what you are reading**. Try writing a summary, outline, or list of key ideas. If you can't, then you have not understood the material.
- **Improve your comprehension of difficult or complicated material**. Writing focuses your attention and clarifies your thinking.
- **Understand relationships between ideas.** When you outline or summarize, you will be forced to see how ideas connect to one another.
- **Create valuable study aids.** Summaries, outlines, lists, study sheets, and vocabulary lists are all essential study aids. Create these and you will not have to reread assigned chapters when an exam is announced.

Writing is not only a good way to test whether you are understanding what you read, but it will also improve your comprehension of difficult or complicated material. When you are reading a complex argument for a logic course, you can improve your understanding by writing a list of the argument's main points. Writing each point forces you to think about each one, so connections and relationships become more apparent. Writing also forces you to spend enough time with the material to understand it fully.

Writing is particularly helpful in mathematics. Writing will increase your understanding of processes. Listing the steps used to solve a problem makes the process "real" and more manageable. Writing makes problem solving practical rather than theoretical. There are many other situations in which writing strengthens comprehension. You can use writing to summarize case studies, explain how a process works, or describe similarities and differences among readings.

EXERCISE 9-1

LEARNING COLLABORATIVELY

Discussing Writing Strategies

Suppose you have been assigned three chapters to read in your psychology textbook. The next exam in psychology will emphasize these three chapters. Because of time limitations, your instructor will not discuss the chapters in class. Form groups of three or four students, and discuss the following issues.

1. How you would learn the chapters' content
2. What writing strategies you would use
3. How you would know when you were adequately prepared for the exam

■ Highlighting and Annotating Textbooks

☑ **Tip for Humanities and Social Science Majors**

Some students find it useful to use different highlighting colors for different purposes. For example, key vocabulary terms might be highlighted in yellow, while the names of important people might be highlighted in pink. (Be sure to use colors that are easy to read through.) Create a system that works well for you and helps you "chunk" your information into manageable amounts.

Highlighting and annotating are excellent means of improving your comprehension and recall of textbook assignments. Highlighting forces you to decide what is important and to sort the key information from less important material. Sorting ideas this way improves both comprehension and recall. To decide what to highlight, you must think about and evaluate the relative importance of each idea. Highlighting has the following added benefits:

- Highlighting keeps you physically active as you read.
- The physical activity focuses your attention and improves your concentration.
- Highlighting helps you discover how ideas are related.
- Highlighting is a good test of whether you understand what you are reading. If you have difficulty deciding what to highlight, it indicates that you are not comprehending the material.

KEY STRATEGY: How to Highlight

To highlight textbook material most effectively, apply these guidelines:

1. **Analyze the assignment.**   Preview the assignment, and define what type of learning is required. This will help you determine how much and what type of information you need to highlight.

2. **Assess your familiarity with the subject.** Depending on your background knowledge, you may need to highlight only a little or a great deal. Do not waste time highlighting what you already know. In chemistry, for example, if you have already learned the definition of a mole, then do not highlight it.

3. **Read first, then highlight.** Finish a paragraph or self-contained section before you highlight. As you read, look for signals to academic thought patterns. Each idea may seem important as you first encounter it, but you must see how it fits in with the others before you can judge its relative importance.

4. **Use the boldfaced headings.** Headings are labels that indicate the overall topic of a section. These headings serve as indicators of what is important to highlight. For example, under the heading "Objectives of Economic Growth," you should be certain to highlight each objective.

5. **Highlight main ideas and only key supporting details.** Try to keep academic thought patterns in mind.

6. **Avoid highlighting complete sentences.** Highlight only enough so that your highlighting makes sense when you reread it.

7. **Move quickly through the document as you highlight.** If you have understood a paragraph or section, then your highlighting should be fast and efficient.

8. **Develop a consistent system of highlighting.** Decide, for example, how you will mark main ideas, how you will distinguish main ideas from details, and how you will highlight new terminology. Some students use a system of symbols such as brackets, asterisks, and circles to distinguish various types of information; others use different colors of highlighters to make distinctions. Experiment, testing various systems, and once you have settled on an effective system, use it regularly.

9. **Use the 15–25 percent rule of thumb.** Although the amount you will highlight will vary from course to course, try to highlight no more than 15 to 25 percent of any given page. If you exceed this figure, it often means that you are not sorting ideas as efficiently as possible. Remember, the more you highlight, the smaller your time-saving dividends will be as you review.

The first three paragraphs of the following textbook excerpt show effective highlighting. Notice that key words, not entire sentences, are highlighted. Also notice that only key information is highlighted. If you read only the highlighted words, can you grasp the key idea of each paragraph?

BIOMES

By using imagination, we can divide the Earth's land into several kinds of regions called biomes, areas of the earth that support specific assemblages of plants. As would be expected, certain kinds of animals occupy each type of biome, since different species of animals are dependent on different sorts of plant communities for food, shelter, building materials, and hiding places. . . .

Tropical rain forests are found mainly in the Amazon and Congo Basins and in Southeast Asia. The temperature in this biome doesn't vary much throughout the year. Instead, the seasons are marked by variation in the amount of rainfall throughout the year. In some areas, there may be pronounced rainy seasons. These forests support many species of plants. Trees grow throughout the year and reach tremendous heights, with their branches forming a massive canopy overhead. The forest floor, which can be quite open and easy to travel over, may be dark and steamy. Forests literally swarm with insects and birds. Animals may breed throughout the year as a result of the continual availability of food. Competition is generally considered to be very keen in such areas because of the abundance of species.

Temperate deciduous forests once covered most of the eastern United States and all of Central Europe. The dominant trees in these forests are hardwoods. The areas characterized by such plants are subject to harsh winters, times when the trees shed their leaves, and warm summers that mark periods of rapid growth and rejuvenation. Before the new leaves begin to shade the forest floor in the spring, a variety of herbaceous (nonwoody) flowering plants may appear. These wildflowers are usually perennials, plants that live and produce flowers year after year. In the early spring, they don't have time to manufacture the food needed to grow and bloom suddenly. Instead, they draw on food produced and stored in underground parts during the previous year. Rainfall may average 75 to 130 centimeters or more each year in these forests and is rather evenly distributed throughout the year.

People who live in temperate deciduous biomes often consider the seasonal changes as both moving and fascinating. They describe a certain joy that swells within them each spring and a secret pensiveness that overcomes them in the fall as the days darken and the forests become more silent. (Perhaps we are exceeding technical descriptions here, but these are my favorite places.)

Taiga (pronounced "tie-gah") is quite unmistakable; there is nothing else like it. It is confined almost exclusively to the Northern Hemisphere and is identified by the great coniferous forests of pine, spruce, fir, and hemlock that extend across North America, Europe, and Asia. Some of these trees are the largest living things on earth.

Taiga is marked by long, cold, wet winters and short summer growing seasons. The forest is interrupted here and there by extensive bogs, or muskegs, which are the remains of large ponds. The forest floor is usually covered by a carpet of needles. In the dim light at ground level, there may be mosses, ferns, and a few flowering plants. One may move silently on the muffling needles through the Canadian taiga observing a host of mammals, including porcupines, moose, bear, rodents, hares, and wolverines.

Tundra is the northernmost land biome. It is covered throughout most of the year by ice and snow. This biome is most prevalent in the far north (arctic tundra), but it may also appear at high elevations in other parts of the world (alpine tundra). For example, in the United States, it may be seen in the high Rocky Mountains. Tundra appears in places where summer usually lasts two to four months, just long enough to thaw a few feet of the soil above the permafrost, or permanently frozen soil. Thaw brings soggy ground, and ponds and bogs appear in the depressions. The plant life consists mostly of lichens, herbs, mosses, and low-lying shrubs and grasses, as well as a few kinds of trees, such as dwarf willows and birches. Such plants obviously must be hardy, but their hardiness disguises their fragility. Once disturbed, these areas take very long periods to restore themselves.

—Wallace, *Biology: The World of Life,* pp. 708, 710, 712–13

EXERCISE 9-2

Practicing Highlighting

Finish highlighting the preceding passage.

Evaluating Your Highlighting

As with any learning strategy, be sure to ask the question "Is it working?" Your final answer, of course, will come when you take your first major examination.

There are two common mistakes you can make when you are highlighting.

Highlighting too much. Using the tired, worn-out "rather safe than sorry" rule, you may tend to highlight almost every idea on the page. Highlighting nearly everything is about as effective as highlighting nothing because no sorting occurs: key ideas are not distinguished from other, less important, ones. Highlighting too much can become a way of escaping or postponing the real issue: deciding what to learn.

Highlighting too little. If you find you are highlighting less than 10 percent per page, this often is a signal that you are having difficulty understanding the material. If you cannot explain the content of a given section in your own words, then you have not understood it.

Evaluate your own highlighting by:

- **Selecting a sample page, highlighting it, and rereading only your highlighting.** Then ask yourself the following questions: "Does my highlighting convey the key ideas of the passage?" "Can I follow the author's train of thought and his or her progression of ideas by reading only my highlighting?" "Is the highlighting appropriate for my purposes?"

- **Comparing your highlighting with that of another student.** Although there will be individual differences, both sets of highlighting should emphasize the same key ideas.

EXERCISE 9-3

Evaluating Highlighting

Evaluate your highlighting in Exercise 9-2 by using one of the preceding suggestions.

Marginal Annotation

In many situations, highlighting alone is not a sufficient means of identifying what to learn. It does not separate the main ideas from the examples, and each of these from new terminology. Nor does it give you any opportunity to comment on or react to the material. Therefore, it is often necessary to make marginal annotations as well as to highlight.

Annotating is an active reading process. It forces you to monitor your comprehension as well as react to ideas. The Key Strategy box "How to Annotate" suggests various ways to annotate a political science textbook chapter.

Annotation as a means of analysis and evaluation is discussed on page 121 in Chapter 4. Review this section now for additional suggestions on how to annotate effectively.

EXERCISE 9-4

LEARNING
COLLABORATIVELY

Annotating

Add annotations to the excerpt that you highlighted in Exercise 9-2 and compare them with those of another student.

EXERCISE 9-5

ACADEMIC
APPLICATION

Highlighting and Annotating

Select a two- to three-page excerpt from one of your textbooks. Read, highlight, and annotate the selection. Do you feel the combination of processes is more effective than highlighting alone? Why or why not?

EXERCISE 9-6

LEARNING
COLLABORATIVELY

Highlighting and Annotating

Working with another student in the class, choose one of the end-of-chapter readings in this text. Assume it is a reading assignment for one of your courses. Each of you should read, highlight, and annotate the selection. Then discuss similarities and differences in your work and evaluate each other's annotations.

KEY STRATEGY: How to Annotate

Marginal Annotation

WAY TO ANNOTATE		EXAMPLE
Circle unknown words		. . . redressing the apparent (asymmetry) of their relationship
Mark definitions	*def*	To say that the balance of power favors one party over another is to introduce a disequilibrium.
Mark examples	*ex*	. . . concessions may include negative sanctions, trade agreements . . .
Number lists of ideas, causes, reasons or events		components of power include ①self-image, ②population, ③natural resources, and geography ④
Place asterisks next to important passages	*	Power comes from three primary sources . . .
Put question marks next to confusing passages	?→	war prevention occurs through institutionalization of mediation . . .
Make notes to yourself	*check def in soc text*	power is the ability of an actor on the international stage to . . .
Mark possible test items	⊤	There are several key features in the relationship. . .
Draw arrows to show relationships		. . . natural resources . . ., . . . control of industrial manufacture capacity
Write comments, note disagreements and similarities	*Can terrorism be prevented through similar balance?*	war prevention through balance of power is . . .
Mark summary statements	*Sum*	the greater the degree of conflict, the more intricate will be. . .

EXERCISE 9-7

ACADEMIC
APPLICATION

Evaluating Highlighting

Choose a two- or three-page section from one of your textbooks and highlight it, using the guidelines suggested in this chapter. Then evaluate the effectiveness of your highlighting in preparation for an objective exam on the material.

■ Note Taking to Organize Ideas

Note taking is a writing strategy that can assist you in organizing information and pulling ideas together. It is also an effective way to pull together information from two or more sources—your textbook and class lectures, for example. Finally, note taking is a way to assess your comprehension and strengthen your recall.

KEY STRATEGY: How to Take Notes

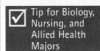 **Tip for Biology, Nursing, and Allied Health Majors**

Many health majors find it useful to use a system in which they fold a sheet of paper in half. On the left side, they write key questions that are based on the headings of textbook chapters. On the right side, they write the answers. Simply writing out this material helps students better learn and retain it. In addition, this system is excellent for exam preparation.

Use the following tips to take good notes:

1. **Read an entire section and then jot down notes.** Do not try to write notes while you are reading the material for the first time.

2. **As you read, be alert for academic thought patterns.** These patterns will help you organize your notes.

3. **Record all of the most important ideas in the briefest possible form.**

4. **Think of your notes as a list of the main ideas and supporting details of a selection.** Organize them to show how the ideas are related or to reflect the organization of the material.

5. **Use words and short phrases to summarize ideas.** Do not write in complete sentences.

6. **Write in your own words; do not copy sentences or parts of sentences from the selection.**

7. **Be highly selective.** Unless you are sure that a fact or idea is important to remember, do not include it. If you are not selective, you will find that your notes are nearly as long as the selection itself and you will save little time when you review the material.

8. **Use an outline system of indentation to separate main ideas and details.** As a general rule, the greater the importance of an idea, the closer it is placed to the left margin. Ideas of lesser importance are indented and appear closer to the center of the page.

Your notes might follow a format such as this:

I. TOPIC
  A. Main Idea
      1. Supporting detail
          a. fact
          b. fact
      2. Supporting detail
  B. Main Idea
      1. Supporting detail
      2. Supporting detail
          a. fact
          b. fact
II. TOPIC

As a further illustration of the techniques of note taking, study the notes shown in Figure 9-1. They are based on the first two paragraphs of the excerpt on biomes that appears on page 256.

FIGURE 9-1   Sample Notes

<u>Biomes</u>
  • Regions of Earth's land
  • Each has own plants and animals

<u>Tropical Rain Forests</u>

  • Amazon & Congo Basins and Southeast Asia
  • Seasons vary according to rainfall amount
  • Trees grow throughout year
        – branches form canopy, forest floor dark, steamy
  • Animals breed throughout year
        – keen competition

EXERCISE 9-8

LEARNING
COLLABORATIVELY

Taking and Evaluating Notes

Write a brief set of notes for the reading selection "New Ways of Administering Justice and Punishment" at the end of this chapter. Working with a classmate, compare, discuss, and revise your notes.

EXERCISE 9-9

ACADEMIC
APPLICATION

Taking Notes

Select a three- to four-page section from one of your textbooks. Write a brief set of notes, including the key ideas.

■ Mapping to Show Relationships

☑ Tip for
Communication/
Graphic Arts
Majors

Using mapping as you read your textbooks is excellent training for your career! Learning how to translate a large amount of text into a concise concept map or diagram is as important as making the final product visually attractive (for example, if you are working for a Web site, newspaper, or magazine).

Mapping is a way of drawing a diagram to show how a topic and its related ideas are connected. It organizes and consolidates information, often emphasizing a particular thought pattern. Mapping is a visual means of learning by writing.

This section discusses four types of maps: conceptual maps, process diagrams, part and function diagrams, and time lines. Each uses one of the thought patterns discussed in Chapter 7.

Conceptual Maps

A conceptual map is a form of outline that presents ideas spatially rather than in list form. It is a "picture" of how ideas are related.

KEY STRATEGY: Constructing a Conceptual Map

Use the following steps to construct a conceptual map:

1. **Identify the topic and write it in the center of the page.**

2. **Identify ideas, aspects, parts, and definitions that are related to the topic.** Draw each one on a line radiating from the topic.

3. **As you discover details that further explain an idea already recorded, draw new lines branching from the idea that the details explain.**

A map of Chapter 1 is shown in Figure 9-2. Take a moment now to refer to Chapter 1 before studying the map.

Process Diagrams

In the technologies and the natural sciences, as well as in many other courses, *processes* are an important part of the course content. A diagram that visually describes the steps, variables, or parts of a process will simplify learning. For example, the diagram in Figure 9-3 visually describes the steps in the search process using online sources.

FIGURE 9–2   Sample Conceptual Map of Chapter 1

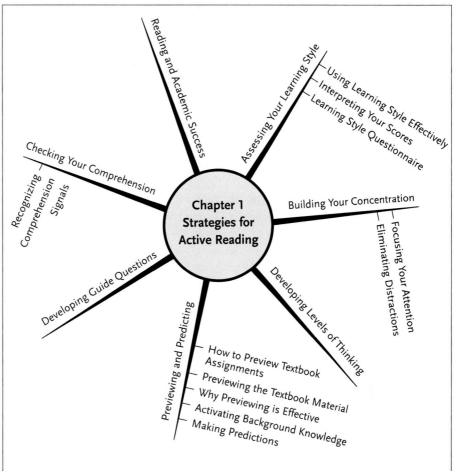

FIGURE 9–3   Sample Process Diagram

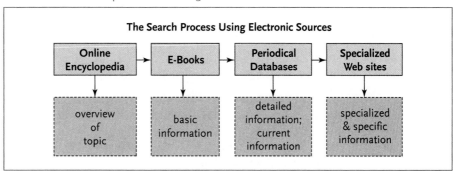

EXERCISE 9–10

Drawing a Map

Draw a conceptual map of Chapter 3 of this book.

EXERCISE 9–11

Drawing a Map

Draw a conceptual map of the reading titled "New Ways of Administering Justice and Punishment" at the end of this chapter.

EXERCISE 9–12

LEARNING
COLLABORATIVELY

Drawing a Process Diagram

The following paragraph describes the sequential effects of taking the psychedelic drug LSD. Read the paragraph, and then draw a process diagram that describes this response sequence. Compare your diagram with those of several other students.

> **Psychedelics** are . . . a group of drugs that produce hallucinations and various other phenomena that very closely mimic certain mental disorders. These drugs include lysergic acid diethylamide (LSD), mescaline, peyote, psilocybin, and various commercial preparations such as Sernyl and Ditran.
>
> Of these, LSD is probably the best known, although its use has apparently diminished since its heyday in the late 1960s. LSD is synthesized from lysergic acid produced by a fungus (ergot) that is parasitic on cereal grains such as rye. It usually produces responses in a particular sequence. The initial reactions may include weakness, dizziness and nausea. These symptoms are followed by a distortion of time and space. The senses may become intensified and strangely intertwined—that is, sounds can be "seen" and colors "heard." Finally, there may be changes in mood, a feeling of separation of the self from the framework of time and space, and changes in the perception of the self. The sensations experienced under the influence of psychedelics are unlike anything encountered within the normal range of experiences. The descriptions of users therefore can only be puzzling to nonusers. Some users experience bad trips or "bummers," which have been known to produce long-term effects. Bad trips can be terrifying experiences and can occur in experienced users for no apparent reason.
>
> —Wallace, *Biology: The World of Life,* pp. 632–33

Part and Function Diagrams: Classification

In courses that deal with the use and description or classification of physical objects, labeled drawings are an important learning tool. In a human anatomy and physiology course, for example, the easiest way to learn the parts and functions of the brain is to draw it. To study, sketch the brain and test your recall of each part and its function.

EXERCISE 9-13

Drawing a Diagram

The following paragraph describes the outer layers of the Earth. Read the paragraph, and then draw a diagram that will help you to visualize how the Earth is structured.

OUTER LAYERS OF THE EARTH

The Earth's crust and the uppermost part of the mantle are known as the *lithosphere.* This is a fairly rigid zone that extends about 100 km below the Earth's surface. The crust extends some 60 km or so under continents, but only about 10 km below the ocean floor. The continental crust has a lower density than the oceanic crust. It is primarily a light granitic rock rich in the silicates of aluminum, iron, and magnesium. In a simplified view, the continental crust can be thought of as layered: On top of a layer of igneous rock (molten rock that has hardened, such as granite) lies a thin layer of sedimentary rocks (rocks formed by sediment and fragments that water deposited, such as limestone and sandstone); there is also a soil layer deposited during past ages in the parts of continents that have had no recent volcanic activity or mountain building.

Sandwiched between the lithosphere and the lower mantle is the partially molten material known as the *asthenosphere,* about 150 km thick. It consists primarily of iron and magnesium silicates that readily deform and flow under pressure.

—Berman and Evans, *Exploring the Cosmos,* p. 145

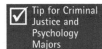

Tip for Criminal Justice and Psychology Majors

In your career you will often need to keep track of the various events in the lives of your clients. Time lines can summarize a good deal of information about an individual person's life in a small amount of space, which can be very helpful in record keeping.

Time Lines

When you are studying a topic in which the sequence or order of events is a central focus, a time line is a helpful way to organize the information. Time lines are especially useful in history courses. To map a sequence of events, draw a single line and mark it off in year intervals, just as a ruler is marked off in inches. Then write each event next to the corresponding year. For example, the time line in Figure 9-4 on page 267 displays major events during the presidency of Franklin D. Roosevelt. The time line shows the sequence of events and helps you to visualize them more clearly.

EXERCISE 9-14

Drawing a Time Line

The following passage reviews the chronology of events in public school desegregation. Read the selection, and then draw a time line that will help you to visualize these historical events.

DESEGREGATING THE SCHOOLS

The nation's schools soon became the primary target of civil-rights advocates. The NAACP concentrated first on universities, successfully waging an intensive legal battle to win admission for qualified blacks to graduate and professional schools. Led by Thurgood Marshall, NAACP lawyers then took on the broader issue of segregation in the country's public schools. Challenging the 1896 Supreme Court decision (*Plessy v. Ferguson*) which upheld the constitutionality of separate but equal public facilities, Marshall argued that even substantially equal but separate schools did profound psychological damage to black children and thus violated the Fourteenth Amendment.

A unanimous Supreme Court agreed in its 1954 decision in the case of *Brown v. Board of Education of Topeka.* Chief Justice Earl Warren, recently appointed by President Eisenhower, wrote the landmark opinion which flatly declared that "separate educational facilities are inherently unequal." To divide grade-school children "solely because of their race," Warren argued, "generates a feeling of inferiority as to their status in the community that may affect their hearts and minds in a way unlikely ever to be undone." Despite this sweeping language, Warren realized that it would be difficult to change historic patterns of segregation quickly. Accordingly, in 1955 the Court ruled that implementation should proceed "with all deliberate speed" and left the details to the lower federal courts.

The process of desegregating the schools proved to be agonizingly slow. Officials in the border states quickly complied with the Court's ruling, but states deeper in the South responded with a policy of massive resistance. Local White Citizen's Councils organized to fight for retention of racial separation; 101 congressmen and senators signed a Southern Manifesto in 1956 which denounced the *Brown* decision as "a clear abuse of judicial power." School boards, encouraged by this show of defiance, found a variety of ways to evade the Court's ruling. The most successful was the passage of pupil-placement laws. . . .

Southern leaders mistook Ike's silence for tacit support of segregation. In 1957, Governor Orville Faubus of Arkansas called out the national guard to prevent the integration of Little Rock's Central High School on grounds of a threat to public order. . . .

Despite the snail's pace of school desegregation, the *Brown* decision led to other advances. In 1957, the Eisenhower administration proposed the first general civil-rights legislation since Reconstruction. Strong southern resistance and compromise by both the administration and Senate Democratic leader Lyndon B. Johnson of Texas weakened the bill considerably. The final act, however, did create a permanent Commission for Civil Rights, one of Truman's original goals. It also provided for federal efforts aimed at "securing and protecting the right to vote." A second civil-rights act in 1960 slightly strengthened the voting-rights section.

—Divine et al., *America Past and Present,* pp. 890–91

■ Summarizing to Condense Ideas

Like note taking, summarizing is an excellent way to learn from your reading and to increase recall. A summary is a brief statement that reviews the key points of what you have read. It condenses and organizes an author's ideas or arguments into sentences written in your own words. A summary contains only the gist of the text, with limited explanation, background information, or supporting detail. Writing a summary is a useful strategy when an overview of the material is needed, as in the following situations:

FIGURE 9-4   Sample Time Line

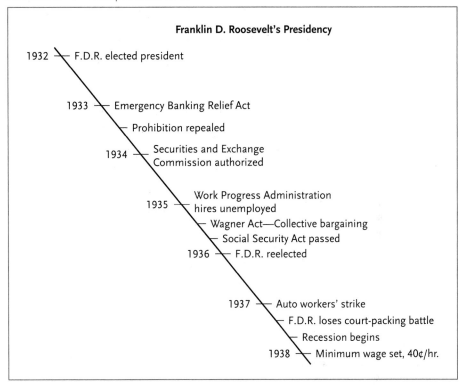

- answering an essay question
- reviewing a film or videotape
- writing a term paper
- recording results of a laboratory experiment or demonstration
- summarizing the plot of a short story
- quickly reviewing large amounts of information

Before writing a summary, be sure that you understand the material and that you have identified the writer's major points.

KEY STRATEGY: How to Summarize

Use the following suggestions to write an effective summary:

1. **As a first step, highlight the material or write brief notes for it.**
2. **Write one sentence that states the writer's overall concern or most important idea.**   To do this, ask yourself what one topic the material is

continued

Key Strategies *continued*

about. Then ask what point the writer is trying to make about that topic. This sentence will be the topic sentence of your summary.

3. **Be sure to paraphrase, using your own words rather than those of the author.**

4. **Next, review the major supporting information that the author gives to explain the major idea.**

5. **The amount of detail you include, if any, depends on your purpose for writing the summary.**   For example, if you are writing a summary of a television documentary for a research paper, it might be more detailed than if you were writing it to jog your memory for a class discussion.

6. **Normally, present ideas in the summary in the same order in which they appear in the original material.**

7. **If the writer presents a clear opinion or expresses an attitude toward the subject matter, include it in your summary.**

8. **If the summary is for your own use only and is not to be submitted as an assignment, do not worry about sentence structure.**   Some students prefer to write summaries using words and phrases rather than complete sentences.

A sample summary of the article on biomes that appears earlier in this chapter is shown in Figure 9-5.

EXERCISE 9-15

LEARNING
COLLABORATIVELY

Writing and Evaluating a Summary

Write a summary of one of the end-of-chapter readings that you have already read. Working with a classmate, compare, discuss, and revise your summaries.

FIGURE 9-5 Sample Summary

> The earth is divided into regions called biomes. Each biome has its own species of plants and animals. Tropical rainforests have consistent temperatures but seasonal variation in rainfall. Trees grow throughout the year and animals breed year round. Both plants and animals are abundant in forests. Temperate deciduous forests have seasonal change in temperature, rainfall is evenly distributed. Tiaga, an area of coniferous pine forests has long wet winters and short summers. Tundra refers to land covered by ice and snow most of the year. Plant life is limited to hardy lichens, herbs, mosses, low-lying shrubs, and dwarf trees.

EXERCISE 9-16

ACADEMIC
APPLICATION

Writing a Summary

Select a five- to six-page section from one of your textbooks. Write a brief summary of the section, using the guidelines suggested above.

■ Brainstorming to Discover Ideas

Brainstorming is a writing and thinking exercise that is particularly effective for generating ideas. It works like this: Suppose you are trying to think of a topic for a three-minute informative speech for your speech class. Begin by making a list of any topics that come into your mind. Write continuously. Do not be concerned about whether you are writing in complete sentences or whether the topics are practical or connected to one another. Write continuously for a set period—two or three minutes. When you have finished, reread what you have written. You will be surprised at the number of different topics you have discovered. Highlight those topics that are worth further exploration.

Brainstorming is also a way to get interested in a topic before beginning to read about it. Suppose you must read several lengthy research articles on the psychological effects of color. Before you start, brainstorm. List every possible effect of color and ways to measure its effects. Then read to confirm what you knew and to find out what you did not know.

EXERCISE 9-17

Brainstorming Ideas

Assume you will be reading several journal articles on drug testing in schools for a sociology class. Brainstorm for three minutes to discover what you already know about the issue.

EXERCISE 9-18

Selecting Writing Strategies

For each of the following statements, suggest one or more writing strategies that would enhance learning.

1. Some math students are having difficulty because they confuse several similar types of problems and choose incorrect solutions.

   _____

2. A political science class does not have a standard textbook. Instead, the instructor assigns weekly library readings on which she bases class discussions and lectures.

   _____

3. An anthropology student is preparing for an essay exam. She plans to predict possible questions and answer them.

   _____

4. A student in a computer literacy course must learn procedures for merging files using word processing software.

_____

5. For an English literature class, a student must write a paper comparing two poems by the same poet.

_____

Self-Test Summary

1. What is a good way to assess and strengthen your reading comprehension?	Self-testing is an effective way to assess and strengthen comprehension. As you read an assignment, write down the main points and write a review of key points when you finish.
2. How can writing help you understand difficult or complex material?	Writing forces you to think about what you read. It helps you to make connections and see the relationships between the main points.
3. Name five writing strategies and describe how each is useful.	Five writing strategies are • highlighting and annotating; they help to distinguish what is important to learn and remember. • note taking; it organizes information and helps pull ideas together. • mapping; it describes how a topic and its related ideas are connected, helping to organize and consolidate information. • summarizing; it condenses ideas and provides a review of key points. • brainstorming; it enables you to discover and clarify ideas, as well as generate interest in a reading assignment.
4. What is a conceptual map?	A conceptual map presents ideas spatially rather than in list form.
5. What is a process diagram?	A process diagram visually describes the steps, variables, or parts of a process.
6. What is a part and function diagram?	A part and function diagram shows labeled parts that aid in the description or classification of physical objects.
7. What is a time line?	A time line is a map showing the sequence in which events occurred.

Criminal Justice

New Ways of Administering Justice and Punishment

Frank Schmalleger

Prereading Questions

1. What do you know about how technology is used in dealing with offenders?
2. What changes do you think are needed in our criminal justice system?

New Ways of Administering Justice and Punishment

1   Technological advances, and the realization that virtually all offenders in prison will return to the community one day after serving their sentences, have spurred the creation of new strategies to deal with offenders. The average prison sentence in the United States is approximately five years, and most offenders in prison were sentenced for drug offenses, robbery, burglary, and other crimes for which release from prison is inevitable. Can prison do more to prepare these offenders for a noncriminal life upon release, and are there more effective and less expensive alternatives to prison for nonviolent offenders?

Technocorrections

technocorrections
The use of technology to monitor offenders and to prevent future crimes.

2   **Technocorrections** is the use of technology to monitor offenders and prevent future crimes. The most popular form of this technology is electronic "bracelets" placed around the ankles of probationers to monitor their whereabouts. A more advanced form of this technology is "probation kiosks," which have been used in New York City. These kiosks are similar to automatic teller machines and are scattered around the city. They identify probationers using a scan of the geometry of the hand on the device and allow the probationer to respond to questions and to schedule meetings with probation officers. These kiosks are designed as a way to monitor low-risk, nonviolent offenders, thereby permitting probation officers to devote closer supervision to higher-risk offenders.

3   Miniaturization of technology will allow for similar experiments with tiny cameras that could be placed in offenders' homes or in high-risk places (such as known drug areas or the residence of a battered spouse). Other technologies are being developed that would be more difficult for offenders to disable and that would permit certain behaviors or movements by offenders to trigger alarms.

Risk-Based Treatment

4   **Risk assessment** involves classifying and evaluating offenders based on their characteristics, crimes, and backgrounds to determine the likelihood of reoffending. Classifying and evaluating offenders has become more sophisticated and accurate over the last two decades.

A probation kiosk in New York City which automates the monitoring of offenders serving probation sentences in the community. Why do you believe automated devices like this have become popular? Do you believe they are effective at monitoring offenders?

Studies have had at least three important findings involving variation, reliability, and statistics. First, there is tremendous variation among offenders and there is no "one size fits all" in trying to isolate the characteristics of an offender. Offender characteristics such as mental health and substance abuse are important considerations, as are situational characteristics that trigger offender predispositions. Second, offenders change over time, so it is necessary for periodic reevaluations in order for risk assessments to be reliable. Third, "gut feelings" about criminal propensities have given way to statistical assessments, which compare the behaviors of groups of offenders in the past to similar offenders under current evaluation. This form of statistical assessment, or statistical profiling, has been shown to be superior to clinical assessments by psychologists.

5   Risk assessments will become even more important in the future because the threshold for violence may be lower now than in times past. In another road rage case, a middle-aged man in Minnesota noticed a car in front of him moving erratically. As he passed the car, the driver swerved to hit him and made an obscene gesture.

Will this encounter escalate into violence leading to criminal liability? How could statistical profiling and risk assessment help in preventing crimes such as road rage assaults and killings?

He returned the gesture. Later, after he arrived home, there was a knock on the door. The man opened the door, and the other driver threw battery acid on him, causing burns to his face. Although these bizarre incidents appear unique, they are now occurring with increasing frequency, permitting the establishment of statistical profiles that will probably be used in the future at trial and in providing treatment to those offenders whose anger results in criminal violence.

Early Life Interventions

6   A fifteen-year-old boy was sentenced to twenty years in prison for participating in a gang rape of a fourteen-year-old girl. It was his first offense. How does someone choose such a serious offense as a first crime? In most cases there is a progression of behaviors from nonserious to serious crime. It is likely that the offender in this case had committed previous, lesser crimes, but had not been caught. Recognition of this progression from nonserious to serious crimes has been the basis for early childhood intervention in preventing later juvenile delinquency.

7   Early life interventions are important because studies have identified childhood risk factors for later delinquency. These include poor language skills, poor attachment to parents and caregivers, poor parenting skills, and multiple stresses on the family. These risk factors lead to failure in school, which is significantly related to delinquency. The Prenatal and Early Childhood Nurse Home Visitation Program is a program that is directed to reduce these identified risk factors that contribute to delinquency. This program builds parenting skills and family unity as it impacts on child rearing. The Boys and Girls Clubs of America is a national network of more than 2,500 clubs that involve more than three million school-age boys and girls in constructive youth development activities, educational support, and adult supervision. A group of researchers convened by the U.S. Office of Juvenile Justice and Delinquency Prevention agreed that "implementing family, school, and community interventions is the best way to prevent children from developing into serious violent juvenile offenders." Although none of the programs described in this section is primarily a crime prevention program, they all have direct implications for the prevention of crime and the involvement of the criminal justice system in the future.

Virtual Prison

8   Despite the best efforts at crime prevention, there always will be offenders who require close supervision. Those who are not dangerous may not require imprisonment, yet something more than probation supervision or an electronic bracelet may be desired. A potential middle ground for close supervision that is less than prison might be "virtual prison." A private company has introduced the Satellite Monitoring and Remote Tracking System (SMART), which is billed as "a virtual prison with an orbiting warden." The offender wears an ankle bracelet and a wireless tracking device that is monitored using Global Positioning Satellites (GPS) and the cellular network. In this way the offender is continuously monitored. The offender can also be signalled instantly when entering a prohibited area, which might be a spouse's neighborhood, school, or drug-trafficking area. Several states are evaluating the system's cost-effectiveness as an alternative to prison.

9   Injected or surgical implants have been proposed as an alternative to electronic bracelets because they cannot be tampered with or defeated effectively. These implants can also be monitored via Global Positioning Satellites. Questions have been raised about the potential for misuse of such Big Brother technology, but it is unlikely that offenders will oppose a technology that offers more freedom than prison.

Writing About the Reading

CHECKING YOUR VOCABULARY

1. For each of the words listed below, use context; prefixes, roots, and suffixes (see Chapter 3); and/or a dictionary to write a brief definition or synonym of the word as it is used in the reading.

   a. miniaturization (para. 3) _____

   b. predispositions (para. 4) _____

   c. propensities (para. 4) _____

   d. threshold (para. 5)_____

   e. convened (para. 7) _____

   f. implications (para. 7) _____

   g. prohibited (para. 8) _____

2. Underline new, specialized terms introduced in the reading (see Chapter 3).

3. Draw a word map of one of the words in the reading.

CHECKING YOUR COMPREHENSION

1. Define the term *technocorrections*.
2. What are "probation kiosks" and how do they work?
3. List three important findings involving variation, reliability, and statistics.
4. Identify four childhood risk factors that contribute to delinquency.

5. According to the reading, what two programs work to reduce childhood risk factors?
6. Describe the Satellite Monitoring and Remote Tracking System (SMART).

THINKING CRITICALLY

1. What is the purpose of this reading?
2. How would you describe the author's tone?
3. What evidence does the author provide? Evaluate its effectiveness.
4. What allusion does the author make in paragraph 9? Discuss its meaning.
5. Study the photograph of the probation kiosk and answer the two questions posed in the caption.

LEARNING/STUDY STRATEGY

Create a map that shows the key ideas of this reading.

MyReadingLab

To practice reading graphics and visuals, go to http://www.myreadinglab .com. Click on "Study Plan," then on "Reading Skills," and then on "Notetaking and Highlighting."

10 Reading in the Social Sciences

The Social Sciences: A Visual Overview

Margaret Mead was an anthropologist who studied adolescence in the South Pacific. Her 1928 work *Coming of Age in Samoa* is one of the most widely read works in the social sciences.

Modern studies in psychology focus not only on behavior but also on evolving research into the brain.

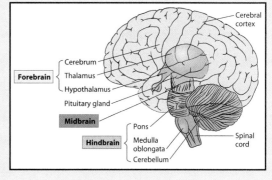

Criminal justice studies not only the prosecution of criminals but also ways to rehabilitate them and give them a second chance.

- To learn what the social sciences are

- To consider whether you should major in a social science

- To discover tips for studying social science

- To learn about characteristics of social science textbooks

- To discover specialized reading techniques for the social sciences

- To learn what common thought patterns to anticipate

- To adapt your study techniques for social science courses

What Are the Social Sciences?

The **social sciences** are concerned with the study of the social, cultural, and behavioral aspects of human interactions. Because of this focus on people, students find they learn a great deal about themselves and those around them. They also learn some answers to many questions they have always wondered about: Why do some people commit violent crimes? Why and how do people fall in love? What factors determine how many jobs are available in a given city?

The social sciences include some of the most popular majors on campus. According to *The Princeton Review*, psychology is the second-most popular major in the United States (the first is business administration); economics is also extremely popular. These disciplines attract many students because they cover a wide range of subfields and provide many job opportunities for graduates. A listing of some of these subfields, as well as career opportunities for majors in the social sciences, appears in Table 10-1.

TABLE 10-1   The Social Sciences: An Overview

DISCIPLINE	SUBFIELDS	JOB AND CAREER OPPORTUNITIES
Anthropology—The study of humanity: Examines concepts, customs, and rules in different societies and cultures.	*Forensic Anthropology*—Seeks to identify human remains through lab techniques	• Forensic scientist • Police lab technician
	Medical and Environmental Anthropology—Studies the factors that influence the health and well being of people	• Environmental worker (local or international) • Public health safety specialist

TABLE 10-1 *continued*

DISCIPLINE	SUBFIELDS	JOB AND CAREER OPPORTUNITIES
Criminal Justice—The study of the governmental systems directed at maintaining social control and deterring and punishing crimes, within the framework of laws that protect individual rights.	*Policing and Law Enforcement*—The study of the proper procedures for identifying, arresting, and interrogating criminals	• Police officer • Detective • Crime scene investigator • Police union representative
	The Court System—The study of the venue where disputes are prosecuted, mediated, and settled	• Court clerk • Process server • Municipal legal worker
	Corrections—The study of the administration of punishment through various methods, such as prison and parole	• Rehabilitation counselor • Parole officer • Corrections officer
Economics—The study of choice: Studies how goods, services, and wealth are produced, consumed, and distributed within societies.*	*Financial Economics*—Studies interest rates and the methods that companies use to raise money to start their businesses or increase their profit	• Stockbroker • Investment counselor • Banker • Insurance agent/broker
	Labor Economics—Looks at trends in job markets and salaries, as well as which industries are expanding and which are shrinking	• Human resource manager • Benefits administrator (health care, pensions) • Union manager or officer
Geography—The study of the surface of the Earth: Focuses on the Earth's divisions, climates, inhabitants, resources, and conflicts.	*Environmental Geography*—Focuses on the care, preservation, or cleaning of the natural environment benefit of for the the planet and its inhabitants	• Forestry technician • Park ranger • Hazardous waste planner
	Urban and Regional Geography—Examines every aspect of a specific city or region in detail	• Urban planner • Transportation planner • Health services planner
Psychology—The study of the mind: Focuses on human mental processes and behavior.	*Clinical Psychology*—Works directly with clients to help them solve problems or improve their lives	• Therapist or counselor • Hospital worker • Hospice worker
	Sports Psychology—Focuses on the study of all aspects of sport, from players through coaches, owners, and spectators	• Team psychologist • Pro or college sports coach • Trainer (with appropriate training in anatomy and physiology)

continued

TABLE 10-1 *continued*

DISCIPLINE	SUBFIELDS	JOB AND CAREER OPPORTUNITIES
	Counseling Psychology— Works directly with people (such as high school or college students) to put them on a path to life success	• School guidance counselor • College counselor • Geriatric (old age) counselor at a retirement home
Sociology—The study of society: Deals with human relationships, social systems, and social institutions.	*Sociology of the Military—* Examines the military as a social group rather than as an organization	• Armed services officer • Military strategist or specialist • CIA/FBI agent
	Sociology of the Family— Studies the family unit	• Family counselor • Social worker

*Economics is also discussed in Chapter 11, "Reading in Business."

Should You Major in a Social Science?

Although each social science focuses on a different aspect of human life, they have much in common. Each is interested in general laws, principles, and generalizations that describe how events, facts, trends, and observations are related. Some students believe that the social sciences are somehow less scientific than the physical and life sciences (such as biology, chemistry, engineering, and physics), but social scientists use the same methods that all scientists do: observation, experimentation, testing of scientific theories (called *hypotheses*), and reporting on the results of experiments. So, if you decide to major in a social science, you should expect to conduct and report on a good amount of your own research, as well as read published studies.

What characteristics and habits will make you a successful social science major?

1. **You are expected to understand the roots of the discipline**. This means that you must learn the history of the field and the contributions of the people who are important in that field. In psychology, for example, you must study the work of major figures like Sigmund Freud and Carl Jung; in sociology and anthropology, you will study the work of Margaret Mead.

2. **You must be able to handle a heavy reading load**. In the physical sciences, many complex concepts can be reduced to simple equations. The study of human beings is much more intricate, however, and the results are not so easily summarized. This means that many of the textbooks you'll be reading will be heavy with text, often in the form of stories and observations.

3. **You must have an adequate grounding in mathematics**. Social science majors are required to have an understanding of statistics and statistical

methods. (For example, all psychology majors are required to take a statistics course.) Do not put off studying math until later in your college career. Start early.

4. **You must be very organized and effective at keeping good records**. The social sciences require you to track a great deal of information that must be properly gathered, organized, and distributed to be considered scientifically valid. Learning how to take effective notes (see Chapter 9, "Using Writing to Learn") will help you to organize and study information.

☑ Special Tip for Psychology Majors

Many students who express an interest in psychology think that they are going to study mostly mental illnesses or theories of personality. However, the study of psychology is much more expansive than these two areas, and from the beginning you will be studying biological concepts like the brain, the central nervous system, sensation, and perception. Before you declare a major in psychology, be sure you understand the kinds of material you will be required to learn.

☑ Special Tip for Criminal Justice Majors

Many careers in the criminal justice system require you to be in good physical condition, so it is a good idea to fill out some of your electives with physical education courses. Also try to find part-time jobs or internships that will give you experience working with community members and leaders.

Tips for Studying Social Science—Even if You Are Not a Major

During college you will take at least two or three required social science courses. Here are some tips for making the most of them.

1. **Make time to read**. Although you will devote more time to your major courses, to get the most out of a social science course, read the assignments when you are feeling fresh and not tired. This allows you to better follow the material and appreciate its narrative approach. It can help to think of your textbook as a novel filled with interesting characters, examples, and case studies.

2. **Focus on the big picture**. You may not remember every detail of your textbook after you've taken the final exam, but each time you read a chapter, make a list of the top three things you have learned. Many social science instructors say they feel quite happy if students leave their course with a general level of awareness, so aim for that very achievable goal.

3. **Think how you can apply the concepts to your major and your life**. Because the social sciences study people, think about the ways the concepts you are studying can apply to yourself, your friends, and your family members. Applying concepts to the world around you helps you remember them better. It also makes you appreciate the contributions of the discipline more.

Social Science Textbooks: The Basics

Social science textbooks tend to share similar characteristics:

1. **The emphasis is on facts.** Especially in introductory courses, an instructor's first task is to acquaint you with known principles, rules, and facts that you can use to approach new problems and situations. Consequently, you must comprehend and retain large amounts of factual information. Refer to "Locating Main Ideas and Supporting Details" in Chapter 2 for specific suggestions, and use a highlighter, take marginal notes, and summarize key information.

2. **Many new terms are introduced.** Each social science has developed an extensive terminology to make its broad topics as objective and quantifiable as possible. To do well on exams, you must understand these terms. Make use of marginal and end-of-text glossaries to test yourself on the meanings of these terms.

3. **Graphics are important.** Social science textbooks include a great deal of information in the form of photographs, diagrams, and other graphics. Be sure to "read" these graphics to learn what they convey about the topic. Refer to Chapter 8, "Reading and Evaluating Graphics and Online Sources," for specific suggestions on how to read and interpret charts, tables, and graphs.

4. **Research references are stressed.** Many texts present research studies as supporting evidence, usually directly in the textbook. In introductory courses, the outcome of the research and what it proves or suggests are usually most important. For majors, it is more important to know about the researchers and their work and methods.

Quotes from a Sociology Professor

Advice for Social Science Students

Robert A. Schwegler, Ph.D., Director of Graduate Studies, University of Rhode Island

66 My students have trouble recognizing the cues that identify a summary of a theoretical approach or research findings. They often read the summaries as statements of fact, not as reports of someone's work, even though they realize that not everything in a textbook or article is fact. I think the problem is that they miss the cues that say, 'This is X's work, etc.' Students need to identify the formal cues, recognize summaries, and deal with the summarized information as the interpretations or conclusions of specific scholars. 99

■ Specialized Reading Techniques

Especially in introductory-level social science courses, you will need to learn a large volume of information. Use the following suggestions to read social science materials and retain as much information as possible.

Identify Key Terms

The key to doing well in any college course is to learn its language: specialized and technical terms unique to the discipline. (Your knowledge of new terminology is often tested on quizzes and exams.) The social sciences use precise terminology to describe observations as well as processes. Terminology in the social sciences includes everyday words with specialized meanings, as well as new words not used elsewhere. Refer to Chapter 3 for specific suggestions for learning specialized terminology.

In social science courses, it is particularly important to learn

- **terms that describe general behavior and organizational patterns.**
  Examples: denial, power, aggression, primary/secondary groups, free trade
- **names of stages and processes.**
  Examples: Piaget's stages of cognitive development, Maslow's hierarchy of needs
- **laws, principles, theories, and models.**
  Examples: figure-ground principles, income/expenditures model, models of attention, Keynesian theory
- **names of important researchers and theorists.**
  Examples: Marx, Freud, Skinner, Durkheim, Mead

Understand Theories

An important part of most social science courses is the study of theories. A theory is a set of propositions that explains a certain phenomenon or occurrence. You might, for example, develop a theory to explain why your roommate cannot fall asleep without music or why your history professor always opens class with the same comment. A theory is a reasoned explanation of an observable occurrence. Theories are often tested using the scientific method. In sociology, you may study exchange theory, which explains social behavior as a series of exchanges or trade-offs involving rewards (benefits) and costs. In economics, you may study the natural rate hypothesis that states that workers do not immediately react to changes in wages.

When studying theories, read to find the following information:

- What is the theory? What is its name?
- Who proposed the theory?
- When was it proposed? (Is it recent or historical?)
- What behavior or occurrence does it explain?
- What evidence or rationale is offered that the theory is correct?
- What use or application does the theory have?

Read the following excerpt from a sociology text. Note how the text has been marked to indicate the answers to each of the questions listed previously.

CONFLICT THEORY

behavior —————— |Conflict| theory also had its origins in early sociology, especially in the work of
origin —————— |Marx.| Among its more recent proponents are such people as |Mills, Coser, and
recent proponents —————— |Dahrendorf.| They share the view that society is best understood and analyzed in
statement of theory   terms of conflict and power.

    rationale   Karl Marx began with a very simple assumption: the structure of society is deter-mined by economic organization, particularly the ownership of property. Religious dogmas, cultural values, personal beliefs, institutional arrangements, class struc-tures—all are basically reflections of the economic organization of a society. Inherent in any economic system that supports inequality are forces that generate revolutionary class conflict, according to Marx. The exploited classes eventually rec-ognize their submissive and inferior status and revolt against the dominant class of property owners and employers. The story of history, then, is the story of class struggle between the owners and workers, the dominators and the dominated, the powerful and the powerless.

    applications   Contemporary conflict theorists assume that conflict is a permanent feature of social life and that as a result societies are in a state of constant change. Unlike Marx, however, these theorists rarely assume that conflict is always based on class or that it always reflects economic organization and ownership. Conflicts are assumed to involve a broad range of groups or interests: young against old, male against female, or one racial group against another, as well as workers against employers. These conflicts result because things like power, wealth, and prestige are not available to everyone—they are limited commodities, and the demand exceeds the supply. Conflict theory also assumes that those who have or control desirable goods and services will defend and protect their own interests at the expense of others.

—Eshleman et al., *Sociology: An Introduction,* p. 46

In some texts, you may find several theories presented to explain a single phe-nomenon. Often, these theories are not compatible, and they may even be contra-dictory. In this case, first make certain that you understand each theory; then examine how they differ and consider the evidence offered in support of each.

EXERCISE 10-1   ## Summarizing a Theory

LEARNING
COLLABORATIVELY

Write a summary of the conflict theory described above. Refer to page 266 for sugges-tions on writing summaries. Compare your summary with those of several classmates.

EXERCISE 10-2   ## Analyzing a Theory

Read this excerpt from a psychology textbook, and answer the questions that follow.

KOHLBERG'S THEORY OF MORAL DEVELOPMENT

How children learn to reason about and make judgments about what is right and wrong is an aspect of cognitive development that has received considerable attention (Darley & Schultz, 1990; Vitz, 1990). Piaget included the study of moral development in his theory, arguing that morality is related to cognitive awareness, and that children are unable to make moral judgments until they are at least 3 or 4 years old (Piaget, 1932/1948).

Lawrence Kohlberg (1963, 1969, 1981, 1985) has offered a theory that focuses on moral development. Like Piaget's approach, Kohlberg's is a theory of stages, of moving from one stage to another in an orderly fashion. Kohlberg's database comes from the responses made by young boys who were asked questions about stories that involve a moral dilemma. A commonly cited example concerns whether a man should steal a drug in order to save his wife's life after the pharmacist who invented the drug refuses to sell it to him. Should the man steal the drug; why or why not?

On the basis of responses to such dilemmas, Kohlberg proposed three levels of moral development, with two stages (or "orientations") at each level. The result is the six stages of moral development. . . . For example, a child who says that the man should not steal the drug because "he'll get caught and be put in jail" is at the first, *preconventional*, level of reasoning because the prime interest of the child is simply with the punishment that comes from breaking a rule. A child who says that the man should steal the drug because "it will make his wife happy, and probably most people would do it anyway" is reflecting a type of reasoning at the second, *conventional*, level because the judgment is based on an accepted social convention, and social approval matters as much as or more than anything else. The argument that "no, he shouldn't steal the drug for a basically selfish reason, which in the long run would just promote more stealing in the society in general" is an example of moral reasoning at the third, *postconventional*, level because it reflects complex, internalized standards. Notice that what matters most is not the choice the child makes, but the reasoning behind the choice.

—Gerow, *Psychology: An Introduction*, p. 290

1. Who proposed the theory?
2. What is it intended to explain?
3. Explain the three levels in your own words.
4. How did Kohlberg arrive at the theory?
5. What practical uses can you see for the theory?
6. Underline terminology in the passage that is important to learn.
7. Construct a story about a moral dilemma, and indicate responses at each of the three levels.

Read Research Reports

Because the social sciences rely heavily on observation, research, and experimentation based on the scientific method, textbooks often include brief descriptions of, or references to, research studies. Writers in the social sciences often give clues rather than directly state that they are about to summarize research. Here are two ways writers tell you that a summary of research is to follow:

- **Use of researcher's name.**
  Example: Margaret's Mead's (1935) classic study of sex and temperament . . .
  Example: According to Turner (2005), teenage gangs . . .

- **Use of parentheses to include author's name and date of research.**
  Example: Children who have been read to at home have fewer reading problems in school (Thompson 2003).

KEY STRATEGY: How to Read Research

When reading reports about research, keep these guidelines in mind:

- Determine who conducted the research.
- Identify its purpose.
- Read reviews of current research in the field of study.
- Find out how the research was done.
- Understand the results of the research.
- Find out what theory the results support or what conclusion was drawn.
- Discover the implications and applications of the research. Ask "Why is it important?"

The following excerpt from a sociology textbook describes research on masculine and feminine behavior. See how the marked passages reflect the guidelines given above.

Although biologically men are men and women are women, roles—that is, definitions of masculine and feminine behavior—differ widely from one culture to another. The discovery of cross-cultural variation in gender was one of the earliest kinds of evidence against the idea that each sex has a "natural" temperament and set of interests. In American culture, for example, it is considered "feminine" to be artistic and emotional, but in other cultures men are supposed to be more emotionally expressive and artistic than women. Margaret Mead's *(Purpose)* (1935) classic study of sex and temperament in three cultures was the earliest study of the variability of gender patterning. In one of the New Guinea tribes, the Arapesh, both men and women were found to be cooperative, unaggressive, and gentle. In contrast, the Mundugumor prescribed what would be a masculine temperament in our culture for both sexes—ruthlessness, aggressiveness, and severity. Neither the Arapesh nor the Mundugumor emphasized a contrast *(Results)* between the sexes. In a third New Guinea tribe, the Tchambuli, however, there was such a contrast, but it was the reverse of sex-role temperament in our culture. Tchambuli women tended to be aggressive, domineering, and managerial, whereas the men tended to be dependent, artistic, and sensitive. In short, the *(Conclusion)* study concludes that sex differences are arbitrary and do not reflect any underlying predisposition.

—Skolnick, *The Intimate Environment: Exploring Marriage and the Family,* pp. 193–94

Not all research in the social sciences involves experiments with numerical results. Some disciplines use more subjective research. These results may be reported as a narrative (story). These include case studies, ethnographies (description of ethnic groups), memoirs, and field studies or reports. When reading these, be sure to focus on the findings and their significance and application to the topics you are studying.

EXERCISE 10-3   ### Analyzing a Research Report

Read the following excerpt from a psychology textbook, and answer the questions that follow.

> Researchers have looked at the relationship between adolescent drug use and psychological health (Shedler & Block, 1990). Participants in this investigation were 18-year-olds who had been under study since they were 3 years old. Based on their level of drug use, they were divided into one of three groups: (1) *abstainers* (N = 29), who had never tried any drug; (2) *experimenters* (N = 36), who had used marijuana "once or twice, or a few times" and who tried no more than one other drug; and (3) *frequent users* (N = 20), who used marijuana frequently and tried at least one other drug. There were no socioeconomic or IQ differences among the groups.
>
> The researchers found that *frequent users* were generally maladjusted, alienated, deficient in impulse control, and "manifestly" distressed. The *abstainers* were overly anxious, "emotionally constricted," and lacking in social skills. These same results were apparent when the researchers examined records from when the same subjects were 7 and 11 years old. Generally, the *experimenters* were better adjusted and psychologically "healthier" than either of the other two groups. The authors of this study are concerned that their data may be misinterpreted—that their data might be taken to indicate "that drug use might somehow improve an adolescent's psychological health." Clearly, this interpretation would be in error. You recognize these as correlational data from which no conclusion regarding cause and effect is justified.
>
> While drug use among adolescents is a matter of great concern, there is evidence that we need not get hysterical about infrequent drug use among teenagers.
> —Gerow, *Psychology: An Introduction,* pp. 305–06

1. Who conducted the research?
2. What was its purpose?
3. What methods were used?
4. What were the results?
5. What did the results demonstrate?
6. What is the practical value of the research?
7. Why did the author feel compelled to caution against misinterpretation?

Read to Make Comparisons and Connections

In the social sciences, the ability to see relationships among different ideas and concepts is a necessary skill. Suppose you are reading about three forms of imperfect economic competition: *monopoly, oligopoly,* and *monopolistic competition.*

TABLE 10-2   Sample Comparison Chart

| | FORMS OF IMPERFECT COMPETITION | | |
	MONOPOLY	OLIGOPOLY	MONOPOLISTIC COMPETITION
Number of sellers	One	Several	Many
Entry	Difficult	Less difficult	Easy
Product	Unique	Homogeneous or differentiated	Differentiated
Price influence	Price makers	Price makers	Limited price makers
Price level	Higher price, lower quantity than competition	Somewhat higher price and lower quantity than competition	Slightly higher price than competition and frequently higher production costs

You would, of course, be expected to understand each form. However, you must also know how they are similar, how they are different, and in what economic situation each is found.

When making comparisons, keep the following question in mind: "What does what I am reading have to do with other topics in the chapter?" Then spend a few minutes thinking about how the topics and ideas in the chapter are connected to one another. Begin by reviewing the chapter using the steps you used to preview it (see the Key Strategy Box, "How to Preview Textbook Assignments," p. 35). Then study your text's detailed table of contents and review the lecture notes that correspond to the chapter. For example, one student connected the forms of imperfect competition to other market variables she had learned in economics: number of sellers, ease of entry, product type, price influence, and price level. Then she drew the chart shown in Table 10-2 to compare the three forms according to the market variables that she identified.

In addition to charts, you can organize comparisons by making outlines or lists or by drawing maps that summarize similarities and differences (refer to Chapter 9).

EXERCISE 10-4	**Making Comparisons**
LEARNING COLLABORATIVELY	*Read the following excerpt from a sociology textbook chapter titled "Religious Groups and Systems," and make comparisons between Hinduism and Buddhism by listing, charting, or mapping. Compare your work with the work of other students, discussing its relative effectiveness.*

HINDUISM

The great majority of Hindus in the world live in India and Pakistan. In India, approximately 85 percent of the population is Hindu. Hinduism has evolved over about 4000 years and comprises an enormous variety of beliefs and practices. It hardly corresponds to most Western conceptions of religion because organization is minimal, and there is no religious hierarchy.

Hinduism is so closely intertwined with other aspects of the society that it is difficult to describe it clearly, especially in regard to castes. . . . Hindus sometimes refer to the ideal way of life as fulfilling the duties of one's class and station, which means obeying the rules of the four great castes of India: the Brahmins, or priests; the Kshatriyas, warriors and rulers; the Vaisyas, merchants and farmers; and the Sudras, peasants and laborers. A fifth class, the Untouchables, includes those whose occupations require them to handle "unclean objects."

These classes encompass males only. The position of women is ambiguous. In some respects, they are treated as symbols of the divine, yet in other ways, they are considered inferior beings. Traditionally, women have been expected to serve their husbands and to have no independent interests, but this is rapidly changing.

Although caste is a powerful influence in Hindu religious behavior, a person's village community and family are important as well. Every village has gods and goddesses who ward off epidemics and drought. Hindu belief holds that the universe is populated by a multitude of gods (polytheism) who behave much as humans do, and worship of these gods takes many forms. Some are thought to require sacrifices, others are worshipped at shrines or temples, and shrines devoted to several gods associated with a family deity are often erected in private homes.

To Hindus, the word *dharma* means the cosmos, or the social order. Hindus practice rituals that uphold the great cosmic order. They believe that to be righteous, a person must strive to behave in accordance with the way things are. In a sense, the Hindu sees life as a ritual. The world is regarded as a great dance determined by one's karma, or personal destiny, and the final goal of the believer is liberation from this cosmic dance. Hindus also believe in *transmigration of souls:* After an individual dies, that individual's soul is born again in another form, as either a higher or lower being, depending on whether the person was righteous or evil in the previous life. If an individual becomes righteous enough, the soul will be liberated and will cease to be reborn into an earthly form and will exist only as spirit.

A fundamental principle of Hinduism is that our perceptions of the external world are limitations. When we think about one thing, we are cut off from the infinite number of things we are not thinking about but could be. If we think of nothing, we become in tune with the universe and freed of these limitations. One means of doing this is through meditation.

The actual belief systems of India are extremely confusing to Westerners, because so many different tribal religions have been assimilated into Hinduism, but the basic nature of polytheism in general and of Hinduism in particular permits new gods to be admitted.

BUDDHISM

It is impossible to precisely determine the number of Buddhists because many people accept Buddhist beliefs and engage in Buddhist rites while practicing other religions such as Shintoism, Confucianism, Taoism, or Hinduism.

Buddhism is thought to have originated as a reaction against the Brahminic tradition of Hinduism in the fifth century B.C. At this time, a prince named Siddhartha Gautama was born in northern India to a prosperous ruling family. As he grew older, he was distressed by the suffering he witnessed among the people. At the age of 29, he left his wife and family to go on a religious quest. One day, sitting under a giant fig tree, he passed through several stages of awareness and became the Buddha, the enlightened one. He decided to share his experience with others and became a wandering teacher, preaching his doctrine of the "Four Noble Truths": (1) this life is suffering and pain; (2) the source of suffering is desire and craving; (3) suffering can cease; and (4) the practice of an "eightfold path" can end suffering. The eightfold path consisted of right views, right intentions, right speech, right conduct, right livelihood, right effort, right mindfulness, and right concentration. It combined ethical and disciplinary practices, training in concentration and meditation, and the development of enlightened wisdom. This doctrine was Buddha's message until the age of 80, when he passed into final nirvana, a state of transcendence forever free from the cycle of suffering and rebirth.

After Buddha's death, legends of his great deeds and supernatural powers emerged. Stories were told of his heroism in past lives, and speculations arose about his true nature. Some groups viewed him as a historical figure, whereas others placed him in a succession of several Buddhas of the past and a Buddha yet to come. Differing views eventually led to a diversity of Buddhist sects in different countries. Some remained householders who set up Buddha images and established many holy sites that became centers of pilgrimage. Others became monks, living in monastic communities and depending on the laity for food and material support. Many monks became beggars, and in several Southeast Asian countries, they still go on daily alms rounds. They spend their days in rituals, devotions, meditation, study, and preaching. Flowers, incense, and praise are offered to the image of the Buddha. These acts are thought to ensure that the monks will be reborn in one of the heavens or in a better place in life, from which they may be able to attain the goal of enlightenment.

In every society where Buddhism is widespread, people combine Buddhist thought with a native religion, supporting the monks and paying for rituals in the temples. These societies are also organized around other religions, however.

Today, the integration of Buddhism into many cultures has resulted in different interpretations of the way to Buddhahood. Yet we can supposedly reach Nirvana by seeing with complete detachment, by seeing things as they really are without being attached to any theoretical concept or doctrine.

—Eshleman et al., *Sociology: An Introduction*, pp. 356–58

Read to Make Practical Applications

In many courses, instructors encourage students to apply what they learn to everyday, practical situations. To do so you need to go beyond what is stated in the text and consider how you can use the information. For example, your psychology instructor may ask this question on a midterm exam:

Five-year-old Sammy tells his grandmother that three dinosaurs are hiding in his closet. Knowing this is not true, his grandmother spanks Sammy. Grandmother should be

a. encouraged to be consistent, spanking Sammy whenever he talks about dinosaurs.
b. reminded that children of this age often confuse fantasy and reality.
c. thanked for acting as a good role model for Sammy.
d. told that her authoritarian response will improve his ability to relate to adults.

Or, in your American government class, the following item might appear on an essay exam:

Project the key political issues that will be involved in the next presidential election.

To be prepared for questions such as these, consider the practical applications of what you read. Try to relate each idea to a real-life situation, and, if possible, connect the material to your own experience.

Focus on Large Ideas

Because many social science courses present a great deal of factual information, it is easy to become convinced that the facts are all you need to learn. Actually, factual information is only a starting point, a base from which to approach the real content of a course. Most social science instructors expect you to go beyond facts to analysis—to consider the meaning of facts and details. Many students fail to understand the overriding concepts of their courses because they are too concerned with memorizing information. Be sure to ask the following questions:

• Why do I need to know this?
• Why is this important?
• What principle or trend does this illustrate?
• What is its significance?

Table 10-3 gives examples of details from a course in American history and the more important trends, concepts, or principles they represent.

To keep your focus on major ideas, use the following steps:

1. **After you preview a chapter, write a list of key topics and concepts you expect to read about.**
2. **After you have read about each one, check it off on your list.**
3. **Before you continue, review what you have learned.**
4. **After completing an assignment, return again to your list to reestablish what is important and recheck your recall.** Restate each idea in your own words; if you can do so, you can be confident that you understand the ideas, rather than just recall the author's words.

TABLE 10-3   Identifying Key Concepts

TOPIC	FACTS	WHY IT IS IMPORTANT
The slavery controversy	On May 22, 1856, Representative Brooks from South Carolina approached Senator Sumner of Massachusetts (who had recently given a speech condemning the South for trying to extend slavery) on the floor of the Senate and beat him with a cane until he was near death.	The antagonism between the North and South had become bitter and violent by 1856.
Annexation of territories to the United States	Texas was annexed in 1845. In 1845 and 1846 a great controversy arose over the Oregon territory. The Democrats wanted to make all of the Oregon territory (stretching north above today's border into British Columbia) part of the United States. The British also claimed this land. A war over the territory was barely avoided.	In the late 1840s a belief called *Manifest Destiny* was widespread. People felt it was the destiny of the United States to spread from the Atlantic Ocean to the Pacific Ocean and eventually take over the entire continent.
Industry	Henry Ford perfected the Model T for manufacture in 1914, and by 1924 more than 40,000 workers were working in the first mass-production, assembly-line factory.	This began the trend toward mass production, which led to the second Industrial Revolution.

■ Thought Patterns in the Social Sciences

Four thought patterns that predominate in the social sciences are comparison and contrast, cause and effect, listing, and definition. Table 10-4 describes the uses of each pattern and includes several examples from a specific discipline.

EXERCISE 10-5

Identifying Thought Patterns

Figure 10-1 on page 293 is a chapter outline from a sociology textbook. Read the headings and subheadings and identify the thought pattern of each shaded section. For some headings, more than one pattern may be identified. Refer to Chapter 7 for a review of thought patterns.

EXERCISE 10-6

Identifying Thought Patterns

LEARNING
COLLABORATIVELY

Form groups of three students, and have each student bring a social science textbook to class. Each group should select one text and, using the table of contents, work together to agree on a list of patterns likely to appear in the first five chapters.

TABLE 10-4   Thought Patterns in the Social Sciences

PATTERN	USES	TOPICAL EXAMPLES
Comparison and contrast	To evaluate two sides of an issue; to compare and contrast theories, groups, behaviors, events	*Anthropology* Limbic and nonlimbic communication Theories of aggression Anatomical comparison: archaic and modern Relative versus chronometric dating methods
Cause and effect	To study behavior and motivation; to examine connections between events, actions, behaviors	*Economics* Price determination Factors affecting individual's demand curve Aggregate effects of taxes Factors influencing consumption and saving
Listing	To present facts, illustrations, or examples; to list research findings	*Sociology* Ways children learn Three sociological research methods Myths about old age Agencies of socialization
Definition	To label and describe behaviors, social systems, laws, cycles, etc.	*Political Science* Coercive power Utilitarian power Capitalism Conservatism

FIGURE 10-1   Chapter Outline

Socialization

Nature Versus Nurture

Becoming Human

The Effects of Social Isolation

Personality Development: A Psychological View

Developing a Concept of Self: A Sociological Approach

Socialization and the Life Course

Childhood Socialization

Adult Socialization

Resocialization

Major Agents of Socialization

The Family

Schools

Religion

Peers

The Workplace

The Mass Media

Socialization: Future Directions

Box 4.1 Sociological Focus:

Nature Versus Nurture:

The Case of Willie Bosket Jr.

Box 4.2 Applied Sociology:

Resocialization in a Marine Corps Boot Camp

SOURCE: Thompson and Hickey, *Society in Focus: An Introduction to Sociology*, p. 81

■ Adapting Your Study Techniques

Use the following suggestions in adapting your study methods to the social science field:

1. **Schedule several two- to three-hour blocks of time per week for reading, review, and study.** Avoid last-minute cramming. Study that is distributed over several periods is more effective than one marathon session.

2. **Recognize that understanding is not the same as learning and recall.** Do not assume that because you have read an assignment, you have learned it. To ensure learning, use writing to organize the information. Refer to Chapter 9 for specific strategies.

3. **Use the SQ3R system, or your own adaptation of it, to learn the material.** See the Key Strategy Box "Steps in the SQ3R System" on p. 45. Writing is useful in the recitation step because it allows for greater retention of information through multiple sensory stimulation.

4. **Make connections between topics and chapters.** Each topic is an essential part of the discipline, as is every chapter. Information gained in one chapter should be used and applied in subsequent chapters.

5. **Use the study guide.** Many social science textbooks have a study guide that may be purchased separately. These guides contain useful reviews, sample test questions, and additional practice materials.

6. **Keep a log of total hours studied per week.** The log will help you maintain your motivation and enable you to see how the grades you are earning are related to the amount of time you spend studying.

Test-Taking Tips
Preparing for Exams in the Social Sciences

Many exams you will take in social science courses will be objective: multiple-choice, true/false, matching, or fill-in-the-blank. Your task in these types of questions is to recognize correct answers. To prepare for objective exams, use the following suggestions:

1. Attend review classes if your instructor conducts them.

2. Prepare study sheets. Organize and summarize important information from your notes and your text on topics you expect the exam to cover.

3. Use index cards to record factual information that you must learn (names, dates, definitions, theories, research findings). Record the name, date, name of theory, and so forth on the front of the card, and record what the person is noted for, the event, or the theory itself on the back. Test yourself by reading the front of the card and trying to recall what is on the back. Shuffle the pack of cards so that you do not learn the material in a fixed order.

4. Review previous exams and quizzes. Look for patterns of errors, and identify kinds of questions you missed (knowledge or critical thinking), as well as topics that you need to review.

Self-Test Summary

1. What is the primary concern of the social sciences?	The social sciences focus on the study of people, their development, and how they function and interact, as well as human behavior, social relationships, or social systems and the laws or principles that govern them.
2. What are some of the disciplines included in the social sciences?	Disciplines include psychology, anthropology, sociology, political science, geography, history, and economics.
3. What is a theory?	A theory is a set of propositions that explains a certain phenomenon or occurrence.
4. What are some guidelines for reading in the social sciences?	The guidelines for reading research are • identify key terms. • understand theories. • read research reports. • read to make comparisons and connections. • read to make practical applications. • focus on large ideas.
5. What are the guidelines for reading research material?	The guidelines for reading research material are • determine who conducted the research. • identify its purpose. • read the reviews of current research in the field of study. • find out how the research was done. • understand the results. • identify the conclusion. • discover the implications and applications.
6. How can you organize information to make comparisons?	Use comparison charts, outlines, lists, or maps.
7. What are the four thought patterns that predominate in the social sciences?	The patterns are comparison and contrast, cause and effect, listing, and definition.

Psychology

Are There "His" and "Hers" Brains?

Carole Wade and Carol Tavris

Prereading Questions

1. Do men and women think differently? How?
2. How are male and female brains different?

1   A second stubborn issue concerns the existence of sex differences in the brain. Historically, findings on male-female brain differences have often flip-flopped in a most suspicious manner, a result of the biases of the observers rather than the biology of the brain (Shields, 1975). For example, in the 1960s, scientists speculated that women were more "right-brained" and men were more "left-brained," which supposedly explained why men were "rational" and women "intuitive." Then, when the virtues of the right hemisphere were discovered, such as creativity and ability in art and music, some researchers decided that *men* were more right-brained. But it is now clear that the abilities popularly associated with the two sexes do not fall neatly into the two hemispheres of the brain. The left side is more verbal (presumably a "female" trait), but it is also more mathematical (presumably a "male" trait). The right side is more intuitive ("female"), but it is also more spatially talented ("male").

2   To evaluate the issue of sex differences in the brain intelligently, we need to ask two questions: Do male and female brains differ physically? And if so, what, if anything, do these differences have to do with behavior?

3   Let's consider the first question. Many anatomical and biochemical sex differences have been found in animal brains, especially in areas related to reproduction, such as the hypothalamus (McEwen, 1983). Human sex differences, however, have been more elusive. Of course, we would expect to find male-female brain differences that are related to the regulation of sex hormones and other aspects of reproduction. But many researchers want to know whether there are differences that affect how men and women think or behave—and here, the picture is murkier.

4   For example, in 1982, two anthropologists autopsied 14 human brains and reported an average sex difference in the size and shape of the *splenium,* a small section at the end of the corpus callosum, the bundle of fibers dividing the cerebral hemispheres (de Lacoste-Utamsing & Holloway, 1982). The researchers concluded that women's brains are less lateralized for certain tasks than men's are—that men rely more heavily on one or the other side of the brain, whereas women tend to use both sides. This conclusion quickly made its way into newspapers, magazines, and even textbooks as a verified sex difference.

5   Today, however, the picture has changed. In a review of the available studies, neuroscientist William Byne (1993) found that only the 1982 study reported the splenium to be larger in women. Two very early studies (in 1906 and 1909) found that it was larger in men, and 21 later studies found no sex differences between the two sexes, differences

that paled in comparison with the huge individual variations *within* each sex (Bishop &
Wahlsten, 1997). Most people are unaware of these findings because studies that find no
differences rarely make headlines.

6   Researchers are now looking for other sex differences in the brain, such as in the
density of neurons in specific areas. One team, examining nine brains from autopsied
bodies, found that the women had an average of 11 percent more cells in areas of the
cortex associated with the processing of auditory information; all of the women had more
of these cells than did any of the men (Witelson, Glazer, & Kigar, 1994).

7   Other researchers are searching for sex differences in the brain areas that are active when
people work on a particular task. In one study (Shaywitz et al., 1995), 19 men and 19 women
were asked to say whether pairs of nonsense words rhymed, a task that required them to
process and compare sounds. MRI scans showed that in both sexes an area at the front of the
left hemisphere was activated. But in 11 of the women and none of the men, the corresponding area in the right hemisphere was also active. These findings are further evidence for a sex
difference in lateralization, at least for this one type of language function. Such a difference
could help explain why left-hemisphere damage is less likely to cause language problems in
women than in men after a stroke (Inglis & Lawson, 1981; McGlone, 1978).

8   Over the next few years, research may reveal additional anatomical and information
processing differences in the brains of males and females. But even if such differences
exist, we must then ask our second question: *What do the differences mean for the
behavior of men and women in real life?*

9   Some popular writers have been quick to assume that brain differences explain,
among other things, women's allegedly superior intuition, women's love of talking about
feelings and men's love of talking about sports, women's greater verbal ability, men's edge
in math ability, and why men won't ask for directions when they are lost. But there are at
least three problems with these conclusions:

10   1 *These supposed gender differences in behavior are stereotypes;* the overlap between
the sexes is greater than the difference between them. Although some differences may be
statistically significant, most are small in practical terms.

11   2 *A biological difference does not necessarily have behavioral implications.* In the rhyme-
judgment study, for example, men and women performed equally well, despite the differences in their MRIs—so what do those brain differences actually mean in practical terms?
When it comes to explaining how brain differences are related to more general abilities,
speculations are as plentiful as ants at a picnic, but at present they remain just that—speculations (Blum, 1997; Hoptman & Davidson, 1994). To know whether sex differences in the
brain translate into significant behavioral differences, we would need to know much more
about how brain organization and chemistry affect human abilities and traits.

12   3 *Sex differences in the brain could be the result rather than the cause of behavioral
differences.* Remember that experiences in life are constantly sculpting the circuitry of
the brain, affecting the way brains are organized and how they function—and males and
females often have different experiences.

13   Thus, the answer to our second question, whether physical differences are linked to
behavior, is "No one really knows." It is important to keep an open mind about new findings on sex differences in the brain, but because the practical significance of these findings (if any) is not clear, it is also important to be cautious and aware of how such results
might be exaggerated and misused.

Writing About the Reading

CHECKING YOUR VOCABULARY

1. For each of the words listed below, use context; prefixes, roots, and suffixes (see Chapter 3); and/or a dictionary to write a brief definition or synonym of the word as it is used in the reading.

   a. existence (para. 1) _____

   b. biases (para. 1) _____

   c. intuitive (para. 1) _____

   d. hemispheres (para. 1) _____

   e. spatially (para. 1) _____

   f. hypothalamus (para. 3) _____

   g. elusive (para. 3) _____

   h. splenium (para. 4) _____

   i. lateralized (para. 4) _____

   j. speculations (para. 11) _____

2. Underline new, specialized terms introduced in the reading (see Chapter 3).

3. Draw a word map of one of the words in the reading.

CHECKING YOUR COMPREHENSION

1. What did researchers decide about the brain once the right hemisphere abilities were discovered?
2. What questions need to be asked to evaluate whether sex is responsible for brain differences?
3. How do male and female brains differ in physical makeup?
4. Why are the differences between male and female brains not as significant as they might seem?
5. What do scientists need to know to determine whether sex differences in the brain are related to general abilities?
6. Explain how sex differences in the brain might actually be the result and not the cause of behavioral differences.
7. Why is it important to keep an open mind about sex differences in the brain?
8. What is the overall thought pattern used throughout the reading?

THINKING CRITICALLY

1. How might the findings about sex differences in the brain be misused?
2. Why do you think the author characterizes some traits as "male" and some as "female"? Is this an accurate characterization? Can you name some other traits that are considered typically male or typically female?

3. Why do you think it is important to understand how male and female brains are different? What possible uses could there be for this information?
4. Why do scientists study which areas of the brain are used for different tasks?
5. Are you convinced by this selection that there are significant differences in male and female brains? Why or why not?
6. Describe other types of physical differences between men and women that impact behavior.

LEARNING/STUDY STRATEGY

Write a summary of this selection.

11 Reading in Business

BUSINESS: A Visual Overview

Billboard usage is an important component of business-related studies in marketing and product management.

Understanding how to read business graphics is an essential part of studying for a business degree.

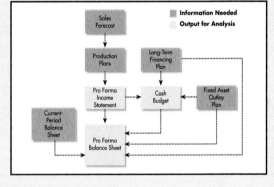

Not all businesspeople wear a business suit to work. Jobs available to business majors range from corporate jobs in sky-scrapers to small business ownership. The woman shown here owns and runs her own garden center.

LEARNING OBJECTIVES

- To learn what the business disciplines are

- To consider whether you should major in business

- To discover tips for studying business

- To become aware of current hot topics in business

- To develop specialized reading techniques for business

- To discover thought patterns commonly used in business

- To adapt study techniques for business courses

What Are the Business Disciplines?

Business administration and management is the top major at U.S. colleges and universities. This is not surprising, because jobs that require business degrees rank in the list of the Top Ten starting salaries for recent college graduates.

In general, a business major encompasses a wide variety of courses intended to give you a sense of every aspect of running a business, from managing the company's money through advertising a product effectively through hiring the right employees. Course work for a business degree often includes requirements in such related fields as computer science, mathematics/statistics, and communications.

Table 11-1 offers an overview of the various types of business courses offered by most colleges and universities. In general, business students must take courses in all these areas and then choose a specialty in which to focus their efforts. Note that the business disciplines can be divided into two general categories: more quantitative areas that deal with numbers, and less quantitative areas that focus on managing, selling, and marketing.

Table 11-1   The Business Disciplines and Career Opportunities

MORE QUANTITATIVE		
DISCIPLINE	**DESCRIPTION**	**CAREER OPPORTUNITIES**
Accounting	Study of the systematic recording, reporting, and analysis of the financial transactions of a business	• Accounts payable clerk • Accounts receivable clerk • Accountant
Finance	Study of raising money and resources (sometimes called *capital*) to begin a business, to invest that business's assets, and to help that business grow or become more profitable	• Banker • Financial planner • Stockbroker • Insurance underwriter

continued

TABLE 11–1 *continued*

DISCIPLINE	DESCRIPTION	CAREER OPPORTUNITIES
Operations Management	Study of the design, execution, and control of a firm's day-to-day operations, including manufacturing and distribution	• Importer • Warehousing specialist • Distributor • Wholesaler
Economics	Study of how goods, services, and wealth are produced, consumed, and distributed	• Banker • Government employee • Public policy analysts • Comptroller

LESS QUANTITATIVE

DISCIPLINE	DESCRIPTION	CAREER OPPORTUNITIES
Management	A general term for the study of how to organize, coordinate, and implement a set of business plans to help achieve the company's goals	• Department manager • Director of nonprofit organization • Agent for actors or sports figures
Marketing	Study of packaging, promoting, advertising, and distributing products and services that consumers want or need	• Advertising executive • Package designer • Publicist • Public relations specialist
Human Resource Management	Study of the activities associated with staffing a business (such as recruitment, selection, appraisal, compensation, and career development)	• Personnel specialist • Recruiter • Human resources manager
Organizational Behavior	Study of the way people and processes interact in the workplace, often with an emphasis on increasing productivity and effectiveness	• Productivity specialist • Management consultant • Labor relations specialist

Should You Major in Business?

The fact that the term *business* encompasses so many areas should provide some insight into what it takes to be a successful business major. Business majors have to be willing to undergo training in the wide variety of areas that are all core parts of running a business. Looking at Table 11-1, you can imagine how a business that doesn't succeed in just one of the areas is likely to fail overall. Your company might have excellent financing and a stellar marketing plan, but if you don't hire the right employees, you will not be successful. Likewise, you might have excellent products and terrific workers, but if you don't spend money wisely and plan for future growth, your business may go bankrupt.

The four-year degrees given in business are sometimes called B.B.A.s, short for Bachelor's of Business Administration. The phrase *business administration* is key here, because it implies that successful businesspeople know how to administer the many aspects of the company and how to keep everything running smoothly.

What characteristics and habits will make you a successful business major?

1. **You should be competitive**. In the business world, there is a huge amount of competition—for the best jobs, for the most lucrative clients, for the best profit levels. The most successful business majors have a strong and healthy sense of competition, a fierce desire to win and be the best. It is probably not surprising that many college athletes go on to successful careers in business.

2. **You should enjoy teamwork**. In very few companies will you ever work alone. Because business operations can be so complex, you will have to work with a number of other people on a regular basis. You'll each have your own job to do as part of a team, so you need to understand effective team dynamics. (If you've ever worked as part of a study group, you can begin to understand how different personalities can affect the team's ability to get the job done.) Business departments recognize this, so you'll be asked to do team research and team presentations on a regular basis.

3. **You should not be afraid of mathematics**. Even if you plan to major in one of the less quantitative business majors, you will still be dealing with numbers on a regular basis, because budgeting and profitability are the responsibility of every manager. Do not put off studying math; start early. (For tips on how to read math textbooks effectively, see Chapter 13, "Reading Mathematics.")

4. **You should be willing to develop people skills**. A business manager's job is to manage not only a process or a product, but also a staff of people. There is also the all-important task of serving your customers. Business majors must have a full set of social skills in their arsenal. They need to know when to be aggressive, when to be gentle, when to be demanding, and when to be motivational. For many business majors, the best place to learn these skills is "on the job" during an internship in junior or senior year.

Tips for Studying Business—Even If You Are Not a Major

All of us are in contact with businesses on a daily basis. When you stop for gas, buy a sandwich, or pick up your cell phone, you are involved in a business transaction. Because the world of business surrounds us, business courses offer a number of advantages.

Even if you do not major in business, it will be very helpful for your career to have a basic understanding of the key business functions. Some schools even offer a business minor to give other majors this type of real-world training. In addition, business courses offer these benefits:

1. **They help you make career decisions.** You will discover a wide range of employment opportunities.

2. **They help you become a successful employee.** Getting a job is only the first step to a successful career; you must be proficient at your job. By learning how businesses operate, you will be able to contribute effectively to your company.

3. **They help you start your own business.** If you plan to start your own company, business courses will give you the knowledge and skills to make your business succeed.

Even if you are required to take only one course titled something like "Business Essentials" or "Business 101," you will benefit from learning the basics of each subdiscipline within business. To make the most of that course, do the following:

- **Apply the concepts to your life and the world around you**. For every concept you learn, you will likely find it easy to give an example from your own life.

- **Read a business magazine like *Business Week* or watch the nightly business report on television**. Business news will often talk about precisely the issues you are studying in your class.

- **Think of your business course as a way of putting money in your wallet**. Good business courses teach you all about opportunities, about ways of saving money and investing it wisely. Make use of this information to start yourself on the road to a successful financial future.

Quotes from a Business Professor

Advice for Business Students

John Ribezzo, Professor of Business, Community College of Rhode Island

❝ Whatever your major concentration of study is, success at the college level is dependent upon several factors, including attending class on a regular basis, being prepared for class, and participating in class discussions. Students in the area of business should not only be concerned with subject content, but should take advantage of the college experience to sharpen their so-called soft skills. Employers are particularly interested in the prospective employee's ability to think critically, communicate orally and in writing, work in teams, lead, and have an overall understanding of how an organization operates. ❞

■ Current Hot Topics in Business

Whenever you take a course, you should always try to discover the trends, issues, and themes that are emphasized. Identifying these "hot topics" will help you predict essay exam questions, choose worthwhile topics for papers and assignments, and make valuable contributions to class discussions.

In business courses, there are at least six current topics:

- **Globalization of Business.** Growing numbers of U.S. companies are doing business with firms in other countries. United States businesses compete in foreign markets, and the number of international trade agreements continues to grow. Consequently, it is important to recognize business as an international venture and understand the role of the United States in the world market.

- **Role of Technology.** As technology continues to develop and change, so must businesses change and adapt to keep pace. The Internet, telecommunications, computers, and robotics all have an impact on business. For example, growing numbers of businesses have Web sites; increasing numbers of employees are telecommuting (working at home); and small robots are used increasingly in manufacturing. Awareness of technology will keep you on the cutting edge of business growth and change.

- **Importance of Diversity.** Today's workforce consists of individuals from a variety of cultural and ethnic groups. A wider range of interests, social customs, and value systems is represented. Diversity can be a strong advantage for a company because it offers a variety of resources and perspectives.

- **Growth and Role of Small Businesses.** Increasingly, small businesses are a major source of employment. Besides providing employment, small businesses provide competition and are responsible for change and innovation. Many people mistakenly think of businesses as only large corporations. By recognizing the role and importance of small businesses, you will approach business courses with a broadened perspective.

- **Importance of Ethical Decisions and Social Responsibility.** There is an increasing emphasis in business on making ethical decisions and demonstrating social responsibility. Business ethics refers to the application of moral standards to business situations. Ethical issues include fairness and honesty, conflict of interest (between personal and business interests), and communication. Using misleading advertising, falsifying information, taking bribes, and endangering a consumer's health are examples of ethical problems that companies should strive to avoid.

- **Accountability and Open Financial Reporting.** There is an increasing emphasis in business on accountability, internal auditing, and financial disclosure. The Sarbanes-Oxley Act of 2002 specifies accounting and auditing procedures. In light of recent large corporate scandals like Bear Stearns, reporting and disclosure guidelines are of significant importance.

■ Specialized Reading Techniques

Business courses often require you to read and work with models, case studies, and specialized graphics. The following sections describe these features and offer strategies for reading each one.

Reading Models

Because business courses focus on organization and management, many texts include models to describe these structures and processes. A model is an overall plan or representation that describes how something is designed, how it functions, or why it occurs.

Models contain general features or characteristics that pertain to many situations. For example, you could construct a model that describes the enrollment/advisement/registration process at your college. It would describe the procedures most students follow from the time they apply for college admission to the time they first attend classes.

Models also may function as explanations of complex processes. For example, you may study models of decision making, information processing, or leadership. These models contain all the pertinent variables, factors, and characteristics that control how something works or explain why it occurs. Diagrams often accompany text descriptions of a model.

The excerpt below and model in Figure A are taken from a business text. They describe how a company develops short-term financial plans. The remainder of the chapter from which this introduction was taken provides detailed information about the process. The excerpt has been annotated to indicate the types of information to look for as you read models.

SHORT-TERM (OPERATING) FINANCIAL PLANS

purpose/function — Short-term (operating) financial plans specify short-term financial actions and the anticipated impact of those actions. These plans most often cover a 1- to 2-year period. Key inputs include the sales forecast and various forms of operating and financial data. Key outputs include a number of operating budgets, the cash budget, and pro forma [document prepared in advance] financial statements. The entire short-term financial planning process is outlined in the flow diagram of Figure A.

time frame —

key parts —

reference to diagram —

Short-term financial planning begins with the sales forecast. From it production plans are developed that take into account lead (preparation) times and include estimates of the required types and quantities of raw materials. Using the production plans, the firm can estimate direct labor requirements, factory overhead outlays, and operating expenses. Once these estimates have been made, the firm's pro forma income statement and cash budget can be prepared. With the basic inputs—pro forma income statement, cash budget, fixed asset outlay plan, long-term financing plan, and current period balance sheet—the pro forma balance sheet can finally be developed. Throughout the remainder of this chapter, we will concentrate on the key outputs of the short-term financial planning process: the cash budget, the pro forma income statement, and the pro forma balance sheet.

summary of model —

—Gitman, *Principles of Managerial Finance*, pp. 580–81

FIGURE A   The Short-Term (Operating) Financial Planning Process

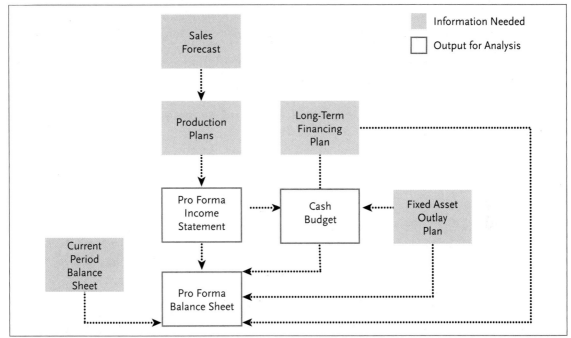

SOURCE: Nickerson, *Business and Information Systems.*

KEY STRATEGY: How to Read Models

When reading and studying models, be sure to:

1. **Find out what the model represents and why it is considered a model.**   In the example above, the model explains the short-term financial planning process and factors that affect it. You should also know who developed the model and when it was developed. A model often is named after the person who proposed it.

2. **Determine how the model was derived.**   Was it developed through study and research (theory), or by observing and working with the actual process (practice)? (In the previous excerpt, the author does not include information on the development of the model under discussion.)

3. **Analyze the model closely.**   Identify each stage or step, and understand the relationship between the parts or steps. If a diagram such as the one shown in the preceding excerpt is not included, try to draw one.

4. **Summarize the model in your own words, including its key features.** This will test your understanding and strengthen your recall (See the Key Strategy box "How to Summarize," p. 267).

continued

5. **Examine the model critically.** Does it account for all aspects or variations of the process? What are its limitations?

6. **Determine the usefulness or application of the model.** How and when can you use it? To what practical situations will it apply? The author may suggest applications or this task may be left to the reader.

7. **If more than one model is presented for a given process, focus on their similarities and differences.**

EXERCISE 11-1   Analyzing a Model

The following excerpt presents a model of group collaboration—the process whereby members of a group work together toward a common goal. Study the model and answer the accompanying questions.

CHARACTERISTICS OF GROUP COLLABORATION

Group collaboration has several characteristics. One characteristic is *when* the collaboration takes place and another is *where* it takes place. This section examines these characteristics to provide a basis for understanding workgroup information systems.

Time and Place of Collaboration

Two of the basic characteristics of group collaboration are *time* and *place*—the "when" and "where" of collaboration. If two or more people collaborate, they may do so at the same time or at different times. To work together at the same time, they could be in a room together or talk by telephone. To collaborate at different times, they could leave voice messages, send faxes, send e-mail, use teleconferencing or send regular mail.

People may also work together at the same place or at different places. They may be in the same room or building, making it possible for them to have direct contact. Alternatively, they may be at widely separated locations, in which case they cannot have direct contact without extensive travel.

There are four possible combinations of these characteristics. People working at the same time and place can collaborate directly. A face-to-face meeting is an example of this type of collaboration. People working at the same time but in different places often use the telephone for collaboration. Conference calls also are common in this situation. When people work at different times but at the same place, they collaborate by leaving messages, either on the telephone or by e-mail. The most complex situation is when people working at different times and places need to collaborate. Voice messages, faxes, e-mail, teleconferencing, and regular mail are used in this situation.

Form of Communication

Another way of characterizing group collaboration is by the *form* that the communication between people takes—the "what" of collaboration. Perhaps the most often used form of communication in business is *audio communication;* people talk to each other, either in person or on the telephone. Audio communication is not only what is said, but also how it is said. Tone, inflection, and other characteristics of speech often express information. In addition to live, verbal communication, recorded sound is used in group collaboration. Voice mail, taped sound, and other recorded sound are part of audio communication.

A second form of communication in group collaboration is *visual communication,* specifically sights of people or other real things. When groups meet in person, the members of the group can see each other. Their facial expressions and body language give visual clues that provide information about what they are saying and thinking. Recorded sights also are used in some collaborative situations. Still pictures or moving images on video tape may be shown to groups for discussion.

A final form of communication used in group collaboration is *document (or data) communication.* Documents may contain text, numbers, table, diagrams, graphs, and other written representations of information. Examples are a report sent to members of a team, a table of data examined by committee members, a diagram of a design examined by several people, and a graph of data discussed by a group.

—Nickerson, *Business and Information Systems,* pp. 263–65

1. What is the model intended to show?
2. Summarize the process described in the model.
3. Evaluate the model. Does the model account for all possibilities? What are its limitations?
4. Of what practical use is the model? When might you use it?

Reading Case Studies

Case studies often are included in business texts. Case studies are reports of single incidents or evaluations of a particular individual, firm, or transaction. They describe how a particular business is organized or how it manages a particular problem or process. They may be intended to introduce a concept, illustrate a principle, describe a situation, or provoke discussion and evaluation. Case studies also give you insights into and experience with actual problems or situations you may face on the job. In some texts, case studies are referred to as "business profiles" or simply as "cases." Other texts include a short case study that provides a brief insight into a particular problem or issue.

The brief case study that follows appears in a marketing text. As you read it, try to discover why it was included in a chapter titled "Catching the Buzz: Promotional Strategy and Integrated Marketing Communication." The excerpt has been annotated to indicate the kinds of information presented.

This case study describes the advertising issues faced by a major credit card company, American Express. The case was included to provide an example of the problems and issues major corporations face in developing advertising strategies.

KEY STRATEGY: How to Read Case Studies

When reading a case study, keep the following questions in mind:

1. **What is the problem** the case study addresses?

2. **What alternative solutions** are proposed or considered, if any?

3. **How do the alternatives compare?** What are the pros and cons of each?

4. **What alternative or solution was selected?** What was the outcome?

5. **What is the case study intended to demonstrate?** For example, does it illustrate practical problems? Discuss limitations? Point out advantages or disadvantages? Demonstrate a process? Describe a management strategy? Demonstrate a particular philosophy or approach?

REAL CHOICES AT AMERICAN EXPRESS

descriptive introduction and background

What do Robert DeNiro, Tiger Woods, Kate Winslet, Laird Hamilton, and Mike Krzyzewski all have in common? Let's see, Robert DeNiro is one of the greatest living actors; Tiger Woods is arguably the best golfer ever; Kate Winslet is a multiple Academy Award nominee; Laird Hamilton is perhaps the greatest surfer to have ever lived; and Mike Krzyzewski is a Hall of Fame basketball coach. However, being famous and best in their field are not the only things these folks have in common. They also all carry the American Express credit card and have been in television or print commercials promoting the card in the company's "My Life, My Card" campaign.

statement of American Express marketing strategy

By using famous and recognizable people in its ads, American Express is trying to capture the attention of current and potential consumers. The fast pace of today's busy lifestyles and the rapid changes in information technology mean that, more than ever, companies like American Express have to rely on the familiar faces of celebrities to get their messages across. Each of the AMEX ads includes brief biographical information on the celebrity such as where they live, profession, greatest triumphs or greatest disappointments, and basic philosophy on life. The final point of each ad is how the American Express card helps enable the individual to pursue what is important to him or her. American Express is communicating to its current and potential customers that they are just like these celebrities—simply trying to live life at its best. So, the slogan of "My Life, My Card" is perfect for the ad campaign.

description of the ad

examples of other marketing strategies

However, advertising is not the only element of the promotion mix that American Express is using to get its message across. In Mexico, for example, AMEX uses sales promotion to offer one free airline ticket for each ticket purchased with the American Express card. In Europe the company has set up "AMEX Travelcast" hubs in tourist areas such as train stations. These hubs take advantage of the growing podcast phenomenon by allowing travelers to download maps and videos to their MP3 players. The maps downloaded feature foreign exchange bureaus and retailers that accept the American Express card. The company also has used the Internet to broadcast

"Webisodes," which are 5-minute video stories featuring comedian Jerry Seinfeld, resulting in over 3 million visitors to its Web site. Finally, AMEX uses personal selling to attract restaurant owners to its Restaurant Partnership Program, which provides savings and benefits to owners that accept the American Express card.

Problem: the competition

Unfortunately for American Express, their "My Life, My Card" advertising campaign isn't without competition. Visa has been running ads for some time now with the slogan of "Life takes Visa," which is a clever variation on the same theme communicated by the American Express ads. American Express's other main competitor, MasterCard, uses its "Priceless" line of commercials that are aimed at encouraging customers to use the card to create priceless moments. Promotional ads expressing the same theme by these competitors diminish somewhat the impact of American Express's ads and have the potential to confuse consumers about which card provides the best means to pursue life's rewards.

question of longevity

The company's previous campaign, "The American Express card, don't leave home without it," had a long run of popularity and is still a well-known advertising saying. But will the current campaign enjoy the same success? How long will people stay connected to the "My Life, My Card" message, along with its accompanying celebrities?

possible solution

Perhaps American Express needs to look for creative ways to utilize other elements of the promotion mix to develop a truly integrated marketing communication strategy that augments its advertisements. Otherwise, over the long haul American Express may end up investing a lot of money in advertising but still fail to achieve its long-term marketing communication goals.

You Make the Call

1. What is the decision facing American Express?
2. What factors are important in understanding the decision situation?
3. What are the alternatives?
4. What decision(s) do you recommend?
5. What are some ways to implement your recommendation?

—Solomon, Marshall and Stuart, *Marketing*, p. 403

EXERCISE 11-2   ## Analyzing a Case Study

Read the following brief case study taken from a business textbook chapter titled "An Overview of Marketing," and answer the questions that follow.

CAMPBELL SOUP SERVES UP VARIETY

Over 120 years ago, the Campbell Soup Company introduced canned condensed soup and gave the world its first convenience food. Since then, those well-known red and white labels and the sigh "Mmmm, mmmm, good" have become symbols of American culture. However, today's increasingly health-conscious consumers often spurn canned soup in favor of those made with fresh ingredients. Although sales of the popular brand total $1.1 billion, earning the line 48.9 percent of the canned soup market, Campbell faces declining domestic sales. Turning to global markets, the company's executives hope, that eventually more than half of the firm's profits will come from sales outside the United States.

Experts caution that strong cultural and regional tastes and preferences make food more difficult to translate to foreign markets than soda or laundry detergent. The editor of *Food and Drink Daily* recently stressed the importance of recognizing the unique characteristics of individual global market segments. Just because Americans love to ladle out clam chowder and tomato soup by the bowl full doesn't mean those same flavors appeal to customers around the world. Marketers at Campbell know that demographics, lifestyle, and geography influence customer choices, with diet especially sensitive to local fancies. To avoid potential pitfalls that differences often create, Campbell conducts extensive research in specific consumer segments before generating and marketing brands.

All over the globe, Campbell's research and taste tests are resulting in new, locally pleasing recipes. In Argentina, consumers don't take to the enduring American favorite, chicken noodle soup, but they do like split pea with ham. Emphasizing *Sopa de Campbell's* fresh ingredients, regional ads proclaim it "the real soup." Polish soup lovers, who eat an average of five bowls each week, can choose from eight varieties of Campbell's *zupa,* including *flaki*—tripe soup spiced with lots of pepper. To please Mexican palates, Campbell came up with hot and spicy Cream of Chile Poblano.

To become a major player in the global market, Campbell will face stiff competition. British consumers, for example, have known and preferred Heinz canned soup for many years. To attract more British shoppers, Campbell is creating new products developed specifically to meet English tastes. To expand its Japanese distribution from Tokyo and Osaka to include all of Japan, the soupmaker recently entered a joint venture with Nakano Vinegar Company of Japan.

Is the world ready for Campbell's soup? The company's CEO believes the answer is a resounding yes. His considerable international experience—as a former marketing executive with Colgate-Palmolive in South Africa and with Parke-Davis in Hong Kong—tells him that responding to consumer preferences leads to increased sales.

—Pride et al., *Business,* pp. 386–87

1. What is the problem the case study addresses?
2. What solution did Campbell pursue?
3. What is this case study intended to demonstrate about global marketing?
4. What does this study tell you about the problems of global marketing?
5. What factors influence consumer choice of soups?

Graphics: Reading Organization Charts

Because the focus in the field of business is on organization and process, business texts frequently include graphs, charts, and tables to synthesize and/or summarize text material that describes those structures and processes. Refer to the Key Strategy box "How to Read Graphics" (p. 224) for a review.

FIGURE 11-1   Organization Chart

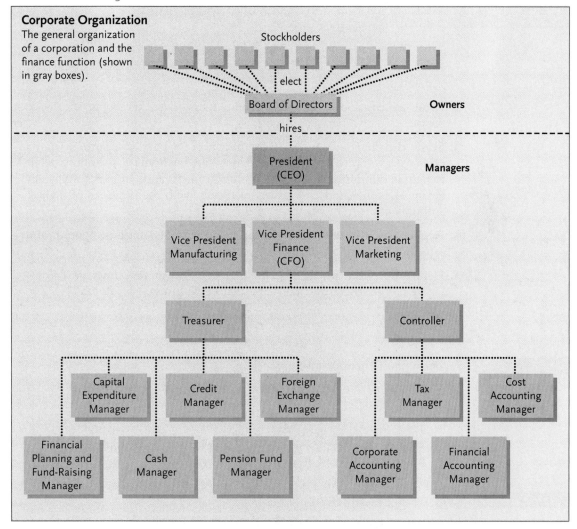

Corporate Organization
The general organization of a corporation and the finance function (shown in gray boxes).

SOURCE: Gitman, *Principles of Managerial Finance,* p. 8

Particularly common in the field of business is the organization chart. Organization charts often are used to reflect structure or to define relationships; they may, for example, show levels of responsibility, roles, or functions. The chart shown in Figure 11-1 describes the organization of a corporation, emphasizing its financial structure.

Organization charts also may be used to describe group behaviors or define employee responsibilities. The impact of decisions or marketing strategies, and the classification of markets, also may be shown on an organization chart.

KEY STRATEGY: How to Read Organization Charts

When reading organization charts, keep in mind the following tips:

1. **Read the text that accompanies the chart.**   It should establish the context and provide details about the chart.

2. **Read the caption or title of the chart.**   Note the key, abbreviations, or coding.

3. **Study the chart carefully.**   Determine how the chart is organized. Charts often use a vertical or horizontal structure, moving from top to bottom or left to right in diminishing degrees of authority, importance, or responsibility. In Figure 11-1, the chart is organized vertically, with the positions of highest authority at the top.

4. **Decide how the items are related.**   In Figure 11-1, each position on the same horizontal line is of equal importance.

5. **Determine what pattern, principle, or concept the chart describes.**   Figure 11-1 describes the financial functions within a corporation.

EXERCISE 11-3   **Analyzing an Organization Chart**

Study the organization chart shown in Figure 11-2 and answer the questions that follow.

1. What is the chart intended to show?
2. Describe how the chart is organized and how the items are related.

EXERCISE 11-4   **Constructing an Organization Chart**

Construct an organization chart that describes the structure of an organization (college, church, club, or business) with which you are familiar.

Graphics: Reading Flowcharts

A flowchart is a specialized diagram that shows how a process or procedure works. Lines or arrows are used to show the direction (route or routes) through the procedure. Various shapes (boxes, circles, rectangles) enclose what is done at each stage or step. You could, for example, draw a flowchart to describe how to apply for and obtain a student loan or how to locate a malfunction in your car's electrical system.

A sample flowchart, taken from a business and information systems text, is shown in Figure 11-3 (p. 316); it describes the information flow related to sales.

FIGURE 11-2   Organization Chart

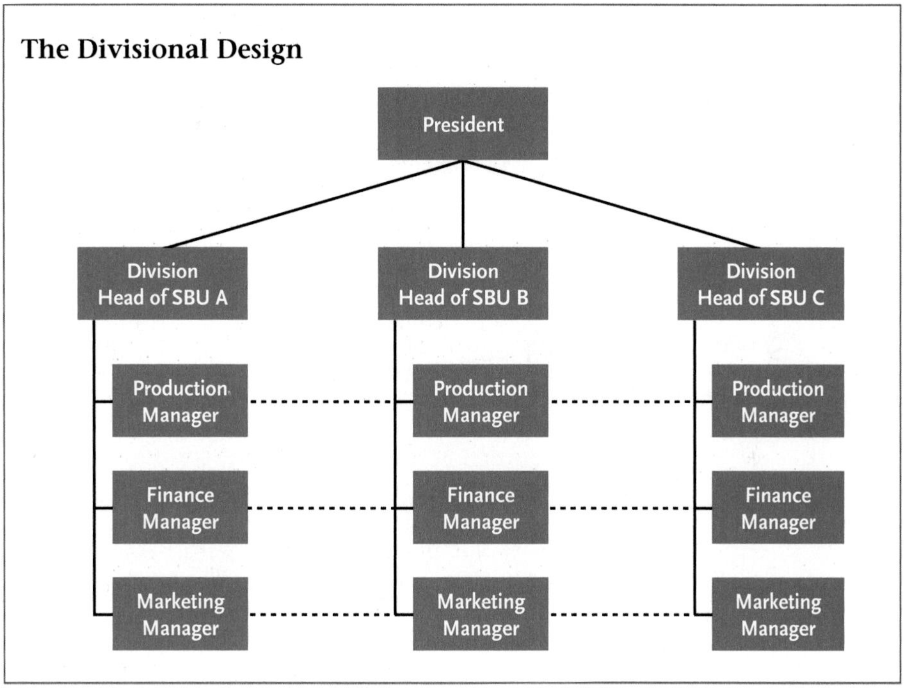

The Divisional Design

SOURCE: Van Fleet, *Contemporary Management,* p. 251

KEY STRATEGY: How to Read a Flowchart

To read flowcharts effectively, use the following suggestions:

1. **Figure out what process the flowchart illustrates.** Figure 11-3 shows the process by which information flows from a sale.

2. **Next, follow the arrows, and read each step in the chart.**

3. **When you have finished, summarize the process in your own words.** Then try to draw the chart from memory without referring to the text. Compare your drawing with the chart, and note any discrepancies.

EXERCISE 11-5   Studying a Flowchart

Study the flowchart in Figure 11-3. Summarize it in your own words and then, without referring to it, list the steps or sketch your own flowchart.

FIGURE 11-3   Sample Flowchart

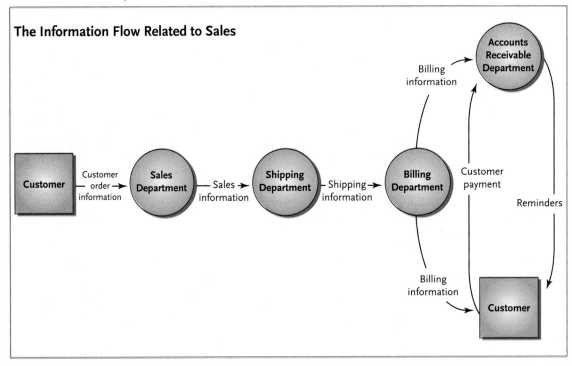

The Information Flow Related to Sales

SOURCE: Nickerson, *Business and Information Systems,* p. 40

■ Thought Patterns in Business

There are three common thought patterns used in business courses:

- **Classification**—subdividing a topic into its parts—is commonly encountered because it is an effective means of describing the components of management.
- **Process**—the study of how events occur—is used frequently because of the focus on *how* a business operates and is managed.
- **Enumeration**, or listing, is a commonly used pattern because much information in the business field is descriptive: listings of characteristics, factors, principles, and theories that affect a business's organization and management.

■ Adapting Your Study Techniques

Because the field of business is diverse and includes courses in a wide range of topics, it is especially important to adapt your study techniques to suit each course you are taking. What follows are a few suggestions for handling your course load:

1. **Begin each class by analyzing course content.** Study course objectives, pay close attention to the course syllabus, and analyze your textbook's preface and individual chapter learning objectives for additional clues.

Then select reading and study strategies for each course. Figure out what types of reading are required and what level of recall is demanded; then identify appropriate reading strategies to use. Refer to Chapter 2 for a discussion of adjusting your reading rate. (See the Key Strategy box "Adjusting Rate to Meet Comprehension Demands," p. 64.) Also select appropriate learning and review strategies and decide how writing could help you with each course. (Refer to Chapter 9 for a review of various strategies.)

2. **Take time to shift gears.** It is important to "shift gears" as you move from studying one course to studying another. Do this by taking a 10- to 15-minute break between study periods. As you begin working on the next course, spend a minute or two focusing your attention on it. You can do this easily by reviewing a previous assignment, your last set of lecture notes, or the last homework assignment you completed. Finally, preview your current assignment, define your goals, and set a time limit to complete the task. Monitor your comprehension as you work by using the suggestions in Chapter 1.

3. **Use available text supplements.** Some business texts have accompanying study guides, CDs, problem sets, Web sites, or simulations. If they are recommended by your instructor, they will guide you in applying chapter content. These guides will also introduce you to the type of questions you may be asked on exams.

4. **Learn formulas and problem-solving strategies.** Some courses, such as accounting, investment, and finance, rely heavily on learning formulas and solving problems. For reading and study strategies useful in these courses, refer to Chapter 13, "Reading Mathematics."

Test–Taking Tips
Objective Exams

Exams in business are often objective. Refer to the test-taking tips in Chapter 10 for suggestions on preparing for objective exams. When taking exams, keep the following suggestions in mind:

1. **Be sure to arrive at the exam on time.** Sit in the front of the room; you will avoid distractions and be able to concentrate more easily.

2. **Preread the exam.** Look through the whole exam before beginning. Then plan your time: decide how much time to spend on each part.

3. **Read the directions carefully.**

4. **Leave nothing blank.** Guess if you are not sure of an answer; circle the question number so you can return to it later if you have time.

5. **Be sure to read all choices before answering a multiple-choice question.** Often, the directions require you to select the "best" choice.

6. **If you are uncertain about a multiple-choice item, eliminate obviously wrong choices.** Then analyze those that remain. When two choices seem similar, analyze how they differ.

7. **Express similar or confusing choices in your own words.** Often, this process will help you discover the right answer.

Self-Test Summary

1. What, in general, is the focus of business courses?	Business courses focus on all aspects of creating and operating a business.
2. What are some of the disciplines included in the broad field of business?	Areas include business management, information systems, accounting, finance, statistics, retailing, advertising, organizational behavior, and corporate strategy.
3. Identify some current "hot topics" or trends in business.	Current hot topics include globalization, the role of technology, diversity, the growth and role of small business, and the importance of ethical decisions and social responsibility in business.
4. In business, what is meant by a "model"?	A model is an overall plan or representation that describes how something is designed, how it functions, or why it occurs.
5. What is a case study? What questions should you ask when reading and evaluating a case study?	A case study is a report of a single company, firm, or individual's business problem, transaction, profit, or decision making. The steps in reading and evaluating a case study are • identify the problem. • determine alternative solutions. • analyze and compare alternatives. • evaluate the alternative selected. • determine what the case study is intended to demonstrate.
6. What is the purpose of an organization chart?	An organization chart reflects structure or defines relationships.
7. What is the purpose of a flowchart?	A flowchart shows how a process or procedure works.
8. What three thought patterns predominate in business texts? Define each.	The three thought patterns are • classification: subdividing a topic into its parts. • process: the study of how events occur. • enumeration: listing of information, such as business characteristics, factors, principles, and theories.

Marketing

New Advertising Techniques
Michael R. Solomon, Greg W. Marshall, and Elnora W. Stuart

Prereading Questions

1. Do you find that word-of-mouth advertising is more credible than media advertising?
2. What product placement have you noticed in television shows and movies?

1   What goes around comes around. The original pre-media advertising, word of mouth, has new currency in techniques that go by the name "buzz communication." The goal is to create buzz about a product. Many buzz campaigns originate on the Internet with the hope of something virus-like. The term *viral advertising* has come into fashion.

Word-of-Mouth Advertising

2   A problem in advertising is credibility. Consumers are hardly blotters who absorb any line laid on them through the mass media. Far more credible are stories from friends and acquaintances who have had a favorable experience with a product.

3   • **Buzz Advertising.** Word-of-mouth testimonials, friends talking to friends, is strong advertising. But how does word-of-mouth advertising get the buzz going? And how can the buzz be sustained? In the advertising industry's desperation in recent years to find new avenues for making pitches, buzzing has turned into an art. Several agencies specialize in identifying individuals with a large circle of contacts and introducing them to a product. These agents sample the product, generally being able to keep the samples for their help in talking them up with family, coworkers and anyone else in earshot. The agents file occasional reports, with the incentive of being eligible for prizes.

4   How does buzz stack up against traditional advertising media? Nobody knows, but it's cheap enough that advertisers have seen it as worth trying.

5   • **Viral Advertising.** Another word-of-mouth tactic is **viral advertising,** so called because, when successful, it spreads contagion-like through the population. Advertisers create clever clips that they hope will prompt visitors to pass them on to friends. People open messages from friends, which tangentially increases an ad's reach at low cost. Viral advertising works particularly well on the Web. Automakers were among the first to experiment with viral techniques. Ford promoted its SportKa in Europe with story lines designed to stir conversation and draw people in for other installments. BMW estimated that 55.1 million people saw its *For Hire* series. Honda could not have been happier with its *Cog* mini-story. Said a Honda executive: "I have never seen a commercial that bolted around the world like *Cog* in two weeks."

• viral advertising Media consumers pass on the message, like a contagious disease, usually on the Internet.

6   On the downside, however, advertisers can't cancel viral ads, which have a life of their own and can float around the Internet for months, even years. An advertisement for beach vacations in Beirut would have been fine in 2005 but grotesquely inappropriate a year later with Israeli air attacks on Hezbollah targets in the city, mass evacuations and hundreds of casualties.

Under-the-Radar Advertising

7   Inundated with advertisements, 6,000 a week on network television, double since 1983, many people tune out. Some do it literally with their remotes. Ad people are concerned that traditional modes are losing effectiveness. People are overwhelmed. Consider, for example, that a major grocery store carries 30,000 items, each with packaging that screams "buy me." More commercial messages are there than a human being can handle. The problem is ad clutter. Advertisers are trying to address the clutter in numerous ways, including stealth ads, new-site ads and alternative media. Although not hidden or subliminal, stealth ads are subtle—even covert. You might not know you're being pitched unless you're attentive, really attentive.

8   • **Stealth Ads.** So neatly can **stealth ads** fit into the landscape that people may not recognize they're being pitched. Consider the Bamboo lingerie company, which stenciled messages on a Manhattan sidewalk: "From here it looks like you could use some new underwear." Sports stadiums like FedEx Field outside of Washington, D.C.," work their way into everyday dialogue, subtly reinforcing product identity.

• **stealth ads** Advertisements, often subtle, in nontraditional, unexpected places

9   • **Product Placement.** In the 1980s advertisers began wiggling brand-name products into movie scripts, creating an additional although minor revenue stream for moviemakers. The practice, **product placement,** stirred criticism about artistic integrity, but it gained momentum. Fees zoomed upward. For the 2005 release of *The Green Hornet,* Miramax was seeking an automaker willing to pay at least $35 million for its products to be written into the script, topping the $15 million that Ford paid for its 2003 Thunderbird, Jaguar and Aston Martin lines to be in the James Bond movie *Die Another Day.*

• **product placement** Writing a brand-name product into a television or movie script

10   Later, placing products into television scenes gained importance with the advent of TiVo and other devices that allow people to record shows and replay them commercial-free at their convenience. By 2004 about 1 million people owned these devices. Their growing popularity worried the television industry, whose business model was dependent on revenue from advertisers to which it guaranteed an audience for ads. With TiVo, audiences no longer were trapped into watching commercials. Was the 30-second spot commercial doomed? The television and advertising industries struck product placement deals that went beyond anything seen before. For a fee, products are being built into scripts not only as props but also for both implicit and explicit endorsement.

11   • **Infomercials.** Less subtle is the **infomercial,** a program-length television commercial dolled up to look like a newscast, a live-audience participation show or a chatty talk show. With the proliferation of 24-hour television service and of cable channels, air-time is so cheap at certain hours that advertisers of even offbeat products can afford it. Hardly anybody is fooled into thinking that infomercials are anything but advertisements, but some full-length media advertisements, like Liz Taylor wandering through CBS sitcoms, are cleverly disguised.

• **infomercial** Program-length broadcast commercial

12   A print media variation is the '**zine**—a magazine published by a manufacturer to plug a single line of products with varying degrees of subtlety. 'Zine publishers,

• 'zine
Magazine whose
entire content,
articles and ads,
pitches a single
product line

including such stalwarts as IBM and Sony, have even been so brazen as to sell these wall-to-wall advertising vehicles at newsstands. One example was a splashy new magazine called *Colors*, for which you paid $4.50. Once inside, you probably realized it was a thinly veiled ad for Benetton casual clothes. *Guess Journal* may look like a magazine, but guess who puts it out as a 'zine: The makers of the Guess fashion brand.

13   Stealth advertisements try "to morph into the very entertainment it sponsors." wrote Mary Kuntz, Joseph Weber and Heidi Dawley in *Business Week*. The goal, they said, is "to create messages so entertaining, so compelling—and maybe so disguised—that rapt audiences will swallow them whole, oblivious to the sales component."

Writing About the Reading

CHECKING YOUR VOCABULARY

1. For each of the words listed below, use context; prefixes, roots, and suffixes (see Chapter 3); and/or a dictionary to write a brief definition or synonym of the word as it is used in the reading.

   a. currency (para. 1) _____

   b. credibility (para. 2) _____

   c. incentive (para. 3) _____

   d. tangentially (para. 5) _____

   e. inundated (para. 7) _____

   f. subliminal (para. 7) _____

   g. proliferation (para. 11) _____

   h. stalwarts (para. 12) _____

   i. brazen (para. 12) _____

2. Underline new, specialized terms introduced in the reading (see Chapter 3).

3. Draw a word map of one of the words in the reading.

CHECKING YOUR COMPREHENSION

1. How does buzz advertising work?
2. Define the term *viral advertising*.
3. What is a disadvantage of viral ads?
4. Identify three types of under-the-radar advertising and describe each type.
5. What is a 'zine?

THINKING CRITICALLY

1. What is the purpose of this reading?
2. How would you describe the author's tone?
3. Why do you think automakers were among the first to try viral advertising?

4. Think of a time when you or a friend created "buzz" about a product. How effective were you as buzz agents?
5. Discuss the use of product placement in movies and on TV. Do you think this practice will continue to grow? Explain your answer.
6. If you were starting a business, which advertising techniques would you consider using? Why?

LEARNING/STUDY STRATEGY

Draw a chart that summarizes the types of advertising discussed in this article. Use the following format.

Type	Definition	Advantages
1. Buzz		
2. Viral		
3. Stealth		
4. Product Placement		
5. Infomercials		

12 Reading in the Liberal Arts, Humanities, and Education

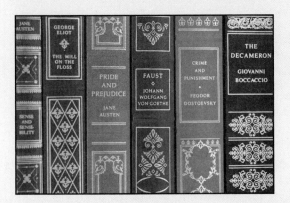

English majors not only read and research the great works of literature from around the world; they may also take courses in creative or expository writing.

Students of art history learn not only about masterworks of painting and sculpture, but also about architecture and the cultural contexts of art. Pictured here: *Guernica*, by Picasso, painted in 1937.

Education majors receive training not only in specific academic disciplines (such as English, science, and math) but also in the methods and techniques of being a good teacher.

LEARNING OBJECTIVES

- To learn what the liberal arts and humanities are

- To consider whether you should major in the liberal arts

- To discover tips for studying the liberal arts

- To learn what is required of education majors

- To learn specialized reading techniques for literature

- To develop an approach to studying visual arts

- To learn to read and use criticism

- To identify predominant thought patterns

- To adapt your learning skills for the humanities and arts

What Are the Liberal Arts and Humanities?

Colleges use the term *liberal arts* to describe a series of courses and disciplines that aim to impart general knowledge and develop critical-thinking skills. Courses in the **humanities** study the human condition from many viewpoints, using methods that are both analytical and critical. A summary of some of the major courses of study available in the liberal arts appears in Table 12-1.

TABLE 12-1   The Liberal Arts and Career Opportunities

DISCIPLINE	DESCRIPTION	CAREER OPPORTUNITIES
Art History	*Art history* courses examine the techniques, styles, and social contributions of the visual arts throughout the ages, often in their cultural contexts. *Studio art* courses actually teach you how to paint, sculpt, and draw.	• Museum acquisitions • Art teacher or therapist • Tour guide • Photographer • Antiques dealer • Historic preservation specialist
Communication Arts Graphic Arts	*Communications* courses focus on how the tools of language can best be used for the benefit of people and society. *Graphic arts* courses teach students how to turn information into visually appealing charts, graphs, and illustrations.	For Communication Arts: • Corporate communications director • Journalist • Publicist • Lobbyist

TABLE 12–1 *continued*

DISCIPLINE	DESCRIPTION	CAREER OPPORTUNITIES
		For Graphic Arts: • Staff artist for newspaper or magazine • Advertising designer or director • Internet/Web designer
English (Language and Literature) **Foreign Languages**	*English* and *foreign language* courses tend to focus on (1) writing and researching, or (2) reading and understanding literature in the form of poems, plays, and novels.	• Novelist • Copywriter • Editor • Fact checker • Speech writer
History/Government*	*History* courses look at a chronological or thematic record of past events. *Government* courses focus on various aspects and types of public governance at all levels, from the local through the national.	• Archivist • Municipal worker • Military careers • Lawyer • Paralegal

*Related to history and government is political science, which is considered one of the social sciences (see Chapter 10). Political science deals with the theory and practice of politics and political behavior. It is sometimes described as the study of "who gets what, when, and how." Many pre-law students choose to major in political science.

Many of those who study the liberal arts do so for sheer love of the subject. Indeed, it is easy to understand why college campuses have so many liberal arts majors. Aspiring writers study English or communication arts, aspiring actors study the performing arts, and aspiring painters study art techniques and art history. Students often report that their liberal arts courses are their favorite classes—the classes in which they learn to read, think, write, and argue a point.

Students who major in the arts and humanities often decide they would like to teach, which requires them to take courses in **education**. Education majors usually specialize in the particular area they would like to teach (such as English, math, or history) and take courses in teaching methods, as well as classes on such topics as classroom control and student motivation.

Should You Major in the Liberal Arts?

People who study the liberal arts are often amazed at how much the disciplines are connected. Religious and historical movements inspire not only great art but also great literature. Literature and social movements inspire philosophers to formulate their ideas, while the governments of today try to learn from the successes and mistakes of history. Those who study the liberal arts come to understand styles of literature, art, and music so well that they can tell when a painting was painted just by looking at it or when a novel was written just by reading the first few pages.

What characteristics and habits will make you a successful liberal arts major?

1. **You should enjoy reading and writing.** Liberal arts courses require a heavy reading load. They also require students to write several papers each semester and take essay exams. To do well in liberal arts courses, you must be willing to read the books (and poems and essays) written by the great thinkers. Even if you major in the visual arts, you will be expected to read a great deal about the society in which the artists lived and worked.

2. **You should be able to see the world from multiple perspectives.** In your course work, you can expect to encounter a wide variety of opinions on the same work or event. For example, in your history courses you will likely study various historians' opinions of the causes of the American Civil War. Literature can be viewed from a variety of perspectives, some of which require special ways of thinking. (For example, feminist perspectives consider the experience of women first and foremost in their analysis.) You must be comfortable with weighing evidence, keeping an open mind, and formulating your own ideas.

3. **You should have a good eye for detail, as well as an ability to see the "big picture."** For example, whether you're analyzing a great painting like the *Mona Lisa* or reading a Shakespeare play, you will see that the richness of the work is evident in its many subtle details.

4. **You should be able to think critically.** Critical thinking is an essential skill for liberal arts majors, who are often asked to synthesize, analyze, and evaluate whatever they are reading. These skills are essential in almost all careers. (For example, many aspiring lawyers study the liberal arts because these courses help sharpen their thinking skills.)

Tips for Studying the Liberal Arts—Even if You Are Not a Major

Even if you are a business, technical, or science major, you will likely be required to take some courses in the liberal arts—at a minimum, English, American or world history, and perhaps art history. If you have no inherent interest in these topics, you can get the most out of these classes by keeping a few things in mind.

1. **Humanities courses focus on the human experience.** For that reason, they can be very personally enriching. When people think about the level of intellectual sophistication they have achieved as a result of attending college, they often realize that their liberal arts courses provided them with the foundation they need to be considered an educated person.

2. **Great works of art and literature have lasted centuries, even millennia, for one main reason: they address or represent universal truths, themes, and yearnings.** Literature, especially, is a creative record of the thoughts, feelings, emotions, and experiences of other people. Look for these universal themes and see how they apply to your own life as well as the world around you.

3. **Though textbooks in disciplines like history and art can seem overwhelming and filled with too many dates and details for you to keep straight, try to take at least three main points away from each chapter you read.** You don't have to memorize every date; just try to retain the most important dates, which will give you a foundation on which to build further knowledge.

The remainder of this chapter focuses on studying literature and the visual arts. For practice in reading selections from communications and history, see pages 98 and 219.

Quotes from a Humanities Professor

Advice for Liberal Arts Students

Patrick Mathias, M.A., Professor of English, Itasca Community College

66 I've found it very useful to use the Internet to do a quick biography of the author (or writer, or artist). Sometimes it yields insights into the life of the writer, time frame, culture, and so forth that really help get a grip on the piece. 99

■ Advice for Education Majors

Education majors by definition have a dual role. Not only must they learn the content of their college courses—so that they can then teach it to others—they must also learn the tools and techniques of teaching effectively. Training to be a teacher requires not only sitting in a college classroom being taught by a professor, but also *student teaching*, in which you teach a class while a more experienced teacher observes you and offers advice on how to improve your teaching style and methods.

As you move through your college courses—both in your major and in your other required courses and electives—it will benefit you to carefully observe and evaluate your own teachers. What things do they do that you find particularly effective? Which of their habits drive you crazy? Which professors make learning enjoyable, and which make it a chore? Try keeping a journal or log of best and worst practices in teaching, and use them to create or develop your own teaching style.

Reading and Analyzing Literature

Literature includes poetry, drama, essays, short stories, and novels. Each is a literary form, or *genre*, through which a writer shares his or her view of the world and of humanity.

Understanding Literature

The focus on reading any form of literature is interpretation. Your goal is to discover what the writer means. You are looking for a statement or message the writer is making about an issue, problem, attitude, or feeling. To do so, you first must understand the literal meaning. Use the suggestions listed in the Key Strategy box below to guide your reading of literature.

KEY STRATEGY: How to Read Literature

1. **Read slowly and carefully.** Literature uses language in unique ways that require interpretation and reaction. Consequently, you must read carefully and slowly, paying attention to numerous language features that provide clues to meaning. For example, observe word choice, syntax, and the order and arrangement of ideas.

2. **Plan on reading the work several times.** Unlike some other types of material, a single reading is *not* sufficient to understand some literary works adequately. During the first reading, try to become familiar with the work and its literal meaning. On the second and subsequent readings, focus on the writer's message, on the significance of the work, and on literary concerns such as the use of language.

3. **Ask questions to establish the literal meaning first; then work on interpretation.** In order to interpret and analyze a literary work, first try to understand it on a literal, or factual, level. An effective approach to reading literature is first to establish "who did what, when, and where." Then ask why the writer wrote the piece and determine the message the writer is conveying.

Who?	Identify the subject or topic.
What is happening?	Describe the basic plot or sequence of events.
When/Where?	Establish the scene, setting, or context (for essays).
Why?	Why did the author write this?
Message?	What is the message the author is conveying and what is its significance?

This questioning approach (p. 328, no. 3) is shown in the following poem, "Mirror," written by Sylvia Plath.

Mirror
Sylvia Plath

I am silver and exact. I have no preconceptions.
Whatever I see I swallow immediately
Just as it is, unmisted by love or dislike.
I am not cruel, only truthful—
The eye of a little god, four-cornered.
Most of the time I meditate on the opposite wall.
It is pink, with speckles. I have looked at it so long
I think it is a part of my heart. But it flickers.
Faces and darkness separate us over and over.
Now I am a lake. A woman bends over me,
Searching my reaches for what she really is.
Then she turns to those liars, the candles or the moon.
I see her back, and reflect it faithfully.
She rewards me with tears and an agitation of hands.
I am important to her. She comes and goes.
Each morning it is her face that replaces the darkness.
In me she has drowned a young girl, and in me an old woman
Rises toward her day after day, like a terrible fish.

—Crossing the Water by Sylvia Plath

QUESTIONS	RESPONSES
Who or What?	A mirror
What is happening?	Plath describes what the mirror reflects.
When/Where?	The mirror is hanging on a wall facing another wall.
Why?	Plath is using the mirror to comment on life and peoples' desire to know how they appear to others or to see their true selves.
Message?	The mirror is exact, accurate, and truthful. Life, in contrast, is affected, untruthful, and cruel.

Annotate as You Read

To understand the message, jot down your reactions, hunches, insights, feelings, and questions. Mark or underline words, sentences, or sections you feel are important statements, and words and phrases that provide clues to meaning. A sample annotation follows.

MIRROR
Sylvia Plath

consumes

reality

reflecting
shows truth
whatever it is

deep, reflective

not usually thought
of as rewards

inescapable reality
of aging

I am silver and exact. I have no <u>preconceptions.</u> ——open—clear view
Whatever I see I swallow immediately
Just as it is, unmisted by love or dislike.—— unemotional, untainted
I am <u>not cruel,</u> only <u>truthful</u>—
The eye of a little god, four-cornered. —— mirror is godlike—all knowing
Most of the time I meditate on the opposite wall.
It is pink, with speckles. I have looked at it so long
I think it is a part of my heart. But it flickers.
Faces and darkness separate us over and over.) obstacles of life
Now I am a lake. A woman bends over me,   searching for truth
<u>Searching my reaches for what she really is.</u>— about herself
Then she turns to those <u>liars,</u> the candles or the moon.—— deceptive, not faithful
I see her back, and <u>reflect it faithfully.</u>
She rewards me with tears and an agitation of hands. she comes and
I am important to her. She comes and goes.)—— goes through reality
Each morning it is her face that replaces the darkness.   mirror
In me she has drowned a young girl, and in me an old woman) holds
Rises toward her day after day, like a terrible fish.   the past

Identify Themes and Patterns

After you have read and annotated, the next step is to study your annotations, looking for themes and patterns. Try to discover how ideas work together to suggest themes. Themes are large or universal topics or subjects that are important to nearly everyone. A study of the Plath poem and annotations indicates that her theme is the realities of life. Possible themes in literature are

- questions, issues, problems raised by the story: moral, political, philosophical, religious.
- abstract ideas: love, death, heroism, escapism, honor.
- conflicts: appearance versus reality, freedom versus restraint, poverty versus wealth, men against women, humans against society, humans versus nature.
- common literary topics: self-realization, inescapability of death, fall from innocence, search for the meaning of life.

EXERCISE 12-1

LEARNING
COLLABORATIVELY

Predicting Exam Questions

Refer to the multilevel thinking skills discussed in Chapter 1 and predict exam questions that might be asked about the Plath poem. Compare your questions with those of another student.

Understanding the Language of Literature

Literature is unique in its extensive use of descriptive, connotative, and figurative language to express images, attitudes, and feelings. In order to succeed in your literature courses, you need to be able to use and understand the specialized vocabulary of literary works.

Descriptive Language   Writers often use words that create sensory impressions or responses. They are intended to help the reader re-create mentally what the author is describing. For example, in describing a stormy night, a poet may write, "Under the thunder-dark clouds, the storm mounts, flashes, and resounds." These terms give you a feeling about the storm and help you imagine its strength. Instead of saying two characters looked at each other, a novelist may write, "their eyes locked momentarily in a gaze, reflecting the strength of their opposing wills." Now, read the following paragraph. Note, in particular, the underlined words.

> Old men, old women, almost 20 million of them. They constitute 10 percent of the total population, and the percentage is steadily growing. Some of them, like <u>conspirators,</u> walk all <u>bent over, as if hiding some precious secret, filled with self-protection.</u> The body seems to gather itself around those vital parts, <u>folding shoulders,</u> arms, <u>pelvis like a fading rose.</u> Watch and you see how <u>fragile</u> old people come to think they are.
>
> —Curtin, "Aging in the Land of the Young," *Nobody Ever Died of Old Age*

Connotative Language   The connotations of a word are the meanings it commonly suggests or implies beyond its primary, denotative meaning. Thus, the word *dinner* denotes an evening meal but connotes a time of conversation, friendship, and interaction. The word *father* means "male parent" but often connotes a person who guides and directs. A connotative meaning may carry either a positive or a negative impression. For example, all of the following words mean an assembled group of people, but they have very different connotations.

crowd, congregation, mob, gang, audience, class

Read the following paragraph, which is taken from Martin Luther King Jr.'s "Letter from Birmingham Jail." He wrote it after being jailed for leading a civil rights demonstration.

> We have waited for more than 340 years for our constitutional and God-given rights. The nations of Asia and Africa are moving with jetlike speed toward gaining political independence, but we still creep at horse-and-buggy pace toward gaining a cup of coffee at a lunch counter. I guess it is easy for those who have never felt the stinging darts of segregation to say, "Wait." But when you have seen vicious mobs lynch your mothers and fathers at will and drown your sisters and brothers at whim; when you have seen hate-filled policemen curse, kick, and even kill your black brothers and sisters; when you see the vast majority of your 20 million Negro brothers smothering in an airtight cage of poverty in the midst of an affluent society; when you suddenly find your tongue twisted and your speech stammering as you seek to explain to your six-year-old daughter why she can't go to the public amusement park that has just been advertised on television, and see tears welling up in her eyes when she is told that Funtown is closed to colored children, and see ominous clouds of inferiority beginning to form in her little mental sky, and see her beginning to distort her personality by developing an

unconscious bitterness toward white people . . . then you will understand why we find it difficult to wait.

—King, "Letter from Birmingham Jail," *Why We Can't Wait,* p. 363

The highlighted words and phrases reveal King's feeling toward segregation and discrimination. For example, notice that King uses the phrase "vicious mobs lynch" rather than "groups of people kill" and "hate-filled policemen curse, kick," instead of "policemen shout and strike." These choices of words are deliberate. King hopes to create an emotional response in his readers.

Figurative Language   Figurative language is a way of describing something that makes sense on an imaginative level but not on a literal or factual level. Many common expressions are figurative:

The exam was a piece of cake.

Sam eats like a horse.

He walks like a gazelle.

In each of these expressions, two unlike objects are compared on the basis of some quality they have in common. Take, for example, Hamlet's statement "I will speak daggers to her, but use none." Here the writer is comparing the features of daggers (sharp, pointed, dangerous, harmful) with something that can be used like daggers—words.

Figurative language is striking, often surprising, even shocking. This reaction is created by the unlikeness of the two objects being compared. To find the similarity and understand the figurative expression, focus on connotative meanings rather than literal meanings. For example, in reading the lines

A sea

Harsher than granite

from an Ezra Pound poem, you must think not only of rock or stone but also of the characteristics of granite: hardness, toughness, impermeability. Then you can see that the lines mean that the sea is rough and resistant. Figurative words, which are also called figures of speech, are used to communicate and emphasize relationships that cannot be communicated through literal meaning. For example, the statement by Jonathan Swift, "She wears her clothes as if they were thrown on by a pitchfork," creates a stronger image and conveys a more meaningful description than saying "She dresses sloppily."

The three most common types of figurative expressions are similes, metaphors, and symbols.

1. **Similes**   Similes make the comparison explicit by using the word *like* or *as.*

We lie back to back.
Curtains lift and fall,
like the chest of someone sleeping.

—Kenyon

Life, like a dome of many-colored glass,
stains the white radiance of Eternity.

—Shelley

2. **Metaphors** Metaphors, on the other hand, directly equate the two objects.

My Life has stood – a Loaded Gun –
In Corners – till a Day
The Owner passed – identified –
And carried Me away –

—Emily Dickinson

. . . his hair lengthened into sunbeams . . .

—Gustave Flaubert

3. **Symbols** Symbols also make a comparison, but only one term of the comparison is stated. A symbol suggests more than its literal meaning. In fact, sometimes more than one meaning is suggested. In your everyday life, a flag is a symbol of patriotism; a four-leaf clover stands for good luck. A writer may describe a character dressed in white to symbolize her innocence and purity, but the words *innocence* and *purity* will not be mentioned. It is left to the reader to recognize the symbol and to make the comparison.

Symbols often are crucial to the writer's theme or essential meaning. For example, Hemingway's short story "A Clean, Well-Lighted Place" describes an aging man who visits a café. In this story, the café symbolizes an escape from loneliness, old age, and death. Hemingway's theme is the inevitability and inescapability of aging and death; the café closes, and the man's escape is short-lived. Melville's novel *Moby-Dick* is the story of a white whale given the name Moby Dick. But the novel is about much more than an aquatic mammal; the whale takes on numerous meanings. The novel's characters imply he is the devil. Later, the whale seems to represent the forces of nature or the created universe.

Symbols, then, are usually objects—concrete items, not abstract feelings such as pity or hate. To recognize symbols, look for objects given a particular or unusual emphasis. The object may be mentioned often, or it may even be suggested in the title. The story or poem may open and/or close with reference to the object. Objects that suggest more than one meaning are possible symbols. Perhaps the best way to identify symbols is to look for objects that point to the author's theme.

EXERCISE 12-2

LEARNING
COLLABORATIVELY

Identifying Figurative Expressions

Working with a group of classmates, make a list of figurative expressions you use in everyday speech.

EXERCISE 12-3   ## Interpreting Figurative Language

Explain the meaning of each of the following figures of speech. Several interpretations are possible.

1. Shall I compare thee to a summer's day?
   Thou art more lovely and more temperate.
   —Shakespeare

2. In plucking the fruit of memory,
   one runs the risk of spoiling its bloom.
   —Joseph Conrad

3. The scarlet of the maples can shake me like a cry
   Of bugles going by.
   —Carman

THE EAGLE

4. He clasps the crag with crooked hands;
   Close to the sun in lonely lands,

   Ringed with the azure world, he stands.
   The wrinkled sea beneath him crawls;
   He watches from his mountain walls,
   And like a thunderbolt he falls.
   —Tennyson

EXERCISE 12-4   ## Analyzing a Poem

Reread Sylvia Plath's poem "Mirror" on page 329. Is the mirror a symbol? If so, what does it symbolize?

EXERCISE 12-5   ## Analyzing a Poem

Read the following poem by Langston Hughes, and answer the questions that follow.

THE NEGRO SPEAKS OF RIVERS
Langston Hughes

I've known rivers:
I've known rivers ancient as the world and older than the flow of
human blood in human veins.
My soul has grown deep like the rivers.

I bathed in the Euphrates when dawns were young.
I built my hut near the Congo and it lulled me to sleep.

I looked upon the Nile and raised the pyramids above it.
I heard the singing of the Mississippi when Abe Lincoln went down to
New Orleans, and I've seen its muddy bosom turn all golden in the
sunset.

I've known rivers:
Ancient, dusky rivers.

My soul has grown deep like the rivers.

—Hughes, *The Collected Poems of Langston Hughes*

1. What does the river symbolize?
2. Explain any metaphors or similes the poem contains.

Reading and Analyzing Poetry

Poetry is a form of expression in which ideas are presented in a unique format. Poems are written in verse—lines and stanzas rather than paragraphs. Often, poetry requires more reading time and greater concentration than other types of material. In reading prose, you could skip a word in a paragraph and your comprehension of the whole paragraph would not suffer; poetry, however, is very compact and precise. Each word is important and carries special meaning. You have to pay attention to each word—its sound, its meaning, and its meaning when combined with other words. Use the guidelines shown in the Key Strategy box below to help you approach poetry effectively.

KEY STRATEGY: How to Read Poetry

1. **Read the poem once straight through, without any defined purpose.** Be open-minded, experiencing the poem as it is written. If you meet an unknown word or confusing reference, keep reading. Read the poem a second time. Identify and correct any difficulties, such as an unknown word.

2. **Use punctuation to guide your comprehension.** Although poetry is written in lines, do not expect each line to make sense by itself. Meaning often flows on from line to line, eventually forming a sentence. Use the punctuation to guide you, as you do in reading paragraphs. If there is no punctuation at the end of the line, consider it as a slight pause, with an emphasis on the last word.

3. **Notice the action.** *Who* is doing *what, when,* and *where?*

4. **Analyze the poem's intent.** Decide what it was written to accomplish. Does it describe a feeling or a person, express a memory, present an argument?

5. **Determine who is speaking.**   Poems often refer to an unidentified "I" or "we." Try to describe the speaker's viewpoint or feelings.

6. **Establish the speaker's tone.**   Is the author serious, challenging, saddened, frustrated? Read aloud; your intonation, your emphasis on certain words, and the rise and fall of your voice may provide clues. You may "hear" a poet's anger, despondency, or elation.

7. **Identify to whom the poem is addressed.**   Is it written to a person, to the reader, to an object? Consider the possibility that the poet may be writing to work out a problem or as an emotional outlet.

8. **Reread difficult or confusing sections.**   Read them aloud several times. Copying these sections word for word may be helpful. Look up unfamiliar words.

9. **Check unfamiliar references.**   A poet may refer to people, objects, or events outside of the poem. These are known as *allusions*.

10. **Look for the poet's meaning or the poem's theme.**   Consider connotative meanings and study figures of speech. Then paraphrase the poem; express it in your own words and connect it to your own experience. Then put all the ideas together to discover its overall meaning. Ask yourself, "What is the poet trying to tell me?" "What is the message?"

Now read the poem "Dream Deferred," by Langston Hughes, applying the above strategies.

DREAM DEFERRED
Langston Hughes

What happens to a dream deferred?

Does it dry up
like a raisin in the sun?
Or fester like a sore—
And then run?
Does it stink like rotten meat?
Or crust and sugar over—
like a syrupy sweet?
Maybe it just sags.
like a heavy load.

Or does it explode?

—Hughes, *The Collected Poems of Langston Hughes*

One key to understanding the poem is the meaning of the word *deferred*. Here, it means put off or postponed. A dream deferred, then, refers to unfulfilled or postponed hopes. A poet questions what happens to a dream that is deferred and offers six alternatives. Note the connotative meanings of the first four choices: "dry up," "fester, "stink," "crust and sugar over." Each of these suggests some type of decay. The term "sags" suggests heaviness and inaction. The last alternative, "explode," is active: posing a threat and implying danger. The poet's purpose is to explore the negative consequences of unfulfilled hopes and to suggest that violent outcomes may result.

EXERCISE 12-6

Analyzing a Poem

Read the following poem by Emily Dickinson, and use the guidelines for analyzing poetry to help you answer the questions below.

Because I Could Not Stop for Death
Emily Dickinson

Because I could not stop for Death –
He kindly stopped for me –
The Carriage held but just Ourselves –
And Immortality.

We slowly drove – He knew no haste
And I had put away
My labor and my leisure too,
For His Civility –

We passed the School, where Children strove
At Recess – in the Ring –
We passed the Fields of Gazing Grain –
We passed the Setting Sun –

Or rather – He passed Us –
The Dews drew quivering and chill –
For only Gossamer,[1] my Gown –
My Tippet[2] – only Tulle –

We paused before a House that seemed
A Swelling of the Ground –
The Roof was Scarcely visible –
The Cornice[3] – in the Ground

Since then – 'tis Centuries – and yet
Feels shorter than the Day
I first surmised the Horses' Heads
Were toward Eternity –

—*The Poems of Emily Dickinson,* ed. by Thomas H. Johnson

[1] A light, thin cloth
[2] Cape
[3] Section beneath roof

1. Summarize the literal action in the poem. Your summary should include answers to the questions given earlier in this chapter (*who, what, where, when,* and *why*).
2. Annotate the poem by marking words and phrases that describe death or the poet's attitude toward it.
3. What message is the author communicating about death?

Reading and Analyzing Short Stories and Novels

A short story is a brief work of prose narrative with an organized plot. It differs from the novel not only in length but also in magnitude: the size and proportion of the story, its scope, its impact, and its effects. A short story may discuss one event that shaped a person's life, whereas a novel describes the numerous actions that contribute to a character's development. Both the short story and the novel share basic features. Study each feature listed in the Key Strategy box below.

KEY STRATEGY: How to Read a Short Story

1. **Plot**   The plot is the basic storyline—the sequence of events as they occur in the work. The plot, however, also consists of the actions through which the work's meaning is expressed. The plot often follows a predictable structure. Frequently, the plot begins by setting the scene, introducing the main characters, and providing background information needed to follow the story. Often, there is a complication or problem that arises. Suspense is built as the problem or conflict unfolds. Near the end of the story, events come to a climax: the point at which the outcome of the conflict will be decided.

2. **Characterization**   Characters are the actors in a narrative story. The characters reveal themselves by what they say—the dialog—and by their actions, appearance, thoughts, and feelings. The narrator, or person who tells the story, also may comment on or reveal information about the characters. Sometimes, the narrator is not the author, in which case you need to consider his or her characterization as well. Be sure to analyze the characters' traits and motives, analyze their personalities, study their interaction, and examine character changes.

3. **Setting**   The setting is the time, place, and circumstances in which the action occurs. The setting provides a framework for the action and establishes an atmosphere in which the characters interact.

4. **Point of View**   The point of view is the way the story is presented or from whose perspective or outlook the story is told. Often, the author of a story is not the narrator. The story may be told from the perspective of a narrator

who is not one of the characters or by one of the characters themselves. In analyzing the point of view, determine the narrator's role and function. Is the narrator accurate and knowledgeable (even all-knowing), or is his or her view limited or restricted? Sometimes the narrator is able to enter the minds of some or all of the characters, knowing their thoughts and understanding their actions and motivations. Other times, a narrator may be naive or innocent, unable to understand the actions or implications of the story.

5. **Tone**   The tone of a story suggests the author's attitude. Like tone of voice, tone in a story suggests feelings. Many ingredients contribute to tone, including the author's choice of details, characters, events, and situations. The tone of a story may be amusing, angry, or contemptuous. The author's feelings are not necessarily those of the characters or of the narrator. Instead, it is through the characters' actions and the narrator's description of them that we infer tone. The style in which a work is written often suggests the tone. Style means the way a writer writes, especially his or her use of language.

6. **Theme**   The theme of the story is the main point or message it conveys through all of the elements above. It is an insight into life revealed by the story. Themes are often large, universal ideas: life and death, human values, or human existence. To establish the theme, ask yourself, "What is the author trying to say about life by telling the story?" Try to explain it in a single sentence. If you are having difficulty stating the theme, try the following suggestions:

- **Study the title.** Now that you have read the story, does it take on any new meanings?
- **Analyze the main character.** Does he or she change? If so, how, and in reaction to what?
- **Look for broad, general statements that a character or the narrator makes about life or the problems the characters face.**
- **Look for symbols, figurative expressions, and meaningful names (for example, Mrs. Goodheart), or objects that hint at bigger ideas.**

Read "The Story of an Hour" by Kate Chopin, paying particular attention to each of the features above.

THE STORY OF AN HOUR

Kate Chopin

Knowing that Mrs. Mallard was afflicted with heart trouble, great care was taken to break to her as gently as possible the news of her husband's death.

It was her sister Josephine who told her, in broken sentences; veiled hints that revealed in half concealing. Her husband's friend Richards was there, too, near her. It was he who had been in the newspaper office when intelligence of the railroad disaster was received, with Brently Mallard's name leading the list of "killed." He had only taken the time to assure himself of its truth by a second telegram, and had hastened to forestall any less careful, less tender friend in bearing the sad message.

She did not hear the story as many women have heard the same, with a paralyzed inability to accept its significance. She wept at once, with sudden, wild abandonment, in her sister's arms. When the storm of grief had spent itself she went away to her room alone. She would have no one follow her.

There stood, facing the open window, a comfortable, roomy armchair. Into this she sank, pressed down by a physical exhaustion that haunted her body and seemed to reach into her soul.

She could see in the open square before her house the tops of trees that were all aquiver with the new spring life. The delicious breath of rain was in the air. In the street below a peddler was crying his wares. The notes of a distant song which someone was singing reached her faintly, and countless sparrows were twittering in the eaves.

There were patches of blue sky showing here and there through the clouds that had met and piled one above the other in the west facing her window.

She sat with her head thrown back upon the cushion of the chair, quite motionless, except when a sob came up into her throat and shook her, as a child who has cried itself to sleep continues to sob in its dreams.

She was young, with a fair, calm face, whose lines bespoke repression and even a certain strength. But now there was a dull stare in her eyes, whose gaze was fixed away off yonder on one of those patches of blue sky. It was not a glance of reflection, but rather indicated a suspension of intelligent thought.

There was something coming to her and she was waiting for it, fearfully. What was it? She did not know; it was too subtle and elusive to name. But she felt it, creeping out of the sky, reaching toward her through the sounds, the scents, the color that filled the air.

Now her bosom rose and fell tumultuously. She was beginning to recognize this thing that was approaching to possess her, and she was striving to beat it back with her will—as powerless as her two white slender hands would have been.

When she abandoned herself a little whispered word escaped her slightly parted lips. She said it over and over under her breath: "free, free, free!" The vacant stare and the look of terror that had followed it went from her eyes. They stayed keen and bright. Her pulses beat fast, and the coursing blood warmed and relaxed every inch of her body.

She did not stop to ask if it were or were not a monstrous joy that held her. A clear and exalted perception enabled her to dismiss the suggestion as trivial.

She knew that she would weep again when she saw the kind, tender hands folded in death; the face that had never looked save with love upon her, fixed and gray and dead. But she saw beyond that bitter moment a long procession of years to come that would belong to her absolutely. And she opened and spread her arms out to them in welcome.

There would be no one to live for her during those coming years; she would live for herself. There would be no powerful will bending hers in that blind persistence with which men and women believe they have a right to impose a private will upon a fellow-creature. A kind intention or a cruel intention made the act seem no less a crime as she looked upon it in that brief moment of illumination.

And yet she had loved him—sometimes. Often she had not. What did it matter! What could love, the unresolved mystery, count for in face of this possession of self-assertion which she suddenly recognized as the strongest impulse of her being!

"Free! Body and soul free!" she kept whispering.

Josephine was kneeling before the closed door with her lips to the keyhole, imploring for admission. "Louise, open the door! I beg; open the door—you will make yourself ill. What are you doing, Louise? For heaven's sake open the door."

"Go away. I am not making myself ill." No; she was drinking in a very elixir of life through that open window.

Her fancy was running riot along those days ahead of her. Spring days, and summer days, and all sorts of days that would be her own. She breathed a quick prayer that life might be long. It was only yesterday she had thought with a shudder that life might be long.

She arose at length and opened the door to her sister's importunities. There was a feverish triumph in her eyes, and she carried herself unwittingly like a goddess of Victory. She clasped her sister's waist, and together they descended the stairs. Richards stood waiting for them at the bottom.

Someone was opening the front door with a latchkey. It was Brently Mallard who entered, a little travel-stained, composedly carrying his grip-sack and umbrella. He had been far from the scene of accident, and did not even know there had been one. He stood amazed at Josephine's piercing cry; at Richards' quick motion to screen him from the view of his wife.

But Richards was too late.

When the doctors came they said she had died of heart disease—of joy that kills.

—Chopin, *The Awakening: Selected Stories of Kate Chopin*

In this short story Mrs. Mallard ponders the death of her husband and relishes the freedom it will bring. The plot involves a surprise ending: she learns that her husband, who she thought had been killed in a railroad disaster, is alive. Upon discovering that her husband is not dead, Mrs. Mallard suffers a heart attack and dies. The key character is Mrs. Mallard; her thoughts and actions after learning of her husband's supposed death are the crux of the story. The setting is one hour in a time near the present in the Mallards' home. The story is told by a third-person narrator who is knowledgeable and understands the characters' actions and motives. In the story's last line, the narrator tells us that doctors assumed Mrs. Mallard died of "the joy that kills."

| EXERCISE 12-7 | **Analyzing a Short Story** |

Answer the following questions about Chopin's "The Story of an Hour."

1. When did you first realize that Mrs. Mallard's reaction to her husband's death would be unusual? Underline words and phrases that led you to suspect her response would be unusual.
2. Explain the meaning of the phrase "the joy that kills."
3. What do Mrs. Mallard's response to the news of her husband's death and the surprise ending suggest about life and death and the nature of true happiness?

■ The Visual Arts: Expression Without Words

A work of art, such as a painting or a sculpture, is the visual expression of an idea. The idea is expressed using a medium—a material such as canvas, clay, fiber, stone, or paint. In a poem, the medium is words; in a sculpture, the medium may be marble. The medium is the vehicle through which the idea is expressed.

Why Study Art?

Many people study art because it is beautiful and they enjoy it. Art can arouse emotions and feelings, stimulate our imaginations, and help us think in new ways. It can enrich our lives. Besides providing enjoyment and enrichment, art also can be a form of communication. By studying the stained glass window in a cathedral, for example, you can learn how, during the Middle Ages, religion was taught to an illiterate population. Art may also have a spiritual (religious) value. Cave drawings may have been used by prehistoric humans to depict animals they valued for food or to magically exert control over them. Finally, art may have a functional value. Some works of art were useful in daily life. Intricately dyed or carved rawhide may have been used to transport personal goods, for instance. By studying works of art, we can learn about a society's religious beliefs and daily living habits.

How to Study Art

To study art, you have to think visually. Use the following suggestions to develop your visual thinking skills. As you read through this section, refer to a photograph taken by Dorothea Lange, *Migrant Mother, Nipomo, California, 1936*, shown on the next page.

See as Well as Look   Looking means taking in what is before you in a physical, mechanical way. Your eyes focus on visual images. Seeing is a more active mental, as well as physical, process. It may require conscious effort. The distinction between looking and seeing is similar to that between hearing and listening. When you hear, you take in sound. When you listen, you understand meaning and grasp the speaker's message. When you see a work of art, you take away some meaning or understanding. What do you *see* in Lange's photograph?

Identify the Subject Matter   Decide who or what the work of art depicts or describes. For example, Michelangelo's *The Creation of Adam* describes, as its title suggests, the biblical creation of the first human. An Inuit stone carving may depict an animal valued by Inuit tribes, such as an eagle or bear. In Lange's photograph, the subject is a mother and her children.

Dorothea Lange, Migrant
Mother, Nipomo, California,
1936.

*Source: Copyright the Dorothea
Lange Collection. The Oakland
Museum, City of Oakland. Gift of
Paul S. Taylor.*

Consider the Title   The title often offers clues that will help you construct an interpretation of the work. You should be aware that not all titles were given to the work by the original artist. The title of Lange's photograph is very revealing. We learn that the woman is a migrant worker and can infer that the children are her children. We also learn that the photograph was taken in California and can infer that the woman was a migrant worker there.

Study the Visual Elements   When you look at a painting the first time, you may notice only a face, or when you study a sculpture, you may notice only its shape. Broaden your study to include the common visual elements. They are line, shape, mass, time, motion, light, color, and texture. Not every element exists within every work of art, but some are important in each.

These elements, sometimes referred to as the form, contribute to the meaning. Small details are important. For example, the grain of marble in a sculpture or the kinds of brush strokes in a painting are meaningful. A painting with deep, heavy, sharply angular lines creates a different impression from one with softly flowing lines.

In Lange's photograph, light seems to be shining on the woman's face and hand. You see harsh, strong lines in her face. Her arm is angular, not graceful. The children seem less sharp.

Write Your Reactions   As you study a work of art, jot down your responses. Write questions, initial reactions, your emotions, and so forth. Do not worry about the order of your ideas or about expressing them in grammatically correct sentences. Just record your impressions. Together, these may help you develop an interpretation of the work. While studying Lange's photograph, one student wrote the following:

- The photo is disturbing—not pleasing.
- The children's faces are hidden—are they ashamed? or perhaps crying? or afraid?
- The woman seems worried. Her hand is at her mouth.
- The children seem highly dependent on her; they seem emotionally close.
- The woman seems to be thinking, but there is no action or movement in the photograph.
- The family seems poor and disheveled.
- The mother seems in control.
- Are they homeless?

Analyze the Work   Analyzing means dividing something into parts in order to understand it. If you are looking at a statue, for instance, you might examine the pose, size, facial expression, medium, gestures, clothing, and so forth. In Lange's photograph, you might first analyze the woman and then the children. Or you might analyze how each is holding his or her body and then how each is dressed. In Lange's photograph, the woman's facial expression is particularly striking.

Consider the Meaning of the Work   An interpretation is a description of a meaning of the work. Many art historians believe that a work of art can have more than one meaning. One meaning is the meaning that it had for the artist; another is the meaning it had for the first people who looked at it. Still another is the meaning it offers to us today. Other art historians argue that a work has no meaning in itself; its only meaning is that given to it by those who view it. This latter viewpoint is known as reader-response theory.

One meaning that Lange's photograph seems to be depicting is the plight of migrant workers, thus suggesting sympathy. Another meaning may be drawn from the similarity of the pose of the woman and her children to traditional paintings of the Madonna and child, perhaps suggesting that the migrant woman is a universal mother figure. Many women share her worry and concern about their place in life.

*Charles White,
1918–1979,
Preacher, 1952.
Pen and black ink
and graphite pencil
on board, Sheet;
22¹³/₁₆ x 29¹⁵/₁₆ x
³/₁₆ in. Whitney
Museum of American
Art, New York, NY.
Purchase 52.25.*

EXERCISE 12-8   Analyzing art

Study the work of art shown above, and answer the following questions.

1. Describe the subject.
2. Identify striking visual elements. For example, consider the size and balance of the preacher's body parts. Consider, too, the background.
3. Write your reactions.
4. Describe the meaning of the work.

■ Reading Criticism

Criticism is writing that discusses, interprets, and evaluates a particular work. Some students erroneously assume that criticism is only negative, or limited to finding fault with a work. Actually, its primary purpose is to analyze and interpret; it may include both positive and negative aspects. Film and book reviews are examples of criticism. Criticism also includes scholarly works that carefully research or closely examine a particular aspect, theme, or approach in literature or art. Often, in order to complete a term paper, you will be required to consult several critical sources. Other times, to understand a work better, you may decide to read several interpretations by critical authorities.

Following is a brief excerpt from a critical work discussing Emily Dickinson's poem "Because I Could Not Stop for Death," which appears on page 337 in this chapter. Read the excerpt, and note that it offers an interpretation of the poem's meaning: the poet fears life and escapes this fear through a journey to death.

> Naive, blank-faced, repelling thought and emotion, the speaker permits herself to be transported to worlds unknown. The first step is easy. The gentleman-caller she calls Death is kindly, civil. The threesome is cozy, he does what she cannot do, the unexamined space of the carriage arouses no anxiety in her, the journey is a leisured one. . . . She has all the time in the world, and in other worlds besides. Remarking on the presence of a third figure, Immortality, she cannot stop to ask herself what this barely personified abstraction, the shard of a disintegrated religious tradition, signifies. Wholly engrossed as she is by her deceptive double, she cannot afford to question whether beneath the smooth, seductive surface his intentions are equally decorous. What she has done is to yield herself up to the power of a dominant obsession. What this obsession is we do not know absolutely. The poem invokes a reason only to dismiss it: "Because I could not . . . He." Thus, although the idea of suicide is implicit in its denial, so too is the idea of controlling this death-wish by displacing it onto another character who is initially capable of masking the deception motif the poem is designed to reveal. In limited terms, perhaps this obsession may be described as the compulsion to repress the anxiety that the circumstances of her life have aroused in her. In its broadest terms, perhaps this obsession may be described as her fear of mortality itself.
>
> —Pollak, *Dickinson: The Anxiety of Gender,* p. 191

To read critical sources effectively, use the guidelines shown in the Key Strategy box below.

KEY STRATEGY: How to Read Criticism

1. **Read the original work carefully and thoroughly before you consult critical sources.**

2. **Make a preliminary interpretation of the work before reading criticism.**   Decide what you think the work means and why it was produced. Record these ideas in note form. If you consult sources before forming your own impressions, your judgment will be colored by what you read and you will have difficulty separating your ideas from those you encounter as you read.

3. **Recognize that not all critics agree.** You may encounter three critics who present three different interpretations of Shakespeare's *Hamlet* or Renoir's "The Luncheon of the Boating Party."

4. **Make certain that the interpretations you read are substantiated with references to the original work.**

5. **Although it is perfectly acceptable to revise your own interpretations on the basis of your reading, do not discard your own interpretation as soon as you encounter one that differs.** Look to the original work to develop support for your interpretations.

6. **Make notes on your readings, recording only key points.**

To locate criticism on a particular literary or artistic work, consult one of these print or online reference sources.

Essay and General Literature Index

The MLA Bibliography

Internet Public Library's Literary Criticism collection
  http://www.ipl.org/div/literit/

Voice of the Shuttle Literary Sources
  http://vos.ucsb.edu/browse.asp?id=2718

EXERCISE 12-9   Analyzing Criticism

The following excerpt provides another critical interpretation of Dickinson's poem "Because I Could Not Stop for Death." Read the excerpt, and answer the questions that follow.

At first reading, the orthodox reassurance against the fear of death appears to be invoked, though with the novelty of a suitor replacing the traditional angel, by emphasizing his compassionate mission in taking her out of the woes of this world into the bliss of the next. 'Death,' usually rude, sudden, and impersonal, has been transformed into a kindly and leisurely gentleman. Although she was aware this is a last ride, since his 'Carriage' can only be a hearse, its terror is subdued by the 'Civility' of the driver who is merely serving the end of 'immortality.' the loneliness of the journey, with Death on the driver's seat and her body laid out in the coach behind, is dispelled by the presence of her immortal part that rides with her as a co-passenger, this slight personification being justified by the separable concept of the soul. Too occupied with life herself to stop, like all busy mortals, Death 'kindly stopped' for her. But this figure of a gentleman taking a lady for a carriage ride is carefully underplayed and then dropped after two stanzas.

The balanced parallelism of the first stanza is slightly quickened by the alliterating 'labor' and 'leisure' of the second, which encompass vividly all that must be renounced in order to ride 'toward Eternity.' So the deliberate slow-paced action that lies suspended behind the poem is charged with a forward movement by the sound pattern, taking on a kind of inevitability in the insistent reiteration of the following stanza:

> We passed the School, where Children strove
> At Recess – in the Ring –
> We passed the Fields of Gazing Grain –
> We passed the Setting Sun –

Here her intensely conscious leave-taking of the world is rendered with fine economy, and instead of the sentimental grief of parting there is an objectively presented scene. The seemingly disparate parts of this are fused into a vivid reenactment of the mortal experience. It includes the three stages of youth, maturity, and age, the cycle of day from morning to evening, and even a suggestion of seasonal progression from the year's upspring through ripening to decline. The labor and leisure of life are made concrete in the joyous activity of children contrasted with the passivity of nature and again, by the optical illusion of the sun's setting, in the image of motion that has come to rest. Also the whole range of the earthly life is symbolized, first human nature, then animate, and finally inanimate nature. But, absorbed 'in the Ring' of childhood's games, the players at life do not even stop to look up at the passing carriage of death. And the indifference of nature is given a kind of cold vitality by transferring the stare in the dead traveler's eyes to the 'Gazing Grain.' This simple maneuver in grammar creates an involute paradox, giving the fixity of death to the living corn while the corpse itself passes by on its journey to immortality. Then with the westering sun, traditional symbol of the soul's passing, comes the obliterating darkness of eternity. Finally, the sequence follows the natural route of a funeral train, past the schoolhouse in the village, then the outlying fields, and on to the remote burying ground.

—Anderson, *Emily Dickinson's Poetry: Stairway to Surprise*, pp. 245–46

1. According to this critic, what is the speaker's attitude toward death?
2. Does the criticism enhance your understanding of the poem? If so, how?
3. How does this critic's interpretation compare with that of the earlier interpretation on page 346? Discuss the similarities and differences.
4. Compare this critic's interpretation with your own interpretation.

■ Thought Patterns in the Liberal Arts and Humanities

Common thought patterns in the liberal arts and humanities include process, chronological order, cause and effect, and comparison and contrast. Table 12-2 on the facing page describes the uses of these patterns and offers examples.

TABLE 12–2   Thought Patterns in the Liberal Arts and Humanities

PATTERN	USES	EXAMPLES
Process	Examining the process through which the writer achieved his or her effect	Studying e.e. cummings's use of space and print size
Chronological order	Sequence of events in fictional works; noting the development of various artists or historical or literary periods	Noting development of Impressionist style of painting
Cause and effect	Examining character motivation, studying effects of various literary and artistic techniques	Evaluating the effect of harsh brush strokes in a painting
Comparison and contrast	Studying two or more artists, works, writers, or schools of thought	Comparing the works of Wordsworth and Coleridge

■ Learning Strategies for Liberal Arts and Humanities Courses

Liberal arts and humanities courses are unique. Grades are often based on papers or essay exams rather than on objective tests or quizzes. Frequently, the focus is on ideas and your interpretation and evaluation of them. Here are several suggestions to help you get the most from these courses:

1. **Learn appropriate terminology.** Learn the names and meanings of literary devices (stream of consciousness, pathos, persona, intrigue). Consult Abrams and Harpham's *A Glossary of Literary Terms*.

2. **Learn classifications.** In literature and art history, works and authors are often grouped or classified, and groupings may be chronological (the Romantic period, 1789–1832; the Victorian period, 1832–1901 in literature; for example). Learn these periods (names, inclusive dates, and characteristics) so that you will understand the historical context of a particular work.

3. **Focus on themes and patterns.** Always analyze and evaluate. Focus on a work's significance and literary merit.

4. **Highlight and annotate as you read.** Mark key figures of speech, global statements by characters, and words and phrases that suggest the theme. Mark confusing sections or unknown references as well.

5. **Write for review.** Write plot summaries of short stories. Make brief outlines of essays. Write a statement of your interpretation of a poem or work or art. These statements will be useful as you prepare for exams or select topics for papers.

6. **Predict exam questions.** Exams are usually in essay form or call for short answers. Prepare for this by predicting questions and drafting outline answers.

7. **Discuss the work with a classmate.** If you are having difficulty with a particular work, consult with your instructor.

Test–Taking Tips
Preparing for Exams in the Liberal Arts and Humanities

In many literature classes, you write papers instead of taking exams, although some instructors do give brief objective tests based on the assigned readings. Most final essay assignments require you to analyze and write about a work or works you have read or viewed.

You may be given several types of writing assignments. It is important to know what is expected in each. Use the following tips:

1. **Explication.** An explication is a full, detailed explanation of the meaning of the work. It proceeds through the work line by line or even word by word, explaining meanings and examining word choices, figures of speech, and so forth. Although it is detailed, it is not limited to a discussion of specifics. Larger concerns such as theme and plot are also discussed.

2. **Analysis.** Analysis involves separating the work into components and then examining and explaining closely one or more of the parts. Usually, analyses are limited to one aspect or element, such as Hawthorne's use of symbolism in *The Scarlet Letter* or an analysis of the point of view in Poe's "The Tell-Tale Heart."

3. **Comparison and Contrast.** Writing assignments may ask you to compare two or more works or two or more authors. To do this, you must examine similarities and differences. If you are given a choice of works or authors, choose two that have much in common; you will find you have more to say than if the two are widely divergent. For suggestions on how to compare two works, refer to Chapter 4, "Synthesize Your Ideas," p. 123. When writing a comparison paper, you should generally integrate your discussion of the works rather than discuss each separately. Select several points or aspects that you will discuss for each work, and then organize your paper to proceed from aspect to aspect.

4. **Synopsis.** Some instructors ask students to write a synopsis or summary of a work. This assignment demands a concise description of major features of the work, such as plot, setting, and characterization. Others ask for a card report (a point-by-point description of various elements, usually on an index card). Generally, some form of evaluation of the work is also expected. If you are not certain what aspects to include or what format to use, ask your instructor.

Self-Test Summary

1. Define the term *genre* and list some examples of different genres.	Genre means a particular type or form of literary, musical, or artistic composition. In literature, examples include poetry, drama, essays, short stories, and novels.
2. What are some of the types of language used in literature?	Literature uses descriptive, connotative, and figurative language to express images, attitudes, and feelings.
3. Give some specific suggestions for reading poetry.	Reread frequently. Note the poem's action, audience, and tone. Analyze the poem's intent, and search for its theme and meaning. Check unfamiliar references.
4. What are the basic features of short stories and novels?	The basic features are plot, characterization, setting, point of view, tone, and theme.
5. What do the visual arts focus on?	Visual arts focus on expressing an idea through a medium, such as canvas, clay, or fiber.
6. How should you study art?	Studying art involves • seeing as well as looking. • identifying the subject matter. • considering the title. • studying the visual elements. • writing reactions. • analyzing the work. • considering meaning.
7. What is criticism?	Criticism is a work that discusses, interprets, or evaluates a piece of art or literature.
8. Name the predominant thought patterns or strategies used when reading literary criticism.	The patterns are process, chronological order, cause and effect, and comparison and contrast.

Leaves

Lloyd Schwartz

Prereading Questions

(Answer after reading the entire poem once.)
1. What is the subject of the poem?
2. Summarize the literal action.

1.

1   Every October it becomes important, no, *necessary*
to see the leaves turning, to be surrounded
by leaves turning: it's not just the symbolism,
to confront in the death of the year your death,
5   one blazing farewell appearance, though the irony
isn't lost on you that nature is most seductive
when it's about to die, flaunting the dazzle of its
incipient exit, an ending that at least so far
the effects of human progress (pollution, acid rain)
10   have not yet frightened you enough to make you believe
is real; that is, you know this ending is a deception
because of course nature is always renewing itself—
      the trees don't *die,* they just pretend,
      go out in style, and return in style: a new style.

2.

15   It is deliberate how far they make you go
especially if you live in the city to get far
enough away from home to see not just trees
but only trees. The boring highways, roadsigns, high
speeds, 10-axle trucks passing you as if they were
20   in an even greater hurry than you to look at leaves:
so you drive in terror for literal hours and it looks
like rain, or *snow,* but it's probably just clouds
(too cloudy to see any color?) and you wonder,
given the poverty of your memory, which road had the
25   most color last year, but it doesn't matter since
you're probably too late anyway, or too early—
      whichever road you take will be the wrong one
      and you've probably come all this way for nothing.

3.

You'll be driving along depressed when suddenly
30   a cloud will move and the sun will muscle through
and ignite the hills. It may not last. Probably
won't last. But for a moment the whole world
comes to. Wakes up. Proves it lives. It lives—
red, yellow, orange, brown, russet, ocher, vermilion,
35   *gold.* Flame and rust. Flame and rust, the permutations
of burning. You're on fire. Your eyes are on fire.
It won't last, you don't want it to last. You
can't stand any more. But you don't want it to stop.
It's what you've come for. It's what you'll
40   come back for. It won't stay with you, but you'll
remember that it felt like nothing else you've felt
or something you've felt that also didn't last.

—Schwartz, "Leaves," *Goodnight, Gracie*

Writing About the Reading

CHECKING YOUR VOCABULARY

1. For each of the words listed below, use context; prefixes, roots, and suffixes (see Chapter 3); and/or a dictionary to write a brief definition or
   synonym of the word as it is used in the reading.

   a. irony (line 5) _____

   b. seductive (line 6) _____

   c. incipient (line 8) _____

   d. vermilion (line 34) _____

   e. permutations (line 35) _____

2. Draw a word map of one of the words used in the reading.

CHECKING YOUR COMPREHENSION

1. In line 3, Schwartz mentions symbolism. To what symbolism is he
   referring?
2. What is the poet's attitude toward human progress (line 9)?
3. To whom does the word *they* refer in line 15?
4. Describe the poem's tone.
5. What is the poem's theme?

THINKING CRITICALLY

Why does the author mention pollution and acid rain in line 9?

LEARNING/STUDY STRATEGY

Annotate the poem using the suggestions for analyzing poetry in the Key Strategy box "How to Read Poetry" on page 335.

13 Reading in Mathematics

MATHEMATICS: A Visual Overview

Studies have shown that people who are interested in music often have a natural ability in mathematics as well.

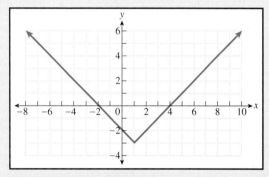

Mathematics is not just about numbers and equations—it is about describing and visualizing problems and their solutions. Most math textbooks will have hundreds of graphics to help you envision the mathematics underlying a given situation.

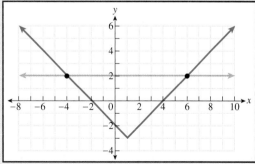

A thorough understanding of mathematics is essential for those who wish to pursue degrees and careers in computer science.

LEARNING OBJECTIVES

- To learn what mathematics is

- To consider whether you should major in mathematics

- To discover tips for studying mathematics

- To develop a systematic approach for reading mathematics textbooks

- To solve word problems in mathematics

- To learn common thought patterns used in mathematics

- To develop study techniques for mathematics

What Is Mathematics?

Many students think of mathematics as the study of numbers and computation, mostly because the courses they've taken in grammar and high school have revolved around basic concepts of arithmetic (adding, subtracting, multiplying, and dividing) and algebra, in which students use mathematical logic to determine the values of unknown variables. (For example, in the equation $2x + 5 = 15$, the letter x is the variable.)

However, college mathematics is much larger in scope. As an academic discipline, **mathematics** involves the study of such ideas as structure, space, and pattern. Calculus, a required math course for most business majors, is the study of change. Statistics is the branch of math dedicated to the collection, analysis, presentation, and explanation of data. It is required not only for business majors, but also for many psychology and social science majors. Computer science is also often considered a branch of mathematics.

Many students tend to see math solely as a requirement that needs to be fulfilled, but the truth is that math is the foundation of many academic disciplines. Think of it as an enabler—a discipline that enables all the other disciplines to function. If you do decide to focus on math as your major area of study, you can feel confident in the fact that many industries hire math majors (see Table 13-1).

Table 13-1   Career Opportunities in Mathematics

INDUSTRY	DESCRIPTION
Mathematical Modeling	Mathematical modelers use math to predict behavior or outcomes. Government agencies use mathematical modelers to predict the effects of various governmental policies. Businesses use mathematical modelers to help them predict their profits and the success of their products.
Biotechnology	Biotechnology companies fuse biology with technology, seeking ways to improve life through science. For example, biotechnology firms have helped farmers by using scientific and mathematical methods to produce genetically engineered seeds that produce fuller, bigger crops than average seeds.
Cryptography	Cryptography is the making and breaking of secret codes, many of which are mathematically based. This is a particularly valuable skill in governmental intelligence and counterintelligence operations.
Banking and Finance	Investment banks and stockbrokers need mathematicians to help them plan their investments wisely.
Mathematics Education	All schools—grammar schools, high schools, colleges, and universities—offer math courses as an important part of their curricula. There is always a need for a new generation of mathematicians to teach math skills to students.

Should You Major in Mathematics?

If you aspire to a career in engineering and certain areas of computer science, you will need strong mathematical skills. Time spent developing these skills is a valuable investment. According to the National Association of Colleges and Employers 2005 salary survey, math and engineering majors earn a salary that is 37.7 percent higher than the average salary for new graduates.

Interestingly, in studies of job satisfaction, mathematicians rank first in terms of how happy they are with their jobs. This is most likely because mathematicians see their math career as an extension of themselves, as something they truly love doing.

What characteristics and habits will make you a successful math major?

1. **You must be a logical, sequential thinker**. Mathematics requires very strong mental discipline. You must be able to follow an equation through in an organized fashion from beginning to end as you develop your thinking. (Of course, computers can and do help greatly, but there is no substitute for understanding how the underlying mathematics works.)

2. **You must be patient.** Many mathematical situations and questions are very complicated. Mathematicians have worked on answering some questions literally for decades. You must enjoy the process of discovery and thinking, not look for the quick and easy answer.

3. **You must enjoy problem solving and thinking theoretically as well as practically.** While many people think of math solely as the solving of equations, in many career applications math is all about solving real-world problems. The importance of problem solving explains why many of your math courses will make use of "word problems" that get you thinking about how to *use* math on a daily basis.

Tips for Studying Mathematics—Even if You Are Not a Major

There is no way around it: during your college career, you will have to take math courses. Here are some tips for making the most of these classes.

1. **View mathematics as essential to your major, and don't put off taking your math courses.** The introductory courses in many disciplines avoid math because the goal is to introduce the material without adding the burden of mathematical knowledge. However, once you move into your major courses, the math requirements kick in rapidly. Take your math courses as soon as you can so that by the time you are taking specialized courses for your major, you understand the required math. For example, nursing majors need math to compute and measure drug dosages. In accounting, you need mathematics to calculate expenses, profits, and losses.

2. **Don't be afraid of math. Try to relax.** Some students have a fear of math. They think of themselves as "incapable" of math, perhaps because numbers don't interest them or because they have not enjoyed previous math courses. With this attitude, the study of math becomes an unpleasant chore. It is much better to approach math as an extremely valuable addition to your set of skills. Employers consistently say that their best performers—the ones most likely to get promotions and earn more money—are those with strong math and writing skills.

3. **Ask for help if you need it.** Many college campuses offer free tutoring in math. If you are struggling, take advantage of any opportunities to help you improve your skills. Remember that your college professors love mathematics, and they want to help you love it too.

4. **Use your progress as a source of encouragement.** One of the things that makes the study of math rewarding is your ability to easily track your progress. You can *see* yourself making progress; you can solve a problem today that you could not solve yesterday. Instead of becoming frustrated by what you can't do, remind yourself of what you *can* do, of what you have already learned—and the fact that you can learn what you need to through hard work and diligence.

Quotes from a Math Professor

Advice for Math Students

Jerry R. Muir, Ph.D., Professor of Math, University of Scranton

66 Reading in mathematics will proceed at a much slower pace than reading in other disciplines. It is a common mistake for students to read a math text as if it were a history or philosophy text. Sometimes a history reading will cover a hundred pages, while a math reading assignment will be as few as ten pages. It shouldn't come as a surprise that, if they read for understanding, these assignments could take the same amount of time. 99

66 When reading a math text, students should literally go sentence by sentence. After each sentence, they should make sure they understand what they have read. If they do not, they should go back to earlier parts of the section that might need to be reread to understand the new point or turn to scratch paper, as perhaps a side calculation is necessary. 99

■ Reading Mathematics Textbooks

To learn from mathematics texts, you must allow plenty of time and work at peak concentration. Mathematics texts are concise and to the point; nearly everything is important. Use the following suggestions to develop a systematic approach for reading in mathematics.

Preview Before Reading

For mathematics texts, your preview should include a brief review of your previous chapter assignment. Because learning new skills hinges on remembering what you have learned before, a brief review of previously learned material is valuable. See the Key Strategy box "How to Preview Textbook Assignments," page 35.

Understand Mathematical Language

One of the first steps to success with mathematics is learning to understand its language. Mathematics uses a symbolic language in which notations, symbols, numbers, and formulas are used to express ideas and relationships. Working with mathematics requires that you be able to convert mathematical language to everyday language. To understand a formula, for example, $I = prt,$ you must translate mathematical language into everyday language: "Interest equals principal times rate times time." To solve a word problem expressed in everyday language, first you must convert it into mathematical language. You might think of equations as mathematical sentences. Just as an English sentence expresses a complete idea, an equation describes a mathematical relationship. Here are a few examples.

SENTENCE	EQUATION
The speed of train A is four times the speed of train B.	$A = 4B$
When I am as old as my mother (m), I shall be five times as old as my daughter (d) is now.	$5d = m$
In a sewing box, there are three times as many pins as needles, and one-third as many buttons as needles; the total number of pins, needles, and buttons is 1,872.	$3n + n + \frac{1}{3}n = 1872$

When you learn a foreign language, it is not sufficient only to learn the new vocabulary; you also must learn the rules of word order, grammar, punctuation, and so forth. To read and understand mathematics, then, you must know not only the signs and symbols (the vocabulary) but also the basic rules for expressing relationships in mathematical form. Figure 13-1 shows six important types of symbols and mathematical language and gives examples of each, taken from introductory algebra.

Figure 13-2 shows a sample page from an introductory algebra textbook. It has been marked to indicate the types of mathematical language used.

FIGURE 13–1 Aspects of Mathematical Language

Type	Function	Example
Punctuation marks	Make clear what parts of a statement are or are not separable; distinguish groups within groups	(0, 1, 2, …) $[3 - (a + b)^2]$
Models (graphs, charts, drawings)	Present a pictorial representation of a relationship or situation	
Numbers	Indicate size, order	3, 7, 9, 11
Variables	Represent a number that is unknown or may vary	x, y
Signs for relations	Indicate relationships	$a = b$ (a equals b) $c > d$ (c is greater than d)
Signs for operations	Give instructions	$15 \div 3$ (divide 15 by 3) $a - b$ (subtract b from a)

FIGURE 13–2 Sample Textbook Page

OBJECTIVE ▶ Inequalities can be used to solve applied problems involving phrases that suggest inequality. The chart below gives some of the more common such phrases, along with examples and translations.

Phrase	Example	Inequality
Is more than	A number *is more than* 4	$x > 4$
Is less than	A number *is less than* –12	$x < -12$
Is at least	A number *is at least* 6	$x \geq 6$
Is at most	A number *is at most* 8	$x \leq 8$

Caution
Do not confuse phrases like "5 more than a number" and statements like "5 *is* more than a number." The first of these is expressed as "x + 5" while the second is expressed as "5 > x."

E X A M P L E   8   **Finding an Average Test Score**
Brent has grades of 86, 88, and 78 on his first three tests in geometry. If he wants an average of at least 80 after his fourth test, what score must he make on his fourth test?
    Let *x* represent Brent's score on his fourth test. To find the average of the four scores, add them and find $\frac{1}{4}$ of the sum.

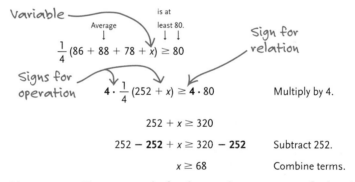

He must score 68 or more on the fourth test to have an average of *at least* 80.

SOURCE: Lial et al., *Introductory Algebra*, pp. 163–64

Much information is packed into small units of mathematical language. Some students find it helpful to translate formulas into words as they read, as is shown in the following equation for a right triangle:

$$c^2 = a^2 + b^2$$

The equation means the square of the hypotenuse of a right triangle is equal to the sum of the squares of the two remaining sides.

In mathematics, you must know the *exact* meaning of both words and symbols. There are several places to find the definition of a new term. If it is from the current chapter, look at the end-of-chapter material, which often includes key vocabulary. You might also check the index to find page numbers or use the glossary to read a brief definition, if one is included. Use the index card system described in Chapter 3 to help you learn the language of mathematics. Record the term or symbol, its meaning, an example, and a diagram, if possible. Also include a page reference to where the term is used in your textbook. Two sample index cards are shown in Figure 13-3.

FIGURE 13–3 Sample Index Cards

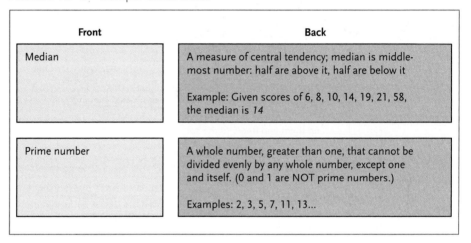

Front	Back
Median	A measure of central tendency; median is middle-most number: half are above it, half are below it Example: Given scores of 6, 8, 10, 14, 19, 21, 58, the median is *14*
Prime number	A whole number, greater than one, that cannot be divided evenly by any whole number, except one and itself. (0 and 1 are NOT prime numbers.) Examples: 2, 3, 5, 7, 11, 13...

EXERCISE 13-1   **Identifying Mathematical Language**

Read the excerpt from an algebra text shown in Figure 13-4 on the next page, and underline five examples of mathematical language that the author assumes you know.

1. Write a definition of each term you have underlined.
2. Write your own definition of the phrase, "evaluating an expression." Include an example to illustrate your definition.

Follow the Chapter Organization

Chapters in most mathematics textbooks contain four essential elements: the presentation or explanation, sample problems, graphs and diagrams, and exercises. Mathematics textbook chapters often use a decimal system for dividing the chapter into sections. For example, Chapter 3 might be numbered 3.1, 3.2, 3.3, and so on. Each number with a decimal is a new section of the chapter.

Reading Chapter Explanations   Each new operation, process, or term is explained in the text. As you read this explanation, focus on *how* and *why* the process works. Discover the reasoning behind the process. If the author refers to a sample

FIGURE 13–4   Excerpt from an Algebra Text

Evaluating an Expression   If you like to fish, you can use an expression (rule) like the one below to find the approximate weight (in pounds) of a fish you catch. Measure the length (in inches) of the fish and then use the correct expression for that type of fish. For a northern pike, the weight expression is shown.

Variable (length of fish) $\dfrac{l^3}{3600}$

where l is the length of the fish in inches.
   To evaluate this expression for a fish that is 43 inches long, follow the rule by calculating

$$\frac{43^3}{3600}$$ Replace l with 43, the length of the fish in inches.

In the numerator, you can multiply $43 \cdot 43 \cdot 43$ or use the $\boxed{y^x}$ key on your calculator. Then divide by 3600.

   Enter 43 $\boxed{y^x}$ 3 $\boxed{\div}$ 3600 $\boxed{=}$ **Calculator shows 22.08527778**

   Base Exponent

The fish weighs about 22 pounds.

   Now evaluate the expression to find the approximate weight of a northern pike that is 37 inches long. (Answer: about 14 pounds.)
   Notice that variables are used on your calculator keys. On the $\boxed{y^x}$ key, y represents the base and x represents the exponent. You evaluated y^x by entering 43 as the base and 3 as the exponent for the first fish. Then you evaluated y^x by entering 37 as the base and 3 as the exponent for the second fish.

Source: Lial and Hestwood, *Prealgebra*, p. 87

problem in the explanation, it is necessary to move back and forth between the explanation and the sample problem. Read a sentence or two and then refer to the sample problem to see how the information is applied. Your purpose is to see how the sample problem illustrates the process being described. The steps to follow in computing the total installment cost and finance charge on a credit card are given in Figure 13-5 on page 364. Then the authors give a sample problem and show how it is solved using the steps they have listed.

   As you read, refer to previous chapters if an operation is unclear or if unfamiliar terms are used. In mathematics, you should expect to look back frequently because much of the material is sequential.

Reading Sample Problems   Sample problems demonstrate how an operation or process works. It may be tempting to skip over sample problems because they require time to work through or because they lack an accompanying verbal explanation. However, careful study of the sample problems is an essential part of learning in mathematics. Follow the steps listed in the Key Strategy box on pages 364–365 to read sample problems effectively.

FIGURE 13–5   Problem Solving Step-by-Step

Since the enactment of the **Federal Truth-in-Lending Act** (Regulation Z) in 1969, lenders must report their **finance charge** (the charge for credit) and their **annual percentage rate.** The truth-in-lending law does not regulate interest rates or credit charges but merely requires a standardized and truthful report of what they are. The individual states set the allowable interest rates and charges.
} back-ground

Find the annual percentage rate by first finding the **total installment cost** (or the **deferred payment price**) and the finance charge on the loan. Do this with the following steps.
overview of process

Finding total in-stallment cost and finance charge

Step 1.   Find the total installment cost.

> **Total installment cost = Down payment**
>
> **+ (Amount of each payment x Number of payments)**

Step 2.   Find the finance charge.
step-by-step procedure

> **Finance charge = Total installment cost – Cash price**

Step 3.   Finally, find the amount financed.

> **Amount financed = Cash price – Down payment**

Example   Diane Phillips bought a motorcycle for $980. She paid $200 down and then made 24 payments of $39.60 each. Find the (a) total installment cost, (b) finance charge, and (c) amount financed.
} sample problem

Solution   (a) Find the total installment cost by multiplying the amount of each payment by the number of payments, and adding the down payment.

$$\text{Total installment cost} = \$200 + (\$39.60 \times 24)$$
$$= \$200 + \$950.40$$
$$= \$1150.40$$

(b) The finance charge is the difference between the total installment cost and the cash price.
} solution

$$\text{Finance charge} = \$1150.40 - \$980$$
$$= \$170.40$$

Phillips pays an additional $170.40 for the motorcycle because it is bought on credit.

(c) The amount financed is
$$\$980 - \$200 = \$780$$

SOURCE: Miller and Salzman, *Business Mathematics*, p. 373

KEY STRATEGY: How to Read Math Problems

1. **Before you read the solution, think of how you would solve the problem, choose a method, and solve the problem.** More than one approach may be possible.

2. **Read the solution and compare your answer with the textbook's.**

3. **Be sure you understand each step; you should know exactly what calculations were performed and why they were done.**

4. **When you have finished reading the sample problem, explain the steps in your own words.** This will help you remember the method later. The best way to verbalize is to write the process down; this forces you to be clear and precise. Figure 13-6 presents two sample problems and shows how a student verbalized each process.

5. **Test your understanding by covering up the text's solution and solving the problem yourself.** Finally, look over the solution, verifying its reasonableness and reviewing the process once again.

FIGURE 13–6 Verbalizing a Process

Problem 1: Find the principal of a loan that gives an interest of $30 at 10% per year for 91 days.

Solution	Verbalization
1. $P = \dfrac{I}{RT}$	1. The formula for computing principal is interest divided by the product of the rate multiplied by the time.
2. $P = \dfrac{30}{.10 \times \dfrac{91}{365}}$	2. The interest is $30. The rate, 10% per year, is converted to a decimal, .10, and the time is expressed as a fraction of a year.
3. $P = \dfrac{30}{.025}$	3. The denominator is simplified.
4. $P = \$1200$	4. The principal is $1200.

Problem 2: $\sqrt{3x + 1} - \sqrt{x + 9} = 2$

Solution	Verbalization
1. $\sqrt{3x + 1} = 2 + \sqrt{x + 9}$	Isolate one radical on one side of the equation.
2. $(\sqrt{3x + 1})^2 = (2 + \sqrt{x + 9})^2$	Square both sides.
3. $3x + 1 = 4 + 4\sqrt{x + 9} + x + 9$	Use formula $(a + b)^2 = a^2 + 2ab + b^2$.
4. $2x - 12 = 4\sqrt{x + 9}$	Isolate the radical.
5. $x - 6 = 2\sqrt{x + 9}$	Factor out 2 on the left side. Divide the equation by 2.
6. $(x - 6)^2 = (2\sqrt{x + 9})^2$ $x^2 - 12x + 36 = 4(x + 9)$	Square both sides.
7. $x^2 - 12x + 36 = 4x + 36$ $x^2 - 16x = 0$ $x(x - 16) = 0$ $x = 16$	Solve for x.

Ignore the solution $x = 0$ because it will not check in the original equation. Extraneous roots can occur when you square both sides of an equation.

SOURCE: Johnson and Steffensen, *Elementary Algebra*, p. 178

EXERCISE 13-2   Verbalizing Problem-Solving

For each of the following problems and solutions, verbalize the process and write each step in your own words. Compare your verbalization with that of another student.

1. Problem: The sum of two numbers is 21 and their difference is 9. Find the numbers.

   Solution: Let x, y be the two numbers.

   $$x + y = 21$$
   $$x - y = 9$$
   $$2x = 30$$
   $$x = 15$$
   $$\text{Then, } 15 + y = 21$$
   $$\text{so, } y = 21 - 15$$
   $$y = 6$$

2. Problem: Solve $x^2 - 6x + 8 = 0$ using the quadratic formula.

   Solution: $a = 1, b = -6, c = 8$

   $$x = \frac{-b \pm \sqrt{b^2 - 4ac}}{2a}$$

   $$= \frac{-(-6) \pm \sqrt{(-6)^2 - 4(1)(8)}}{2(1)}$$

   $$= \frac{6 \pm \sqrt{36 - 32}}{2}$$

   $$= \frac{6 \pm \sqrt{4}}{2} = \frac{6 \pm 2}{2}$$

   $$x = \frac{6 + 2}{2} = \frac{8}{2} = 4$$

   or

   $$x = \frac{6 - 2}{2} = \frac{4}{2} = 2$$

   $$x = 4, 2$$

Reading and Drawing Graphs, Tables, and Diagrams   Graphs, tables, and diagrams are often included in textbook chapters. These are intended to help you understand processes and concepts by providing a visual representation. Treat these drawings as essential parts of the chapter. Here are a few suggestions on how to use them:

1. **Study each drawing closely, frequently referring to the text that accompanies it.** Test your understanding of the drawing by reconstructing and labeling it without reference to the text drawing; then compare drawings.

2. **Use the drawings in the text as models on which to base your own drawings.** As you solve end-of-chapter problems, create drawings similar to those included in the text. These may be useful as you decide how to solve the problem.

3. **Draw your own diagrams to clarify or explore relationships.** For example, an algebra student drew the following diagram of the trinomial equation:

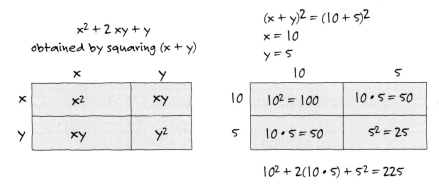

Another student drew the following diagram to explain why the formula for finding the area of a parallelogram is $A = bh$.

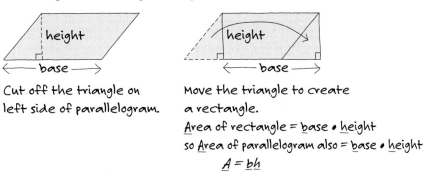

4. **Use tables to organize and categorize large amounts of complicated data.** For example, a student made the following table to solve a frequency distribution problem in statistics, in which she was asked to identify the frequency of female Democrats and male Republicans. She was provided with the following information: Of a sample of 150 people, 62 males and 31 females are Democrats. Thirty-eight males and 19 females are Republicans.

	DEMOCRAT	REPUBLICAN	TOTALS
Male	62	38	100
Female	31	19	50
Totals	93	57	150

Solving Word Problems Most textbook chapters have numerous problem-solving exercises; quizzes and exams also consist primarily of problems. Often, the problems are expressed in words and are not conveniently set up for you in formulas or equations. Solving word problems is a seven-step process as shown in the Key Strategy box on page 368. In your textbook, be sure to work through exercises as they occur in the chapter. Do not wait until the end and try to work them all at once.

KEY STRATEGY: How to Solve Word Problems

1. **Identify what is asked for.**   What are you supposed to find?

2. **Locate the information that is provided to solve the problem.**   (Some math problems may include irrelevant information; if so, underline or circle pertinent data.)

3. **Draw a diagram, if possible.**   Label the diagram.

4. **Estimate your answer.**   If possible, make a guess about what the answer should be. Be sure your guess is reasonable and logical.

5. **Decide on a procedure to solve the problem.**   Recall formulas you have learned that are related to the problem, and look for clue words that indicate a particular process. For example, the phrase "how fast" means *rate;* you may be able to use the formula $r = d/t$. If you do not know how to solve a problem, look for similarities between it and sample problems you have studied.

6. **Solve the problem.**   Begin by choosing variables to represent the unknown quantities. Then set up an equation.

7. **Verify your answer.**   Compare your answer with your estimate. If there is a large discrepancy, this is a signal that you have made an error. There are three possibilities: (1) the solution is correct, but the estimate was off base, (2) the solution is wrong, but the estimate is good, or (3) both the solution and estimate are wrong. Check to be sure your estimate is reasonable and logical. Then check your problem-solving strategy and your arithmetic.

Figure 13-7 gives an example of how this problem-solving process works.

EXERCISE 13-3   **Solving Word Problems**

Complete each of the following problems using the procedure outlined above. Label each step.

1. Samantha receives an 11% commission on her sales of cosmetics. During one week, her daily sales were $482.10, $379.80, $729.62, $524.24, and $310.40. Find her gross earnings for the week.

2. If a microwave oven costs the retailer $325 and the markup is 35%, find the selling price.

3. Two joggers start jogging from the same point on a highway. One is running north, and the other is running south. One jogs 2 miles per hour faster than the other. They are 24 miles apart after 3 hours. At what rate is each jogging?

FIGURE 13–7 *Sample Word Problem*

Problem: A four-ton passenger paddleboat goes 210 miles down the Mississippi River in the same time it can go 140 miles upriver. The speed of the current is five miles per hour. Find the speed of the boat in still water.

Steps	Solution
1. Identify what is asked for.	speed in still water
2. Locate given quantities.	210 miles down 140 miles up
3. Draw a diagram.	

down → 5 mph → 210 miles

up → −5 mph → 140 miles

} equal time

4. Estimate the answer.	Estimate: 20 mph
5. Decide on a procedure; recall formulas.	$d = rt$ (distance = rate x time)
6. Solve the problem.	x = speed in still water time up = time down $d = r \times t$ downstream $210 = (x + 5)t$ upstream $140 = (x - 5)t$
(a) Solve for t.	$d = rt$ $t = d/r$
(b) Determine t values.	$t \text{ (downstream)} = \dfrac{210}{(x + 5)}$ $t \text{ (upstream)} = \dfrac{140}{(x - 5)}$
(c) $t = t$	$\dfrac{210}{(x + 5)} = \dfrac{140}{(x - 5)}$
(d) Multiply both sides by $(x + 5)(x - 5)$.	$(x + 5)(x - 5)\dfrac{210}{(x + 5)} = (x + 5)(x - 5)\dfrac{140}{(x - 5)}$
(e) Solve the equation.	$210(x - 5) = 140(x + 5)$ $210x - 1050 = 140x + 700$ $70x = 1750$ $x = 25$
7. Compare with estimate and check arithmetic.	answer 25 mph (estimate was 20 mph)

SOURCE: Johnson and Steffenson, *Elementary Algebra*.

4. A collection of nickels and dimes is worth $2.85. If there are 34 coins in the collection, how many of each type of coin are there?

5. One number is 6 larger than another. The square of the larger is 96 more than the square of the smaller. Find the numbers.

EXERCISE 13-4

LEARNING
COLLABORATIVELY

Writing and Solving Word Problems

Write three sample word problems. Exchange your problems with another student, and solve each other's problems.

Using End-of-Chapter Material   Many mathematics texts include useful review material at the end of the chapter. Typically, there is a summary of key ideas from the chapter, often with sample worked examples; key terms; review exercises; and a chapter test. Use these materials to test yourself.

Use Writing to Learn

As in most disciplines, reading is not sufficient for learning mathematics. Highlighting and marking are the strategies students generally use to enhance learning; however, these techniques do not work well in mathematics. Mathematics texts are concise; everything is important. Writing, instead of highlighting, is a useful learning strategy in mathematics. Writing in your own words will force you to convert mathematical language to everyday language. It will also demonstrate what you understand and what you do not. The Key Strategy box below suggests a few ways to use writing to increase your understanding and learning in mathematics.

KEY STRATEGY: How to Use Writing to Learn Mathematics

1. **Definitions.**   Read the textbook definition; then close the book and write your own. Compare it with the textbook definition, noticing and correcting discrepancies. Rewrite your definition until it is correct and complete.

2. **Class notes.**   Rewrite your notes, including more detail and explanation. Focus on process; include reasons and explanations. Include information from the corresponding textbook section.

3. **Questions.**   Write lists of questions based on chapter assignments, homework assignments, and your class notes. Seek answers from classmates, your instructor, a review book, or the learning lab or tutorial services.

4. **Problems.**   Once you think you understand a particular problem or process, write down what you understand. To test your recall, write several questions based on your written explanation. Put aside both your explanation and your questions for several days. Then take out the question sheet and, without reference to your explanation, try to answer your questions. Compare your answers with your original explanation.

5. **Tests.**   When preparing for an exam, construct and answer sample questions and problems. It is also effective to exchange self-constructed problems with a classmate and solve them.

6. **Diagrams.** Draw diagrams of sample problems as you read, and diagram actual problems before you attempt a solution. Describing the situation in visual terms often makes it more understandable.

7. **Review.** Review your course weekly. Write a description of what you have learned in the past week. You might compare your description with those of your classmates. Keep your weekly descriptions; they will be useful as you review for tests and final exams.

EXERCISE 13-5   Analyzing a Mathematics Excerpt

Read Figure 13-8 on page 372, an excerpt from a basic college mathematics textbook on the Pythagorean Theorem. Then complete each of the following steps.

1. List the terminology that is essential to understand when reading this excerpt.
2. Without referring to the text, write a definition of *hypotenuse*. Make a diagram to illustrate your definition. Compare your definition and diagram with the text excerpt. Revise your definition and diagram, if necessary.
3. Without referring to the text, describe how to use the Pythagorean Theorem to find the unknown length of the hypotenuse in a right triangle. Compare your description with the text excerpt. Revise your description if necessary.
4. Find the unknown length in the following right triangles.

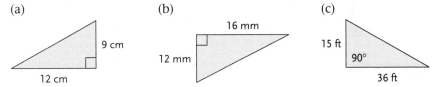

(a)   9 cm   12 cm

(b)   16 mm   12 mm

(c)   15 ft   90°   36 ft

Expect Gradual Understanding

Mathematics is a reasoning process: a process of understanding relationships and seeing similarities and differences. Consequently, mathematics is not an "either you understand it or you don't" discipline. Your understanding will develop by degrees; it grows as you work or "play with" problems. Here is how you can work toward developing your understanding as you read:

1. **Plan on reading, and then reading and solving, and finally re-solving, problems.** As you reread and re-solve problems, you often will come to a new understanding of the process involved. (This is similar to seeing a film or reading a novel a second time; you will notice and discover things you did not see the first time.)

2. **Experiment with the chapter's content.** The style of most textbooks is concise, but this does not mean that there is no room for creativity or experimentation. Try various solutions to problems. As you experiment, you will come to a new understanding of the problems and solutions.

FIGURE 13–8   Pythagorean Theorem

OBJECTIVE ▶   One place you will use square roots is when working with the *Pythagorean Theorem*. This theorem applies only to *right* triangles (triangles with a 90° angle). The longest side of a right triangle is called the **hypotenuse** (hy-POT-en-oos). It is opposite the right angle. The other two sides are called *legs*. The legs form the right angle.

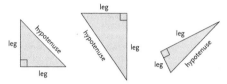

Examples of right triangles

Pythagorean Theorem

$$(\text{hypotenuse})^2 = (\text{leg})^2 + (\text{leg})^2$$

In other words, square the length of each side. After you have squared all the sides, the sum of the squares of the two legs will equal the square of the hypotenuse.

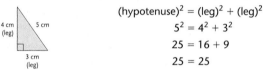

$$(\text{hypotenuse})^2 = (\text{leg})^2 + (\text{leg})^2$$
$$5^2 = 4^2 + 3^2$$
$$25 = 16 + 9$$
$$25 = 25$$

If you know the lengths of any two sides in a right triangle, you can use the Pythagorean Theorem to find the length of the third side.

Pythagorean Theorem

To find the hypotenuse, use this formula:

$$\textbf{hypotenuse} = \sqrt{\textbf{(leg)}^2 + \textbf{(leg)}^2}$$

EXAMPLE 2   Finding the Unknown Length in a Right Triangle
Find the unknown length in this right triangle.

The length of the side opposite the right angle is unknown. That side is the hypotenuse, so use this formula.

$\text{hypotenuse} = \sqrt{(\text{leg})^2 + (\text{leg})^2}$ Find the hypotenuse.

$\text{hypotenuse} = \sqrt{(3)^2 + (4)^2}$ Legs are 3 and 4.

$\qquad\qquad = \sqrt{9 + 16}$ $3 \cdot 3$ is 9   and $4 \cdot 4$ is 16

$\qquad\qquad = \sqrt{25}$

$\qquad\qquad = 5$

The hypotenuse is 5 ft. long.

Note: You use the Pythagorean Theorem to find the *length* of one side, *not* the area of the triangle. Your answer will be in linear units, such as ft, yd, cm, m, and so on (*not* ft², cm², m²).

SOURCE: Lial et al., *Basic College Mathematics*, pp. 548–49

3. **Take risks.** Attempt a solution to a problem even if you do not fully understand it. As you work, you may discover more about how to arrive at the correct answer.

4. **Be active.** Active reading (see Chapter 1) is essential in mathematics. Get involved with the ideas, ask questions, and search for applications.

5. **Study mathematics frequently.** Because learning is gradual, it is better to study mathematics frequently rather than in large blocks of time. For example, studying one hour a day for six days is much better than studying three hours on two different days.

■ Thought Patterns in Mathematics

In mathematics there are three commonly used patterns:

- **Process**—Your goal in many situations is to see *how* a problem is solved or *how* a theory applies. As you make notes on chapters and as you rewrite class notes, explain, in your own words, how and why things work. Include reasons, explain relationships, and state why a particular operation was selected or why one problem-solving strategy was chosen over another.

- **Problem solving**—Problem solving in mathematics involves creativity and even playfulness. It is not, as many students think, a matter of merely plugging numbers into a preselected formula and completing the necessary computations. Instead, problem solving is the process of assessing a situation (problem) and assembling and applying what you have learned that fits the problem. As you attempt to solve problems, do not immediately reach for a formula. Instead, analyze, think, and experiment while you work. Try several approaches and decide which one works best.

- **Comparison and contrast**—Understanding and solving problems often requires you to see the similarities and differences among problem types and to study variations of sample problems. Often, you must look at a series of examples and detect a pattern (similarities) and then find a way to state this pattern as an equation or formula or rule. As you read and study, then, make notes about similarities and differences as they occur to you. Write, in your own words, how one problem differs from, or is a variation of, a type of problem you have previously learned about.

■ Studying Mathematics

Be certain to attend all classes. Because mathematics is sequential, if you miss one specific skill, that gap in your understanding may cause you trouble all term. Expect regular homework assignments and complete them on time, even if your instructor does not require you to turn them in. Practice is an essential element in all mathematics courses. Never let yourself get behind or skip assignments. Try to study mathematics at least three times a week—more often, if possible. Use the following suggestions to learn mathematics more effectively.

Preparing for Class

1. **Emphasize accuracy and precision.** In mathematics, knowing how to solve the problem is not enough; you must produce the right answer. A small error in arithmetic can produce a wrong answer, even when you know how to solve the problem. Use a calculator if your instructor allows it.

2. **Read the chapter carefully before working on exercises.** Do not worry if you do not understand everything right away. Then, as you work on the problems, refer to the chapter frequently.

3. **Before you begin a new chapter or assignment, always review the preceding one.** If you take a break while working on an assignment, do a brief one-minute review when you resume study.

4. **Read the portion of your textbook that covers the next day's lecture before attending class.** The lecture will be more meaningful if you have some idea of what it is about beforehand.

5. **In your class notes, be sure to record sample problems that your instructor solves in class.** If you get behind in taking notes, leave some blank space; then fill in what is missing later by working with a classmate or asking your instructor. After class, review and organize your notes, rewriting them if necessary. Add your own observations and ideas from your textbook as well.

6. **Rework sample problems solved in class.** This is an excellent means of review.

7. **Find a study group and work together to solve problems immediately after class.** Get the phone numbers of a few people in class whom you can call if you have missed an assignment or are stuck on a problem.

8. **Keep your homework in a special notebook.** Star the problems you have trouble with. Bring this notebook with you when you ask your instructor for help so that you can go immediately to those problems. When you review for a test, study the starred problems.

Preparing Sample Tests

One of the best ways to learn mathematics is to create your own sample tests. Use index cards to write your questions. Try to create three or four test question cards for each section of the chapter as you go along. Write the problem, including the directions, on the front of the card; write the solution and a page number reference to your text on the back. When preparing for a test, shuffle the cards so you are forced to work the problems out of order. Try to simulate test conditions; give yourself a time limit, allow yourself the same equipment (such as a calculator), and so forth.

Building Your Confidence

1. **Approach mathematics confidently.** Both men and women can suffer what has come to be known as "math anxiety." Math anxiety often reflects a negative self-concept: "I'm not good at math." Some students think,

incorrectly, that one either has or does not have a mathematical mind. This is a myth. Some people may find the subject easier than others, but the average student can learn mathematics.

2. **If you feel uncomfortable about taking your first math course, consider taking a basic refresher course in which you are likely to be successful.** You may not earn college credit, but you will build your confidence and prove to yourself that you can handle math. Other students find working with computerized review programs helpful when catching up on fundamentals. The machine is nonthreatening, offers no time pressures, and allows you to review a lesson as many times as you want. Many campuses offer workshops on overcoming math anxiety. To find out what help is available, check with your instructor, the learning lab, or the counseling center. A particularly useful book is *Conquering Math Anxiety*, by Cynthia Arem.

Test-Taking Tips
Preparing for Exams in Mathematics

Exams in mathematics usually consist of problems to solve. Use the following tips to prepare for exams in mathematics:

1. **When studying for exams, pay attention to what your instructor has emphasized.** Predict what will be on the exam, make a sample test that includes all the important topics, and practice completing it.

2. **When studying for an exam, review as many sample problems as possible.** Do not just read the problems; practice solving them. Try to anticipate the variations that may appear. For example, a variation of the paddleboat problem shown in Figure 13-7 may give you the rate but ask you to compute the distance.

3. **Identify problems that are most characteristic of the techniques presented in the chapter you are studying.** Record these on a study sheet, and summarize in your own words how you worked them. Compare your study sheet with that of a friend.

4. **As you solve homework problems and review returned exams and quizzes, search for a** pattern of errors. Is there one type of problem you frequently have trouble with? Do you make mistakes when setting up the equation, in factoring, or in computation? If you identify such a pattern, pay special attention to correcting these errors.

5. **If you are having trouble with your course, get help immediately.** Once you get behind, it is difficult to catch up. Consult with your instructor during his or her office hours. Check with the learning lab for tutoring or computer-assisted review programs.

6. **If you find you are weak in a particular fundamental such as fractions, correct the problem as soon as possible.** If you do not, it will interfere with your performance.

7. **Obtain additional study aids.** Schaum's *College Outline Series* offers excellent study guides. Check with your instructor for additional references.

8. **When a test is returned, rework the problems on which you lost points to find out exactly what you did wrong.**

Self–Test Summary

1. What are four useful techniques for reading mathematics?	Four useful techniques for reading mathematics are • previewing before reading. • learning mathematical language. • following chapter organization (including explanations, sample problems, diagrams, and graphs). • learning to solve word problems.
2. In mathematics, how are ideas and relationships expressed?	Ideas and relationships are expressed through notations, symbols, numbers, and formulas.
3. List the seven steps used in solving word problems.	Seven steps for resolving word problems are • identifying what is being asked for. • locating the information that is provided to solve the problem. • drawing a diagram, if possible, and labeling it. • estimating your answer. • deciding on a procedure to use to solve the problem. • solving the problem. • verifying the answer.
4. List seven ways to use writing to help you learn mathematics.	Use writing for • writing your own definitions of terms. • rewriting class notes. • writing questions based on assignments and class notes. • recording problem-solving methods. • preparing sample problems for tests. • drawing diagrams as you read. • reviewing your learning.
5. List five techniques that will help you gradually understand mathematics.	To gradually understand mathematics, • plan on rereading and re-solving problems. • experiment with chapter content. • take risks. • read actively. • study frequently.
6. What are the three most common thought patterns used in mathematics?	The three patterns are process, problem solving, and comparison and contrast.
7. List three tips for studying mathematics.	Three tips for studying mathematics are • prepare for class. • prepare sample tests. • build your confidence.

Statistics

Introduction to Statistics: Mean, Median, and Mode

Margaret L. Lial and Diana L. Hestwood

Prereading Questions

1. Preview this selection. On the basis of your preview, write a sentence describing its contents.
2. How difficult do you predict it will be to complete the exercises at the end of this selection?

1   The word *statistics* originally came from words that mean *state numbers.* State numbers refer to numerical information, or *data,* gathered by the government such as the number of births, deaths, or marriages in a population. Today the word *statistics* has a much broader meaning; data from the fields of economics, social science, science, and business can all be organized and studied under the branch of mathematics called *statistics.*

2   **Objective** ▶ Making sense of a long list of numbers can be hard. So when you analyze data, one of the first things to look for is a *measure of central tendency*—a single number that you can use to represent the entire list of numbers. One such measure is the *average* or **mean.** The mean can be found with the following formula.

Finding the Mean (Average)

3

$$\text{mean} = \frac{\text{sum of all values}}{\text{number of all values}}$$

EXAMPLE 1 Finding the Mean

4   David had test scores of 84, 90, 95, 98, and 88. Find his average or mean score. Use the formula for finding mean. Add up all the test scores and then divide by the number of tests.

$$\text{mean} = \frac{84 + 90 + 95 + 98 + 88}{5} \quad \begin{array}{l} \leftarrow \text{Sum of test scores} \\ \leftarrow \text{Number of tests} \end{array}$$

$$= \frac{455}{5} \quad \text{Divide}$$

$$= 91$$

David has a mean score of 91.

5   **Objective** ▶ Some items in a list of data might appear more than once. In this case, we find a **weighted mean,** in which each value is "weighted" by multiplying it by the number of times it occurs.

EXAMPLE 2 Understanding the Weighted Mean

6   The following table shows the amount of contribution and the number of times the amount was given (frequency) to a food pantry. Find the weighted mean.

Contribution

Value	Frequency
$ 3	4
$ 5	2
$ 7	1
$ 8	5
$ 9	3
$10	2
$12	1
$13	2

7   The same amount was given by more than one person: for example, $5 was given twice and $8 was given five times. Other amounts, such as $12, were given once. To find the mean, multiply each contribution value by its frequency. Then add the products. Next, add the numbers in the *frequency* column to find the total number of values.

Value	Frequency	Product
$ 3	4	$(3 \cdot 4) = \$12$
$ 5	2	$(5 \cdot 2) = \$10$
$ 7	1	$(7 \cdot 1) = \$ 7$
$ 8	5	$(8 \cdot 5) = \$40$
$ 9	3	$(9 \cdot 3) = \$27$
$10	2	$(10 \cdot 2) = \$20$
$12	1	$(12 \cdot 1) = \$12$
$13	2	$(13 \cdot 2) = \$26$
Totals	20	$154

Finally, divide the totals.

$$\text{mean} = \frac{\$154}{20} = \$7.70$$

The mean contribution to the food pantry was $7.70.

8   A common use of the weighted mean is to find a student's *grade point average*, as shown by the next example.

EXAMPLE 3 Applying the Weighted Mean

9   Find the grade point average for a student earning the following grades. Assume A = 4, B = 3, C = 2, D = 1, and F = 0. The number of credits determines how many times the grade is counted (the frequency).

Course	Credits	Grade	Credits · Grade
Mathematics	3	A (= 4)	3 · 4 = 12
Speech	3	C (= 2)	3 · 2 = 6
English	3	B (= 3)	3 · 3 = 9
Computer Science	3	A (= 4)	3 · 4 = 12
Lab for Computer Science	2	D (= 1)	2 · 1 = 2
Totals	14		41

It is common to round grade point averages to the nearest hundredth. So the grade point average for this student is shown below.

$$\frac{41}{14} \approx 2.93$$

10 **Objective ▶** Because it can be affected by extremely high or low numbers, the mean is often a poor indicator of central tendency for a list of numbers. In cases like this, another measure of central tendency, called the **median** (MEE-dee-un), can be used. The *median* divides a group of numbers in half; half the numbers lie above the median, and half lie below the median.

11 Find the median by listing the numbers *in order* from *smallest* to *largest*. If the list contains an *odd* number of items, the median is the *middle number*.

EXAMPLE 4 Using the Median

12 Find the median for the following list of prices.

$7, $23, $15, $6, $18, $12, $24

First arrange the numbers in numerical order from smallest to largest.

Smallest → 6, 7, 12, 15, 18, 23, 24 ← Largest

Next, find the middle number in the list.

6, 7, 12, 15, 18, 23, 24

Three are below | Three are above
Middle number

The median price is $15.

13 If a list contains an *even* number of items, there is no single middle number. In this case, the median is defined as the mean (average) of the *middle two* numbers.

EXAMPLE 5 Finding the Median

14 Find the median for the following list of ages.

74, 7, 15, 13, 25, 28, 47, 59, 32, 68

First arrange the numbers in numerical order. Then find the middle two numbers.

Smallest → 7, 13, 15, 25, 28, 32, 47, 59, 68, 74 ← Largest

Middle two numbers

The median age is the mean of these two numbers.

$$\text{median} = \frac{28 + 32}{2} = \frac{60}{2} = 30 \text{ years}$$

15 **Objective ▶** The last important statistical measure is the **mode,** the number that occurs most often in a list of numbers. For example, if the test scores for 10 students were

↓   ↓   ↓

74, 81, 39, 74, 82, 80, 100, 92, 74, and 85

then the mode is 74. Three students earned a score of 74, so 74 appears more times on the list than any other score.

16   A list can have two modes; such a list is sometimes called *bimodal*. If no number occurs more frequently than any other number in a list, the list has *no mode*.

Measures of Central Tendency

17 The **mean** is the sum of all the values divided by the number of values. It is the mathematical average.

The **median** is the middle number in a group of values that are listed from smallest to largest. It divides a group of numbers in half.

The **mode** is the value that occurs most often in a group of values.

—Lial and Hestwood, *Prealgebra,* pp. 347–50

Writing About the Reading

CHECKING YOUR VOCABULARY

1. For each of the words listed below, use context; prefixes, roots, and suffixes (see Chapter 3); and/or a dictionary to write a brief definition of the word as it is used in the reading.

   a. state numbers (para. 1) _____

   b. data (para. 1)_____

   c. values (para. 3)_____

   d. frequency (para. 6) _____

2. Underline new, specialized terms introduced in the reading.

3. Draw a word map of one of the words in the reading.

CHECKING YOUR COMPREHENSION

1. To assess your comprehension, define each of the following terms in your own words without reference to the reading: *statistics, measure of central tendency, mean, median, mode.* Verify your definitions by comparing them with the definitions in the reading.
2. What is the difference between a mean and a mode?
3. What is the difference between a mean and a median?

THINKING CRITICALLY

1. List the names and ages of 15 friends or classmates. (Estimate the ages, if necessary.)
   a. Find the mean age and the median age.
   b. Are the mean and median ages similar or different? Why did that happen?
2. List the names and ages of ten family members or relatives. Try to include one very young person or one very old person (but not both). Estimate the ages, if necessary.
   a. Find the mean age and the median age.
   b. Are the mean age and median ages similar or different? Why did that happen?
3. List the courses you are taking at this time and the number of credits for each course.
   a. List the highest grade you think you will earn in each course. Then find your grade point average.
   b. List the lowest grade you think you will earn in each course. Then find your grade point average.
4. Suppose you own a gift shop. Last summer, you stocked T-shirts in five different sizes, but they took up too much shelf space. This summer, you want to order only one size. Using last summer's sales, should you find the mean size, median size, or mode size? Explain your answer.

LEARNING/STUDY STRATEGIES

1. Write a summary of the process involved in finding
   a. the mean.
   b. the median.
   c. the mode.
2. What overall thought pattern(s) is or are used in the reading?

14 Reading in the Life and Physical Sciences

THE LIFE AND PHYSICAL SCIENCES: A Visual Overview

Geologists study natural processes that affect the earth. For example, the awe-inspiring Grand Canyon was created by the natural flow of the Colorado River over a period of millions of years.

All science textbooks include dozens of diagrams aimed toward helping the reader understand a process. Here, the diagram shows how ocean currents distribute warmth from the equator to northern and southern coastal areas.

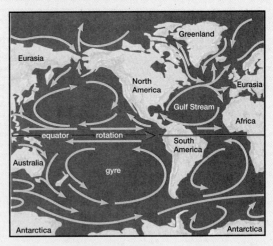

Students learn scientific techniques through required lab work in which they conduct experiments and report on the results.

LEARNING OBJECTIVES

■ To learn what the life and physical sciences are

■ To consider whether you should major in the life and physical sciences

■ To discover tips for studying the life and physical sciences

■ To develop specialized reading techniques for the sciences

■ To learn to work with process, cause and effect, classification, and problem/solution patterns

■ To adapt study strategies for the sciences

What Are the Life and Physical Sciences?

The **life sciences** are concerned with the study of living organisms: how they grow, develop, function, and reproduce. Biology is considered the "catch-all" term for the study of life, but it is subdivided into many more specialized areas such as anatomy, botany, genetics, and zoology. The **physical sciences** are concerned with the properties, functions, structure, and composition of matter, substances, and energy. They include astronomy, chemistry, geology, and physics. (Computer science, a common college major, is often considered more of a mathematical science than a natural science.) Together, the life and physical sciences are known as the **natural sciences** (as opposed to the social sciences, which are the subject of Chapter 10).

While each discipline varies in its focus and emphasis, all the natural sciences have several things in common. First, their goals are the same: to explain the natural phenomena that affect our daily lives. Second, they are all built on knowledge resulting from scientific investigation. Through a process known as the **scientific method,** scientists ask well-defined questions and then use carefully designed experiments to investigate and draw conclusions.

Consider, for example, the disease called AIDS. In ongoing scientific research, scientists have asked questions such as:

- What causes it?
- How is it transmitted?
- What is its incubation period?
- What are its precise effects on the immune system?
- How can it be treated or cured?

Because the emphasis is on observation and experimentation, most science courses have a weekly lab requirement in which you are given the opportunity to observe, experiment, and report on your results. The lab gives you direct

TABLE 14-1   The Natural Sciences and Career Opportunities

LIFE SCIENCE: BIOLOGY

DISCIPLINE	DESCRIPTION	CAREER OPPORTUNITIES
Anatomy	The study of the structure of living things (bones, muscles, tissues, etc.)	• Physical therapist • Athletic trainer • Personal trainer
Botany	The study of plant life and development	• Farming • Owner of greenhouse or garden center • Conservationist
Zoology	The study of animals	• Zookeeper • Veterinary assistant

PHYSICAL SCIENCES

DISCIPLINE	DESCRIPTION	CAREER OPPORTUNITIES
Astronomy	The study of celestial objects (planets, stars, galaxies) beyond Earth	• Astronaut • Observatory worker • Space program worker
Chemistry	The study of the composition, structure, and properties of matter	• Pharmacist or pharmacy "tech" (assistant) • Water purity specialist • Crime lab analyst
Geology	The study of Earth	• Cartographer (mapmaker) • Meteorologist • Oil or gas industry worker
Physics	The study of energy, force, mass, and motion	• Airline pilot • Energy industry worker

experience with the scientific method while reinforcing, explaining, or demonstrating theories and principles presented in the course lectures.

Table 14-1 summarizes the natural sciences and some of the career opportunities available in each field.

Should You Major in the Life and Physical Sciences?

The life and physical sciences investigate the physical world around us and attempt to answer many important questions:

• Is there extraterrestrial life?

• Why do leaves change color in the fall?

• Why do volcanoes erupt?

The life and physical sciences also explore questions essential to our well-being and progress:

- How can cancer be cured or prevented?
- What synthetic substitutes can prevent depletion of our natural resources?
- How can water pollution be reduced or prevented?

Most students who choose to major in science do so because they are fascinated by the physical world around them. They will stare at the wings of a butterfly, or the patterns of bark on a tree, and wonder about them. An abiding curiosity is one of the hallmarks of a successful scientist.

What characteristics and habits will make you a successful major in the life and physical sciences?

1. **You must be willing to become proficient in math and to study other scientific disciplines.** Scientific majors often require advanced study in mathematics, and most of the sciences are informed by the other sciences. Career options often require a strong base in at least two of the natural sciences. For example, those who work for pharmaceutical firms developing new drugs have often studied both biology and chemistry.

2. **You must enjoy the process of experimentation, lab work, and fieldwork.** Because science is based on experiments, you should enjoy working in labs. In addition, a true mastery of the sciences requires you to get out of the laboratory and into "the field," a term that professionals use for experiencing natural phenomena where they occur. Geologists visit areas all over the Earth, while oceanographers spend time in various locations studying marine life.

3. **You must be a strong team player.** While it is true that many of the great scientific discoveries were made by individuals (such as Albert Einstein or Isaac Newton), today's careers in science often require a team approach to experimenting and finding solutions. The ability and desire to collaborate are very important to success in a scientific career.

4. **You must understand the importance of memorization.** The sciences, especially biology, are filled with hundreds of new words and concepts whose meanings you must learn and apply. Work actively to develop your note-taking and memorization skills (see Chapter 9) and use homemade flash cards (or Web sites) to test yourself. Creating your own concept maps, tables, and outlines can help, too.

Tips for Studying the Life and Physical Sciences—Even if You Are Not a Major

To ensure that your education is well rounded, you will need to fulfill at least one or two science requirements. If you are not a science major, here are some suggestions for making the most of your science courses.

1. **Carefully explore the science course options on your campus.** Talk with your advisor about finding the course that best matches your interests and background. For example, many campuses have a science course jokingly called "Science for Poets," because it is intended for liberal arts majors rather than science majors. These types of courses often focus on current topics of interest (such as nutrition and health), and they often have no lab requirement.

2. **Talk with other students about their experiences with various professors.** As in other disciplines, having the right professor can make all the difference in a science course, which challenges you to think in ways you may not be accustomed to. Energetic science professors usually succeed in making the material interesting and relevant to students who don't normally have a strong interest in science.

3. **Focus on the big picture.** While you will have to memorize details for your examinations, try to come away from each lecture (and each chapter of your textbook) with a few key points to take with you throughout life. One way to do this is to apply the concepts to your everyday life. For instance, if you are studying the genetics section of your biology textbook, you may find it interesting to ask why you have green eyes when both your parents have brown eyes.

4. **Attend review sessions.** Many instructors offer "review sessions" before examinations to help students focus on the most important material and to answer any questions they may have. These sessions are extremely valuable, but they require a time commitment on your part.

5. **Be careful with terminology.** Your science courses will often use words that you already know, but in a different context. For instance, you usually think of the word "dominant" as meaning powerful or overbearing. But in genetics, a "dominant gene" does not mean one that will take over. Rather, it is a form of a gene whose trait is expressed even if you inherit only one copy of that gene.

Quotes from a Science Professor

Advice for Natural Science Students

William J. Straits, University of California, Long Beach

66 I always encourage my students to ask themselves, 'What concepts would I test about if I were the instructor?' and to then compare their ideas with two or three classmates. I find collectively a small group of students is nearly always able to identify the most important ideas. 99

66 Controversy seems to be *the new issue* in science today. Students need to be able to, and need to be open to, reading information about the science related to bioengineering, evolution, global warming, etc., regardless of their individual beliefs about the appropriateness of these issues in society. Students often get sidetracked in the

politicized aspects of an issue; they want to discuss what they 'feel.' In science classes these personal opinions, while important, must be informed by an understanding of what the scientific community 'knows.' 99

■ Specialized Reading Techniques

Reading scientific material requires specialized techniques, as does each of your other courses, but once you develop an effective approach, you will find science courses to be interesting and challenging, as well as manageable.

Use the following strategies to strengthen your approach to scientific reading.

Preview Before Reading

Because scientific material is often detailed and unfamiliar, previewing is even more important than in other courses. (Refer to the Key Strategy box "How to Preview Textbook Assignments," p. 35) Your preview should include looking at problems at the end of the chapter and the chapter summary because they will provide clues about principles and formulas emphasized in the chapter.

Adopt a Scientific Mind-Set

To read effectively in a science course, it is essential to adopt a scientific way of thinking. The usual concerns (such as "What is important to learn?" and "How much supporting information do I need to learn?") may be of only secondary importance. Instead, to be successful, you must adopt the scientific mind-set of asking questions and seeking answers, analyzing problems, and looking for solutions or explanations. Use the questions listed in the Key Strategy box below to guide your thinking.

KEY STRATEGY: Questions to Ask as You Read

- **What does this mean? What does it *not* mean?**
- **Does this make sense to me?**
- **Why is this so?**
- **How do we know this?**
- **How does this happen?**
- **What does this show?**
- **Are alternative explanations plausible?**
- **What laws govern or affect this?**

To illustrate this process, Figure 14-1 below shows the questions a student asked as she read a page of her chemistry textbook.

Sometimes, the questions you ask will be answered as you continue reading. Other times, you may need to seek answers yourself by referring to another chapter, by asking your instructor, or by talking with classmates. Asking and answering these questions will get you involved with the material and direct you toward scientific critical thinking.

FIGURE 14-1   Scientific Thinking

MARS

How far away is it?

Why?

Mars is the only planet whose surface features can be seen through Earth-based telescopes. Its distinctive rust-colored hue makes it stand out in the night sky. When Mars is near opposition, even telescopes for home use reveal its seasonal changes. Dark markings on the Martian surface can be seen to vary, and prominent polar caps shrink noticeably during the spring and summer months.

6-7 Earth-based observations originally suggested that Mars might harbor extraterrestrial life

Is it similar in other ways, as well?

The Dutch physicist Christian Huygens made the first reliable observations of Mars in 1659. Using a telescope of his own design, Huygens identified a prominent, dark surface feature that re-emerged roughly every 24 hours, suggesting a rate of rotation very much like the Earth's. Huygens' observations soon led to speculation about life on Mars because the planet seemed so similar to Earth.

In 1877 Giovanni Virginio Schiaparelli, an Italian astronomer, reported seeing 40 lines criss-crossing the Martian surface. He called these dark features *canali*, an Italian term meaning "water channels." It was soon mistranslated into English as *canals*, implying the existence on Mars of intelligent creatures capable of substantial engineering feats. This speculation led Percival Lowell, who came from a wealthy Boston family, to finance a major new observatory near Flagstaff, Arizona. By the end of the nineteenth century, Lowell had allegedly observed 160 Martian canals.

What evidence did he offer?

Why was it fashionable?
Who did this?

What causes them?

It soon became fashionable to speculate that the Martian canals formed an enormous planet-wide irrigation network to transport water from melting polar caps to vegetation near the equator. (The seasonal changes in Mars' dark surface markings can be mistaken for vegetation.) In view of the planet's reddish, desertlike appearance, Mars was thought to be a dying planet whose inhabitants must go to great lengths to irrigate their farmlands. No doubt the Martians would readily abandon their arid ancestral homeland and invade the Earth for its abundant resources. Hundreds of science fiction stories and dozens of monster movies owe their existence to the canali of Schiaparelli.

SOURCE: Kaufmann and Comins, *Discovering the Universe,* pp. 144–45

EXERCISE 14-1   **Asking Questions**

Read the following excerpt from a human physiology textbook. What questions could you ask about the excerpt? Write them in the margin.

COLLOIDS IN THE CAFETERIA

The next time you are in a cafeteria, look closely at the colorful gelatin dessert. It appears to be a transparent, wobbly solid, yet it consists primarily of water. The chocolate pudding nearby is also mainly water. Is it a solid or a liquid? When you fill your glass with milk, can you determine whether it is a solution or a mixture? Like most foods, these are *colloids,* suspensions of particles ranging from 20 µm to 100 µm in diameter, in a solvent. Colloidal particles are much larger than most molecules but are too small to be seen with a microscope. Colloids thus are often classified between homogeneous solutions and heterogeneous mixtures. The small particles give the colloid a homogeneous appearance but are large enough to scatter light. The light scattering explains why milk is white, not transparent.

A colloid that is a suspension of solids in a liquid is called a *sol,* and a suspension of one liquid in another is called an *emulsion.* For example, skim milk is a suspension of solids, mainly proteins, in water, so it is a sol; mayonnaise has small droplets of water suspended in oil, so it is an emulsion. When we whip cream, milk rich in butterfat, or beat egg whites to form meringues, we make *foams,* suspensions of a gas in a liquid or solid. When we separate the fat from milk and churn it into butter, we create a *solid emulsion,* a suspension of a liquid, in this case, milk, in a solid, butterfat. Gelatin desserts are a type of solid emulsion called a *gel,* which is soft, but holds its shape.

Aqueous colloids can be classified as hydrophilic or hydrophobic. Suspensions of fat in water, such as milk and mayonnaise, are hydrophobic colloids, because fat molecules have little attraction for water molecules. Gels and puddings are examples of hydrophilic colloids. The macromolecules of the proteins in gelatin and the starch in pudding have many hydrophilic groups that attract water. The giant protein molecules in gelatin uncoil in hot water. Their abundant amide groups form hydrogen bonds with water. When the mixture cools, the protein chains link together again, but now they enclose many water molecules within themselves, as well as molecules of sugar, dye, and flavoring agents. The result is an open network of protein chains that hold the water in a flexible solid structure.

—Atkins and Jones, *Chemistry: Molecules, Matter, and Change,* p. 444

Learn Terminology and Notation

Physics: wave-particle duality, torque, tangential acceleration, $v = dx/dt$

Physiology: hemagglutination, ventricular diastole, myocardial infarction, DNA

Chemistry: NaCl

Astronomy: mass-luminosity relation, eclipsing binaries, bok globules

How many of these terms are familiar? They are only a few of the new terms and notations encountered in each of these courses. You must understand the meaning of specialized and technical words in order to understand the ideas and concepts being presented.

In some courses, such as physics and chemistry, formulas and notation are important as well. Symbols, abbreviations, and formulas are used to represent objects and concepts in abbreviated form. You might think of these as short-hand systems for naming elements and quantities and describing their interaction. As you read and study, avoid memorizing formulas; instead, focus on understanding what they mean and how to apply them.

A course master file, described in Chapter 3, is extremely valuable in science courses. Mapping also works well, especially in the life sciences. Finally, as you learn the meaning of each new term, also learn its correct pronunciation and spelling.

Learn Symbols and Abbreviations

Symbols and abbreviations are frequently used in the sciences. The abbreviation "g" is a shortcut expression for a unit of mass, called a gram. The symbol "g" can also stand for the gravitational constant, 9.8N/kg, for the surface of the Earth. Textbooks use different kinds of type to distinguish types of quantities. For instance, "*v*" (in italics) means speed while "**v**" (in boldface) means velocity. Watch for clues your textbook provides.

Special Meanings of Everyday Words

Scientists sometimes attach specialized meanings to ordinary words. For example, *power, pressure, force,* and *impulse* are everyday words, but they have very specific meanings to a physicist. Power, for instance, is a measure of how fast work is done or energy is transformed and is represented by the formula:

Power = work ÷ time

Note that its meaning in science is different from its meaning in mathematics, too, where *power* refers to a number multiplied by itself. *Pressure,* another everyday term, in physics means the amount of force per area over which the force is distributed.

Because you are familiar with these words, it is easy to overlook them when studying or to assume you already know them. Be sure to include these terms in your course master file, along with the other specialized terminology and notations.

Learn Common Prefixes, Roots, and Suffixes

As you discovered in Chapter 3, many words in our language contain prefixes, roots, and suffixes. In most science courses, you will discover a common core of these word parts that are used as the basic building blocks of a specialized terminology. In physics, for example, units of measurement take prefixes.

PREFIX	MEANING
micro-	millionth
milli-	thousandth
centi-	hundredth

deci-	tenth
deka-	ten
hecto-	hundred
kilo-	thousand
mega-	million
giga-	billion

In physiology, roots and suffixes unlock the meaning of numerous frequently used terms.

ROOT	SUFFIX	WORD
hem(a)—blood	-logy (study of)	hematology
	-oma (growth, tumor)	hematoma
	-thermal (heat)	hemathermal

Similarly, in chemistry, astronomy, and biology you will find sets of core prefixes, roots, and suffixes. Include these in your master file, as suggested in Chapter 3.

Read Section by Section

Chapters in science texts are usually lengthy. Because the material is so complex, try not to read an entire chapter in one sitting. Instead, divide the chapter into sections and read one portion at a time. Look for end-of-chapter problems or questions that apply to the sections you are reading. Mark them and remember to work them out after you have read the section. Be sure to make connections between sections.

Study Sample Problems

In the physical sciences, sample problems are often included in the text to demonstrate a problem-solving process. Read the sample problems carefully, alternating between the text explanation and the mathematical solution. Next, explain the process in your own words. Doing so will solidify it in your memory. If you are unable to express the process in your own words or if you must refer back frequently to the text, this indicates that you do not fully understand the process. Do not expect to get it all the first time. These are difficult subjects, and understanding may come gradually.

Study and Draw Diagrams

Science texts contain numerous diagrams and drawings of structures and processes. These drawings often clarify a principle or concept; a diagram of a gun firing and recoiling, for example, makes the concept of conservation of momentum clear. Diagrams also are used to show forces, conditions, shapes, directions, processes, or positions. Diagrams provide a visual representation of an object or occurrence, and they increase your ability both to understand and to retain information. Diagrams are also important in answering questions and solving problems. Consult Chapter 8 of this text to learn how to read and study graphics and visuals.

Many students do not pay enough attention to the diagrams included in their texts. Take time to study each drawing as you read. As you review, use the drawings to refresh your recall of key concepts and processes. Test your recall by closing the book and drawing the diagram from memory. Compare your drawing with the one in the text, noting errors, missing parts, or discrepancies. Do not be concerned if your drawings seem poor in comparison to the text; your ability to draw will improve as you practice.

You will also find diagrams useful in laboratory situations. Draw brief sketches of your equipment setup, techniques, and observations. These will help as you write your lab reports.

Brush Up on Math Skills

Mathematics is an integral part of many science courses, especially chemistry and physics. Many instructors assume you have taken algebra, which is often needed to solve equations and problems. If your math background is weak or if it has been a number of years since you studied algebra, you may need to brush up on your skills. You might consider taking a review course, purchasing a skills practice book, or using computer-assisted instructional programs in the learning lab. Talk with your instructor, and ask for recommendations.

■ Thought Patterns in the Life and Physical Sciences

Four thought patterns are common in the life and physical sciences: process, cause and effect, classification, and problem/solution.

The Process and Cause and Effect Patterns

Many of the sciences are concerned with how and why things happen: how a tadpole turns into a frog, what makes light reflect, how the tides work, how our metabolism functions, and so forth. Process and cause and effect patterns are often used to explain natural phenomena. Process and cause and effect patterns are logically linked to each other. In a process, the steps may be linked in a cause and effect chain. You may find that you need to read process descriptions more than once. Read the description the first time to get an overview; then read it at least once more to understand the steps and the connections between them.

Use the following strategies to read process material:

1. **List the steps.** Either in the text margin or in your notebook, write a step-by-step summary of the process in your own words. Figure 14-2 on page 393 shows the notes a student wrote for a physics textbook chapter on plate tectonics, explaining how islands and mountains are formed.

FIGURE 14-2   Sample Summary

PLATE TECTONICS

Summary:

1. Earth's crust has approx. 12 large plates = lithosphere. These rest on the asthenosphere.

2. These plates spread and sink (subduction).

3. When a continental plate and an ocean plate collide, a trench and island arc will form.

4. When ocean plates collide, they create a marginal or inland sea.

5. When continental plates collide, folding and faulting of sediment and rock occurs, creating mountain ranges.

Recent ideas concerning seafloor spreading and the origin and evolution of the ocean basins are incorporated into an even more encompassing concept called plate tectonics. In plate tectonics theory, Earth's entire crust is composed of about a dozen large plates, up to 160 km (100 miles) thick. These plates make up the lithosphere. Each moves essentially as a rigid block over Earth's surface. The lithosphere rests upon the less rigid part of Earth called the **asthenosphere.**

The plates can be visualized as curved caps covering a large ball, or perhaps as sections of peel on an orange. Boundaries of the individual plates are usually areas of high seismic (earthquake) activity. Deformation, such as faulting, folding, or shearing mainly occurs at the boundaries between the plates. Because the surface area of Earth is essentially constant, spreading in one place must be balanced by sinking or **subduction** somewhere else.

The appearance of the edge of a continent is often influenced by its relation to areas of seafloor spreading or subduction. If a continent's edge is at the boundary of a subducting oceanic plate, a trench will form, and sometimes an **island arc** or coastal mountain range (Figure a). A **trench** is a deep, long narrow depression in the seafloor, with very steep slopes. An island arc is a curved pattern of mainly volcanic islands and a trench. It is

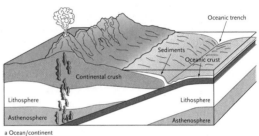

a Ocean/continent

generally curved in a convex direction (bows out) toward the ocean, with the trench on the seaward side. The Aleutian Islands and Aleutian Trench in the north Pacific is a good example of a trench-island arc system.

The subducting plate forms the trench. In the process of submerging beneath the other plate, much of its sediment is scraped off onto the landward side of the trench. This material and the subducting plate may be reheated, perhaps even melted, eventually becoming part of the continental plate and forming a coastal mountain range. These are events that occur when oceanic crust is subducted beneath lighter continental crust. A similar sequence occurs during the collision of two ocean plates. The main difference is that an inland or marginal sea may form behind an island arc (Figure b).

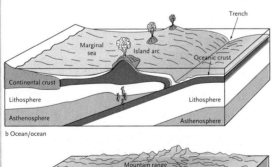

b Ocean/ocean

Results can be quite different when two plates of continental composition collide. In this case, both plates are of similar density, so neither easily overrides the other. The result is unusually intense folding and faulting of the sediments and rocks, often leading to the formation of a major mountain range (Figure c). The Himalayan Mountains are still being formed in this manner by the collision of India (continental crust) with Asia (continental crust).

c Continent/continent

SOURCE: Ross, *Introduction to Oceanography*, pp. 51–52

2. **Draw diagrams or maps.** Diagrams, maps, or flowcharts help you visualize the process and will enhance your recall as well. Chapter 9 describes several types of mapping. Figure 14-3 below shows a diagram a biology student drew to describe how convection currents stir the air and create winds.

3. **Describe the process aloud.** Assume you are explaining the process to a friend who is not taking the course, or better yet, actually study with a friend. By forcing yourself to explain the process in a nontechnical way, you can test whether you really understand it and are not simply rephrasing the technical language used by the author.

FIGURE 14-3   Sample Diagram

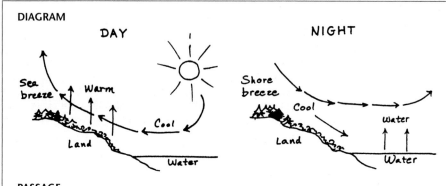

DIAGRAM

DAY   NIGHT

Sea breeze   Warm   Shore breeze   Cool

Cool   Water

Land   Land

Water   Water

PASSAGE

Convection currents stirring the atmosphere result in winds. Some parts of the Earth's surface absorb heat from the sun more readily than others, and as a result the air near the surface is heated unevenly and convection currents form. This is evident at the seashore. In the daytime the shore warms more easily than the water; air over the shore is pushed up (we say it rises) by cooler air from above the water taking its place. The result is a sea breeze. At night the process reverses because the shore cools off more quickly than the water, and then the warmer air is over the sea. Build a fire on the beach and you'll notice that the smoke sweeps inward during the day and seaward at night.

SOURCE: Hewitt, *Conceptual Physics*, pp. 274–75

EXERCISE 14-2

LEARNING COLLABORATIVELY

Writing a Summary

Read the following excerpt from an earth science textbook. Working with a classmate, one student should write a summary of the greenhouse effect while the other draws a diagram. Exchange your work, and draw a diagram based only on your partner's summary, or write a summary based only on his or her diagram. Then compare the results with the whole excerpt.

CARBON DIOXIDE AND THE GREENHOUSE EFFECT

The possible relationship between carbon dioxide in the atmosphere and climate warming was proposed by Svante Arrhenius, one of the early winners of the Nobel

Prize in chemistry (1903). Arrhenius knew a great deal about geology as well as chemistry, and he was familiar with the effects of glaciation on the terrain of his native Sweden. He was also aware of the growing discussion of the causes of glaciations that enlivened many geologists' meetings at the end of the nineteenth century. He reasoned that the small amount of carbon dioxide in the atmosphere (now about 345 ppm) could affect climate because the carbon dioxide molecules strongly absorb heat rays from the Earth.

Here is how it works. The atmosphere is relatively transparent to the incoming visible rays of the Sun. Much of this radiant energy from the Sun is absorbed by the Earth's surface and then reemitted as invisible infrared heat rays. Just as a hot pavement radiates heat as it is warmed by the Sun, the Earth's surface radiates heat back to the atmosphere. The atmosphere, however, is not transparent to these infrared rays, because carbon dioxide and water molecules strongly absorb the infrared instead of allowing it to escape to space. As a result, the atmosphere is heated and radiates heat back to the surface. this is called the *greenhouse effect,* by analogy to the warming of a greenhouse, whose glass lets in visible light but lets little heat escape.

The more carbon dioxide, the warmer the atmosphere; the less carbon dioxide, the colder. Without any greenhouse effect, Earth's surface temperature would be well below freezing and the oceans would be a solid mass of ice. Geologists now have evidence that, aside from glaciations, climates ranged from warm to cool in the geological past. It is likely that some of these changes were related to changes in the amount of carbon dioxide in the atmosphere.

—Press and Siever, *Understanding Earth,* p. 348

The Classification Pattern

In the life sciences, classification is an important pattern. As a means of studying life forms or species, biologists classify them into groups or types based on shared or similar characteristics. Organisms are first divided into three domains. Those domains are subdivided into groups called kingdoms, and then into phyla classes, orders, families, genera, and species.

Other examples of classification include types of cells, methods of reproduction, and types of tissues.

Classification is also used in the physical sciences. In chemistry, elements are grouped and listed by groupings on the periodic table. In physics, matter is classified into gases, liquids, plasmas, and solids.

When reading material written in this pattern, first determine what is being classified and what the types or groups are. Look for a topic or summary sentence that states what is being classified. Next, discover why or on what basis the classification was made. That is, determine what characteristics members of the group share. For example, the following excerpt from a biology textbook describes the classification of animal eggs.

TYPES OF EGGS

The three basic types of animal eggs are roughly categorized according to the amount of *yolk* they have. The amount of yolk is critical since it is the embryo's food supply, at least for a time. In some species, the embryo needs only a small supply of yolk since it soon switches to nutrients derived from the mother's blood, as is the case with humans. We only need enough to last until the embryo has implanted in the wall of the uterus. In contrast, birds leave their mother's body at a very early developmental stage, and they must carry their entire embryonic food supply with them. So, whereas a human egg is smaller than the period at the end of this sentence, it would be hard to hide an ostrich egg with this whole book. Interestingly, both the young and the adults of these two species are about the same size.

Other kinds of animals have a moderate yolk supply. In these, the young must begin to find its own food long before it has reached its final body organization. The frog is an example. The frog egg has just enough yolk to get the developing embryo to the tadpole stage; after that, the tadpole can survive on food stored in its tail for a time, but it must soon begin to eat on its own.

—Wallace, *Biology: The World of Life,* pp. 446–47

In this excerpt, the basis of classification is directly stated in the first sentence: eggs are classified according to the size of the yolk.

EXERCISE 14–3

Analyzing the Classification Pattern

Read this excerpt from a physiology textbook, and answer the questions that follow.

TYPES OF SMOOTH MUSCLE

The smooth muscle in different body organs varies substantially in its (1) fiber arrangement and organization, (2) responsiveness to various stimuli, and (3) innervation. However, for simplicity, smooth muscle is usually categorized into two major types: *single-unit* and *multiunit smooth muscle.*

Single-Unit Smooth Muscle

Single-unit smooth muscle, commonly called **visceral muscle,** is far more common. Its cells (1) contract as a unit and rhythmically, (2) are electrically coupled to one another by *gap junctions,* and (3) often exhibit spontaneous action potentials. All the smooth muscle characteristics described so far pertain to single-unit smooth muscle. Thus, the cells of single-unit smooth muscle are arranged in sheets, exhibit the stress-relaxation response, and so on.

Multiunit Smooth Muscle

The smooth muscles in the large airways to the lungs and in large arteries, the arrector pili muscles attached to hair follicles, and the internal eye muscles that adjust your pupil size and allow you to focus visually are all examples of **multiunit smooth muscle.**

In contrast to what we see in single-unit muscle, gap junctions are rare and spontaneous and synchronous depolarizations infrequent. Multiunit smooth muscle, like skeletal muscle, (1) consists of muscle fibers that are structurally independent of each other; (2) is richly supplied with nerve endings, each of which forms a motor unit with a number of muscle fibers; and (3) responds to neural stimulation with graded contractions. However, while skeletal muscle is served by the somatic (voluntary) division of the nervous system, multiunit smooth muscle (like single-unit smooth muscle) is innervated by the autonomic (involuntary) division and is also responsive to hormonal controls.

—Marieb, *Human Anatomy and Physiology*, p. 294

1. What does this excerpt classify?
2. Describe each type of smooth muscle.
3. On what basis is the classification made?

The Problem/Solution Pattern

Textbook chapters, homework, and exams in the physical sciences often contain problems. To solve these problems, you must apply the concepts, laws, and formulas presented in the chapter. Use the steps listed in the Key Strategy box below to solve problems.

KEY STRATEGY: How to Solve Problems

1. **Read the problem and identify what is given and what is asked for.** In word problems, mark or underline critical information. Next, restate the information using the symbols you will use as you solve the problem. Be certain not to use the same symbol to represent different quantities. For example, if there are two objects in a situation with different masses, do not use m for both masses. Use m_1 and m_2 to distinguish between the two masses.

2. **If possible, make a drawing of the problem.** Label known quantities with the correct symbols; using the symbols may suggest which equation to use in solving the problem, if you are not certain.

3. **State the principle that is related to the problem, and write the general equation that embodies the principle.**

4. **Calculate the solution.** Always write the units after each number (seconds, moles, liters, etc.).

5. **Analyze your answer.** Does it make sense? Compare your solution with similar sample problems and determine whether you followed the correct procedure. Check the units as well as the numerical values.

6. **Review your solution process.** Especially if you had difficulty with the problem, pause after you solve it to figure out what you should have done or known in order to solve it more easily. Did you overlook a step or ignore a key concept? Analyzing your solution process will help you solve similar problems more easily in the future.

Here is an example of the use of this problem-solving procedure:

PROBLEM: A cat steps off a ledge and drops to the ground in ½ second. What is the cat's speed on striking the ground? What is the cat's average speed during the ½ second? How high is the ledge from the ground?

Steps	Example

1. Identify what is given and what is asked for.	Given: drops in ½ sec, $t = $ ½ sec
	Asked for: 1. speed (velocity) (v)
	                 2. average speed (average velocity) ($\overline{v}$)
	                 3. height (distance) (d)

2. Draw a diagram.	$t = $ ½ sec

3. Determine the principle and formula.	Principle: acceleration and motion of free-falling bodies
	Formulae: $v = gt$, $d = \overline{v}t$
	             $g = 10$ m/s^2
	             $\overline{v} = \dfrac{\text{beginning } v + \text{final } v}{2}$

4. Calculate the solution.	$v = gt$ $v = 10$ m/s$^2 \times$ ½ s $= 5$ m/s $\overline{v} = \dfrac{0 \text{ m/s} + 5 \text{ m/s}}{2} = 2.5$ m/s
5. Analyze the answer.	$d = \overline{v}t = 2.5$ m/s$^2 \times$ ½ s $= 1.25$ m
6. Review the solution process.	Had to know acceleration of free-falling bodies is 10 m/s^2

—Hewitt, *Conceptual Physics*, p. 30

■ Adapting Your Study Techniques

Because of the unique content of science courses, it is especially important to adapt your study habits. Use the following suggestions for studying in the sciences.

1. **Complete reading assignments before attending lectures.** Because of the unfamiliar subject matter, you can understand lectures better if you know something about the topic. You may not understand everything you

read (and it will be necessary to reread after the lecture), but you will have an advantage during the lecture because the terms, concepts, and principles will be more familiar.

2. **Highlight your textbook selectively.** Everything looks important in scientific texts, and it is easy to fall into the habit of over-highlighting. Avoid this pitfall by reading a paragraph or section before highlighting. Then go back and mark only key terms and concepts. Do not try to highlight all useful facts. Refer to Chapter 9 for suggestions on how to highlight effectively.

3. **Integrate your lab work with the text and lectures.** Most science courses have a required lab. Because the lab is scheduled separately from the lecture and has its own manual, you may fail to see the lab as an integral part of the course. The lab is intended to help you understand and apply principles and research techniques used in your course, as well as providing you with an opportunity to ask pertinent questions. Use the following tips for handling lab work:

   - **Be prepared before going to lab.** Read the experiment once to understand its overall purpose and a second time to understand the specific procedures. Make notes or underline key information.
   - **Ask questions before you make a mistake.** Lab procedures can be time-consuming to repeat, so ask questions first.
   - **Be sure you understand the purpose of each step before you perform it.**
   - **Analyze your results and do the lab report as soon as possible.** The best time to study your results is while the experiment and procedures are still fresh in your mind. If you finish the lab work early, stay and discuss results and interpretations with other students or your lab instructor.
   - **Follow the required format closely when writing your report.**

4. **Use chapter problems as guides.** The end-of-chapter problems in your textbook help you determine what it is important to learn. Do the problems even if they have not been assigned by your instructor. As you read the problems, note the variables (temperature, pressure, volume, etc.) that appear in the problems. Then be certain to learn definitions, concepts, principles, and formulas pertaining to these variables.

5. **Develop a weekly study plan.** Science is best studied on a daily basis. Devise a weekly plan that includes time every day for previewing text assignments, reviewing lecture notes, reading text assignments, preparing for and writing up labs, and—most important—reviewing in such a way as to integrate lectures, the text, and lab sessions.

6. **Prepare for exams.** Exams and quizzes in the sciences require you to learn factual information as well as develop problem-solving ability and apply your learning to practical situations. To be prepared for exams,

   - Make lists of types of problems you have studied and key facts about their solution.

- Identify key laws, principles, and concepts.
- Determine where your instructor placed her or his emphasis.
- Prepare a practice test, using problems from your text, and take it as though it were an actual exam.
- Consider forming a study group with classmates.

■ If You Are Having Difficulty

If the sciences are typically a difficult field of study for you, or if you suddenly find yourself not doing well in a science course, try the following survival tactics:

Use available resources. Visit your instructor during office hours to discuss your performance or to get help with particular problems. Check to see whether tutoring is available through the department office or the college's learning center.

Make changes in your learning strategies. If you are a non-science major taking your one or two required science courses, you may feel as strange as if you were in a foreign country. First, you must revise your approaches and strategies. Plan on making the changes already described in this section.

Learn from classmates. Talk with and observe the strategies of students who are doing well in the course. You are likely to pick up new and useful procedures.

Double your study time. If you are having trouble with a course, make a commitment to spend more time on it and to work harder. Use this added time to revise and try out new study strategies. Never spend time using a strategy that is not working.

Use ancillary materials. Many major science texts have study guides or problem-solving guides to accompany them. These may be in print or electronic form. Also check the book's Web site for useful study aids.

Finally, here are some specific tips to help you "pull the course together":

1. **Review your lecture notes and text assignments frequently; discover how they work together and where they seem to be headed.**

2. **As you review, make a list of topics you do understand and a list of those you do not.**

3. **Decide whether you are experiencing difficulty as a result of gaps in your scientific background.** Ask yourself whether the instructor assumes you know things when you do not. If so, consider finding a tutor.

4. **Make a list of specific questions and ask for help from both your classmates and your instructor.**

Test-Taking Tips
Preparing for Exams in the Life and Physical Sciences

Exams in the sciences require you to learn factual information as well as to develop problem-solving ability and apply your learning to practical situations. To be prepared for exams, use the following tips:

1. **Identify key laws, principles, and concepts.** Prepare review sheets on which you summarize important information.

2. **Make lists of types of problems you have studied.** For example, in chemistry, for a chapter on gases, you might identify problem types such as pressure and volume, temperature and pressure, and temperature and volume. For each problem type, list steps in the solution. Practice solving each problem type by using exercises in the text or by constructing your own problems.

3. **Consider forming a study group with classmates.** Quiz each other, and work through sample problems.

4. **Prepare a practice exam using problems or review questions from your text, and take it as though it were an actual exam.**

5. **Do not review by simply rereading your text and notes.** The material will look familiar, and you will think you have learned it. Instead, test yourself: Ask yourself questions and answer them. Use guide questions (see Chapter 1).

Self-Test Summary

1. What do the life and physical sciences focus on?	The life sciences are concerned with the study of living organisms. The physical sciences are concerned with the properties, functions, structure, and composition of matter, substances, and energy. Together, the life and physical sciences are known as the natural sciences.
2. List six specialized techniques for reading in the natural sciences.	The six techniques are • previewing before reading. • adopting a scientific mind-set. • learning terminology and notation. • reading section by section. • studying sample problems. • studying drawings and diagrams. • brushing up on math skills.
4. Identify the four thought patterns that predominate in the natural sciences.	The patterns are process, cause and effect, classification, and problem/solution.
5. List the ways in which you might adapt your usual study techniques to the sciences.	Ways to adapt study techniques are • complete reading assignments before attending lectures. • highlight the textbook selectively. • integrate lab work with the text and lectures. • use chapter problems as guides. • develop a weekly study plan. • prepare for exams.
6. What should you do if you are having difficulty in a science course?	If you are having difficulty, you should • meet with your instructor; check about tutors. • change your learning strategies. • learn from classmates. • double your study time. • use ancillary materials.

The Promise of Stem Cell Research

Michael Bay and Matt Ford

Prereading Questions

1. What do you already know about stem cell research?
2. Why is the use of stem cells controversial?

1　Chances are very good you've heard about stem cells. Whether from reports of their almost miraculous ability to cure and restore, or very public controversies over their source or the research itself, stem cells have been a hot topic in the news for years.

2　The use of stem cells as therapy isn't new. "The curative component in bone marrow transplantations, which have been used to treat certain blood cancers for more than 40 years," says CNN Future Summit Nominating Committee Member Alan Colman, "is the small proportion of stem cells present." Colman is the CEO of E. S. Cell International in Singapore, and was part of the team that cloned "Dolly" the sheep.

3　We all have stem cells. They're an integral part of our bodies. Long before you were born, they were creating the tissues and organs that make you who you are. At the core of the research is the desire to use the unique way stem cells behave to heal a range of illnesses and ailments. These cells have the potential to develop into any of the 220 cell-types in the human body, and serve as a kind of natural repair mechanism. Theoretically they can keep dividing and re-dividing as long as an organism is alive, producing red blood cells, skin cells, muscle cells or whatever the body needs to keep going. Understanding precisely how this process works and how these cells specialize could have a huge impact on healthcare. Ultimately it should be possible to use stem cells to replace any other cells in the body that have been damaged or harmed by accident and disease.

4　Many scientists believe the treatment of strokes, heart disease, cancer and birth defects could benefit from stem cell research, along with Parkinson's and Alzheimer's disease. "I do believe that Alzheimer's disease will be a target in the future." Colman says. "I don't think that people suffering from the disease can expect to get memories back that they have lost because those neurons, responsible for those memories, will have long been lost. But it will afford them a quality of life in their terminal years, which they wouldn't have without the use of stem cells."

5　Unfortunately, adults don't have a lot of stem cells available. And there's a difference between stem cells in adults and those in embryos just days old. Colman explains that both embryonic and adult stem cells are important. "I think that we will find that each type of stem cell is good for some purposes and bad for others. Embryonic stem cells have the benefit that they can grow indefinitely in culture. Adult stem cells generally cannot do that."

6   "But on the other hand, adult stem cells," Colman says, "are nearer, if you like, to the end product than the embryonic stem cell. I think researchers should be backing both areas of research at the moment and the public also should support both types of research," Researchers have been working to manipulate stem cells, in pursuit of treatments for a broad range of illnesses and ailments. The cells can be applied directly in the body, or used to grow replacement tissue in a laboratory.

The Possibilities of Stem Cell Therapy

7   Stem cell research promises to help fill gaps where current medicine falls short. "We believe that stem cells have uses in diabetes patients," says Colman, "where they have lost the ability to make insulin." There are things called mesenchymal stem cells which can be found in the bone marrow," says Colman, "which can replace cartilage."

8   Colman believes stem cells may have a role in heart patients as well. "Bone marrow stem cells are now being used to repair hearts of people who have had myocardial infarctions." One of those people is Ian Rosenberg, who suffered a heart attack in 1985. By 2003, time was running out. "My heart was in such bad shape," Rosenberg told CNN last year, "That they told me I had only two and a half months to live." Rosenberg underwent treatment at a hospital in Germany, and says, "My heart is pretty good now. I can go cruising, travel to America where I spend about six months of the year and walk a lot further than previously." "These are big unmet clinical needs," he [Coleman] says, "and we believe these are needs which can be met by stem cells in the next few years."

9   Repairing bone is something Colman believes "will be conquered in the next few years." And he thinks Alzheimer's patients may also benefit. "Not to give people back the memories that are lost, but just to allow them, as they go into their latter years, an increased quality of life."

How Stem Cells Are Being Used Today

10   The concept of using stem cells to repair damage to the spine or nervous system has been successful in animals. Last year, researchers at the University of California at Irvine announced they had successfully used adult human neural stem cells to treat mice with spinal injuries. Surgeons in London have been working to use stem cells to treat patients with damage to their nervous system. They'll take stem cells from the noses of their patients, which will mean there is no chance of rejection. If all goes well, the cells will patch a broken connection between nerves in the patient's arms and their spinal cord.

11   Dorairajan Balasubramanian, Chairman of the National Task Force on Stem Cell Research and a member of the CNN Future Summit Nominating Committee, has been using stem cells to treat patients at the L.V. Prasad Eye Institute in Hyderabad. Last year, Edward Bailey described to CNN how the use of stem cells helped restore sight in his left eye.

12   Seeking to understand stem cell development, British scientists earlier this year sought permission to fuse human cells with rabbit eggs. The scientists hope that the resulting embryos would allow them to better understand stem cell development. The embryos would not be allowed to develop. The matter is now being considered by the Human Fertilization and Embryology Authority.

Challenges and Controversies

13　There are some significant challenges ahead in the research. Colman says identifying the right stem cells and converting them properly to the cells you need are the first task. "Then we have to ensure that once transplanted the cell behaves properly and integrates with the neighboring cells and tissues and that it doesn't run amuck." At question is whether stem cells grown in a laboratory will "respond to the cues in the body that say enough is enough. Stop growing now, you are at the right number."

14　The use of embryonic stem cells has become a social issue in some societies. Many religious groups find the idea of using cells from human embryos morally unacceptable. Others believe the ability to heal the living outweighs those concerns. "My own view is that the embryo does have a moral status," says Colman, "but it's not equivalent to that of a living person, particularly not that of a sick living person."

15　Another controversy involving stem cell research erupted last year when it was learned that South Korean researcher Hwang Woo-suk faked results in nine of the 11 stem cell lines he claimed to have created. That news stunned scientists and those who follow stem cell research. Colman says the incident in South Korea "gives the impression that all scientists, working in what is already a controversial area, are similarly. If you like, scurrilous and prone to fraud." Colman says that's unfair. "Most scientists have great integrity and the experiments they do are fairly reported and there is no fraud attempted."

16　Balasubramanian says there must be an on-going conversation between scientists and the rest of society. "The role of scientists as interpreters," he says, "about advances in stem cell therapy, genetics and such is vital."

Writing About the Reading

CHECKING YOUR VOCABULARY

1. For each of the words listed below, use context; prefixes, roots, and suffixes (see Chapter 3); and/or a dictionary to write a brief definition or synonym of the word as it is used in the reading.

   a. curative (para. 2) _____

   b. integral (para. 3) _____

   c. fuse (para. 12)_____

   d. amuck (para. 13) _____

   e. scurrilous (para. 15) _____

   f. vital (para. 16) _____

2. Underline new, specialized terms introduced in the reading (see Chapter 3).

3. Draw a word map of one of the words in the reading.

CHECKING YOUR COMPREHENSION

1. List at least four uses for stem cells that are described in the reading. Use a C to indicate current uses and a P to indicate potential uses.

2. Identify two differences between embryonic and adult stem cells.
3. What does Alan Colman say is the first task regarding stem cell research?
4. What was the controversy surrounding stem cell research in South Korea?

THINKING CRITICALLY

1. What is the purpose of this reading?
2. What types of evidence do the authors use? Evaluate their effectiveness.
3. Identify examples of fact and opinion in this reading. How can you tell which is fact and which is opinion?
4. If you were to write a paper or a speech on this issue, where would you look for additional information?
5. What kind of government intervention do you think is needed or appropriate regarding stem cell research?

LEARNING/STUDY STRATEGY

Draw a chart that summarizes the uses of and problems with stem cells.

15 Reading in Technical and Applied Fields

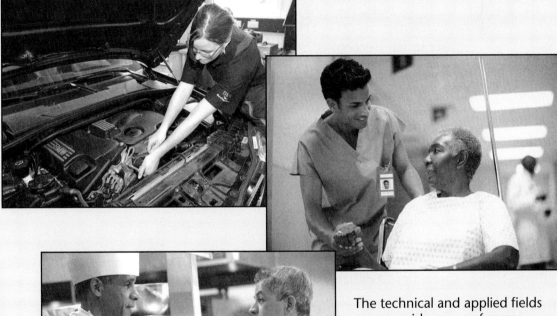

The technical and applied fields cover a wide range of career opportunities that ask you to "roll up your sleeves" and get to work. These include fields such as (1) auto mechanics, (2) nursing and allied health professions, and (3) service professions such as hotel and restaurant management.

LEARNING OBJECTIVES

■ To learn what the technical and applied fields are

■ To consider whether you should major in a technical/applied or allied health field

■ To develop specialized reading techniques for technical material

■ To learn processes and develop problem-solving strategies

■ To adapt your study strategies for technical material

What Are the Technical and Applied Fields?

Our society has become a technological one, in which there is a heavy reliance on automation and computerization. Consequently, more technical knowledge and expertise are required. Many students are thus pursuing degrees in a variety of **technical fields**, including computer information systems, environmental technology, mechanical and electrical technology, and computer-assisted drafting.

Many colleges also offer degrees in **applied fields** such as EKG and X-ray technology, air conditioning and refrigeration, food service, and horticulture. Unlike the academic majors, which focus on research and theory, these applied fields actively seek to apply knowledge in specialized areas that are of value to society. Table 15-1 summarizes some of the technical and applied fields and a few of the career opportunities available in each.

Table 15-1   Career Opportunities in the Technical and Applied Fields

AREA	CAREER OPPORTUNITIES
Automotive	• Mechanic • Auto factory worker • Car sales
HVAC (Heating, Ventilation, and Air Conditioning)	• Heating systems specialist • Public utilities worker • Refrigeration specialist
Computer Information Systems	• Database specialist • Computer repairperson • Help desk worker • Data security worker
Environmental Technology	• Pollution control worker • Sanitation specialist

TABLE 15-1 *continued*	
AREA	**CAREER OPPORTUNITIES**
Hotel and Restaurant Management	• Hotel manager • Restaurant or catering manager
Child Care	• Teacher's aide • Daycare center worker, manager, or owner

One of the largest of the applied fields is the area known as **allied health**, a catch-all term for clinical health-care professions that support the medical and dental industries. One of the most popular allied health majors is nursing, but there are many other types of allied health professionals, from nutritionists to radiology workers.

Should You Major in a Technical/Applied Field?

The result of many two-year programs in the technical fields is a certificate or license that gives you the credentials you will need to get hired in the career of your choice. If you are working toward a degree in a technical field, you will take two basic types of courses: the technical courses in your major and required courses in other disciplines.

What characteristics and habits will make you a successful major in your chosen area?

1. **You should enjoy working with your hands.** Grading and evaluation in technical courses is often performance-based. In addition to traditional exams and quizzes, instructors use hands-on exercises to evaluate your performance. In an auto mechanics course, for example, you may be asked to diagnose the problem with an engine.

2. **You should like solving problems.** The technical fields often require you to fix something that's broken—for example, eliminating a problem with someone's computer or repairing a clogged plumbing system. You should be someone who thinks on your feet and knows how to apply your learning.

3. **You should be comfortable working with instruments, equipment, and tools.** Many fields involve the use of instruments and equipment; others require measurement and recording of data. In both cases, you must be good about following procedures carefully and exactly.

4. **You should understand that a successful career in these fields requires you to do good work in your nontechnical courses as well.** Sometimes

technical majors enjoy the technical part of their major so much that they ask questions like "Why do I have to take this English course?" or "Why do I have to study history?" Your other college courses are intended to help you become a better writer and a better thinker—two qualities that are very much in demand by employers. Keep an open mind in these other courses; you may be surprised by how much you enjoy them.

Should You Major in an Allied Health Field?

Many students find themselves drawn to the allied health fields because they want to work with people. This is a wise decision from a career perspective, as allied health is one of the fastest growing fields in the United States. Table 15-2 lists just a few of the dozens of job opportunities for allied health majors.

Those of you who have considered majoring in nursing may be interested to know that nurses are usually voted the most trusted profession in opinion polls. Nursing and allied health majors truly do make a difference in people's lives.

Tips for Being a Successful Allied Health Major

1. **Understand that you'll be learning in three places: the classroom, the lab, and the field.** Because the allied health fields are all about helping people live healthier and better lives, there's only so much you can learn from a textbook. Much of your training will be conducted with real people in places such as hospitals, medical offices, and training facilities.

2. **Plan your study time very carefully.** The amount of information you will be required to learn in the health fields, particularly nursing, can feel intimidating. The best way to learn is to craft a system and a schedule that work for you, and to carefully plan and utilize your time. Study groups can be particularly helpful in terms of helping you memorize terminology and procedures.

TABLE 15-2   Job Opportunities in the Allied Health Professions

• Athletic trainer	• Nutritionist
• CAT scan technician	• Occupational therapist
• Dental hygienist, technician, or assistant	• Pharmacist
• Doctor's assistant	• Public health worker or advocate
• Forensics worker	• Radiologist
• Lab worker	• Rehabilitation counselor
• Medical billing specialist	• Speech therapist
• Medical transcriber	• Sports coach or sports medicine specialist
• Nurse	• X-ray technician

3. **Stay physically as well as mentally healthy.** Health workers should model good behavior and habits for their patients and clients. This means taking good care of yourself physically, getting enough sleep and exercise, and eating right. Of course, the benefits of physical health extend far beyond your career as well!

Quotes from an Engineering Professor

Advice for Students Taking Technical Courses

Jim White, Dean, Industrial and Engineering Technology, Central Carolina Technical College

66Some documentation [manuals, etc.] accompanying equipment or equipment-related software may be difficult to read, as it may have originally been written by people whose native language is not English.99

66Technology obviously changes at an incredible rate. As a result, the half-life of knowledge learned today is even shorter than 15 to 20 years ago. Students must learn how to approach problem solving step-by-step, or they will be overwhelmed.99

■ Reading Technical Material

Textbooks in technical fields are highly factual and packed with information. Compared to other textbooks, technical writing may seem "crowded" and difficult to read. In many technical courses, your instructor requires you to read manuals as well as textbooks. These are even more dense and, on occasion, poorly written. Use the following suggestions to help you read and learn from technical writing.

Read Slowly

Because technical writing is factual and contains numerous illustrations, diagrams, and sample problems, adjust your reading rate accordingly. Plan on spending twice as long reading a technical textbook as you spend on reading other, nontechnical texts.

Reread When Necessary

Do not expect to understand everything the first time you read the assignment. It is helpful to read an assignment once rather quickly to get an overview of the processes and procedures it presents. Reread it to learn the exact steps or details.

Have a Specific Purpose

Reading technical material requires that you have a carefully defined purpose. Unless you know why you are reading and what you are looking for, it is easy to become lost or to lose your concentration. Previewing is particularly helpful in establishing purposes for reading.

Pay Attention to Illustrations and Drawings

Most technical books contain illustrations, diagrams, and drawings, as well as more common graphical aids such as tables, graphs, and charts. (Refer to Chapter 8 for suggestions on reading graphics and visuals). Although graphics can make the text appear more complicated than it really is, they actually are a form of visual explanation designed to make the text easier to understand. Read the following excerpt from a building design and construction textbook describing the framing of roof rafters.

ROOF RAFTERS

Once the ceiling joists are nailed in place, the **roof rafters** can be installed. Common sizes for roof rafters include 2 in. × 6 in., 2 in. × 8 in., or 2 in. × 10 in. members spaced 12 in., 16 in., or 24 in. o.c., depending upon the width of the house and the magnitude of the dead and live loads imposed on the roof.

The rafters from both sides are usually connected at the top to a ridge board (Fig. A). Due to the angle cut in the rafters, the ridge board must be a larger size than the rafter. The ridge board runs the entire length of the roof and helps to distribute the roof load among several rafters. The location where the rafter bears on

FIGURE A   Roof Rafter/Ceiling Joist Roof Framing System

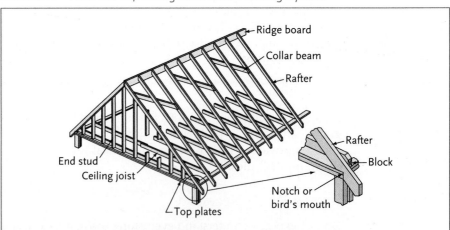

SOURCE: Gerald E. Sherwood and Robert C. Stroh, *Wood Frame House Construction*, p. 81 (Mineola, NY: Dover Publications, Inc. 1989)

the exterior wall is notched to form a snug fit. The notch is commonly known as a "bird's mouth." The end of the roof is known as the gable and is the location where the roof and wall join.

Collar beams (i.e., collar ties) are often required when roof spans are long and the slopes are flat. Steeper slopes and shorter spans also may require collar beams, but only between every third rafter pair. Collar beams are usually 1 in. $\times$ 6 in. or 2 in. $\times$ 4 in. members.

—Willenbrock et al., *Residential Building Design and Construction,* pp. 171–72

Now, study the diagram and reread the passage above. Does the diagram make the passage easier to understand? Use the suggestions in the Key Strategy box below to help you read illustrations and diagrams.

KEY STRATEGY: How to Read Illustrations and Drawings

1. **Note the type of illustrations or diagrams included in the assignment when you preview the chapter.**

2. **Look over each illustration, and determine its purpose.**   The title or caption usually indicates what it is intended to show.

3. **Examine the illustration first.**   Alternate between the text and the illustrations; illustrations are intended to be used with the paragraphs that refer to them. You may have to stop reading several times to refer to an illustration. For instance, when collar beams are mentioned in the preceding example, stop reading and find where they are placed in the diagram. You may also have to reread parts of the explanation several times.

4. **Look at each part of the illustration and note how the parts are connected.**   Notice any abbreviations, symbols, arrows, or labels.

5. **Test your understanding of illustrations by drawing and labeling an illustration of your own without looking at the one in the text.**   Then compare your drawing with the text. Note whether anything is left out. If so, continue drawing and checking until your drawing is complete and correct. Include these drawings in your notebook and use them for review and study.

EXERCISE 15-1

Analyzing Technical Writing

Read the following excerpt on ignition coils from an automotive technology textbook, and answer the questions that follow.

IGNITION COILS

The heart of any ignition system is the **ignition coil.** The coil creates a high-voltage spark by electromagnetic induction. Many ignition coils contain two separate but electrically connected windings of copper wire. Other coils are true

FIGURE B

Internal construction of an oil-cooled ignition coil. Notice that the primary winding is electrically connected to the secondary winding. The polarity (positive or negative) of a coil is determined by the direction in which the coil is wound.

Secondary tower

Electrical connection primary connected to secondary winding

Primary winding

Secondary winding

Laminated soft-iron core

Case

transformers in which the primary and secondary windings are not electrically connected. See Figure B.

The center of an ignition coil contains a core of laminated soft iron (thin strips of soft iron). This core increases the magnetic strength of the coil. Surrounding the laminated core are approximately 20,000 turns of fine wire (approximately 42-gauge). These windings are called the **secondary** coil windings. Surrounding the secondary winding are approximately 150 turns of heavy wire (approximately 21-gauge). These windings are called the **primary** coil windings. In many coils, these windings are surrounded with a thin metal shield and insulating paper and placed in a metal container. Many coils contain oil to help cool the ignition coil. Other coil designs, such as those used on GM's **high energy ignition (HEI)** systems, use an air-cooled, epoxy-sealed **E coil** named for the *E* shape of the metal laminations inside the coil.

—Halderman and Mitchell, *Automotive Technology: Principles, Diagnosis, and Service,* pp. 382–83

1. What is the purpose of the illustration?
2. Does the diagram make the text easier to understand? Briefly describe how.
3. Sketch a diagram of an ignition coil without referring to the drawing above.

Use Visualization

Visualization is a process of creating mental pictures or images. As you read, try to visualize the process or procedure that is being described. Make your image as specific and detailed as possible. Visualization will make reading these descriptions easier, as well as improve your ability to recall details. Here are a few examples of how students use visualization:

A nursing student learned the eight family life cycles by visualizing her sister's family at each stage.

A student taking a computer course was studying the two basic methods of organizing data on a magnetic disk: the sector method and the cylinder method. She visualized the sector method as slices of pie and the cylinder method as a stack of dinner plates.

Now read the following description of an optical disk system from a computer science textbook, and try to visualize as you read.

OPTICAL DISKS

Optical technology used with laser disk systems is providing a very high capacity storage medium with the **optical disk,** also called a **videodisk.** Videodisks will open new applications, since they can be used to store data, text, audio, and video images.

Optical disk systems look like magnetic disk systems. Each has a rotating platter and a head mechanism to record information. However, optical systems differ because they use light energy rather than magnetic fields to store data. A high-powered laser beam records data by one of two methods. With the **ablative method,** a hole is burned in the disk surface. With the **bubble method,** the disk surface is heated until a bubble forms.

The laser beam, in a lower power mode, reads the data by sensing the presence or absence of holes or bumps. The light beam will be reflected at different angles from a flat or disfigured surface. A series of mirrors is used to reflect the light beam to a photodiode, which transforms the light energy into an electric signal. The photodiode process works like the automatic doors at your local supermarket. As you walk toward the door, you deflect a light beam, which signals the doors to open.

—Athey et al., *Computers and End-User Software,* pp. 122–23

Did you visualize the disks with tiny holes or bumps?

EXERCISE 15-2   Visualizing

Read the following passage describing a standard bumper jack. As you read, try to visualize the jack. After you have finished, draw a sketch of the jack as it is described in the passage, without looking at the diagram. After you have completed your sketch, compare it with Figure C on page 416.

DESCRIPTION OF A STANDARD BUMPER JACK
Introduction—General Description

The standard bumper jack is a portable mechanism for raising the front or rear of a car through force applied with a lever. This jack enables even a frail person to lift one corner of a 2-ton automobile.

The jack consists of a molded steel base supporting a free-standing, perpendicular notched shaft. Attached to the shaft are a leverage mechanism, a bumper catch, and a cylinder for insertion of the jack handle. Except for the main shaft and leverage mechanism, the jack is made to be dismantled and to fit neatly in the car's trunk.

The jack operates on a leverage principle, with the human hand traveling 18 inches and the car only $\frac{3}{8}$ of an inch during a normal jacking stroke. Such a device requires many strokes to raise the car off the ground, but may prove a lifesaver to a motorist on some deserted road.

Five main parts make up the jack: base, notched shaft, leverage mechanism, bumper catch, and handle.

Description of Parts and Their Function

Base

The rectangular base is a molded steel plate that provides support and a point of insertion for the shaft. The base slopes upward to form a platform containing a 1-inch depression that provides a stabilizing well for the shaft. Stability is increased by a 1-inch cuff around the well. As the base rests on its flat surface, the bottom end of the shaft is inserted into its stabilizing well.

Shaft

The notched shaft is a steel bar (32 inches long) that provides a vertical track for the leverage mechanism. The notches, which hold the mechanism in its position on the shaft, face the operator.

The shaft vertically supports the raised automobile, and attached to it is the leverage mechanism, which rests on individual notches.

Leverage Mechanism

The leverage mechanism provides the mechanical advantage needed for the operator to raise the car. It is made to slide up and down the notched shaft. The main body of this pressed-steel mechanism contains two units: one for transferring the leverage and one for holding the bumper catch.

The leverage unit has four major parts: the cylinder, connecting the handle and a pivot point; a lower pawl (a device that fits into the notches to allow forward and prevent backward motion), connected directly to the cylinder; an upper pawl, connected at the pivot point; and an "up-down" lever, which applies or releases pressure on the upper pawl by means of a spring. Moving the cylinder up and down with the handle causes the alternate release of the pawls, and thus movement up or down the shaft—depending on the setting of the "up-down" lever. The movement is transferred by the metal body of the unit to the bumper-catch holder.

The holder consists of a downsloping groove, partially blocked by a wire spring. The spring is mounted in such a way as to keep the bumper catch in place during operation.

Bumper Catch

The bumper catch is a steel device that attaches the leverage mechanism to the bumper. This 9-inch molded plate is bent to fit the shape of the bumper. Its outer $\frac{1}{2}$ inch is bent up to form a lip, which hooks behind the bumper to hold the catch in place. The two sides of the plate are bent back 90 degrees to leave a 2-inch bumper-contact surface, and a bolt is riveted between them. This bolt slips into the groove in the leverage mechanism and provides the attachment between the leverage unit and the car.

Jack Handle

The jack handle is a steel bar that serves both as lever and lug-bolt remover. This round bar is 22 inches long, $^5/_8$ inch in diameter, and is bent 135 degrees roughly 5 inches from its outer end. Its outer end is a wrench made to fit the wheel's lug bolts. Its inner end is beveled to form a blade-like point for prying the wheel covers and for insertion into the cylinder on the leverage mechanism.

Conclusion and Operating Description

One quickly assembles the jack by inserting the bottom of the notched shaft into the stabilizing well in the base, the bumper catch into the groove on the leverage mechanism, and the beveled end of the jack handle into the cylinder. The bumper catch is then attached to the bumper, with the lever set in the "up" position.

As the operator exerts an up-down pumping motion on the jack handle, the leverage mechanism gradually climbs the vertical notched shaft until the car's wheel is raised above the ground. When the lever is in the "down" position, the same pumping motion causes the leverage mechanism to descend the shaft.

FIGURE C   Sample Diagram

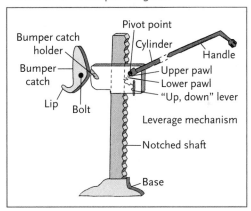

—Lannon, *Technical Writing*, pp. 419–21

Mark and Highlight

You may find your textbooks to be valuable reference sources for lab or on-site experiences; you may also use them when you are employed in your field. Take special care, then, to mark and highlight your textbooks for future reference. Marking will also make previewing for exams easier. Develop a marking system that uses particular symbols or colors of ink to indicate procedures, important formulas, troubleshooting charts, and so forth. Refer to Chapter 9 for additional suggestions on how to highlight effectively.

Learn to Read Technical Manuals

Many technical courses require students to operate equipment or become familiar with computer software. Study of and frequent reference to a specific manual are additional requirements in some technical courses. Unfortunately, many technical manuals are poorly written and organized, so you need to approach them differently from textbooks. Use the suggestions in the Key Strategy box below when reading technical manuals.

KEY STRATEGY: How to Read Technical Manuals

1. **Preview the manual to establish how it is arranged and exactly what it contains.** Does it have an index, a troubleshooting section, a section with specific operating instructions? Study the table of contents carefully and mark sections that will be particularly useful.

2. **Do not read the manual from cover to cover.** First, locate and review those sections you identified as particularly useful. Concentrate on the parts that describe the overall operation of the machine: its purpose, capabilities, and functions.

3. **Next, learn the codes, symbols, commands, or terminology used in the manual.** Check to see if the manual provides a list of special terms. Many computer software manuals, for instance, contain a list of symbols, commands, or procedures used throughout the manual. If such a list is not included, begin making your own list on a separate sheet of paper or on the inside cover of the manual.

4. **Begin working with the manual and the equipment simultaneously,** applying each step as you read it.

5. **If the manual does not contain a useful index, make your own by jotting down page numbers of sections you know you will need to refer to frequently.**

6. **If the manual is overly complicated or difficult to read, simplify it by writing your own step-by-step directions in the margin or on a separate sheet of paper.**

■ The Allied Health Fields

This section of the chapter offers suggestions for reading, learning, and studying in allied health courses.

Learn Medical Terminology

Medical terminology is the vocabulary of technical terms used in medicine. These terms are used in written and oral communication in all allied health settings including labs, hospitals, doctors' offices, and other treatment facilities. In order to be part of a medical team and to communicate with your team's members, you must be able to "speak the language." This means you must be able to read, write, and speak using medical terminology.

Medical terminology is specialized and precise. Specific words are used to refer to diseases, procedures, equipment, and parts of the body. As medical science advances, new terms are introduced to describe new procedures, diseases, and drugs, thereby expanding the store of medical terminology. Here are a few suggestions for learning this new vocabulary.

Learn Word Parts   The key to understanding medical terminology is to learn the meaning of word parts commonly used in medicine. Think of word parts as the key to unlocking the code of medical terminology. Learning the meaning of word parts, which are used in many words, is a much more efficient way of mastering terminology than memorizing the meaning of each individual word you need to learn. Word parts are discussed in detail in Chapter 3 of this book. Be sure to review this section to help you get started using word parts to decipher unfamiliar medical terms.

Quotes from a Nursing Professor

Advice for Allied Health Students

Jim Foley, RN, BSN, Nursing Instructor, Minneapolis Community Technical College

"The goal of classroom work is to allow you to reason out your actions and articulate your reasoning."

"Students should learn to reread sections (probably up to six times). Each rereading should have a specific goal."

Many long and complicated medical terms can be broken down into parts. The word *bilateral* has three word parts:

bi means two
later means side
al means pertaining to

So you can figure out that *bilateral* refers to something that is two-sided.

To learn a large number of word parts, many students find it effective to use index cards. Record the word part on the front and its meaning on the back. Create packs of cards that pertain to various topics you are studying, such as the various body systems—the skeletal system, the nervous system, and so forth. This index card system is explained in Chapter 3 on page 78.

Learn Eponyms   **Eponyms** are words that are based on a person's name. In medicine, they are often used to describe diseases, drugs, or structures discovered or described by particular individuals. For example, Hodgkin's lymphoma is a type of cancer first described by a physician named William Hodgkin.

Learn Acronyms   **Acronyms** are words created from the first letters of a group of words. CAT scan, for example, stands for <u>c</u>omputed <u>a</u>xial <u>t</u>omography scan. STD stands for <u>s</u>exually <u>t</u>ransmitted <u>d</u>isease, and MRI stands for <u>m</u>agnetic <u>r</u>esonance <u>i</u>maging.

Develop Your Mathematics Skills

Mathematics skills are vital in allied health fields because making correct measurements, such as medication dosages, is very important. Three types of skills are involved in math-related tasks that are essential in allied health fields.

- **You have to have knowledge.** For example, you need to know what certain drugs are used for, what are safe dosages of them, and how often they can be given to a patient.
- **You need good reasoning skills.** You need to be able to make inferences and draw conclusions about different situations.
- **You need to be able to make simple calculations.**

Here is an example of a common math problem that involves these skills:

Sample Problem

According to the manufacturer's recommendations, children 9 to 10 years old should not receive more than 2 grams of acetaminophen in a 24-hour period. If you are using acetaminophen solution containing 160 milligrams in 3.33 milliliters, how many milliliters per day would you give to reach the maximum dose?

In this problem situation, which a nurse may typically encounter, you have to understand what acetaminophen is and what it is used to treat. You also need to be able to reason out how to calculate the number of milliliters you can administer without exceeding the maximum dose for a 24-hour period, and then do the actual calculations.

Pay Attention to Processes and Procedures

Processes and procedures are important in all allied health fields. Processes are particularly complicated to understand when there is more than one option for treatment in a particular situation. As you read your textbooks, be sure to mark or highlight processes and procedures. To learn and remember how processes and procedures work, it may be helpful to construct a diagram or flowchart that details the options and shows what action to take depending on a given situation.

Figure 15-1 is an example of a flowchart that details the procedures to follow when rechecking the temperature of a patient who is suffering from hyperthermia (unusually high body temperature).

FIGURE 15-1   Response to Hyperthermia

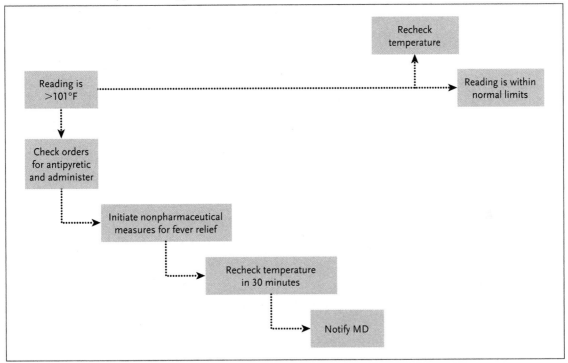

Polish Your Reasoning Skills

Learning in the allied health fields goes far beyond memorizing facts. While it is essential to acquire a solid base of knowledge, that is not all that will be expected of you. Rather, you must use your factual knowledge base to reason out what must be done in specific situations, and be able to explain your reasoning to others. Skills such as making inferences, drawing conclusions, and evaluating data and evidence are essential. (Refer to Chapter 4 of this book for a review of these skills.) For example, if you are working as an ER nurse, you must use your knowledge of what vital signs mean to reason out what immediate action is appropriate for you to take when a patient is first admitted.

Develop Skills in Informatics

Informatics is the use of information and computer technology to support medical diagnosis and treatment, as well as to manage a medical office. Think of informatics as the managing of information and records. All workers in the allied health fields are involved with informatics, since accurate record keeping is essential to communication and quality care. Here are a few examples of the types of information nursing care professionals need to manage: documentation of patient care and discharge, computerized patient records, online drug information, and the monitoring of devices that record patient vital signs.

Here is what you can do to be prepared:

- **Polish your computer literacy and keyboarding skills.**
- **Learn medical terminology so you are prepared to "speak the language."**
- **Take any training classes or workshops, either in real time or online, that are available.**
- **Develop an awareness of patient confidentiality.** Patient records are protected by privacy laws, and you must take steps to insure privacy regulations are followed.

Use Practicum Experiences to Your Advantage

Many allied health fields require practicum experiences. A practicum is a work experience in a medical setting where you learn practical, on-the-job skills and apply the skills and knowledge you have learned in the classroom. Be sure to treat this experience seriously; it is an important part, if not *the* most important part of your training. The Key Strategy box below explains how to succeed in and use practicum experience to your advantage.

KEY STRATEGY: Learning from Practicum Experience

- **Prepare in advance.** Do not just show up on the assigned day. Learn about the facility; consider visiting it before your first day.
- **Take notes during or after each day at work.** Record information that you are expected to know and use; it is annoying to supervisors if you keep asking the same questions. Also, record what you have learned. Many students find keeping a journal helpful. Avoid personal thoughts: instead record your experience in a factual manner.
- **Expect to be evaluated.** Your performance will be evaluated by a supervisor. Ask for and expect feedback on your work. Remember, too, that a positive evaluation may lead to a job offer.
- **Use the practicum to learn about where you would like to work.** Your practicum can provide you with valuable information about the types of patients you enjoy working with, the kind of facility in which you would like to work, and the area of the health field you would like to specialize in.

■ Thought Patterns in Technical Fields

The two thought patterns most commonly used in technical fields are process and problem/solution. Each is used in textbooks and manuals as well as in practical, hands-on situations.

FIGURE 15-2   Sample Summary Sheet

> **Venipuncture**
>
> 1. Wash hands, explain procedure to patient, assess patient status
> 2. Assemble equipment
> 3. Locate puncture site
> 4. Apply tourniquet, cleanse site
> 5. Place thumb distal to puncture site
> 6. Insert needle 30° angle aspirate desired amount
> 7. Remove tourniquet, place dry compress on needle tip & withdraw
> 8. Remove needle from syringe and place specimen in container; label

Reading Process Descriptions

Testing procedures, directions, installations, repairs, instructions, and diagnostic checking procedures all follow the process pattern. To read materials written in this pattern, you must not only learn the steps but also learn them in the correct order. To study process material, use the following tips:

1. **Prepare study sheets that summarize each process.** For example, a nursing student learning the steps in venipuncture (taking a blood sample) wrote the summary sheet shown in Figure 15-2 above.

2. **Test your recall by writing out the steps from memory.** Recheck periodically by mentally reviewing each step.

3. **For difficult or lengthy procedures, write each step on a separate index card.** Shuffle the pack and practice putting the cards in the correct order.

4. **Be certain you understand the logic behind the process.** Figure out why each step is performed in the specified order.

EXERCISE 15-3

LEARNING
COLLABORATIVELY

Writing a Process Summary

Read the following excerpt describing acid rain. After you have read it, write a process summary of each stage of the acid rain process. Compare your process summary with that of a classmate.

HOW ACID RAIN DEVELOPS, SPREADS, AND DESTROYS

Introduction

Acid rain is environmentally damaging rainfall that occurs after fossil fuels burn, releasing nitrogen and sulfur oxides into the atmosphere. Acid rain, simply stated, increases the acidity level of waterways because these nitrogen and sulfur oxides combine with the air's normal moisture. The resulting rainfall is far more acidic than normal rainfall. Acid rain is a silent threat because its effects, although slow, are cumulative. This report explains the cause, the distribution cycle, and the effects of acid rain.

Most research shows that power plants burning oil or coal are the primary cause of acid rain. The burnt fuel is not completely expended, and some residue enters the atmosphere. Although this residue contains several potentially toxic elements, sulfur oxide and, to a lesser extent, nitrogen oxide are the major problem, because they are transformed when they combine with moisture. This chemical reaction forms sulfur dioxide and nitric acid, which then rain down to earth.

The major steps explained here are (1) how acid rain develops, (2) how acid rain spreads, and (3) how acid rain destroys.

The Process

How Acid Rain Develops

Once fossil fuels have been burned, their usefulness is over. Unfortunately, it is here that the acid rain problem begins.

Fossil fuels contain a number of elements that are released during combustion. Two of these, sulfur oxide and nitrogen oxide, combine with normal moisture to produce sulfuric acid and nitric acid. (Figure D illustrates how acid rain develops.) The released gases undergo a chemical change as they combine with atmospheric ozone and water vapor. The resulting rain or snowfall is more acid than normal precipitation.

Acid level is measured by pH readings. The pH scale runs from 0 through 14—a pH of 7 is considered neutral. (Distilled water has a pH of 7.) Numbers above 7 indicate increasing degrees of alkalinity. (Household ammonia has a pH of 11.) Numbers below 7 indicate increasing acidity. Movement in either direction on the pH scale, however, means multiplying by 10. Lemon juice, which has a pH value of 2, is 10 times more acidic than apples, which have a pH of 3, and is 1,000 times more acidic than carrots, which have a pH of 5.

Because of carbon dioxide (an acid substance) normally present in air, unaffected rainfall has a pH of 5.6. At this time, the pH of precipitation in the northeastern United States and Canada is between 4.5 and 4. In Massachusetts, rain and snowfall have an average pH reading of 4.1. A pH reading below 5 is considered to be abnormally acidic, and therefore a threat to aquatic populations.

FIGURE D   How Acid Rain Develops

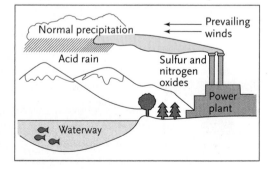

How Acid Rain Spreads

Although it might seem that areas containing power plants would be most severely affected, acid rain can in fact travel thousands of miles from its source. Stack gases escape and drift with the wind currents. The sulfur and nitrogen oxides are thus able to travel great distances before they return to earth as acid rain.

For an average of two to five days, the gases follow the prevailing winds far from the point of origin. For example, estimates show that about 50 percent of the acid rain that affects Canada originates in the United States; at the same time, 15 to 25 percent of the U.S. acid rain problem originates in Canada.

The tendency of stack gases to drift makes acid rain such a widespread menace. More than 200 lakes in the Adirondacks, hundreds of miles from any industrial center, are unable to support life because their water has become so acidic.

How Acid Rain Destroys

Acid rain causes damage wherever it falls. It erodes various types of building rock such as limestone, marble, and mortar, which are gradually eaten away by the constant bathing in acid. Damage to buildings, houses, monuments, statues, and cars is widespread. Some priceless monuments and carvings already have been destroyed, and even trees of some varieties are dying in large numbers.

More important, however, is acid rain damage to waterways in the affected areas. (Figure E illustrates how a typical waterway is infiltrated.) Because of its high acidity, acid rain dramatically lowers the pH of lakes and streams.

Although its effect is not immediate, acid rain can eventually make a waterway so acidic it dies. In areas with natural acid-buffering elements such as limestone, the dilute acid has less effect. The northeastern United States and Canada, however, lack this natural protection, and so are continually vulnerable.

The pH level in an affected waterway drops so low that some species cease to reproduce. In fact, a pH level of 5.1 to 5.4 means that fisheries are threatened; once a waterway reaches a pH level of 4.5, no fish reproduction occurs. Because each creature is part of the overall food chain, loss of one element in the chain disrupts the whole cycle.

In the northeastern United States and Canada, the acidity problem is compounded by the runoff from acid snow. During the cold winter months, acid snow sits with little melting, so that by spring thaw, the acid released is greatly concentrated. Aluminum and other heavy metals normally present in soil are released by acid rain and runoff. These toxic

FIGURE E   How Acid Rain Destroys

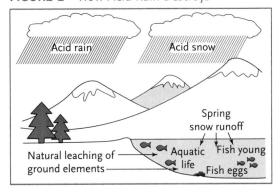

substances leach into waterways in heavy concentrations, affecting fish in all stages of development.

Summary

Acid rain develops from nitrogen and sulfur oxides emitted by industrial and power plants burning fossil fuels. In the atmosphere, these oxides combine with ozone and water to form acid rain: precipitation with a lower-than-average pH. This acid precipitation returns to earth many miles from its source, severely damaging waterways that lack natural buffering agents. The northeastern United States and Canada are the most severely affected areas in North America.

—Lannon, *Technical Writing*, pp. 452–55

Problem–Solving Strategies

In technical fields, you will encounter hypothetical problems to solve that require you to apply formulas and work with procedures. More important, you will face simulated problems in labs and actual problems throughout your career. A systematic approach is helpful to improve your problem-solving abilities.

It is easy to panic when a piece of equipment fails or a procedure does not produce the expected results. Using a systematic approach to solving problems will help you in these situations. A problem is basically a conflict between "what is" (the present state) and "what should be" or "what is desired" (the goal state). For example, a medical office assistant has a problem when she cannot calm a frightened child in order to take her blood pressure. The steps listed in the Key Strategy box below can help you attack problem situations.

KEY STRATEGY: How to Approach Problems

Step 1: Specify the problem. Do this by evaluating the present state and determining how it differs from what is desired. The more specific you can be, the more likely that you will be able to identify working solutions. For example, if you are faced with a machine that does not function properly, figure out what part or feature is malfunctioning. Do not simply say the machine does not work; instead, determine that the robot arm does not remain in position to complete the task. If your patient will not cooperate when you need to take her blood pressure, try to discover why she is unwilling.

Step 2: Analyze the problem. Analysis is a complex critical thinking skill. Begin by learning as much as you can about the problem. For instance, it may be necessary to find out why your young patient is frightened in order to be able to calm her down. To analyze a problem, it may be necessary to look beyond the obvious solution—to stretch your imagination and reach for creative options.

For example, you may discover the child is frightened because you are wearing white and the child's dentist, of whom she is frightened, also wears white. When analyzing a problem, use the following suggestions:

- **Be flexible in your analysis.** Do not eliminate possibilities because they seem unlikely or never have happened in the past.
- **Brainstorm about all the possibilities.** Except for problems that must be solved immediately, spend a few minutes listing anything you can think of that is remotely related to your problem. Sort through the list later, preferably the next day. You probably will discover the seeds of a solution.
- **Talk with others about the problem.** By putting the problem into words (to a classmate or your instructor), you may hear yourself say things that will lead to further understanding.
- **Research problems for which you lack complete information.**

Step 3: Formulate a solution path. Identify a possible solution to the problem. For some problems, such as a machine malfunction, there is only one correct solution. For others, such as an uncooperative patient, various solutions may be feasible.

Step 4: Evaluate possible solution paths. If you have identified more than one solution path, the next step is to weigh the advantages and disadvantages of each one. You will need to think through each solution path in detail, considering how, when, and where you could accomplish each. Consider the likelihood of success with each solution, and weigh both short- and long-term effects. Thinking aloud may help you realize why various solutions will not work.

Step 5: Implement the solution. If your solution does not solve the problem, analyze what went wrong and repeat the problem-solving process. A trial-and-error process may be necessary. Be sure to use a logical, systematic approach and keep track of your results for each trial.

EXERCISE 15-4

LEARNING
COLLABORATIVELY

Developing Problem-Solving Strategies

Form groups of four or five students and discuss and develop a strategy for solving each of the following problems.

1. A computer will not boot the program when the disk is inserted in the second disk drive.
2. A student in a science laboratory technology course gets a different result for his lab experiment from other students conducting the same experiment.

■ Study Techniques for Technical Courses

Use the following suggestions to adapt your study skills to technical courses.

Pronounce and Use Technical Vocabulary

Understanding the technical vocabulary in your discipline is essential. For technical and applied fields, it is especially important to learn to pronounce technical terms and to use them in your speech. To establish yourself as a professional in the field and to communicate effectively with other professionals, it is essential to speak the language. Use the suggestions in Chapter 3 for learning specialized terminology.

Draw Diagrams and Pictures

Although your textbook may include numerous drawings and illustrations, there is not enough space to include drawings for every process. An effective learning strategy is to draw diagrams and pictures whenever possible. These should be fast sketches; be concerned with describing parts or processes, and do not worry about artwork or scale drawings. For example, a student studying air conditioning and refrigeration repair drew a quick sketch of a unit he was to repair in his lab before he began to disassemble it. He then referred to sketches he had drawn in his notebook as he diagnosed the problem.

Reserve Blocks of Time Each Day for Study

Daily study and review are important in technical courses. Many technical courses require large blocks of time (two to three hours) to complete projects, problems, or drawings. Technical students find that taking less time is inefficient because if they leave a project unfinished, they have to spend time rethinking it and reviewing what they have already done when they return to the project.

Focus on Concepts and Principles

Because technical subjects are so detailed, many students focus on these details rather than on the concepts and principles to which they relate. Keep a sheet in the front of your notebook on which you record information to which you need to refer frequently. Include constants, conversions, formulas, metric equivalents, and commonly used abbreviations. Refer to this sheet so you will not interrupt your train of thought in order to search for these pieces of information. Then you can focus on ideas rather than specific details.

Make Use of the Glossary and Index

Because of the large number of technical terms, formulas, and notations you will encounter, often it is necessary to refer to definitions and explanations. Place a paper clip at the beginning of the glossary in your textbook and a second at the index so you can find them easily.

Test-Taking Tips
Preparing for Exams in Technical Courses

Exams in technical courses may consist of objective questions or of problems to solve. (For suggestions on preparing for and taking these types of exams, see the test-taking tips in Chapters 10, 11, and 13.) Other times, exams may take the form of a practicum. A practicum is a simulation, or a rehearsal, of some problem or task you may face on the job. For example, a nursing student may be asked to perform a procedure while a supervisor observes. Or an EKG technologist may be evaluated in administering an EKG to a patient. Use these suggestions to prepare for practicum exams:

1. Identify possible tasks you may be asked to perform.

2. Learn the steps each task involves. Write summary notes, and test your recall by writing or mentally rehearsing them without reference to your notes. Visualize yourself performing the task.

3. If possible, practice performing the task, mentally reviewing the steps you learned as you proceed.

4. Study with another student; test and evaluate each other.

Self-Test Summary

1. Identify six specific techniques for reading technical writing.	Six techniques for reading technical writing are • reading slowly. • rereading when necessary. • setting a specific purpose for reading. • studying illustrations and drawings. • using visualization. • marking and highlighting.
2. Which two patterns of thought predominate in technical and applied fields?	The two thought patterns are process and problem/solution.
3. List the five steps in the problem-solving process.	The five steps in the problem-solving process are • specify the problem. • analyze the problem. • formulate a solution path. • evaluate possible solution paths. • implement the solution.
4. How should you adapt your study skills for technical courses?	You can adapt your study skills to read technical material by • pronouncing and using technical vocabulary. • drawing diagrams and pictures. • reserving large blocks of time in which to study. • focusing on concepts and principles, rather than just details. • making use of your textbook's glossary and index.

Nursing

Telehealth: Promise or Peril?
Linda Q. Thede

Prereading Questions

1. What do you know about telehealth?
2. How has technology made a difference in your own health care?

1   As you walk down the hall of the clinic, you see thorough the window millions of jewels as the sun is reflected off the ice on the Bering Sea. You enter the consultation room and greet your patient, Missy Becker. You have arranged for a consult with Dr. Sarah McKinnon about a lesion that Missy has. Turning on the computer you tell Missy that Dr. McKinnon, a dermatologist in Chicago, will be examining her today. When the computer monitor comes alive, you say hello to Dr. McKinnon and introduce her to Missy. You set up the camera that has finger like probes so that Dr. McKinnon can manipulate both the camera and probes. Using these touch-sensitive probes she examines Missy's lesion just as she would if she were physically with you in the consultation room. "Good news," Dr. McKinnon says after a thorough examination, "As far as I can tell now, the lesion is benign. Do a biopsy and put it under the telemicroscope so I can see it." The fact that Dr. McKinnon is in Chicago and you and Missy are separated by over 3,000 miles does not even evoke a comment.

2   The above scenario exemplifies one of the promises of telehealth, providing top-specialist care to those who live at a distance from the specialist. There are others, who if asked about telehealth would see some of the perils. Some fear that telehealth will reduce the number of nurses and other healthcare professionals needed; others worry about privacy and legalities. Regardless of one's beliefs, telehealth is not likely to go away. [This article] will examine some of these perils as well as some of the promises.

3   Telehealth is defined as the use of electronic communication networks to transmit date or Information that focuses on health promotion, disease prevention, diagnosis, consultation, education, and/or therapy. In one of its many forms telehealth has been practiced ever since the advent of the telephone. Telehealth in patient care covers many areas, but can be divided into two distinct parts, the technology and the provider/client relationship. On the technology side are many different technologies including advanced image and audio capabilities that range from high resolution still images to sophisticated interactive tele-conferencing systems. Technology is now available that allows a virtual simulation of tissues and blood flow. Use of the Internet to transmit the feel of a lesion, or even muscles and bones, prior to surgery will happen soon.

4   The telehealth technology is relatively simple compared to the telehealth provider/client relationship. This provider/client relationship encompasses not only direct care, but also the content of Information that is made available electronically in Web sites to both patients and healthcare professionals. As a result, there are many complex issues surrounding telehealth. These include reimbursement, privacy, licensure, jurisdiction and standards.

5   The issue of who is to pay and for what has slowed down the development of tele-health. Dr. Puskin, in her article "Telemedicine—Follow the Money" addresses payment issues starting with the flawed Balanced Budget Act (BBA) of 1997 through the Medicare, Medicaid, and SCHIP Benefits Improvement Act of 2000 (BIPA), which became effective October 1, 2001. The BBA, although providing a beginning for telehealth payment," . . . did not work because it was predicated on a very limited view of how telemedicine is actually practiced. These limitations fell into four categories: (a) who can receive services; (b) what is covered; (c) who gets paid; and (d) how are services reimbursed." The BIPA, although not fully endorsing telehealth, addresses some of these shortcomings by enlarging the number of people eligible to receive telehealth consults and adding a few methods in which telehealth can be conducted. The BIPA also required a study to identify issues that are unresolved such as who is covered and what services can be provided. Various sides of other issues such as home health care, store and forward technology and quality are also explored in this article. The author makes a case for nurses, as those who will manage and be a part of much of telehealth, to be involved in forthcoming legislation that will determine policies such as whether reimbursement should be offered for preventive telehealth.

6   Kumekawa in her article "Health Information Privacy Protections: Crisis or Common Sense" looks at the privacy, confidentiality, and security issues. The effects of the Health Information Privacy and Accountability Act of 1996, whose rules are fairly well promulgated (although several pressure groups are arguing to nullify or weaken some provisions) are thoroughly addressed by this author. One of the problems in this issue is the dilemma that appears when state laws are more stringent than federal. This author advances the thought that telehealth requirements in basic administrative procedures, physical safeguards, and technical security mechanisms present special needs for privacy that involve more than just the patient, care giver, and third party payers. Shortfalls in security by consumers who divulge personal information to online medical sites are also discussed. Although not often considered, nurses who set up web pages focusing on certain diseases, as well as healthcare agencies who provide healthcare Information on the Internet, will find themselves involved in these privacy Issues. The desire of Americans for the latest healthcare and healthcare information, together with a concern about privacy of medical information, creates issues that, although they have no easy answers, will need to be addressed.

7   Hutcherson addresses the added legal concerns that become very important in tele-health as explained in her article "Legal Considerations for Nurses Practicing in a Telehealth Setting." One of the questions she addresses is, "Who should have jurisdiction over healthcare; the states or the federal government?" Prior to the advent of multi-state delivery systems and nursing call centers, regulatory functions for most healthcare matters were given to the states based on the Tenth Amendment. This answer, however, became more uncertain with the enactment of the Balanced Budget Act of 1997 and the issuance of federal grants designed to use telehealth to increase access for rural and underserved areas to quality healthcare. Another facet of this question that she presents is, "Where is the location of care when the patient and provider are in different geographical locations?" The answer of course is very relevant to the issue of licensure. State Boards of Nursing have grappled with this problem; currently the National Council of State Boards of Nursing has proposed a mutual recognition model of licensure in which a nurse licensed in one state can practice in another state if she or he abides by the Nursing

Practice Act of that State (See www.ncsbn.org/public/regulation/mutual_recognition_state.htm). Another issue that she believes will be debated is whether there is enough difference in practice to warrant credentialing for those engaged in telehealth practice. Regardless of the outcome of these issues, it is imperative that standards be developed and employed that encompass safe and effective direct care and the provision of health information.

8   The article "Windows of Opportunity for Home Care Nurses: Telehealth Technologies" by Russo focuses on the opportunities for nurses as technology becomes more prevalent in healthcare and the population ages. As the author reports, these opportunities that increase the need for nurses come at a time when half of all registered nurses are over 44 years old and nursing school enrollments have been down for the last five years. Technology, this author believes, can be used to improve the situation. She describes how it has provided nurses with the opportunity for educational experiences in their own home and on an as-needed basis. The author discusses the importance of the Internet to Seniors who use it to find healthcare information. These Seniors find higher satisfaction with telehealth and have the potential for better health outcomes using telehealth. On the technology side, the author discusses use of interactive video in telehealth which has offered many clients immediate access to care, care that prevents serious problems from developing and gives homebound clients a sense of security. Correctional institutions are another place where telehealth is very beneficial. The question the author leaves us with is "Will we take advantage of the opportunities provided by the new technology, or will we be run over by it"?

9   Telehealth has the potential to make a difference in the health care of not only Americans, but people all over the world. Whether it achieves its potential may depend on the resolution of the issues addressed in these articles. In the near future, however, do not expect to see consensus in many of these areas. One thing that is certain, given the present and future advances in technology, telehealth is here to stay. The question then becomes, how will it be used and who will benefit?

— Online Journal of Issues in Nursing

Writing About the Reading

CHECKING YOUR VOCABULARY

1. For each of the words listed below, use context; prefixes, roots, and suffixes (see Chapter 3); and/or a dictionary to write a brief definition or synonym of the word as it is used in the reading.

   a. evoke (para. 1) _____

   b. advent (para. 3) _____

   c. predicated (para. 5) _____

   d. promulgated (para. 6) _____

   e. nullify (para. 6) _____

   f. stringent (para. 6) _____

   g. divulge (para. 6) _____

   h. prevalent (para. 8)_____

2. Underline new, specialized terms introduced in the reading (see Chapter 3).

3. Draw a word map of one of the words in the reading.

CHECKING YOUR COMPREHENSION

1. What is telehealth?
2. What are the two distinct parts of telehealth in patient care? Give an example of each.
3. In this reading, the author cites four articles that focus on important issues surrounding telehealth. List each title and identify the issue that is addressed in the article.

THINKING CRITICALLY

1. What is the purpose of this reading?
2. Who do you think is the primary audience for this reading?
3. Evaluate the effectiveness of the opening paragraph. How else might the author have captured your attention?
4. Why do you think the author does not expect to see consensus in many of the areas addressed in the reading?
5. What issues do you think represent the most promise and the most peril in the field of telehealth? Explain your answer.

LEARNING/STUDY STRATEGY

Prepare a study sheet that summarizes each of the issues and how they are addressed in the corresponding articles.

Credits

Photo Credits

Page xxii, 1st row: Big Stock Photo; xxii, 2nd row, left to right: Big Stock Photo; Dreamstime; iStockphoto; xxii, 3rd row, left to right: Dreamstime; Big Stock Photo; Big Stock Photo; xxii, 4th row, left to right: Big Stock Photo; Big Stock Photo; iStockphoto; 1: Yellow Dog Productions/Getty Images; 21: i love images/Alamy; 50: Mary Kate Denny/PhotoEdit, Inc.; 54: Al Bello/Getty Images; 69: Jeff Greenberg/Alamy; 71: Spencer Grant/PhotoEdit, Inc.; 75: joSon/Getty Images; 98: Zigy Kaluzny/Getty Images; 103: Courtesy of Peta; 116: AP Images; 130: Julio Donoso/Corbis; 154: AP Images; 177: Phillipe Gendreau/Corbis; 219: National Baseball Hall of Fame Library; 222: Scott McKiernan/Black Star; 234: Tribune Media Services, Inc. All Rights Reserved. Reprinted with Permission.; 235: Bob Campbell/Gorilla Organization; 252: Influx Productions/Getty Images; 272: Joel Gordon Photography; 273: Time Life Pictures/Getty Images; 277, top to bottom: AP Images; Scott Shaw/The Plain Dealer/Landov; 282: Courtesy of Professor Robert A. Schwegler; 300, top to bottom: Joel Gordon Photography; Masterfile; 304: Courtesy of Professor John Ribezzo; 323, top to bottom: BroadSpektrum/Alamy; "Guernica" by Pablo Picasso, The Print Collector/Alamy, © Estate of Pablo Picasso/Artists Rights Society (ARS), NY; Superstudio/Getty Images; 327: Courtesy of Professor Patrick Mathias; 343: Library of Congress; 355, top to bottom: Richard A. Brooks/Getty Images; Eric Dreyer/Getty Images; 359: Courtesy of Professor Jerry R. Muir; 382, top to bottom: Big Stock Photo; Masterfile; 386: Courtesy of Professor William J. Straits; 407, clockwise from top left: Stefan Kiefer/Vario Images/Alamy; Brooklyn Production/Corbis; Masterfile; 411: Courtesy of Professor Jim White; 419: Courtesy of Professor Bradley Foley.

Text Credits

Chapter 1 33: Josh R. Gerow, from *Psychology: An Introduction*, 5th Edition, pp. 217–219. Copyright © 1997 by Addison-Wesley Educational Publishers, Inc. Reprinted by permission of Pearson Education, Inc. 33: Weaver, *Understanding Interpersonal Communication*, pp. 423–426, © 1996. Reproduced by permission of Pearson Education, Inc. 37: Gronbeck, *Principles of Speech Communication*, pp. 38–39. Reproduced by permission of Pearson Education, Inc. 43: Weaver, *Understanding Interpersonal Communication*, pp. 423–426, © 1996. Reproduced by permission of Pearson Education, Inc. 43: Jerry A. Nathanson, P.E., *Basic Environmental Technology*, 3rd Edition, Upper Saddle River, New Jersey: Prentice-Hall, 2000, p. 351. 46: Weaver, *Understanding Interpersonal Communication*, pp. 423–426, © 1996. Reproduced by permission of Pearson Education, Inc. 50: Gerow, *Psychology: An Introduction,* 1st ed., © 1992. Electronically reproduced by permission of Pearson Education, Inc., Upper Saddle River, New Jersey.

Chapter 2 55: Leon Baradat, *Understanding American Democracy*, Pearson Education, 1992. Used by permission of Pearson Education. 56: Thompson/Hickey, *Society in Focus: An Introduction to Sociology*, p. 131, © 2005, 2002, 1999, 1996 HarperCollins College Publishers Reproduced by permission of Pearson Education, Inc. 57: Joseph DeVito, *Human Communication: The Basic Course*, 7th Edition, Longman, 1998, p. 182. 57: Gerow, *Psychology: An Introduction,* 1st ed., © 1992. Electronically reproduced by permission of Pearson Education, Inc., Upper Saddle River, New Jersey. 57: Robert Wallace, *Biology: The World of Life*, 6th Edition, Pearson Education, 1992. Used by permission of Pearson Education. 58: James Coleman and Donald Cressey, *Social Problems*, 6th Edition, HarperCollins College Publishers, Inc., 1996, p. 277. 58: Jeffrey Bennett, et al., *The Cosmic Perspective*, Brief Edition, Addison Wesley Longman, 2000, p. 28. 58: Gerow, *Psychology: An Introduction*, 1st ed., © 1992. Electronically reproduced by permission of Pearson Education, Inc., Upper Saddle River, New Jersey. 59: Timberlake, Karen C., Chemistry: *Intro General Organic Biological Chemistry*, 6th ed., © 1996. Electronically reproduced by permission of Pearson Education, Inc., Upper Saddle River, New Jersey. 59: Michael Mix, Paul Farber, and Keith King, *Biology: The Network of Life*, 2nd ed., Pearson Education, 1996. Used by permission of Pearson Education.

2002. **137:** Christine Haugen, "Logging Illogic," *World Watch*, September/October, 2002. **142:** Editorial, "Raising the September 11 Generation," *Chicago Tribune*, September 8, 2002. **142:** Russ O'Hearn, "School's First Week Provides a Few Bright Exceptions," Letter to the Editor, *Toronto Star*, September 6, 2002. **143:** "From the Hip; Gun Control," *The Economist*, November 23, 2002. **143:** Editorial "Steroids Should be Tagged Out," *San Jose Mercury News*, June 3, 2002. **143:** Editorial, "Sign of Civilization," *Providence Journal*, August 15, 2002. **146:** Rebecca Jaycox, "Rural Home Schooling and Place-Based Education," *ERIC Digest*, December 1, 2001. **146:** "Endangered Species," *Funk and Wagnall's New World Encyclopedia*, EBSCO Online Reference System. **148:** Frank Grazian, "How Much Do Words Really Matter," *Public Relations Quarterly*, Summer 1998, p. 37. **151:** Reprinted with permission of *Wall Street Journal*, Copyright © 2009 Dow Jones & Company, Inc. All Rights Reserved Worldwide. License number 2183141423397 and 2152690211876.

Chapter 6   155, 162: Billitteri, T. J. (2008, May 2). "Cyberbullying." *CQ Researcher*, 18, Pg. 401. Copyright © 2008 CQ Press, a division of SAGE Publications, Inc. Reprinted by permission. **165:** Barry Lynn, "Pornography's Many Forms Not All Bad," *Los Angeles Times*, May 23, 1985. **165:** Jane Rule, "Pornography Is a Social Disease," *The Body Politic*, Jan/Feb 1984. **169, 170:** *USA Today*. June 6, 2005. Reprinted with permission. **172:** "Internet Accuracy: Pro/Con," *The CQ Researcher*, Aug 1, 2008, Vol. 18, No. 27. Copyright © [2008] CQ Press, a division of SAGE Publications, Inc.

Chapter 7   180: Michael Mix, Paul Farber, and Keith King, *Biology: The Network of Life*, 2nd ed., Pearson Education, 1996. Used by permission of Pearson Education. **181:** Elaine Marieb, *Essentials of Human Anatomy and Physiology*, 6th ed., Pearson Education, 2000, p. 3. **181:** Richard Janaro and Thelma Altshuler, *The Art of Being Human*, 4th ed., Pearson Education, 1993. Used by permission of Pearson Education. **181:** Davis, Stephen F., Palladino, Joseph J., *Psychology*, 3rd ed. © 2000. Electronically reproduced by permission of Pearson Education, Inc., Upper Saddle River, New Jersey. **182:** Joseph DeVito, *Human Communication: The Basic Course*, 8th ed., Longman, 2000, p. 124. **183, 184:** Gerard Tortora, *Introduction to the Human Body: The Essentials of Anatomy and Physiology*, Second Edition, Copyright John Wiley & Sons, Inc.

Reproduced with permission of John Wiley & Sons, Inc. **183, 184, 185:** Tarbuck, Edward, Lutgens, Frederick K., *Earth Science,* 9th ed., © 2000. Electronically reproduced by permission of Pearson Education, Inc., Upper Saddle River, New Jersey. **187:** Wilson, R. Jackson; Gilbert, James; Kupperman, Karen Ordahl; Nissenbaum, Stephen; Scott, Donald M., *The Pursuit of Liberty*, Vol. II, 3rd ed. © 1996. Electronically reproduced by permission of Pearson Education, Inc., Upper Saddle River, New Jersey. **187:** Zimbardo, *Psychology and Life*, 14e, text on pp. 115 and 501, © 2002, 1999, 1996 Allyn & Bacon Reproduced by permission of Pearson Education, Inc. **188:** Thio, *Sociology,* 4e, excerpt of text on pp. 255 and 534, © 1998, 1996 HarperCollins College Publishers. Reproduced by permission of Pearson Education, Inc. **188:** Michael Mix, Paul Farber, and Keith King, *Biology: The Network of Life*, 2nd ed., Pearson Education, 1996. Used by permission of Pearson Education. **189:** Gerard Tortora, *Introduction to the Human Body: The Essentials of Anatomy and Physiology*, Second Edition, Copyright John Wiley & Sons, Inc. Reproduced with permission of John Wiley & Sons, Inc. **189:** George Edwards, Martin Wattenberg, and Robert Lineberry, *Government in America*, 9th ed., Pearson Education, 2000. Used by permission of Pearson Education. **190:** Rebecca Donatelle, *Access to Health*, 7th ed., Benjamin Cummings, 2002. Used by permission of Pearson Education. **190:** Elaine Marieb, *Essentials of Human Anatomy and Physiology*, 6th ed., Pearson Education, 2000, p. 55. **191:** Wilson Dizard, *Old Media, New Media*, 3rd ed., Longman, 2000, p. 179. **191:** Bergman, Edward F.; Renwick, William H., *Introduction to Geography: People, Places, and Environment*, Updated Edition, 2nd ed., © 2003. Electronically reproduced by permission of Pearson Education, Inc., Upper Saddle River, New Jersey. **192:** George Edwards, Martin Wattenberg, and Robert Lineberry, *Government in America*, 9th ed., Pearson Education, 2000. Used by permission of Pearson Education. **193:** Rebecca Donatelle, *Access to Health*, 7th ed., Benjamin Cummings, 2002. Used by permission of Pearson Education. **195:** Thio, *Sociology,* 4e, excerpt of text on pp. 255 and 534, © 1998, 1996 HarperCollins College Publishers. Reproduced by permission of Pearson Education, Inc. **197:** Paul Hewitt, *Conceptual Physics*, 7th ed., Pearson Education, 1993. Used by permission. **197, 198, 199:** Rebecca Donatelle, *Access to Health*, 7th ed., Benjamin Cummings, 2002. Used by permission of Pearson Education. **200:** Kinnear, *Principles of Marketing*, 4th ed., © 1995. Reproduced by permission of Pearson Education, Inc., Upper Saddle River, New Jersey. **201:** Leon Baradat, *Understanding American Democracy*, Pearson Education, 1992. Used by permission of Pearson Education. **201, 202:** Henslin, *Social Problems*, excerpts on pp. 154, 74, © 1994, 1996, 2000, 2003, 2006 Pearson Education, Inc. Reproduced by permission of Pearson Education, Inc. **202:** Davis, Stephen F.; Palladino, Joseph J., *Psychology*, 3rd ed., © 2000. Electronically reproduced by permission of Pearson Education, Inc., Upper Saddle River, New Jersey. **204:** From Pride, *Business*, 5e Student Text, © 1996 South-Western, a part of Cengage Learning, Inc. Reproduced by permission. www.cengage.com /permissions. **205:** Leon Baradat, *Understanding American Democracy*, Pearson Education, 1992. Used by permission of Pearson Education. **205:** Henslin, *Social Problems*, excerpt on p. 252, © 1994, 1996, 2000, 2003, 2006 Pearson Education, Inc. Reproduced by permission of Pearson Education, Inc. **206:** George Edwards, Martin Wattenberg, and Robert Lineberry, *Government in America*, 9th ed., Pearson Education, 2000. Used by permission of Pearson Education. **206:** Smith, Sandra F.; Duell, Donna; Martin, Barbara C., *Clinical Nursing Skills: Basic to Advanced Skills*, 7th Edition, © 2008, p. 510. Reprinted by permission of Pearson Education, Inc., Upper Saddle River, New Jersey. **208:** Rebecca Donatelle, *Access to Health*, 7th ed., Benjamin Cummings, 2002. Used by permission of Pearson Education. **208, 209:** Tarbuck, Edward; Lutgens, Frederick K., *Earth Science*, 9th ed., © 2000. Electronically reproduced by permission of Pearson Education, Inc., Upper Saddle River, New Jersey. **211:** Bergman, Edward R.; Renwick, William H., *Introduction to Geography: People, Places, and Environment*, Updated Edition, 2nd ed., © 2003. Reproduced by permission of Pearson Education, Inc., Upper Saddle River, New Jersey. **213:** Wilson Dizard, *Old Media, New Media*, 3rd ed., Pearson Education, 2000, p. 169. **213:** Davis, Stephen F.; Palladino, Joseph J., *Psychology*, 3rd ed., © 2000. Electronically reproduced by permission of Pearson Education, Inc., Upper Saddle River, New Jersey. **214:** Bergman, Edward F.; Renwick, William H., *Introduction to Geography: People, Places, and Environment*, Updated Edition, 2nd ed., © 2003. Electronically reproduced by permissions of Pearson Education, Inc., Upper Saddle River, New Jersey. **215:** Rebecca Donatelle, *Access to Health*, 7th ed., Benjamin Cummings, 2002. Used by permission of Pearson Education. **215, 216, 217:** Henslin, *Social Problems*, excerpts on pp. 93, 336, 91, © 1994,

1996, 2000, 2003, 2006 Pearson Education, Inc. Reproduced by permission of Pearson Education, Inc. **216:** Wilson Dizard, *Old Media, New Media*, 3rd ed., Pearson Education, 2000, pp. 87, 157. **216:** Clayborne Carson, et al., *African American Lives: The Struggle for Freedom*, Longman, 2005, pp. 490–491. **217:** Joseph DeVito, *Human Communication: The Basic Course*, 8th ed., Pearson Education, 1998, p. 103. **217:** Bergman, Edward F.; Renwick, William H., *Introduction to Geography: People, Places, and Environment*, Updated Edition, 2nd ed., © 2003. Electronically reproduced by permissions of Pearson Education, Inc., Upper Saddle River, New Jersey. **217:** H.L. Capron and J.A. Johnson, *Computers: Tools for an Information Age*, 7th ed., Prentice Hall, 2002, p. 328. **219:** Carnes, Mark C.; Garraty, John A., *American Destiny: Narrative of a Nation*, Concise Edition, Combined Volume, 3rd Edition, © 2008, pp. 528–530. Reprinted by permission of Pearson Education, Inc., Upper Saddle River, New Jersey.

Chapter 8   224: Conger, *Adolescence & Youth: Psychological Development in Change*, pp. 296–297, © 1991, 1997 Harper & Row Publishers, Inc. Reproduced by permission of Pearson Education, Inc. **226:** Curtis Byer and Louis Shainberg, "Table 24.8: The Intensity of Some Common Sounds," *Living Well: Health in Your Hands*, 1995. Jones and Bartlett Publishers, Sudbury, MA. www.jbpub.com. Reprinted with permission. **227:** (Fig. 8-4) Pew Research Center, Spending Time With the News. **228:** Solomon, Michael R., *Consumer Behavior*, 8th Edition, © 2009, p. 160. Reprinted by permission of Pearson Education, Inc., Upper Saddle River, New Jersey. **229:** Bar Graph: Rate of Extinction from Coreen Belk and Virginia Borden, *Biology: Science for Life*, 2e, Benjamin Cummings, 2008. Used by permission of Pearson Education, Inc. **231:** McKnight, Tom L., *Physical Geography: A Landscape Appreciation*, 4th ed., © 1993. Electronically reproduced by permission of Pearson Education, Inc., Upper Saddle River, New Jersey. **232:** Henslin, *Essentials of Sociology: Down to Earth Approach*, © 2007 Pearson Education, Inc. Reproduced by permission of Pearson Education, Inc. **235:** Robert Wallace, *Biology: The World of Life*, 6th Edition, Pearson Education, 1992. Used by permission of Pearson Education. **245:** Brennan, Scott R., *Environment: The Science Behind the Stories*, 1st ed., © 2005. Electronically reproduced by permission of Pearson Education, Inc., Upper Saddle River, New Jersey.

Chapter 9   **256, 264:** Robert Wallace, *Biology: The World of Life,* 6th Edition, Pearson Education, 1992. Used by permission of Pearson Education. **265:** Louis Berman and J. C. Evans, *Exploring the Cosmos,* Pearson Education. Used by permission of Pearson Education. **265:** Divine, et al., *America Past and Present,* 4e. Reproduced by permission of Pearson Education, Inc., Upper Saddle River, New Jersey. **271:** Schmalleger, Frank, *Criminal Justice Today: An Introductory Text for the 21st Century,* 9th Edition, © 2007, pp. 428–431. Reprinted by permission of Pearson Education, Inc., Upper Saddle River, New Jersey.

Chapter 10   **277:** Campbell, et al., *Biology: Concepts and Connections,* 5e, San Francisco: Pearson/Benjamin Cummings, 2008, p. 579. **284:** Ross Eshleman, et al., *Sociology: An Introduction,* 4th ed., Pearson Education, 1993, p. 46. Reproduced by permission of Pearson Education, Inc. **284, 287:** Gerow, *Psychology: An Introduction,* 1st ed., © 1992. Electronically reproduced by permission of Pearson Education, Inc., Upper Saddle River, New Jersey. **286:** Arlene Skolnick, *The Intimate Environment: Exploring Marriage and the Family,* 5th ed., Pearson Education, 1992, pp. 193–194. **289:** Ross Eshleman, et al., *Sociology: An Introduction,* 4th ed., Pearson Education, 1993, pp. 356–358. Reproduced by permission of Pearson Education, Inc. **293:** Thompson/Hickey, *Society in Focus: An Introduction to Sociology,* p. 81, © 2005, 2002, 1999, 1996 HarperCollins College Publishers. Reproduced by permission of Pearson Education, Inc. **296:** Wade, Carole; Tavris, Carol, *Psychology,* 6th ed., © 2000. Electronically reproduced by permission of Pearson Education, Inc., Upper Saddle River, New Jersey.

Chapter 11   **300, 307:** Nickerson, Robert C., *Business and Information Systems,* 2nd ed., © 2001. Reproduced by permission of Pearson Education, Inc., Upper Saddle River, New Jersey. **306:** Gitman, *Principles of Managerial Finance,* 9th Edition, © 2000. Lawrence J. Gitman. Reproduced by permission of Pearson Education, Inc. **308:** Nickerson, Robert C., *Business and Information Systems,* 2nd ed., © 2001. Reproduced by permission of Pearson Education, Inc., Upper Saddle River, New Jersey. **310:** Solomon, Michael R.; Marshall, Greg; Stuart, Elnora, *Marketing: Real People, Real Choices,* 5th Edition, © 2008, p. 403. Reprinted by permission of Pearson Education, Inc., Upper Saddle River, New Jersey. **311:** From Pride, *Business,* 5e, Student Text, 5e. © 1996 South-Western, a part of Cengage Learning,

Inc. Reproduced by permission. www.cengage.com /permissions. **313:** Gitman, *Principles of Managerial Finance,* 9th Edition, © 2000. Lawrence J. Gitman. Reproduced by permission of Pearson Education, Inc. **315:** From Van Fleet, *Contemporary Management,* 2e © 1991 South-Western, a part of Cengage Learning, Inc. Reproduced by permission. www.cengage.com/permissions. **316:** Nickerson, Robert C., *Business and Information Systems,* 2nd ed., © 2001. Reproduced by permission of Pearson Education, Inc., Upper Saddle River, New Jersey. **319:** From Vivian, John, *The Media of Mass Communication,* 9e. Published by Allyn & Bacon/Merrill Education, Boston, MA. Copyright © 2009 by Pearson Education. Reprinted by permission of the publisher.

Chapter 12   **329:** All lines from "Mirror" from *Crossing the Water* by Sylvia Plath. Copyright © 1963 by Ted Hughes. Originally appeared in the *New Yorker.* Reprinted by permission of HarperCollins Publishers and Faber and Faber. **331:** Martin Luther King, Jr., *Why We Can't Wait.* New York: Harper & Row Publishers, Inc., 1964. **331:** Sharon Curtin, "Aging in the Land of the Young," *Nobody Ever Died of Old Age,* Little, Brown, 1972. **332:** Jane Kenyon, excerpt from "The Suitor" from *Collected Poems.* Copyright © 2005 by the Estate of Jane Kenyon. Used by the permission of Graywolf Press, Saint Paul, Minnesota. www.graywolf.org. **333:** Reprinted by permission of the publishers and the Trustees of Amherst College from *The Poems of Emily Dickinson,* Thomas H. Johnson, Ed., Cambridge, Mass: The Belknap Press of Harvard University Press, Copyright © 1951, 1955, 1979, 1983 by the President and Fellows of Harvard College. **334:** Print—"The Negro Speaks of Rivers" from *The Collected Poems of Langston Hughes* by Langston Hughes, edited by Arnold Rampersad with David Roessel, Associate Editor, copyright © 1994 by the Estate of Langston Hughes. Used by permission of Alfred A. Knopf, a division of Random House, Inc. Elec—By permission of Harold Ober Associates Incorporated. **336:** Print—"Harlem (2) ["What happens to a dream deferred . . ."]" from *The Collected Poems of Langston Hughes* by Langston Hughes, edited by Arnold Rampersad with David Roessel, Associate Editor, copyright © 1994 by the Estate of Langston Hughes. Used by permission of Alfred A. Knopf, a division of Random House, Inc. Elec—By permission of Harold Ober Associates Incorporated. **337:** Reprinted by permission of the publishers and the Trustees of Amherst College from *The Poems of Emily Dickinson*, Thomas H. Johnson, Ed., Cambridge, Mass: The Belknap Press of Harvard University Press, Copyright © 1951, 1955, 1979, 1983 by the President and Fellows of Harvard College. **346:** Vivian Pollack, *Dickinson: The Anxiety of Gender*, Cornell Univ. Press, 1986. **347:** Charles Anderson, *Emily Dickinson's Poetry: Stairway to Surprise*, Doubleday, 1960. **352:** Lloyd Schwartz, "Leaves," from *Goodnight Gracie*. Used by permission of the author.

Chapter 13   355: Woodbury, *Intermediate Algebra,* Example 2 p. 637, © 2009. Reprinted by permission of Pearson Education, Inc. **361:** Lial/Miller, *Introductory Algebra*, 6e, © 1998 by Pearson Education, Inc. Reproduced by permission of Pearson Education, Inc. **363:** Lial, *Prealgebra* 1e, © 1999 Addison Wesley Longman Inc. Reproduced by permission of Pearson Education, Inc. **364:** Miller/Salzman, *Business Mathematics*, Excerpt of text on p. 373, © 1987 Pearson Education, Inc. Reprinted by permission of Pearson Education, Inc. **365:** Johnson, *Elementary Algebra 2*, p. 178, © 1985. Reproduced by permission of Pearson Education, Inc. **372:** Lial at al, *Basic College Mathematics*, 5e, "Geometry," pp. 548–549, 1998 Pearson Education, Inc. Reproduced by permission of Pearson Education, Inc. **377:** Lial, *Prealgebra*, 1e, © 1999 Addison Wesley Longman Inc. Reproduced by permission of Pearson Education, Inc.

Chapter 14   388: William Kaufmann and Neil Comins, "Mars," *Discovering the Universe*, 4e, WH Freeman, 1999, pp. 144–145. **389:** Peter Atkins and Loretta Jones, "Colloids in the Cafeteria," *Chemistry: Molecules, Matter and Change*, 3e, WH Freeman, 1997, pp. 444–445. **393:** David Ross, *Introduction to Oceanography*, Pearson Education, 1995. Used by permission of Pearson Education. **394:** Paul Hewitt, *Conceptual Physics*, 8th ed., Pearson Education, 1998.

Used by permission of Pearson Education. **394:** Frank Press and Raymond Siever, "Carbon Dioxide and the Greenhouse Effect," *Understanding Earth*, 2e, WH Freeman, 2001, p. 348. **395:** Robert Wallace, *Biology: The World of Life*, 6th ed., Pearson Education, 1992. Used by permission of Pearson Education. **396:** Elaine Marieb, *Human Anatomy & Physiology*, 4e, Pearson Education, 1992. Used by permission of Pearson Education. **398:** Paul Hewitt, *Conceptual Physics*, 8th ed., Pearson Education, 1998. Used by permission of Pearson Education. **403:** Michael Bay and Matt Ford, "The Promise of Stem Cell Research: A CNN Future Summit Technology Profile," Science & Space, CNN.com International, April 18, 2006. Used by permission of CNN.

Chapter 15   412: Willenbrock, Jack H.; Manbeck, Harvey; Suchar, Michael G.; Anbeck, Harvey, *Residential Building Design and Construction*, 1st ed., © 1998. Electronically reproduced by permission of Pearson Education, Inc., Upper Saddle River, New Jersey. **412:** Gerald Sherwood and Robert Stroh, "Figure A: Roof Rafter/Ceiling Joist Roof Framing System," *Wood Frame House Construction*, Dover, 1989. **413:** Halderman, James D; Mitchell, Chase D., *Automotive Technology:Principles of Diagnosis and Service*, 1st ed. © 1999. Electronically reproduced by permission of Pearson Education, Inc., Upper Saddle River, New Jersey. **415:** Athey, et al., *Computers and End-User Software*, © 1992. Reproduced by permission of Pearson Education, Inc., Upper Saddle River, New Jersey. **415 424, 425:** John Lannon, *Technical Writing*, 6e, Pearson Education, 1994. Used by permission of Pearson Education. **431:** "Telehealth Overview and Summary: Promise or Peril?" was first published in *OJIN: The Online Journal of Issues in Nursing*, Volume 6, Number 3. OJIN has granted permission to reprint this article. www.nursingworld.org/ojin.

Index